The POPULAR ENCYCLOPEDIA *of* WORLD RELIGIONS

RICHARD WOLFF

HARVEST HOUSE PUBLISHERS

EUGENE, OREGON

Cover by Dugan Design Group, Bloomington, Minnesota

Cover photos © iStockphoto

Back cover author photo © Debbie Bartlett Cantor

THE POPULAR ENCYCLOPEDIA OF WORLD RELIGIONS
Copyright © 2007 by Richard Wolff
Published by Harvest House Publishers
Eugene, Oregon 97402

www.harvesthousepublishers.com

Library of Congress Cataloging-in-Publication Data
Wolff, Richard, 1927-
The popular encyclopedia of world religions / Richard Wolff.
    p. cm.
Includes bibliographical references.
ISBN-13: 978-0-7369-2007-0
ISBN-10: 0-7369-2007-2
1. Religions—Encyclopedias. I. Title.
BL31.W65 2007
200.3—dc22

                                                                    2007002937

Printed in the United States of America

07 08 09 10 11 12 13 14 15 / LB-SK / 11 10 9 8 7 6 5 4 3 2 1

To Sook…a gift from the Far East

CONTENTS

INTRODUCTION

ANCIENT MAPMAKERS WITH ONLY fragmentary knowledge of the world filled the gaps on their maps with drawings of dragons or inserted a note of caution that would warn, "Beyond this point there be monsters." But today, we know better—there are no monsters, only people who don't speak our own language. The ancient Greeks would have called them barbarians. The Greek word refers to someone who speaks a language that is not understood. Did not all civilized people speak Greek? The conclusion is obvious: such a person must be uneducated, a barbarian.

And of course in ages past the Chinese knew perfectly well that anyone not familiar with *their* culture was a barbarian. All foreigners were barbarians.

Fear fills the unknown with monsters; pride looks down on barbarians. Now that the whole world has become a "global village" and technology has annihilated distance, we all seem to live next to each other. It's time for us to slay the imaginary monsters and to understand the "barbarians."

History books focus on political or economic developments and usually pay scant attention to religion. Books on world religions repay the compliment and, by and large, ignore history. But history is more than a collection of dates. There is a context. History does not operate in a vacuum. There is a culture, a civilization, and that means values. At this point, history and religion intersect. Professor Samuel Huntington of Harvard University observed that "religion is a central defining characteristic of civilizations...the great religions are the foundations on which civilization rests."[1] Confucius or Buddha cannot be understood outside of their cultural setting. We need to understand the civilization of their day, the values of their society. Instead of filling the gaps of knowledge with imaginary dragons or secretly looking down upon the barbarians, let us get acquainted with our new neighbors in the global village and learn to love them. This book is an endeavor to make a small contribution to the village dialogue through historic and religious information.

ISLAM

*Your hearts are taken up with worldly gain
from the cradle to the grave.*

*But you shall know. You shall before long come
to know.*

*Indeed, if you knew the truth with certainty,
you would see the fire of Hell:
you would see it with your very eyes.*

*Then, on that day, you shall be questioned
about your joys.*

Koran, *Sura* 102

ISLAM

WITH 1.2 BILLION MUSLIMS, Islam is the second largest religion in the world. The three largest Muslim population centers are Indonesia, Pakistan, and Bangladesh. None of these have a large Arab population. Most Muslims are not Arabs; only about 15 to 20 percent of Muslims are Arab. Compared to the total Muslim population, the terrorist groups are small, but they dominate the headlines. Because of them, many see Islam through a distorted lens. It is unfortunate but understandable.

Muslims are not limited to the Near East or Asia. In Europe, the native population is aging and declining, and governments fear that in time, there may not be enough workers to sustain the economy. To solve the problem, immigration has been facilitated. Germany is home to three million Muslims, mostly Turks. They make up 5.7 percent of the total population. In France it is estimated that five to ten percent profess Islam, mostly people from North Africa. Statistics are unreliable, but there are probably between four to five million Muslims in France, where they outnumber Protestants. In Holland, six percent of the population follows Islam (mostly Indonesians and Moluccans)—over one million out of 15.5 million people. There are perhaps five million Muslims in the United States, mostly in California, New York, and Illinois. The fact that there are approximately 1,500 mosques in the United States means Islam cannot be ignored.

Professor Samuel Huntington of Harvard University speaks of religion as "a central defining characteristic of civilizations." He stresses that the great religions are the foundations on which civilization rests, pointing out that "in the modern world religion is central, perhaps the central force that motivates and mobilizes people."[1] Since Christianity and Islam are the two major religions of the world, he fears that clashes may come from the interaction of Western arrogance and Islamic intolerance. It is perhaps an unduly pessimistic outlook, but he is not alone in his evaluation.

In January 2006, President Chirac of France spoke of new threats and specifically mentioned a "confrontation of civilizations."[2] Philip Jenkins, Distinguished Professor of History and Religious Studies at Pennsylvania University, writes that by and large, U.S. foreign policy has ignored the power of religious motivation and points to Iran and Iraq as the latest examples of this failure to understand deep-seated convictions nourished by faith.[3] Perhaps the people involved in foreign policy do not have strong religious convictions and therefore fail to understand this type of motivation? Maybe it is due to a deep-seated conviction regarding the separation of church and state? Jenkins believes that out of the world's 25 largest nations, 20 will be predominantly or entirely Christian or Muslim in about 50 years. According to him, "the fundamental question here is whether Islam and Christianity can co-exist." He believes that across history "there is no question that the threat of intolerance and persecution chiefly comes from the Islamic side of the equation" and states without hesitation that if Muslims insist that their faith demands the establishment of Islamic states, a collision is unavoidable.[4] Unfortunately this is exactly the position of many jihadist movements today, including terrorist organizations such as al-Qaida.

Islamic rule does not automatically exclude religious tolerance. Suleiman the Magnificent (1529–1566) at the height of the Ottoman Empire and Akbar the Great (1556–1605) of the Mogul Empire are shining examples of religious tolerance.

A clash of ideology is one thing, but to envision armed conflict as the only or ultimate solution is an extraordinary viewpoint. According to Daniel Pipes, former instructor at the University of Chicago and Harvard University, "there is nothing *inherently* antagonistic between the faith of Islam and good American citizenship"[5] (emphasis added).

It is essential to gain a better understanding of the great world civilizations and religions, especially of Islam, given its worldwide importance. Jenkins laments the "parochialism of Western public opinion."[6] With increasing instant international communication and global trade so much a part of our world today, a parochial attitude is irresponsible. As Toynbee put it, given the "annihilation of distance" by modern technology, local or regional problems have now become worldwide problems.[7]

In a genuine desire to improve mutual understanding, key personalities have encouraged interfaith dialogue. This is undoubtedly useful—within certain limits. All too often the agenda is determined in the West and the "dialogue" is more in the nature of a monologue. Clever labels hide profound differences and disagreements are papered over for the sake of harmony. The temptation is to ignore serious disagreements and to find compatibility where there is little or none. It is better to recognize the differences and maintain mutual respect.

In an effort to build bridges of understanding, the Roman Catholic Church has taken a new look at Islam. In 1964 the Second Vatican Council issued a carefully crafted document affirming that "the Church looks with esteem upon Muslims. They adore one God, living and enduring, merciful and all-powerful, Maker of heaven and earth and Speaker to men." God's "will of salvation also embraces those who recognize God as Creator, especially Muslims who confess the faith of Abraham and worship one God with us, the Merciful, who judges men in the Last Judgment."[8] This is a remarkable statement coming from a body that, in the past, professed that outside of the Roman Catholic Church there is no salvation.

None of the above addresses the issue of Muslim fundamentalism or movements such as al-Qaida. Does Muslim fundamentalism present the true face of Islam? How and where did Islam develop? Are there points of contact with Christianity? What exactly do Muslims believe, and what do we really know about Muhammed?

THE SETTING IN WHICH ISLAM BEGAN

IN THE DAYS OF Muhammed, the Arabian Peninsula lay at the margin of the civilized world. It was largely ignored because of the extreme climate, the arid desert, and the frequent tribal raids. From time to time a few caravans loaded with spices crossed Arabia—sometimes these were comprised of more than 1,000 camels. Arabia was in decline; chaos prevailed. Small client states at the edge of the peninsula depended on the Byzantine Empire (Eastern Rome), Persia (Iran), or Abyssinia (Ethiopia). The occasional ship reached the coastal cities of Aden or Jeddah. Centuries later, Arabia was still ignored. Ibn Battuta (1304–c. 1368), a tireless Arabian traveler, was one of the few who crossed the peninsula. The Chinese Admiral Cheng Ho (1371–1435) reached the coast of Arabia on his seventh sea voyage. Central Arabia was closed to foreigners, but Niebuhr (1733–1815), a German explorer, visited a small corner of the Arabian Peninsula, mostly Yemen. The Swiss orientalist Burckhardt (1784–1817) managed to visit Mecca in disguise. The British contribution came from Burton (1821–1890), another secret visitor to Mecca.

At the time Muhammed came upon the scene, the small buffer states at the edge of Arabia had been eliminated in the seesaw battles between the two empires of Byzantium or Eastern Rome and Persia. As the major regional powers exhausted each other through endless wars, Mecca grew in importance as a caravan and pilgrim center. The city was on one of the trade routes between India and the Mediterranean, and commerce was thriving. Mecca even became an export center for Arabian products such as frankincense and myrrh, a gum resin. Finally, because of the sacred black stone, the Kaaba, pilgrims flocked to Mecca from all quarters of Arabia.

It is important to take a closer look at the people who lived in Arabia in the days of Muhammed.

Jews played an important role in the life of Muhammed. Several Jewish tribes lived in Yathrib (Medina) and the surrounding area. In Yemen a Jew seized the throne, proclaimed himself independent of Christian Abyssinia (Ethiopia), and called himself King Dhu Nuwas. He tried to impose Judaism on the people and attacked Najran, an important Christian center. Aretes and his 340 Christian companions were killed. This provoked retaliation from Abyssinia. King Ellesbaas (A.D. 552) launched a successful military campaign. Later Persia took control of the area (A.D. 575) till the Muslim conquest.

The peninsula was home to the small *Christian* center of Najran. Isolated Nestorian Christians* were scattered across the Arabian Peninsula.

Most interesting are the *Hanifim* (searchers after God), Arabian monotheists who firmly rejected idol worship. For that matter, even idolaters had a sense of a supreme God. As the Koran put it, "If you ask them who it is that has created the heavens and the earth and subjected the sun and the moon, they will say: 'Allah' (God). How then can they turn away from Him?"[9] and worship idols alongside of Allah. The supreme God was known as Allah. Muhammed's father was called *Abdullah,* incorporating the word *Allah,* or God, in his name. Muhammed complained of the pagans who, "when they embark they

---

* See the section on Christianity for details regarding the Nestorian Christians.

pray to Allah with all fervor; but when He brings them safe to land, they serve other gods besides Him."[10] The influence of both Jews and Hanifim on the general population was significant.

The *idolaters* worshipped ancestors and local clan and tribal deities who were thought to reside in sacred stones. The center of this stone worship was the black stone in Mecca, the Kaaba, an important pilgrimage center to this day. A few idols commanded broader allegiance throughout Arabia—especially Venus, the morning star.

It is reasonable to assume that *Jewish Christians* were also represented in Arabia. Some scholars are reasonably sure on this point, because the picture of Jesus presented in the Koran echoes the beliefs of some Jewish-Christian sects that stood outside of the orthodox Christian framework. They accepted Christ's teaching and thought of him as the Messiah, but denied his deity. This includes the Ebionites (the poor), who maintained that Jesus was merely a man, a prophet of God. Other Jewish Christians were called Nazarites. They accepted Jesus as the Messiah, the Son of God, and held his teachings to be superior to those of Moses, but also insisted that Christian Jews should observe elements of the Jewish law, such as the Sabbath and circumcision. In the Koran, Christians are called Nazarites. Further afield were the Elchasaites with a mixture of Jewish, Christian, and Gnostic elements. They held the law in high regard (except for the sacrifices), thought of Jesus as the Messiah, added astrology and magic to the mix, and believed that Adam went through a series of incarnations that eventually culminated in Jesus. We can't be certain how much contact Muhammed had either directly or indirectly with Jewish

Christians, but contact with the Ebionites might have been a source of Muhammed's knowledge about Jesus.

THE LIFE OF MUHAMMED

A BRIEF CHRONOLOGICAL overview of Muhammed's life may be helpful:

YEAR	EVENT	AGE
570	Birth of Muhammed	
595	Marriage to Kadija	25
610	The call	40
613	Public sermons	43
617	Muslims leave for Ethiopia	45
619	Death of Kadija	49
621	Agreement with Medina	51
622	**Hegira**	**52***
624	Battle of Badr	54
	Expulsion of the Qainuqa, a Jewish tribe	
625	Battle of Uhud	55
	Expulsion of the Nadir, a Jewish tribe	
626	Marriage to Zainab	56
627	Massacre of the Quraiza, a Jewish tribe	57
628	Treaty of Hudaybiya	58
629	Battle of Muta	59
630	Conquest of Mecca	60
630	Last marriage	60
632	Death	62

*Muslim chronology begins with the Hegira, the year A.D. 622.

MUHAMMED'S EARLY YEARS

Muhammed was born in Mecca, a city ruled by the Quraysh tribe. Each tribe consisted of several clans. The Umayyad clan was the most important of the Quraysh tribe. They played an important role in the history of Islam. The Quraysh controlled the Kaaba, a sanctuary that housed 360 idols. It was a magnet for all the tribes of Arabia. Pilgrims were a common sight in Mecca. The ancient pagan pilgrimage featured many of the elements that were incorporated into the *hajj*, the Muslim pilgrimage.

Muhammed was born into a lesser clan of the Quraysh tribe, the Banu Hashim or Hashemite clan. Thanks to Muhammed, this clan has gained enormous prestige. The roots of the royal family of Jordan go back to the Hashemite clan, and the official name of the country is the Hashemite Kingdom of Jordan.

Muhammed came into the world in A.D. 570. His father died before he was born, and he was orphaned at age six when his mother, Amina, died. The Koran recalls the event. "Did He [God] not find you an orphan and give you shelter?"[11] His grandfather, Ahmed ben-Mottalib, already 76 years old, accepted the responsibility of educating the boy. When he died, Muhammed ended up in the care of his uncle, Abu Talib. It is possible that when Muhammed was 12, he accompanied his uncle to Syria, where he may have met a Christian monk, Bahira. Exact facts about the life of Muhammed are difficult to ascertain. Ibn Ishaq, who died about A.D. 768, produced the earliest biography of Muhammed. Unfortunately, his work survived only through quotes from later historians. Buchari (810–870) created a major work regarding Muhammed, and finally there was the effort of Tabari (838–923), which, unfortunately, is incomplete. All three historians lived at least 100 years

after the death of Muhammed, and in spite of their sincere efforts, it is difficult to know what information can be accepted as authentic.

Muhammed worked for a wealthy widow, Kadija, and led her caravans across the desert. He obtained an excellent reputation for integrity and truthfulness and was called al Ameen, the Trustworthy. Muslim scholars unanimously agree that Muhammed could neither read nor write and conclude that the creation of the Koran is the one and only great miracle performed by Muhammed. At first sight it seems that the Koran confirms this when it speaks of the "unlettered prophet,"[12] but the exact meaning of the Arabic word is uncertain and several other meanings have been suggested. Arberry translates this phrase "prophet of the common folk." This text is not decisive and fails to settle the issue. Could Muhammed function properly, especially as caravan leader, without at least a rudimentary knowledge of reading, writing, and arithmetic? It is difficult to be certain, and it would seem that it hardly matters, except that for Muslims it is an article of faith. For Muslims, the Koran is a miracle because Muhammed was illiterate.

It was almost unavoidable that Muhammed, in the course of his travels, would encounter Jews, Christians (Nestorians), and Hanifim. No doubt he heard biblical stories from them that were later incorporated into the Koran. To what degree these stories accurately reflect the Scriptures and how much was due to traditional lore is another question. In several instances the details recorded in the Koran are in perfect agreement with the Talmud (but not with the Bible), the collection of Jewish laws. It points to contacts with Jews.

MUHAMMED'S CALLING

At 25 years of age, Muhammed married Kadija, the well-to-do widow for whom he had worked. She was 15 years older than him. They were married for 26 years, and throughout the marriage, Muhammed maintained a monogamous relationship. Kadija bore him three sons and four daughters. Although tradition has firmly established that Kadija was 40 at the time of her marriage, she seems rather old to have given birth to so many children. Unfortunately, all Muhammed's sons died in infancy. In due time his daughters married. Thanks to his marriage to Kadija, Muhammed was at ease financially. The same text that recalls his orphaned childhood reads, "Did he [God] not find you poor and enrich you?"[13] Perhaps Muhammed used his newfound leisure to meditate and ponder religious questions. Few people would doubt that he had a serious religious disposition. We are told that he often retired to a cave in Mount Hira. At age 40, in the month of Ramadan, on the "Night of Qadr" (Power),[14] he heard a voice that he accepted as God's revelation. It seems that the call, mediated by the angel Gabriel, came to Muhammed in his sleep (unless he was in a trance?). Three times he heard the angels say,

Recite in the name of your Lord,
    the Creator,
who created—created man from
    clots of blood.
Recite! Your Lord is the Most Bountiful One,
who by the pen has taught man what
    he did not know.[15]

Muhammed's age at that time is indirectly confirmed when, speaking of his calling, he said, "A whole lifetime I dwelt among you before its coming."[16]

Muhammed was extremely uncomfortable with his commission and even fearful of possession by a jinn, a supernatural being thought to influence humans. His wife reassured him and became the first believer in his prophetic mission. She got in touch with a cousin, Waraqa, a Bible-reading Christian who reassured Muhammed that he would be a prophet to his own people and that his call was legitimate. Muhammed was relieved and thus dismissed his fears.

Muhammed then adopted his cousin, Ali, who became a believer at age ten. He was followed by Zaid, a freedman who had been ransomed by Kadija and Muhammed. The next disciple was Abu Bakr, a prominent merchant who played a key role in the development of Islam and became the first caliph or successor to Muhammed. Abu Bakr involved a few other prominent people, who became Muhammed's "companions" and later assumed a special role. At first there were very few converts, mostly poor people and slaves. Pagan opposition in Mecca was almost a foregone conclusion. The city was the commercial and religious center of pagan Arabia and the Quraysh tribal chiefs derived considerable income from the pilgrims. It was hardly the right moment to proclaim a strict monotheism, denounce idols, and threaten the prosperity of Mecca. The Kaaba, which had 360 idols, attracted a lot of business. Not that the idea of Allah, of a supreme God, was altogether new. The word *Allah* was already used to designate the highest God, but not necessarily to the exclusion of other deities. Allah may have been one of the tribal gods of the Quraysh and was perhaps fairly well known because the Quraysh were the guardians of the Kaaba and exercised considerable influence. It was the idea of excluding all other gods that was unacceptable.

As the number of followers increased, persecution intensified. Finally, in 717, it was decided that a group of believers should move to Abyssinia (Ethiopia) where the Negus, a Christian ruler, received them kindly. It is difficult to determine the exact number of believers who emigrated, but it probably involved 50 to 100 persons.

A greater calamity for Muhammed than the local persecution was the death of Kadija when Muhammed was 49, followed rapidly by the death of his uncle, Abu Talib, who had never embraced the new faith but felt an obligation to defend a member of his clan. Without his protection, Muhammed was at the mercy of his opponents. The new leader of the clan was another uncle of Muhammed, Abu-Lahab. The Koran has harsh words for Abu-Lahab: "May the hands of Abu-Lahab perish! May he himself perish! Nothing shall his wealth and gains avail him. He shall be burnt in flaming fire [a pun on the meaning of Abu-Lahab, father of flames], and his wife, laden with faggots, shall have a rope of fiber around her neck!"[17]

For Muhammed, life had become precarious. There was a plot to assassinate him. He decided to leave Mecca and find refuge in the mountainous area of Taif, southeast of Mecca. But he was not well received. Perhaps the people were fearful of the possibility of vengeance from those at Mecca. Muhammed was ridiculed and had no choice but to return to Mecca.

A CRITICAL JUNCTURE

Greatly discouraged, it may have been at this critical moment that Muhammed briefly vacillated. This would explain the famous controversial "satanic verses" found in *Sura* 53:20. The text there mentions Al-Lat, Al-Uzza, and Manat, who were Arabian idols worshipped as daughters of God. Perhaps it was while Muhammed was under considerable pressure that he momentarily wavered and admitted the existence of other deities. As one Muslim scholar put it, "What wonder that a momentary thought crossed his mind to end the conflict by making a light concession to the bigotry of his enemies...it was his first and last concession. He recited a revelation to the Quraysh in which he spoke respectfully of the three moon-goddesses, and asserted that their intercession with God might be hoped for. His audience was overjoyed at the compromise, bowed down and worshipped the God of Muhammed...the whole city was reconciled to the double religion."[18]

Muhammed could not remain untrue to himself. He retracted what he had said and admitted that the devil had tempted him—hence the title of "satanic verses." But it is more than "a slight concession" for one to admit the existence of several deities, and the text has always been an embarrassment to Muslims.

Some Muslim traditionalists have a different explanation and allege that an idolater was present when Muhammed prayed—an idolater that tradition has converted into a devil—and he called out, "They are exalted damsels and their intercession with God may be hoped for." These words were interjected (by the devil) to appear as if they were part of the prophet's revelation, but when Muhammed heard what had happened, he immediately declared, "These are but empty names." Some of these explanations are farfetched, and there is no reason to doubt that momentarily, Muhammed briefly yielded to the pressure of the Quraysh. Muhammed quickly recovered and added, "Is He [God] to have daughters and you sons? This is indeed an unfair distinction!" How can you attribute daughters to God—given the low opinion of the female sex in Arabia at that time—when you yourselves prefer sons?

This was not the only time Muhammed dealt with temptation; we find echoes of his struggles in the Koran. "They sought to entice you from Our revelations…. Indeed had We* not strengthened your faith you might have made some compromise with them." And again, "Never have We sent a single prophet or apostle before you with whose wishes Satan did not tamper. But Allah abrogates the interjections of Satan and confirms His own revelations."[19] Perhaps this came to Muhammed after his temporary lapse and recognition of idols.

Some Meccans were ready to assassinate Muhammed, who, at one point, hid for three nights in a cave three miles from Mecca. He was accompanied by one loyal follower, Abu Bakr, and the incident is mentioned in Koran 9:40.

From time to time people from Yathrib (better known as Medina) came to Mecca as pilgrims. Because the city of Yathrib was home to several Jewish tribes, even idol worshippers had gained some knowledge of the Old Testament stories and were no strangers to the idea of monotheism. The people from Yathrib were therefore more inclined to listen to the monotheistic proclamations of Muhammed. Seventy-five men from Medina came to Mecca and pledged to defend Muhammed against all enemies. This was significant because once Muhammed accepted the proposal, he replaced tribal or clan loyalty with the support of people not connected by blood. It was the beginning of the *umma,* the believing community, replacing tribal

structure. Muhammed saw the wisdom of exchanging the meager protection of his own clan for the strength of a larger community of believers. This would ultimately lead to his relocation in Medina.

One reason the people in Yathrib would call upon Muhammed to help sort out problems was his good reputation. Tribal disputes in the city could not be resolved, and delegates from Yathrib asked Muhammed to come and settle matters. Muhammed resolved to move his small community of believers from Mecca to Yathrib. Some 200 followers moved with him to Yathrib, which is now called Medina, the city of the prophet. Muhammed followed a bit later, accompanied only by Abu Bakr. It is true that he left a desperate situation behind, but the move, now known as the *hegira,* was not so much a flight as it was a migration. This momentous event took place on June 8 in A.D. 622, which became the starting point of the Islamic calendar.

MUHAMMED'S CONQUESTS

With the move to Medina Muhammed entered a totally new and different phase of life. His prophetic role continued, and his proclamations based on ongoing revelations from Allah via Gabriel lasted from 610 to his death, a period of 22 years. In Medina he became the head of a community and mediated disputes between the *muhagirun,* or fellow-migrants, and the new converts in Medina. The burden of social organization and political leadership fell upon his shoulders.

Muhammed had high hopes that the three Jewish tribes in Medina would accept him as one more prophet in the long line of God's messengers. He was severely disappointed by their refusal. The *kiblah,* the

---

* The Koran always uses the royal plural. In other words, when God speaks, he uses *Our* or *We* to speak of Himself.

direction that the Muslim faces in prayer, was changed from Jerusalem to Mecca so that Muslims could face the Kaaba. Muhammed's followers wondered about the sudden change, but the Koran reminds us that only

> the foolish will ask: "What has made them turn away from their *kiblah?*" Say: 'The east and the west are Allah's. He guides whom He will to the right path.... We decreed your former *kiblah* only in order that We might know the Apostle's true adherents and those who were to disown him. It was indeed a hard test, but not to those whom Allah has guided.... We will make you turn toward a *kiblah* that will please you. Turn towards the Holy Mosque; wherever you be, face towards it.' "[20]

The "Holy Mosque" is a reference to the Kaaba; at that time it was still a center of idolatry.

Once Muhammed had gained a dominant position in Medina, raids were organized. Perhaps this was an economic necessity. Most of those who had come from Mecca were poor and a burden on their fellow believers in Medina. Raids and the acquisition of booty were "normal procedures," with the chief receiving 20 percent of the spoils. Nevertheless, one raid was roundly criticized. By common agreement and Bedouin tradition, every year all warfare stopped for a period of four months. But on the last day of the period of peace, the last day of the month of Rajab, Muhammed organized a raid. With 300 men he attacked a caravan moving from Syria to Mecca. The commander of the caravan heard about the projected attack, changed his route and sent to Mecca for

help. The Quraysh sent 900 men to defeat the Muslims, but lost the battle. The upset victory under the personal leadership of Muhammed was a tremendous boost for the Muslim cause. Yet people raised questions about this breach of customary law, and Muhammed received a special revelation to deal with the issue. "They ask you about fighting in the sacred month. Say: 'To fight in this month is a great offence; but to debar others from the path of Allah, to deny Him, and to expel His worshippers from the Holy Mosque, is far more grave in His sight. Idolatry is worse than carnage.' "[21] Muhammed justified the raid by observing that the Quraysh in Mecca did not allow Muslims to visit the Kaaba as pilgrims and that they refused to accept his message. According to Muhammed, in the light of the great transgressions of Mecca, the minor sins of the Muslims paled into insignificance. It is an interesting bit of reasoning, and a revelation was needed to calm the situation.

The victory consolidated the power of Muhammed, who could afford to allow a few executions to take place, especially of poets who had reviled him. A Muslim was sent secretly to assassinate Kab ibn al-Asraf, who, in his poems, had ridiculed Muhammed. It should be understood that these poets were the communicators of the day, taking the place of today's daily paper or television news. Others who had been a thorn in the side of Muhammed were also killed. Some of the details are gruesome, but perhaps not historically accurate. Regardless of how the executions were carried out, Muhammed was the instigator. Nothing happened without his approval. According to Muslim scholars, Muhammed believed a swift and secret execution was the only way to deal with problem people. There was no police, no judicial tribunal to consider individual crimes. To arrest people openly would have provoked unnecessary bloodshed and led to clan warfare. The blood avengers would have started a long cycle of violence. Thus it was better to carry out such assignments secretly (which seems a poor justification for doing this).

Now that Muhammed had absolute control, he expelled the Qainuqa, one of the Jewish tribes in Medina. The background story is rather peculiar. A young girl from the country came to the Jewish market of the Qainuqa to sell milk and was grossly insulted by Jewish youths. A Muslim sided with the girl and, in the ensuing commotion, the Jewish instigator of the affair was killed. The Jews now rose as one man and killed the Muslim, and a free-for-all followed. Muhammed rushed to the spot and tried to calm everyone. As he saw it, the Jews had deliberately infringed upon the terms of a firm compact. Actually, Muhammed would never hesitate to break a treaty if he thought that the other party might violate it. He believed in preventive warfare, retaliation before the enemy moved. "If you fear treachery on the part of an ally, you may retaliate by breaking off your treaty with them. Allah does not love the treacherous."[22]

The Qainuqa had the choice to accept Islam or leave Medina. They defied Muhammed and shut themselves up in their fortress. Within two weeks they surrendered and were expelled. About 700 people were forced to leave their possessions behind, and the spoils fell to the victor.

After the lost Battle of Badr, Mecca was out for revenge, and the next year (625), the Battle of Uhud took place. The armies clashed a few miles outside of Medina.

This time the Muslims were defeated and Muhammed was wounded.

A few months later Muhammed accused another Jewish tribe, the Nadir, of collusion with the enemy, the Quraysh of Mecca. The siege of the Jewish fortress lasted only a few weeks, but in the course of the attack Muhammed allowed palm trees to be cut down. It was another serious breach of Bedouin tradition. This action was justified when Muhammed received a revelation that "it was Allah who gave you leave to fell or spare their palm trees, so that He might humiliate the evildoers." A reminder of the large booty immediately followed this text: "As for those spoils of theirs, which Allah has assigned to His apostle, you spurred neither horse nor camel to capture them."[23] The Jews capitulated and were allowed to emigrate, and the Muslims took over their properties.

In 626–627 the Meccans launched a major offensive, but 10,000 men were unable to pierce the trenches that had been dug to defend Medina, and the Meccans abandoned the effort to crush the Muslims. The last remaining Jewish tribe, the Quraiza, were now accused of giving aid to the enemy, or Mecca. Over a period of a few days 600 men of the tribe were slain and the women and children given to the conquerors as legitimate spoils of war. Muhammed received 20 percent of the booty and sold some of the women and children into captivity in exchange for horses and weapons. The Koran refers to these events: "Allah turned back the unbelievers [of Mecca] in their rage, and they went away empty-handed." In reference to the Quraiza the Koran says that God "brought down from their stronghold those who had supported them [the Meccans] from among the People of the Book [the Jewish tribe] and cast terror into their hearts, so that some you slew and others you took captive. He made you masters of their land, their houses, and their goods."[24]

It is difficult to evaluate these incidents because the documentation comes exclusively from Muslim sources, which, if at all biased, would be in favor of Islam. Some of the military actions can perhaps be explained. It is possible, for instance, that Muhammed considered the attack against the Quraiza a military necessity to prevent a possible alliance between the Jewish tribe and Mecca. The same may be alleged about attacks against the other Jewish tribes following the Battle of Uhud and the Trench War. Both threatened Muslim survival. The Jewish tribes were attacked not because of their Jewish faith, but because they were a foreign body in the midst of the Muslim community. It could perhaps be claimed that the slaughter of the Quraiza was customary. Muslim scholars insist that even the smallest betrayal might have tipped the balance in favor of Mecca against Muhammed. But even when all these mitigating circumstances are taken into consideration, one can hardly avoid the conclusion that Muhammed failed to rise above the ethical standards of his generation. The picture of Muhammed that emerges is not one of love and gentleness.

Muhammed finally suggested that peace should prevail with Mecca and that caravans should be able to pass by unmolested. In return he requested that his followers be allowed to perform the pilgrimage to Mecca—although at the time the Kaaba still housed hundreds of idols. The Meccans insisted on one year of peace before they were willing to sign the treaty; they wanted Muhammed to demonstrate serious intent. They finally came to terms, and

Muhammed greatly surprised his followers when he agreed to a ten-year truce in the Treaty of Hudaybiya. The treaty compelled Muslims to surrender every idolater who came over to their cause without permission of their chief. Since women were not mentioned in the treaty, they were not returned. There was sharp disagreement among Muhammed's followers regarding the very idea of a treaty with Meccan unbelievers as well as the specifics of the treaty. A revelation settled the matter. Muhammed proclaimed that "it was He [Allah] who made peace between you in the Valley of Mecca."[25] It was a diplomatic compromise. Mecca rejected Muhammed's prophetic claim. The official treaty was with Muhammed, son of Abdullah, not with Muhammed the prophet.

Muhammed now turned his attention to attacks against the Jews of Khaibar, who lived northeast of Medina. After a vigorous defense and the death of almost 100 soldiers, the Jews surrendered. Except for the leaders, survivors were spared, but all property was forfeited. Muhammed took yet another wife, a woman who had been engaged to the dead leader. Safiya, the Jewess, was 17; Muhammed by this time was 58.

Shortly afterward, Muhammed dispatched envoys to neighboring rulers and invited them to embrace Islam. Delegations were sent to the emperor at Byzantium and to the Court of Persia, as well as to leaders of smaller countries and tribes. We are told that one of the ambassadors was ill-treated at the court of a Ghassanide prince who was a feudal subject of the Byzantine emperor. The historic details are not crystal clear. Muslim authors claim that Sharabhil, chief of Muta, killed the Muslim envoy. Muslims held Byzantium responsible.

Supposedly the incident was at the root of the war that placed Islam in conflict with all Christendom. Whatever really happened, it was hardly such an isolated incident that took place in a remote corner of the Byzantine Empire that ignited or explains the conflict between Islam and Christendom. If the murder took place, it was neither unusual nor unique. When a band of 50 Muslims was sent to the Bani Suleim demanding the people's allegiance to Islam, the Muslims were greeted with a cloud of arrows and only a few escaped and returned to Medina. There were many skirmishes of this nature, some successful and others failures. In 629 the murder of an envoy was used to justify an expedition of 3,000 men to exact reparation from Muta. It was not the first time that Muhammed organized incursions acrosss the Syrian border. A defensive alliance had been formed to resist the Muslim invasions. The Muslim army fought heroically but was devastated, and the remnants were forced to retreat to Medina. Jafar, leader of the army and cousin of Muhammed, was among the dead. Muhammed's prestige suffered from this setback, which compelled him to use armed forces to quell the unrest taking place along the Syrian border.

In 629 and in line with the Treaty of Hudaybiya, some 2,000 Muslim pilgrims entered Mecca and walked around the Kaaba, which was still full of idols. A year later Muhammed claimed that the Quraysh had violated the truce and marched on Mecca with 10,000 men. It is possible that someone from the Quraysh tribe was involved in an attack against the Bani Khuzaa, who stood under the protection of Muhammed. To Muhammed it was evidence that the Meccans had broken the truce. Mecca offered the customary compensation but Muhammed rejected the offer. Technically he may have been right to do so, but from a moral standpoint the war was unjustifiable. Such raids were common throughout Arabia and carried out by all sides, including the Muslims.

In 630 Muhammed entered Mecca unopposed and declared a general amnesty. There was remarkably little looting and killing. He cleansed the Kaaba by removing the idols. He spared a picture—probably an icon—of Jesus on his mother's knee. If the story is authentic, then Muhammed might not have approved the legislation by Muslim scholars who opposed representations of the human form.

At age 60, Muhammed's triumph was finally complete. The city that had ridiculed and despised him had no choice but to receive him with open arms. He lived another two years to enjoy the fruits of his labor. It was perhaps two years before his death when Xisna, Bishop of Najran in Yemen, sent a delegation to Muhammed to find out more about both the person and the message.

CONTROVERSIES REGARDING MUHAMMED

Aside from those already mentioned, several other events in the life of Muhammed have been controversial. One incident is referred to in the Koran: "He [Muhammed] frowned and turned his back when the blind man came towards him."[26] Muslim commentators remark that the incident reflects the highest honor on the prophet's sincerity since he reveals "a false step" in the blind man's mission.[27] Commentators offer lengthy explanations and furnish many reasons why Muhammed turned away from a man in need. We really don't have enough information to evaluate the situation.

No doubt one of the most controversial aspects of Muhammed's life concerns his marriages. For 26 years he lived in a monogamous union with Kadija, but after her death, when Muhammed was 51, everything changed. Muslim commentators claim that he married widows who were bereft of their natural protectors, and that each time the marriage was an act of charity. This is hardly accurate and definitely not the case for Aisha, the daughter of Abu Bakr, to whom Muhammed was betrothed when he was 50 and Aisha seven. She became his favored wife and he died in her arms when she was a teenager. Safiya, the Jewess, has already been mentioned. He also accepted Mary, a Christian slave, presented to him by the Negus of Abyssinia. She gave birth to a son in the last year of Muhammed's life, but the baby died in infancy.

Since Muslims were limited to four wives and Muhammed had 11, it took a divine message to explain the difference. The revelation was received when Muhammed had nine wives, not counting slave girls. "We have made lawful to you the wives whom you have granted dowries and the slave-girls whom Allah has given you as booty; the daughters of your paternal and maternal uncles and of your paternal and maternal aunts who fled with you; and the other women who gave themselves to you and whom you wish to take in marriage. This privilege is yours alone, being granted to no other believer."[28] Muslim scholars have suggested that the restriction of polygamy to four wives came after all Muhammed's marriages had been contracted.

Because Muhammed favored Aisha and slept with her more often than any of the other wives, he received another divine communication that set him free from the necessity of regular rotation: "You may put off any of your wives you please and take to your bed any of them you please. Nor is it unlawful for you to receive any of those whom you have temporarily set aside. That is more proper, so that you may be contented and not vexed, and may all be pleased with what you give them."[29] In the same sura Allah informed Muhammed that it was unlawful for anyone to marry one of his wives after his death. As it turned out, Aisha was only 18 when Muhammed died, and this edict condemned her to a long life of celibacy.

One of the most questionable and perhaps scandalous situations arose when Muhammed, at age 56, married Zainab, who had been the wife of Zaid, one of Muhammed's first converts. Muhammed himself had arranged Zaid's marriage, but according to Muslim commentators, Zaid and his wife were incompatible. Zaid divorced his wife. The exact circumstances are veiled in obscurity. Did Zaid overhear Muhammed praising Zainab's beauty and feel duty-bound to divorce her in order to set her free? Be that as it may, in spite of Muhammed's misgivings, the divorce took place and Muhammed married Zainab. The situation is addressed in the Koran because it created a sensation among the pagans who objected to the marriage of the wife of an adopted son:

> You [Muhammed] said to the man [Zaid, your adopted son] whom Allah and yourself have favored: "Keep your wife and have fear of Allah." You sought to hide in your heart what Allah was to reveal [i.e., your intention to marry Zaid's wife]. You were afraid of man, although it would have been more right to fear Allah.

And when Zaid divorced his wife,
We gave her to you in marriage,
so that it should become legitimate for true believers to wed the
wives of their adopted sons if they
divorced them. Allah's will must
needs be done.[30]

So the legitimacy of marrying the divorced wives of son-in-laws was settled once for all. One Muslim commentator compares the situation to that of Henry VIII, whose marriages may have been dictated by the desire for male offspring, and adds that Muhammed may have felt the natural wish to leave sons behind.

Finally, at about age 60, Muhammed received this word: "It shall be unlawful for you to take more wives or to change your present wives for other women, though their beauty please you, except where slave-girls are concerned."[31]

The Koran relates yet another interesting incident in the family life of Muhammed. He had promised Hafsa, one of his wives, that he would no longer sleep with a Coptic slave, but he was subsequently discovered with her. Hafsa promptly informed Aisha, and this is when Muhammed heard the following message: "Prophet, why do you prohibit that which Allah has made lawful to you, in seeking to please your wives. Allah is forgiving and merciful. Allah has given you absolution from such oaths."[32] To free Muhammed from his promise was perhaps the purpose of this chapter, but Muslim commentators claim a totally different historic setting.

THE FAMOUS NIGHT JOURNEY

Another remarkable event is the famous mystic night journey alluded to in the Koran, when God "made His servant go by night from the Sacred Mosque [the Kaaba at Mecca] to the farther Mosque [the temple of Jerusalem]."[33] Some Muslim commentators offer a literal interpretation of the text, while others assume that Muhammed had a vision. Details abound. Muhammed rode on a winged steed with a human face, called al-Buraq, or the Lightning. At the gate of the temple in Jerusalem he dismounted and, with Gabriel, entered the Sacred Rock. There, Muhammed met Abraham, Moses, and Jesus, as well as several prophets. From the Sacred Rock Muhammed ascended on a ladder of light into heaven and enjoyed a vision of paradise. He moved through seven heavens till he finally stood before Allah and received injunctions regarding the prayers his followers were to perform. Muhammed then returned to Mecca before the day ended. There was no mosque in Jerusalem at the time, and the obscure reference has allowed colorful speculations. The story was later used by Sufi Muslims to justify their mystic ascensions into the presence of God.

MUHAMMED'S ACCOMPLISHMENTS AND INFLUENCE

Muhammed died of a high fever on June 8, 632. He had unified the Arabian Peninsula, led 27 campaigns, and fought in nine battles. He had firmly implanted monotheism throughout the peninsula and virtually eliminated idolatry. He saw himself as the last one in a long line of prophets. It was perfectly natural that he would appropriate for himself words spoken by Noah: "'Will you have no fear of Allah?' said Noah, their compatriot, to them. 'I am indeed your true apostle. Fear Allah, then, and follow me.'"[34] Muhammed claimed he did not present a different message: "I am no bringer of new-fangled doctrine"—or, as another translator puts it, "I am not an innovation among the

Messengers." He also saw himself as "the Seal of the Prophets."[35] Even as a document is sealed when it is completed, so Muhammed's message is complete and no further additions are allowed.

According to Muhammed, Jesus spoke of a messenger to come, whose name would be Ahmed.[36] This enigmatic text is a reference to John 14:16, where Jesus promises the coming of a "Comforter" *or paraklete* (in Greek). According to Muslim commentators, the text has been corrupted. The original word, *periklytos,* was accidentally or deliberately changed to *paraklete.* Finally we are told that *periklytos* has the same meaning as Ahmed, which is another name of Muhammed, meaning "the Praised One." However, there is not a shred of textual evidence to suggest there was a change from *periklytos* to *paraklete.* Perhaps Muhammed had heard something about the promise of the coming *paraklete* and applied it to himself. He had spoken of himself as the one "described in the Torah and the Gospel."[37] And ever since, Muslim commentators have had no choice but to defend this interpretation of the biblical texts.

Muhammed functioned as a prophet and a statesman. In his person, religious truth and political power were linked. He was the leader of the *umma,* or community of believers. He also presented himself as a pattern of conduct: "You have a good example in God's Messenger." Given what we know of his life based on Islamic sources, this is a questionable proposition.

It has been claimed that Muhammed incorporated some elements of pre-Islamic paganism into Islam, such as the pilgrimage to Mecca and the veneration of the Kaaba, but these are relatively minor matters. Like every reformer, Muhammed was initially reviled and persecuted, and at times lived in fear of his life. The unbelievers "plotted against you. They sought to take you captive or have you killed or banished."[38] Muhammed's opponents spoke of his revelations as a forged calumny, "an invented falsehood," and to them, the Koran was nothing but "manifest sorcery" or plain magic.[39] But Muhammed persevered and triumphed. He was a genuine seeker after God who hated corrupt superstitions. McNeill observes that "never before or since has a prophet won such success so quickly; nor has the work of a single man so rapidly and radically transformed the course of world history."[40] Anderson offers this fairly balanced characterization of Muhammed: "That he was in the main simple in his tastes and kindly in his disposition there can be no doubt; he was generous, resolute, genial and astute: a shrewd judge and a born leader of men. He could, however, be cruel and vindictive to his enemies; he could stoop to assassination; he was undeniably sensual."[41]

THE KORAN, ISLAM'S HOLY BOOK

THE OPENING SURA OR chapter of the Koran is one of the most beautiful and is used by Muslims in their prayers:

In the Name of Allah,
the Compassionate,
the Merciful
Praise be to Allah, Lord of the Creation,
the Compassionate, the Merciful,
King of the Last Judgment!
You alone we worship, and to You alone
we pray for help.
Guide us to the straight path,

the path of those You have favored,
not of those who have incurred Your wrath,
nor of those who have gone astray.

Jews pointed to the books of Moses, and Christians relied on the Gospels. There were no sacred texts in Arabia. Muhammed keenly felt the lack of such a book in the Arab world. But finally, there was "an Arabic Koran, wherein there is no crookedness" (translation of A.J. Arberry) or "free from all faults."[42] At age 40 Muhammed heard the word, "Recite" (*Sura* 96) and he listened to the same voice again and again over the next 22 years. The Koran presents itself as a collection of revelations received by Muhammed and transmitted by him orally. Tradition informs us that shortly after Muhammed's death someone recited all 114 chapters or suras of the Koran, and a few people took notes. These formed the basis of several private recollections. According to the same tradition Muhammed's successor, the first caliph, Abu Bakr, asked Zayd Ibn Thabit to create a complete collection. Fragments of speeches preserved on palm leaves, bones, stones, leather, and wood pieces were gathered and sorted, and from these the first compilation was created. At the death of Abu Bakr this material was handed over to the next caliph, Omar, and at his death the material was turned over to Hafsa, one of the widows of the prophet. Under the next caliph, Othman, this material became the foundation of an "authorized version." To eliminate disputes about the Koranic text, all copies that did not conform to this standard text were eliminated. In 1972 thousands of manuscript fragments were discovered during the restoration of the Great Mosque of Saana in Yemen. These fragments go back to the seventh

and eighth centuries and show some small variations from the authorized text.

Othman ordered four copies made of the standard text and sent them to Damascus, Kufa, Basra, and Mecca. The earliest surviving copies of the Koran date from the ninth century, 300 years after the initial revelations. Across the centuries the text was copied with care. The first printed version appeared in 1801 only after overcoming considerable resistance. Traditionalists felt strongly that the text should always be copied by hand.

KEY PERCEPTIONS REGARDING THE KORAN

After endless controversy it became the official orthodox position that the Koran existed from all eternity. Muhammed had declared, "We have revealed the Koran in the Arabic tongue that you may grasp its meaning. It is a transcript of Our eternal book…[it is] a glorious Koran, inscribed in a hidden book which none may touch except the purified…. it is inscribed on a preserved tablet."[43] Thus Muslim scholars concluded that the Koran is uncreated and eternal. Later it was argued that if the Koran were uncreated it would be co-eternal with Allah and destroy the divine unity. The issue became highly controversial. Finally the idea of a created Koran was declared heretical. It was equated with rationalism and roundly condemned.

In Islam the divine Word became a book, in Christianity the Word became flesh. As Phipps put it, "in Islam the Quran is primary and Muhammed is a secondary material witness to it; in Christianity, Jesus is primary, and the Bible is a secondary material witness to him."[44] Since Muslims believe that Muhammed was illiterate, the Koran is the one and only—but most glorious—miracle of the prophet. If his opponents say, "He has invented it himself," and claim that it is not the result of divine revelation, then "let them produce a scripture like it."[45] Arberry, a translator/interpreter of the Koran, speaks of "the wild charm of the Arabic" but also mentions the "mysterious inconsequences of the Koranic rhetoric."[46] Arabs never cease to praise the majestic rhythm of the language. Some speak of flashing images and inexorable measures that go directly to the brain and intoxicate it. The English reader does not get the same impression. The historian Will Durant claims that "the nature of the book doomed it to repetition and disorder."[47]

Initially there was fierce resistance against all efforts to translate the Koran into other languages, and even now every "translation" is called an "interpretation." The fact of the matter is that the majority of Muslims have to read the Koran in "translation" since they do not speak Arabic. Today the book is available in over 100 languages. Peter the Venerable (1122–1157), Abbot of Cluny, sponsored a translation into Latin in 1143. By the sixteenth century the Koran was available in Italian and a bit later in French, German, and other languages.

THE CONTENTS OF THE KORAN

Even the average native Arab speakers find it difficult to read the Koran, since the language has changed over the centuries. Sometimes the text itself defies understanding. Muslim scholars are aware of the difficulties and obscurities of the text. Schoeps opines that "in language and style [the Koran] is exceedingly uneven,"[48] and Bouquet finds it "formless, full of trepidation, sometimes terse, often rambling and prolix."[49] Speaking of the Koran, Muhammed declares that "some

of its verses are precise in meaning—they are the foundation of the Book—and others ambiguous."[50] The Koran mixes narrative and exhortation and occasionally offers legislative wisdom. There is no overall structure, and some topics are connected without obvious reason. Commentators have tried to identify the occasions on which Muhammed made certain pronouncements and have been relatively successful in this endeavor.

Like the letters of Paul in the Bible's New Testament, the Koran is not organized chronologically, but by the length of each chapter. The shortest chapters are therefore found at the end of the book. These go back to the earliest proclamations of Muhammed, when he was still in Mecca. The much longer suras came with more extensive practice and, although found at the beginning of the book, are part of his work in his later years, in Medina. In some instances we have no idea of the situation that provoked a particular speech.

The Koran tells us far more about Abraham (Sura 14 is named after him) and Moses than about Muhammed. This is especially true of Moses, who is referred to more than 200 times. Muhammed has far more in common with Moses than with Christ. Many biblical characters appear, including Adam, Noah (Sura 71 is named after him), Lot, Isaac and Ishmael, Joseph (Sura 12 is named after him), Pharaoh, Aaron, Saul, David and Goliath, Solomon, Elijah and Elisha, Jonah (Sura 10 is named after him), and others. The Koran's information about the Bible probably came from Jews and Christians who were living in Arabia at the time. Some of the pagans claimed that " 'a mortal taught him.' But the man to whom they allude speaks a foreign tongue, while this Koran is in plain Arabic."[51] We know nothing about this foreigner mentioned by Muhammed's opponents. A Persian has been suggested, or perhaps a monk.

Muhammed's audience obviously already knew many of the biblical stories, and Muhammed only draws conclusions about them. However, the koranic stories do not always correctly reflect the Bible's Old Testament accounts. There are occasional confusions. "Pharaoh said, 'Haman, build me a tower,'" and in the same sura God "sent forth Moses with Our signs and with clear authority to Pharaoh, Haman, and Korah."[52] Saul is associated with Gideon: "When Saul marched out with his army, he said: 'God will put you to the proof at a certain river. He that drinks from it shall cease to be my soldier.'"[53] We are also informed that Solomon was tested "and We placed a counterfeit upon his throne, so that he at length repented."[54] Job was told to "take a bunch of twigs and beat your wife with it; do not break your oath."[55] According to Muslim commentators, Job had sworn to punish his wife with 100 blows. God now suggests that he keep the oath by giving her one blow with 100 twigs. Muslim scholars have concluded this means that one can be released from an oath rashly taken.

Muhammed twice refers to an incident when God turned some of the Jews into "apes and swine,"[56] an event not mentioned in the Bible's Old Testament. In *Sura* 19:28, the mother of Jesus is called "sister of Aaron." Muslim commentators point out that, in context, this simply means "virtuous woman." This is barely possible at best. These and similarly confusing koranic texts have made life difficult for Muslim commentators.

Again and again Muhammed referred to the Torah (the five books of Moses) and the gospel as messages from God. "He has revealed to you the Book with the truth, confirming the scriptures which preceded it; for He has already revealed the Torah and the Gospel for the guidance of mankind, and the distinction between right and wrong."[57] He admonishes the Jews to "have faith in my revelations, which confirm your Scriptures."[58]

When Christians pointed out the discrepancies between the Bible and the Koran, they were accused of concealing many things of the Book and "effacing many things."[59] But no textual change, no matter how radical, can reconcile historical errors such as associating Pharaoh with Haman and Korah, as done in the Koran. As far as the Old Testament is concerned, one would have to assume that the changes were made before the time of the Dead Sea Scrolls because the scrolls contain the same text that appears in Bibles today. Can anyone seriously suggest that changes were made perhaps as early as 700 B.C. and that the correct text appeared in the Koran some 1,300 years later? Speaking to Jews, Muhammed pointed out that "there is [notice the present tense] light in the Torah which We have revealed"[60] and suggested that they should read the Torah because it is reliable.

THE KORAN AND THE BIBLE

The idea of textual changes having occurred in the New Testament after the Koran was written is totally impossible. By the time of Muhammed, innumerable quotations from the Bible had already appeared in the writings of the church fathers. One would have to assume that changes were made before the time of the church fathers, and Clement of Rome wrote his letter to the Corinthians before the end of the first century. The Epistles of Ignatius also go back to the first century. Early on the New Testament was translated into different languages. One would have to assume that these translations were all based on a falsified text. But thousands of manuscripts with the biblical texts were already in circulation, and some of the earliest go back to the early second century. And the Koran wasn't written until well after this time. How could the Bible have been corrupted if the texts before and after the writing of the Koran are the same? For Muslim scholars there is only one radical answer. Supposedly there was only one single Gospel text based on the teaching of Jesus. This Gospel was lost. Only fragments survived here and there…and were incorporated into the Koran. Muslim scholars have no choice but to defend the idea that the Gospels we have today do not reflect the teaching of Christ. This is an utterly impossible supposition for which there is not one shred of manuscript evidence, one that needs no refutation. It is a counsel of desperation.

As might be expected, there are excellent admonitions in the Koran reminiscent of the Old Testament: Show kindness to parents and to orphans, to the poor and to fellow workers, to strangers and to slaves. "Be steadfast in prayer, enjoin justice, and forbid evil…. Do not treat men with scorn nor walk proudly on the earth."[61] Pay the alms and perform the prayers, be equitable, safeguard the property of orphans. Homosexuality is condemned,[62] and thrift is recommended because "squanderers are brothers of Satan."[63] The Koran praises chastity and those "who restrain their carnal desire (save with their wives and the slave-girls, for these are lawful to them: he that lusts after other than these is a transgressor)."[64]

THOUGHTS AND THEMES IN THE KORAN

A text about "arrow shuffling" may seem bizarre at first sight. It refers to the casting of lots by means of marked arrows, which is more or less the equivalent of a lottery. Yet based on *Sura* 2:219, all gambling is prohibited. So is the usage of alcoholic beverages, although the issue might be debated. Early on, in Mecca, Muhammed spoke of the fruit of the palm and the vine "from which you derive intoxicants and a provision fair."[65] When the question regarding wine was raised in Medina, the answer was diplomatic: "There is great harm in both [drinking and gambling], although they have some benefit for men; but their harm is far greater than their benefit."[66] That is not an outright condemnation, but (presumably) later yet the condemnation is unequivocal: "Believers, wine and games of chance, idols and divining arrows, are abominations devised by Satan. Avoid them, so that you may prosper."[67] Is this a case of later correction, or perhaps progressive revelation? Nevertheless, in paradise, the righteous will be given pure nectar to drink, "a pure wine, securely sealed, whose very dregs are musk for this let all men emulously strive; a wine tempered with the waters of Tasnim, a spring at which the favored will refresh themselves."[68] According to one orthodox school, liquor produced by means of honey, wheat, barley, or millet is lawful.

One of the difficulties in understanding the Koran is that a later revelation can overrule an earlier one. The aforementioned verses about wine are a good illustration. "Allah confirms or abrogates what he pleases."[69] He "blots out" or "confirms" because with him is the Mother of the Book, the original foundation of all revelation. Elsewhere we read, "If We abrogate any verse or cause it to be forgotten, We will replace it by a better one or one similar."[70] Because of such changes, some accused Muhammed of forgery or of being an impostor.[71] There is nothing wrong with progressive revelation, but according to al-Sututi, changes appear in anywhere from five to fifty verses, and other scholars mention hundreds. It has even been suggested that an earlier text can abrogate a later one in the same sura. This, of course, complicates the understanding of the text.

One of the most important themes in the Koran is the Day of Judgment. Much space is devoted to the story of Noah and the flood. Hell is depicted vividly, and so are the delights of paradise, which is complete with *houris,* or dark-eyed virgins—bashful, untouched by any man, and "high-bosomed maidens."[72] Some modern Muslim interpreters inform us that all these suras belong to an intermediate period, before the mind of the teacher had attained full development. Others say that it was necessary for Muhammed to use simple language to describe the bliss of heaven or the pain of hell. Still, the graphic promise of *houris* does not depict spiritual joys characteristic of heaven.

One strange aspect of the Koran concerns the oaths found in the headings of many suras: "By the light of day and by the fall of night…I swear by the declining day…by the glow of sunset, by the moon…by the dawn."[73] There is no apparent connection between these oaths and the text itself. Were they part of the language used by professional seers? Twenty-nine suras begin with letters of the alphabet. For instance, the opening of *Sura* 10, entitled "Jonah," reads "Alif Lam Ra"—but there is no explanation given for these three letters.

THE KORAN AND JESUS

What does the Koran have to say about Jesus, who is mentioned more than 20 times? First of all, positively, it says that he was born of the Virgin Mary. *Sura* 19 is entitled "Mary" and offers details regarding the birth of Christ, who "shall be a sign to mankind." Mary, in the throes of childbirth, heard a voice: "Do not despair. Your Lord has provided a brook that runs at your feet, and if you shake the trunk of this palm-tree it will drop fresh ripe dates in your lap." Jesus spoke in the cradle and mentions the days of his death and resurrection. Elsewhere he is called the Messiah. "He shall be noble in this world and in the next…. he shall preach to men in his cradle and in the prime of manhood, and shall lead a righteous life."[74] In the days of Muhammed, many stories circulated about the childhood of Christ. It was tempting to fill in the gaps of information, especially those about Christ's infancy and early childhood. Some of the stories from the Apocrypha found their way into the Koran. In the *Sura* just quoted, Muhammed relates how Jesus used clay to create the likeness of a bird and breathed life into it. Some of the miracles of Jesus—his healing of the blind, his restoring of the lepers, and his bringing the dead to life—are also mentioned in this *Sura.* Jesus is called *rasul*—Messenger or Apostle—a respectful title he shares with Muhammed, Abraham, and Noah. According to the Koran, Noah, Abraham, Jesus, and Muhammed presented the same message.[75]

On the negative side, the reality of Christ's death on the cross is denied. The Jews "uttered a monstrous falsehood against Mary. They declared: 'We have put to death the Messiah, Jesus son of Mary, the apostle of Allah.' They did not kill him, nor did they crucify him, but they thought they did [or "he was made to resemble another for them"].... Allah lifted him up to His presence."[76] At first sight this may seem strange, but the Ebionites mentioned previously held similar beliefs. Docetism, an early Christian heresy, denied the humanity of Christ and taught that he, like a phantom, only appeared as man in a human body. Those who held this view thought of matter as evil and concluded that God could not possibly be linked to matter in any way. To them the idea of incarnation was impossible. Since Christ had a phantom body, he could not possibly die. These ideas may seem strange today, but at the time they percolated throughout the East. It seems that, at some point, this information was related to Muhammed. Irenaeus (A.D. 120–202) informs us that Docetists claimed that Simon of Cyrene, who helped carry the cross, was made to look like Jesus, and that Jesus took the shape of Simon and laughed as he stood by the cross.[77] Muhammed accepted the idea that Jesus did not die and that a stand-in, a disciple named Sergius, took his place.*

Among Muslim commentators, there seems to be some confusion regarding the death of Christ. Ali declares that "the end of his life [is] a mystery."[78] One text in the Koran declares, "They plotted, and Allah plotted. Allah is the supreme plotter. He said: 'I am about to cause you to die and lift you up to Me.'"[79] Since the death of Christ on the cross for the forgiveness of sin is a cardinal point of Christian truth, this denial goes against the heart of Christianity.

Most Muslims believe that Christ did not die, but lives in his body in heaven waiting to reappear in the last days to defeat *al-Dajjal,* the Antichrist. Muslims await the return of Jesus; Muhammed saw Jesus as "a portent of the Hour of Doom."[80] There is some question about the exact meaning of this text, but some Muslim commentators find a reference here to the second coming of Jesus. The Antichrist will rule 40 days and then be killed by Jesus. Wars with Gog and Magog are part of the end scene. In Muslim tradition the Antichrist is depicted as misshapen and blind in one eye. He will deceive the faithful, work miracles, and try to put a man on God's throne. He will revive some of the dead and claim to be God. There are dim echoes here of Judeo-Christian traditions regarding the end times.

Sometimes Jesus is seen as the Mahdi, the Muslim Messiah, but for most Muslims they are two different persons. The Mahdi will be of the house of Muhammed. Both the Mahdi and Jesus will die and "then all things will perish," except God.[81] This is perhaps followed by a renewal of creation—but the matter is not altogether clear.

Muslims emphatically deny the deity of Christ. It is possible that Muhammed did not have a clear understanding of the Trinity. He said that in the Day of Judgment God would question Jesus and say, "Did you ever say to mankind: 'Worship me and my mother as gods beside

---

* Ghulam Ahmad (1980) claimed that he found the tomb of Jesus in Kashmir. Supposedly Jesus escaped somehow, migrated to India looking for the ten lost tribes, and died of old age and was buried at Srinagar, where his tomb has been found. Some believe that one of Jesus' disciples took his place on the cross, others suggest that Jesus lost consciousness on the cross but was revived. Ghulam Ahmad presented himself as the promised Messiah, the divine light who would guide the world to the path of righteousness. His teaching combined elements of Islam and Hinduism. The Ahmadiyya movement spawned by him has a missionary outreach, and the followers claim to be Muslims, an assertion firmly rejected by most Muslims. These followers have thus been persecuted as apostates.

Allah?'"[82] What's more, did Muhammed think that Mary was part of the Trinity? At first glance this might seem absurd, but this strange idea may be due to the Collyridians, who adored Mary and were centered in Arabia in the fourth century. It is uncertain how much Muhammed really knew about Jesus and what he might have been told by Christians or heretics he met here and there, or by Jews, who did not accept Christ as the Messiah.

Muhammed repeatedly stressed the point that God has no son. "Allah forbid that He Himself should beget a son...those who say 'The Lord of Mercy has begotten a son,' preach a monstrous falsehood at which the very heavens might crack, the earth split asunder and the mountains crumble to dust."[83]

The reality of Christ's death on the cross and Christ's deity are the two cardinal issues on which Islam and Christianity disagree.

THE BASIC TEACHINGS OF ISLAM

Muslims say the first Muslim was Adam, and that "Abraham in truth was not a Jew neither a Christian; but he was a Muslim and one of pure faith." Therefore, "follow the faith of saintly Abraham: he was no idolater."[84] Adam or Abraham could not possibly be followers of Muhammed, but the word *Muslim* simply means "one who resigns himself to God," and thus Adam and Abraham are said to be Muslim.

THE FIVE PILLARS OF ISLAM

All Muslims accept the five pillars of Islam.

1. *The Creed.* "There is no God but God, and Muhammed is the prophet of God" is proclaimed over and over again in the call to prayer that is heard five times a day from the minarets in Muslim lands. This short confession of faith is known as the *shahada.*

2. *Prayer.* Five times a day the *muezzin* calls Muslim believers to prayer. In the days of Muhammed, there were no clocks. Christians used bells to alert the faithful, and Jews used a ram's horn. Muslims used a *muezzin,* or town crier. The stated times of prayer are dawn, noon, mid-afternoon, sunset, and after dark. The believer prays in Arabic (a prayer not understood by the vast majority of Muslims) and follows a set form of words. Each prayer contains 17 small units. Ritual details cover every aspect of prayer. The bodily postures (standing, bowing, kneeling, prostration, sitting), ablutions that precede prayer, the rinsing of hands (forearm to elbow) and face (ears, mouth, and nostrils), and the passing of wet hands over head and feet. Believers observe the *kiblah;* they face the direction of Mecca. Because girls mature earlier than boys, they are required to pray five times a day when they reach nine years of age. Boys must meet the requirement at 13.

Congregational prayer takes place in the mosque on Friday at noon. "Believers, when you are summoned to Friday prayers...cease your trading.... Then, when the prayers are ended, disperse and go your way in quest of God's bounty."[85] After the service, normal activities can be resumed. There is no clergy in Sunni Islam; there are no priests. It is an *ulema,* a Muslim scholar, a professional, who preaches the sermon. The mosque ("place of prostration") features a prayer niche that faces Mecca and a raised pulpit for the speaker. The floor is covered with prayer carpets. Worshippers are to remove their shoes, and women either sit apart or occupy separate rooms. There are no musical instruments.

3. *Fasting.* This includes abstinence from smoking and sensual pleasures (including sex) and lasts from dawn to dusk. Believers fast the entire month of Ramadan, the month in which Muhammed received his first revelation. A joyful three-day feast, Eid ul Fitr, is observed at the end of Ramadan.

4. *Almsgiving.* This is a sacred duty, called *zakat.* Usually it means 2.5 percent of one's money and merchandise, and a different percentage for agricultural goods. Today (because of modern taxation), free-will offering or *sadaqa* are perhaps more common. According to some orthodox schools, *zakat* is due only for animals, agricultural products, precious metals, and objects intended for sale. Almsgiving, like everything else, is carefully regulated. Rules and regulations are endless and cover every aspect of every issue. *Zakat* is due only when the property has reached a certain value and has been in the possession of that person for one whole year. For instance, the taxable minimum of sheep is 40 heads, at which point one goat is due. At 121 sheep two goats are due, and at 201 sheep three goats are due…and the list goes on.

5. *Pilgrimage* to Mecca, or the *hajj.* Every Muslim is enjoined to visit the Kaaba in Mecca at least once in a lifetime. According to an old tradition, "every step in the direction of Mecca and the sacred Kaaba blots out a sin." The Koran informs us that Abraham and Ishmael came to Mecca and raised up the foundations of the Kaaba, an area that is now considered sacred territory and is closed to non-

Muslims. "We made the House [the Kaaba] a resort and a sanctuary for mankind, saying: 'Make the place where Abraham stood a house of worship.' We enjoined Abraham and Ishmael to cleanse Our House for those who walk round it."[86] It is almost inconceivable, however, that Abraham and Ishmael traveled to Mecca. Yet for Muslims, this is an article of faith.

For *hajj,* Muslim pilgrims dress in white and walk through an eight-mile long valley to reach the actual starting point. Seven times they walk around the Kaaba and kiss the Black Stone while reciting *Sura* 112: "Say: 'Allah is One, the Eternal God. He begot none, nor was He begotten. None is equal to Him.'" To re-enact Hagar's search for water, the pilgrim rushes seven times between two hills, moving faster and faster. On Mount Arafat the pilgrim offers prayers of repentance and asks for mercy and renewal. Pebbles are collected and cast at three stone pillars—this is a symbolic stoning of Satan where he had tempted Abraham. The pilgrimage ends with an animal sacrifice. The four-day feast of Eid al-Adha follows. It is one of the most important feasts observed throughout the Islamic community. It recalls the test of Abraham and his readiness to sacrifice his son who—according to Muslim sources—was Ishmael. Usually a sheep is offered in sacrifice, occasionally a goat or a camel. One third of the meat is used for the family, one third for the poor, and the last third for friends or neighbors. The sacrifice has nothing to do with the idea of atonement.

TRADITIONS IN ISLAM

There are many traditions—or *hadith*—that play a key role in Islam and that supplement the occasional utterances of

Muhammed found in the Koran. Early on, an effort was made by Muhammed's followers to collect traditions regarding Muhammed from living witnesses. This began with about 60 Muslims who had known or seen Muhammed. They became the first link in a long chain of witnesses. According to Sunni Muslims, even people who had briefly been in Muhammed's presence could become witnesses, even though they might have been blind or infants. Some believe that more than 100,000 had been in Muhammed's presence—making them all witnesses. Shiites, however, reject any traditions transmitted by Muslims who were not "just." They interpret the *hadith* differently from the Sunni. This is one the many areas of disagreement between Sunni and Shia.

Muhammed is said to be the ultimate model for all, and that his behavior should be imitated: "There is a good example in Allah's apostle for those who look to Allah."[87] One of the first (and perhaps most reliable) collections of traditions was published by al-Bukhari (d. 870), long after Muhammed's death. By this time, there were already 7,275 traditions. Al-Hajjaj (d. 875) offered a collection of 9,200. An effort was made to authenticate each one through a chain of witnesses or *isnad,* a list of transmitters going back to the days of Muhammed. Over time the *hadith* gained more and more authority till it was seen as secondary only to the Koran itself.

The *hadith* embraces the words, actions, and daily practices of Muhammed. Even his silence was significant, for a lack of objection implies tacit approval. More and more *hadith* appeared, literally tens of thousands, covering every possible situation. Traditions were divided into 1) genuine or sound traditions; 2) acceptable or fair traditions;

3) weak traditions. Koranic teaching and the *hadith* combined to form the Muslim law or *sharia.* For Sunni Muslims, the *sharia* has four principal elements: 1) the Koran; 2) the directions of Muhammed or *sunna* recorded in the *hadith;* 3) the consensus (*ijma*) of qualified legal scholars; and 4) analogical reasoning (*qiyas*) for cases not covered in any other way—for instance, the presentation of human images on television. The validity of consensus was based on the idea that no one "follows a path other than that of the faithful,"[88] bolstered by a tradition that "the *umma* (community of Muslims) will never agree on an error."

As with all legalistic systems, innumerable rules and regulations control every aspect of life. Precepts are categorized into acts that are obligatory, meritorious, permissible, objectionable, and forbidden. Independent, personal reasoning (*ijtihad*) was once acceptable, but the results were not binding. Later, after the four schools of orthodox thinking had been firmly established, all independent thinking was banned.

There are four orthodox schools of jurisprudence, and each one reached slightly different conclusions. These schools go back to the eighth and ninth centuries.

1. Hanafi, originally a Shiite scholar, allowed some room for private judgment (a typical Shiite position). This relatively liberal school of thought is popular in Iraq and western Iran, Central Asia, Egypt, and Turkey.

2. Ahmad ibn Hanbal gave rise to the Hanbali school of thought found in northern Iraq, the United Arab Emirates, and Syria. The Hanbali inspired the Wahhabi, who made a deep impact on Saudi Arabia. They are the "red hot puritans." These purists often persecute other

Muslims and comprise the most traditional and literalist of all the schools. They denounce learning, science, and rationalism. Their passionate preaching often leads to rioting and bloodshed in the streets.

3. Shafi'i was a Syrian. His teaching is prominent in Lower Egypt, Syria, Baghdad, and western Iran, as well as southeast Asia and East Africa. Shafi'i steered a middle course and accepted the rules of analogy. He also relied on consensus as long as it was linked to the judgment of the community *(umma)*.

4. Malik ibn Anas was a traditionalist. Maliki thinking is honored in Egypt and North Africa. The principle of consensus is accepted.

Rationalists were called *mutazili,* a word that means "to leave" or "abandon," because Wasil ibn Ata "left" the teaching of his masters after a theological dispute. Rationalists hoped to reconcile Islamic thinking with Greek philosophy. The big question of the day concerned the origin of the Koran. Was the book created or somehow eternal? They also discussed the problems of evil, predestination, what will happen to sinning Muslims, and how the Koran should be interpreted—always literally, or sometimes allegorically? The rationalists absolved God of all injustice, insisted on a measure of free will, and took an interesting intermediate position between those who say that all sinners will be condemned to hell forever and those who proclaim that sinners will not be punished. Their thinking had broad intellectual appeal, but was restricted to an elite. They lost all credibility when these allegedly liberal people persecuted those who disagreed with them. They imprisoned and tortured Ahmad ibn Hanbal because he affirmed the eternity of the Koran. As a school of thought the *mutazili* have

disappeared. Recently attempts to revitalize the movement, especially in opposition to the Wahhabi and Salafi, have failed.

By the tenth century, all four schools agreed that the days of independent interpretation were closed—an idea not accepted by Shiites, and more recently hotly disputed by reformers.

The interpretation and application of Muslim law, the *sharia,* varies enormously. Some Muslim countries—such as Indonesia, Bangladesh, and Pakistan—have a secular constitution, and Islamic law is largely limited to family law. Many countries feature a dual system, such as Saudi Arabia. Islamic law is usually applied to marriage and inheritance. In Northern Nigeria and elsewhere, an effort has been made to impose the *sharia* on the entire population, including the Christians who live there. By contrast, Abu Bakr, the highly revered first successor of Muhammed, allowed Christians and Jews the freedom to follow their own laws.

Some aspects of Muslim teaching are of particular interest at the present time.

JIHAD AND ISLAM

JIHAD DEFINED

Webster defines *jihad* as "a holy war waged on behalf of Islam as a religious duty," and "a crusade for a principle or belief," (*Merriam-Webster's Collegiate Dictionary,* 11th ed.).

What does the *sharia,* this great body of law, teach about jihad? A few Muslim scholars insist that jihad only refers to the internal struggle of the soul and has no reference to military action against an external enemy or another religion. A few passages in the Koran might perhaps be interpreted in this manner, but definitely not all of them. The occasional reference to the "struggle in His way" might conceivably be understood as a moral struggle, although the context is dubious at best. The same *Sura* adds, "Whether unarmed or well-equipped, march on and fight for the cause of Allah, with your wealth and with your persons," and finally, "Prophet, make war on the unbelievers and the hypocrites."[89] This takes jihad out of the realm of mere internal struggle.

> Let those who would exchange the life of this world for the hereafter, fight for the cause of Allah; whoever fights for the cause of God, whether they die or conquer, We shall richly reward them…the true believers fight for the cause of God, but the infidels fight for idols.[90]

At one point it seems that Muhammed declared war on Jews and Christians unless they embraced Islam: "Fight against such of those to whom the Scriptures were given as believe neither in Allah nor the Last Day…[who] do not embrace the true faith until they pay tribute out of hand and are utterly subdued."[91] That can hardly be taken to refer to an internal struggle! The call to kill idolaters is crystal clear: "When the sacred months [four months out of the year] are over slay the idolaters wherever you find them. Arrest them, besiege them, and lie in ambush everywhere for them. If they repent, and take to prayer and pay the alms-tax, let them to go their way. God is forgiving and merciful."[92]

FIGHTING ENCOURAGED

In the Koran, vigorous warfare is encouraged: "When you meet the unbelievers in the battlefield strike off their heads, and when you have laid them low, bind your captives firmly. Then grant them their freedom or take ransom from them." The Koran explicitly states that a different rule prevails for fellow Muslims. "He that kills a believer by design, shall burn in Hell for ever." Those who embrace Islam and then desert it are to be seized "and put them to death wherever you find them."[93] An apostate can be killed outright. War is lawful against infidels and apostates, and these wars count as jihad.

Across history there have always been martyrs in search of a glittering paradise, the faithful who "will fight for His cause, slay and be slain. Such is the true pledge [of paradise] which He has made them in the Torah, the Gospel and the Koran…. Rejoice then in the bargain you have made. That is the supreme triumph."[94] In other words, killing in God's name will secure a place in heaven.

When Muhammed proclaimed, "Fight for the sake of Allah those that fight against you, but do not attack them first. God does not love aggressors,"[95] he did not give a green light to terrorism. Seemingly Muhammed encouraged tolerance when he said, "No compulsion is there in religion," although it is not clear whether the text means that one cannot or should not force another person to become a Muslim. After all, "if God intends to guide a man, He opens his bosom to Islam. But if He pleases to confound him [lead him astray] He makes his bosom small and narrow" because "strive as you may to guide them, Allah will not guide those whom He misleads."[96] The idea of predestination is a controlling factor in Muslim thinking.

Whereas idolaters and apostates can be killed, Jews and Christians (or the People of the Book) are in a special category. They are the *dhimmi,* or protected minorities. No thought is given to equality; the *dhimmi* could never be on a level playing field with Muslims. They should at least pay a special tax.

In spite of these legal demands, pragmatism prevailed at times. In India the small Muslim elite could not possibly exterminate the immense number of Hindu "idolaters." To solve the problem, the Hindus were simply placed in the same category as "the People of the Book" and legally became part of the protected monotheistic(!) minorities. Now, at least, they could be taxed. A later Sultan, Aurangzeb (1618–1707), who fiercely opposed idol worship, reversed this "enlightened" policy of the Indian emperor Akbar.

JIHAD UNDERSTOOD

Regardless of the interpretation and exact meaning of jihad, an "individual" military jihad has never been sanctioned by the *umma,* the community at large. The very idea of jihad involves the community in a holy war. Individual action is never contemplated; that is inconceivable. The individual suicide bomber is not a typical Muslim personality regardless of proclamations of martyrdom and promises of paradise. In Muslim law, suicide is illegal and suicide bombers break Islamic law and are condemned to hellfire and damnation.

Traditionally, only an *ulema* can declare armed jihad. The killing of fellow Muslims is strictly prohibited, not to mention children and women. It is possible that some Sunnis do not recognize Shiites as fellow believers and therefore treat them like apostates who can legitimately be killed. Shiites may have the same conviction regarding Sunnis, and religious extremists are certain that everyone not part of their group is an apostate. Often jihad cloaks personal ambition, vengeance, financial considerations, and even baser motives. There is never a legitimate justification for the indiscriminate killing and senseless slaughter of entire families.

WOMEN IN ISLAM

WE SHOULD GIVE CREDIT where it is due and be grateful that the Koran forbids infanticide: "You shall not kill your children for fear of want."[97] Muhammed ended the custom of burying alive unwanted newborn girls.

MUHAMMED'S HOUSEHOLD

It is impossible to consider the position of women without reference to the household of Muhammed, for he is the ultimate model for all Muslims. Abdullah Yusuf Ali, in his commentary on *Sura* 66:1, points out that "the Prophet's household was not like other households. His 'Consorts of Purity' were held to a higher standard in behavior than ordinary women."

Given the large number of wives Muhammed had, it is not surprising that difficulties arose from time to time in his household. The behavior of his beloved Aisha created so many problems that Muhammed renounced the society of his wives for a while. Reference has already been made to the special revelation that allowed Muhammed to deviate from the regular rotation of conjugal rights. A seemingly authentic tradition quotes the irrepressible young Aisha as commenting, "God is in a hurry to fulfill your desire." That was surely true of Muhammed's relationship with the Coptic slave mentioned previously.

THE RESTRICTIONS REGARDING THE VEIL

Muhammed received special rules regarding his wives. He was told, "Prophet, enjoin your wives, your daughters, and the wives of true believers to draw their veil close round them. That is more proper, so that they may be recognized and not be molested." Some claim that this admonition addressed only Muhammed's wives. Others disagree. The general topic reappears in *Sura* 24:31:

> Enjoin believing women to turn their eyes away from temptation and to preserve their chastity; to cover their adornments (except such as are normally revealed); to draw their veils over their bosoms and not to reveal their finery except to their husbands, their fathers, their husbands' fathers, their sons, their step-sons, their brothers' sons, their sisters' sons, their women servants, and their slave girls; male attendants lacking in natural vigor, and children who have no carnal knowledge of women. And let them not stamp their feet in walking so as to reveal their hidden trinkets.[98]

Traditional interpreters of this text conclude that a woman should cover everything except the face and the hands. Some contemporary commentators see it differently. They believe that modesty must be interpreted in line with contemporary moral standards. The koranic requirements can be understood only in the light of the prevailing immorality of the pre-Islamic society of Arabia. Regardless of the text, it seems that the veil did not become widespread for several generations. There are Muslims scholars who claim that the veil was customary in the pre-Islamic society of Arabia and was considered a badge of honor, since veiled women could not possibly work in the field. According to them, the veil was a status symbol.

Unfortunately, the traditional interpretation of this text is the most common. The Taliban in Afghanistan did not allow women to receive normal hospital treatment because they wanted to prevent bodily exposure to male hospital staff and doctors. Recently, male doctors were forbidden to practice at the gynecological hospital in Sadr City, Baghdad. A clinic where male technicians performed ultrasound examinations of pregnant women was threatened with closure and two doctors were slain in 2005 for treating Iraqi women.

The actual situation varies from country to country. For example, there is a world of difference between Saudi Arabia and Algeria. In recent years the veil has become a political issue in the West and made into a test of flexibility and tolerance by Muslims. As long as *Sura* 24:31 is in the Koran, the veil will always be a contentious issue.

THE ISSUE OF POLYGAMY

Muhammed limited a husband to four wives, but he added, "but if you fear that you cannot maintain equality among them, marry one only or any slave-girls you may own."[99] The number of slave girls a man could marry was not restricted, but these girls would never be on the same level as wives. As far as polygamy is concerned, Muslim commentators point out—perhaps not without reason—that the requirement to love and treat all equally is impossible, and that for all practical purposes, monogamy is recommended. Polygamy has recently been abolished in Morocco, and the age at which it is permissible to wed raised to 18. Polygamy is not permitted in

Turkey or Tunisia. Elsewhere, a number of restrictions limit polygamy. For instance, the Maliki school of thought insists that new spouses must be informed about the existence of another wife. In some countries the woman may insist on a clause in the marriage contract that stipulates the union will be dissolved if a second marriage is contracted.

We are told that Muhammed married many more than four wives because there were so many widows after the Battle of Uhud and he felt impelled to marry several of them. It seems that none of his followers, however, had the same benevolent impulse. As Muslim commentators claim, the four-wife limit came later. We are also told that Muhammed might have received the four-wife restriction *after* he had already married many more.

In the past, Muslim women were not allowed to marry a non-Muslim man, but Muslim males were free to take a wife from the People of the Book.[100] For example, Muhammed took a Jewish wife who had been taken prisoner.

THE MATTER OF AUTHORITY

One text often quoted by critics of Islamic morality is found in *Sura* 4:34:

> Men have authority over women because Allah has made the one superior to the other, and because they spend their wealth to maintain them. Good women are obedient. They guard their unseen parts because Allah has guarded them. As for those from whom you fear disobedience, admonish them and forsake them in beds apart, and beat them.

Muslim commentators insist that the text here merely means "spank them lightly," but there is no sound reason to change the meaning of the word "beat." Other commentators have suggested that the husband should beat his wife lightly, with his hands, avoiding her face and other sensitive parts. In no case should he resort to using a stick or any other instrument that might cause injury. These liberal interpretations, however, have not improved the position of Islamic women.

Then there is what's called *mut'a,* or marriage for a fixed period of time. According to the Sunni, Muhammed initially allowed such temporary marriages, but later decided against unions with a time limit. For Shiites such marriages are perfectly legal, and a great deal of legislation has been created to establish with whom *mut'a* can be carried out and under what conditions. It has been suggested by some that such marriages might only last a few hours and justifies legalized prostitution. Perhaps temporary marriages were justified because of long absences due to travel. In ancient times, depending on the destination, travel could involve years, and even a relatively short distance might require a few weeks. Nevertheless, this is hardly a justification for the practice of *mut'a*.

CONTROVERSIES REGARDING WOMEN

Honor killings are mentioned in the news from time to time, but they are not part of official Islamic teaching, although that does not make them any less horrible. Such killings have occurred with alarming frequency in Pakistan as well as in Iraq.[101] In Germany a Turkish-based women's group has documented 40 instances of so-called honor killings since 1996. It is often the youngest son of the family who does "the honor." On January 26, 2007, the Associated Press reported one such killing. This barbaric custom emerges out of an atmosphere of ultra-religious zeal on the part of misguided people.

Many African Muslims insist on female circumcision, although the majority of Muslims do not think that this practice has any basis in Islam. It is a fairly common practice in the Sudan. France considered the problem sufficiently serious enough that it passed legislation outlawing female circumcision.

Muslim women are at a distinct disadvantage when it comes to matters of inheritance. Sometimes she is altogether excluded (Maliki school) or has restricted rights (Hanafi school). Divorce is basically a male prerogative, but the divorced woman can keep her dowry (if there was one) and receive child support till the child is weaned. At that point the child may be returned to the father. While this matter is for the court to decide, in traditional Islamic law, the child goes to the father.

On the other hand, Muhammed allowed women to testify at trials, although he said their testimony had only half the value of a man's. Still, this was progress. He also allowed women to receive an inheritance. In a few areas of life Muhammed improved the position of women, but in others they fared worse.

Today the legal situation varies from country to country. Some versions of Islamic law allow a husband to prevent his wife from working. He may even forbid her to leave the house for any reason other than studying Islam. In Saudi Arabia women are not allowed to drive a car. In Jordan women are legally equal to men and the legal code is committed to liberal humanism. In Iraq, a law enacted in 1959 set the marriage age at 18. In Iran, after the revolution of 1979, the age permissible for marriage was lowered to nine and polygamy became permissible. In spite of Islamic law, family planning has entered upon the scene, and in some Muslim countries contraceptives are available. Tunisia has gone so far as to permit abortion.

Strictly speaking, it is at the sole discretion of the husband to decide whether the spouse is free to work outside of the home. And overall, the role and position of Muslim women remains bleak. Everything is in the hands of the husband, who seemingly has unlimited authority over the extended family.

THE SUFIS

WHO THEY ARE

In all religions there are groups of people who are dissatisfied with the mere observance of rules and regulations. They are in search of something deeper, including a relationship with God rooted in love. This is the case with Islamic mystics, who are called *Sufis*. It is possible that *Sufi* is derived from a word meaning "wool" and refers to the simple woolen cloak originally worn by Sufis, perhaps in imitation of Jesus, according to Islamic tradition. Was there an early connection with certain Christian monks who lived the ascetic life? Mystics usually live a peaceful, tranquil life of contemplation, but the Sufi have played and continue to play a very important public role in their society. Isolated koranic texts have been used by Sufis to justify their attitude: "To Allah belongs the east and the west. Whichever way you turn there is the face of Allah."[102] The Koran also declares that God is closer to man than his jugular vein.[103] The Sufi also found encouragement in the mysterious night journey of Muhammed.

The ultimate goal of the mystic is union with God. The exact nature of this union is a matter of debate. Sufis yearn for a "passing away" from the self into a higher consciousness, a survival in God. They describe four or perhaps seven stages on the way to *fana,* the passing away. This goal can be reached through meditation on the names and attributes of God. Many Sufis entertain unorthodox interpretation of the Koran, looking for hidden meanings only known to initiates. Orthodox Muslims have been distrustful of these mystics and have frequently persecuted and even killed them.

One of the first-known mystics was Hasan Al-Basti, for whom *fana* meant the annihilation of the self. By the twelfth century, individual Sufis in Iraq banded together in groups and followed a leader. The disciples abandoned themselves into the hands of a master who exercised total control over them.

Such mystical fervor, the transport out of the self into God, gave rise to extremes. From the idea of union with God it was a simple step to merge into the deity, enabling one to say, "I am God." At that point the distinction between good and evil becomes meaningless. Accused of heresy and blasphemy, some Sufis were executed. The so-called intoxicated mystics came out of Persia; they used ritual and dance to reach ecstasy. They saw dance movements as an echo of the order and motion of the heavenly spheres.

This mysticism was formalized and reduced to a system that could be taught. Masters defined 50 stations or steps toward God. Older texts mention only seven: repentance, abstinence, renunciation, pov-

erty, patience, trust in God, and acquiescence in the will of God. The stations are followed by different states, including states of hope, fear, and love. The mystic followed a long and lonely path.

The most famous mystic was al-Ghazali, a renowned orthodox theologian who turned to mysticism for answers in life and became one of the greatest Sufi philosophers. He tried to bridge the gap between orthodox Islam and the Sufi movement.

THE KEY BROTHERHOODS

From 1200 to 1500—the so-called Golden Age of Islam—Sufiism spread from Baghdad to the rest of the Muslim world. Sufis were ardent missionaries and largely responsible for the conversion of the central Asian Turks to Islam. Sufi brotherhoods became powerful, organized revolutions, and governed cities. Some of the most important brotherhoods are…

1. The Quadiri, founded by Abd al Jilani (1077–1166). This Sufi order is widespread, perhaps because it always stayed within the limits of orthodoxy. The Quadiri flourished in India, Pakistan, and Turkey. One of their sheiks led the Algerian resistance against the French. They have many followers in northern Nigeria and among the Chechen. Many Sufi orders are politically active.

2. The Naqshbandi is one of the few Sufi orders that traces its origin to Muhammed through Abu Bakr, not Ali. This order has been most active in Chechnya and Pakistan.

3. The Mevlevi order goes back to Rumi, whose tomb in Konya is the most important place of pilgrimage in all of Turkey. The order is best known for its dancing dervishes.

4. The oldest surviving group is the Chishti order, founded by a Syrian, Khaja

Abu Ishaq Shami, who died about A.D. 940. Members of the order settled in India and Afghanistan.

The difference between these various schools of thought is not so much dogmatic as practical, in the area of methodology. For all, the central point is love seen as a projection of the very essence of God.

WHAT THEY TEACH

For most Sufis, all of creation is a manifestation of one single reality—God. The duality between Creator and creation is dissolved in unity through an awakening that leads to meditation. The most common method is called *dhikr,* a collective experience of chanting and dancing till a state of trance is achieved. The same result can be reached through endless repetition of the divine names, sacred formulas, or breathing exercises.

The Sufis say there is more than one path to union with God. The Naqshbandi suggest more than 40, and claim that 70,000 veils between us and "the station of the Prophet" have to be removed one by one. The goal of Sufism is not easily reached.

Some Sufis have spoken of "the idea of Muhammed" almost in the same way Christians have spoken of the *Logos,* the Word of God. Most Sufis have prudently maintained that the union with God is not an actual merging. They have tried to remain within the limits of orthodoxy with the exception of veneration of Muhammed. For a while, among Sufis, irrationality reigned supreme and the sober speculation of the true mystics was forgotten. Magic and miracles moved into the forefront, and worldly learning was despised. As a result, Sufism went into a temporary decline.

The main orders of Sufis continue to exist and are active even in the West. They have formed powerful brotherhoods and cannot be ignored politically or socially, not to mention spiritually.

A word should perhaps be added about the Bektashi communities in Turkey and Albania. Although founded in the thirteenth century by Bektash Wali, the movement did not reach its present form till the sixteenth century. Both Shiites and the Orthodox Church influenced the Bektashi, who believe in a "Trinity" of Allah/Muhammed/Ali, whom they venerate excessively. Like all mystics, they pursue the "Unity of Being." They worship in monasteries *(teke)* and mausoleums *(turbe)* rather than in mosques. They oppose literalism and seek an understanding of the inner meaning of the Koran. Bektashi ignore many of the rules of conventional Islam. They do not face Mecca in prayer, are free to drink alcohol and eat pork, and revere Jesus as a "Vessel of the Divine Spirit."

There are levels of initiation all the way up to dervish and *baba* (father), and even a few "grand fathers." For centuries the Bektashi maintained a loose connection with the Janissaries of the Ottoman army. Banned by a progressive Sultan in 1826, they regained freedom till they were banned—along with all other Sufi orders—by Kemal Ataturk in 1925. The Bektashi moved on to Albania, where perhaps as many as 20 percent of the population have some connection to the Bektashi. Since 90 percent of the population in Kosovo is Albanian, it is reasonable to assume that some are Bektashi.

News reports seldom have anything to say about the Alewis—yet another Shiite group—although it not unreasonable to believe that they constitute as much as 25 percent of the Turkish population. Because they have suffered considerable prejudice, they have resorted to legal dissimulation. The Alewis combine Sufiism and Shiism, and their veneration of Ali borders on deification. They reject the literal interpretation of the Koran, do not observe the five daily prayers, Ramadan fasting, or the pilgrimage to Mecca. Alewis see Muhammed as the announcer and Ali as the preserver of the truth. Like the Shiites, they are waiting for the Mahdi, the Savior who will set everything right.

For a while the Alewis thought of Ataturk—the first president of the Republic of Turkey—as yet another divine emanation because he liberated them from the yoke of Sunni orthodoxy and promoted a secular state. Later, in his drive for secularization, Ataturk turned against the Alewis. The Turkish government would like to integrate the Alewis into the Sunni framework, but its success has been limited. In recent years—and with greater freedom—the Alewis have experienced renewal.

THE EARLY DAYS OF ISLAM AND THE SHIITES

THE ISSUE OF A SUCCESSOR

Events that took place in the early days of Islam are extremely important because they directly impact our generation. The death of Muhammed produced instant chaos. No provision had been made for a successor. His death unleashed a round of fighting across Arabia because 1) many Bedouin tribes believed that their loyalty was not to Islam but to Muhammed, and ended with his death; 2) there were pretenders who claimed to have a prophetic mission; and 3) competing factions within the Muslim community had their eye on

the seat of power. It was understood that Muhammed was the last of the prophets, but still there was a need for a spiritual successor, and someone had to fill the role of head of State.

Among the claimants were 1) the original converts who had come with Muhammed from Mecca to Medina and occupied a place of honor; 2) the group of early supporters in Medina who had invited Muhammed to the city; 3) the leaders of the Quraysh tribe in Mecca, who hoped to regain preeminence; and 4) Ali, the cousin and son-in-law of Muhammed, an immediate family member, who was certain that the leadership should fall on his shoulders and stay within the family.

A compromise was agreed upon in a meeting of the companions of Muhammed and the earliest converts. How the final choice was made at that meeting remains unknown. Abu Bakr emerged as the caliph or successor and had excellent credentials. He was the father of Aisha, Muhammed's favorite wife and one of his earliest converts. In a moment of extreme danger, Abu Bakr was the only one willing to hide with Muhammed in a cave. Abu Bakr had been chosen by Muhammed to lead the traditional prayers, which was almost as good as an official designation. He was caliph from 632–634.

The Sunni, however, claim that Muhammed deliberately declined to name a successor. Shiites are equally certain that Muhammed designated Ali, a family member. But Ali willingly submitted to Abu Bakr and his two successors. Shiites argue that this was just a meaningless gesture for the sake of unity and that Ali withdrew from public life in quiet protest. The germ of the Sunni/Shia split is found here, a split that has provoked many wars and has recently torn Iraq apart. Shiites believe that successors to Muhammed should be family members, whereas Sunnis do not.

THE IDENTITY OF THE SUCCESSORS

Abu Bakr showed remarkable administrative ability. The new caliph managed to quell unrest among the Bedouin tribes in Arabia and reasserted the central authority of Mecca. Many tribes had undergone a halfhearted conversion and resented the tax that had been imposed by Muhammed and refused payment. Others returned to idol worship. In response, Abu Bakr launched the Wars of Apostasy.

Muhammed had not been unaware of the superficial allegiance of some tribes. "The Arabs of the desert declare: 'We are true believers.' Say: 'You are not.' Rather say: 'We profess Islam,' for faith has not yet found its way into your hearts."[104] Abu Bakr allowed the People of the Book, Jews and Christians, a large degree of freedom. They were ruled by their own civil code. Two years later, Abu Bakr died, either of natural causes or by poisoning. The issue of succession came to life again.

When Omar (634–644) was chosen as the second caliph, Ali objected vehemently. Those who believed that only a member of the family should be a caliph spurned Omar and accepted the leadership of Ali. This was the beginning of an open break in Islam that never healed. Omar was the true founder of the Arab Empire; he belonged to the Quraysh clan of Mecca, and the center of the empire's gravity shifted from Medina to Mecca. Omar was wise enough to tolerate the social and religious arrangements of the conquered tribes and nations, but he definitely favored the interests of Mecca and the Quraysh over against the old companions of Muhammed.

THE CONQUESTS BY THE SUCCESSORS

Once control had been reestablished over the Bedouin tribes and the Arab Peninsula, Syria was attacked (636) and conquered rapidly, followed by the fall of Iraq one year later. In those days, many converts to Islam adopted Arabic and came to be regarded as Arabs.

In Byzantium, the Eastern Roman Empire, civil war raged, and ten kings ruled over a four-year period (628–632). The Byzantines underestimated the Muslim threat and assumed that Arab incursions were no more than the customary raids for spoils. They did not anticipate the establishment of garrison cities, among them Basra and Kufa. In the occupied areas the Arabs became a military elite separate from the rest of the population. They were never landowners or laborers, only conquerors. Arab victories were greatly facilitated by the alienation of the population, thanks to the oppression of the Byzantine court. The official Orthodox Church tried to convert followers of Bishop Nestorius by force, so the persecuted groups actually welcomed the Muslim invaders. Circumstances could not have been more favorable for Omar: The weak military situation of Byzantium, the inspiration of a newfound faith with a promise of paradise for those killed on the battlefield, and the allure of enormous spoils was an unbeatable combination.

Gradually the attitude Muslims exhibited toward Jews and Christians changed. In 641 Caliph Omar decreed that they should all be removed from Arabia, except for those in the southern and eastern fringes. It should be said in all fairness that the expulsion—unreasonable as it was—was carried out with compassion. Many of the Jews and Christians were resettled in newly conquered Syria and Iraq.

Omar came to his end when a Persian slave struck him down in a mosque. The choice of successor was now between Ali and Othman (644–656), an early convert from the powerful Umayyad tribe who had married one of Muhammed's daughters. Once Othman became caliph, he increased central control over provincial revenues. Inevitably, of course, tensions arose between the precepts of religion and political reality. Since church and state were never separated, the collision of interests was unavoidable.

Persia (Iran) was next on the list of conquered nations, and by 651, the last resistance was overcome. Christians and Jews had to pay a special poll tax, but compared to the fiscal demands of the Byzantine emperor, they were actually better off, and the Nestorian "heretics" were no longer exposed to ridicule and persecution. Christians were even allowed to build churches—and that is more than can be said of Turkey and Saudi Arabia today. There was one limitation, however: Church spires could not exceed the height of minarets.

The spoils from the conquest of Persia helped to finance a dozen more Muslim campaigns, including one against Egypt. The Christian population, which had been persecuted by Byzantium because of theological differences, received the Muslim invaders as liberators. It seems that Muslim forces conquered Egypt with less than 2,000 men.

The problems Othman faced in his administration were internal. An army of rebels demanded his abdication. Some resented his innovations, others objected to his alleged laxity and misrule. He was surrounded in his palace and hacked to death. Again, succession became a major issue.

FURTHER CONTROVERSY REGARDING SUCCESSORS

After the murder of Othman, the split between Sunni and Shiite became permanent. Some approved the assassination, while others condemned it. Neutrality was unacceptable. The time had come for Ali to assert himself. At this crucial moment of Ali's career, Aisha, one of Muhammed's widows, deserted Ali and accused him of complicity in the murder of Othman. Ali left the unfriendly confines of Mecca and made Kufa, in Iraq, his new capital. Muawiya, a cousin of Othman and commander of the army in Syria, took it upon himself to avenge the murder and to wage war against the Shia or partisans of Ali.

Because Ali came to power as a consequence of the assassination of Othman, many believed him to be guilty by association even though he was not directly involved in the killing. Unrest persisted throughout his reign, and not everyone accepted him as the legitimate ruler. Civil war broke out. Ali defeated his enemies at the Battle of the Camel (656), but nothing was settled. A year later the Battle of Siffin took place and Ali's opponents were on the verge of defeat when the Syrians dramatically lifted copies of the Koran on their lances and made an appeal for arbitration. Ali agreed, but those who supported Ali saw it as an unacceptable compromise. How could the legitimacy of the caliphate be submitted to negotiation? Had not the Koran proclaimed, "If two parties of believers take up arms the one against the other, make peace between them. If either of them commit aggression against the other, fight against the aggressors till they submit to Allah's judgment"?[105] Radicals accused Ali of repudiating the Koran, and the arbitration of 659 was unfavorable to Ali. The murder of Othman was declared unjustified and a council was asked to elect a new caliph. Ali rejected these conclusions, but by this time his coalition had disintegrated. Unpopular in Basra, he moved his headquarters to Kufa, where the radical Khariji, who were opposed to the very idea of arbitration, assassinated him in 661. Hasan, Ali's son, accepted a large pension and retired to Medina. Leadership now fell on the shoulders of Hasan's brother, Husayn. The situation was chaotic. People in Medina resented the influence of Kharijis. These extremists tolerated Jews and Christians as People of the Book, but fellow Muslims who held divergent beliefs were treated as apostates and killed. The uncompromising Khariji split into several sects, and one of them, the Ibadi, has survived in the modern Muslim country of Oman.

The Shiites hoped to gain control of the caliphate and to install Husayn as the successor, but Muawija was also in the running, and he headed a large army. Husayn left Medina with a small following—mostly his own family—and set out for Kufa, the new Shiite headquarters, to be installed as the new caliph. Perhaps he assumed that he would be safe as Muhammed's only living grandson. But his little band was surrounded, deprived of water, and after ten days, cut down to the last man. The death of Husayn took place in Karbala on October 10, 680. Ever since, Karbala in Iraq has been a most important place of pilgrimage for Shiites. One of the key dates on the Shiite calendar is the festival of Muharram Ashourah, which commemorates the death of Imam Husayn, complete with "passion plays." It is a day of deep mourning, fasting, and often self-flagellation. Forty days later another commemorative day is dedicated to the suffering

of the women and children of the family of Husayn. The death of Husayn was not the end of the fratricidal wars; later, a grandson of Husayn led a revolt and was killed.

THE DIFFERENCES BETWEEN SUNNIS AND SHIITES

ASIDE FROM THE DISAGREEMENT over who can properly be chosen as Muhammed's successors, there are several dogmatic differences between the Sunnis and the Shiites:

1. Shiites accept the idea that the Koran was created.

2. Shiites reject traditions that have been handed down through their enemies, such as Aisha (who betrayed Ali).

3. Shiites have accepted the principle of *taqiya,* the right to dissimulate in times of peril—i.e., to pretend not to be a Shiite. It seems to be sanctioned by the Koran. "Those who are forced to recant while their hearts remain loyal to the faith shall be absolved."[106] It makes it difficult to know how many Shiites live in Saudi Arabia, a country that is predominantly Sunni. The government would like to have a better handle on the situation because most of the (known) Shiites live in the areas where the oil fields are located.

4. Shiites accept the validity of temporary marriages.

5. There are legal differences between Sunnis and Shiites. This complicates the attempt to write a constitution in countries such

as Iraq, where both groups are heavily represented. Even if Islam were the official religion of the state, it would not automatically resolve disagreements between major population groups. In some Islamic countries it is permissible to opt out of the secular civil law on issues such as marriage, inheritance, or divorce in order to follow Muslim law. The choice has practical consequences. For instance, under Islamic rule, a brother receives twice as much inheritance as his sister. That is not the case under civil law. In the case of a "mixed" marriage between a Sunni and a Shia, the problem is compounded.

6. Aside from the intercession of Muhammed, Shiites rely on the prayers of "the House of the Prophet," meaning Muhammed, Ali (especially) and his wife Fatima, and their sons Hassan and Husayn. The 12 Imams are also intercessors. Imams are believed to be infallible and sinless.

7. If Ali is the spiritual ancestor of the Shiites, Husayn is the great martyr. Shiites observe a special feast day recalling the occasion when Muhammed announced the Imamate of Ali—of which the Sunnis fail to find a trace. The festival of al-Muhabila celebrates a meeting between the household of Muhammed and a Christian deputation from Najran.

8. The most essential difference between Sunni and Shia is the matter of succession to Muhammed. According to Shiite scholars, Muhammed more than once appointed Ali as his suc-

cessor. They reject the legitimacy of the first three caliphs who followed Muhammed. It would be tedious and beyond the scope of this book to follow the many reasons for the divisions among Shiites, but the divisive factor was usually the apostolic succession of the Imams. The "twelvers" have dominated Iran for over 500 years. They look back to Ali and the first 12 Imams as authoritative. The so-called "seveners" and "fivers" (not to mention others) have their own lists of Imams.

THE IMAMS

	Twelvers	Fivers	Seveners/Ismaili
1.	Ali	same	same
2.	Hasan	same	same
3.	Husayn	same	same
4.	Ali	same	same
5.	Muhammed	Zayd	Muhammed
6.	Jafar		same
7.	Musa		Ismail
8.	Ali		
9.	Muhammed		
10.	Ali		
11.	Hasan		
12.	Muhammed		

The largest group of Shiites is the twelvers. When the eleventh Imam died in 874, his son, Muhammed, was the logical successor. We are told that at the time his father was a prisoner. When the young boy searched for his father, he entered a cavern not far from the house and never returned. He was the twelfth and last of the Imams. For hundreds of years Shiites assembled at the entrance of the cave praying for the return of the child. Shiites believe that he did not die but is in "occultation," or that he was hidden away by God. In due time he will return (perhaps with Jesus) and be called the Mahdi ("the guided one"). Till the Mahdi appears, governments are tolerated as temporary necessary evils that will someday be replaced by the rule of the Mahdi. To some degree this explains the tumultuous history of the Shiites, which has been marked by anti-government uprisings, including some in this era.

Shiites have not been able to agree on the succession of the Imams. The fivers only accept the first five successors. The seveners trace their origin back to Ismail, the oldest son of the sixth Imam. The Ismailis are seveners. The twelvers cannot accept Ismail; they claim that Ismail died or was often inebriated and unfit to be an Imam regardless of blood connection. They selected Ismail's younger brother Musa as the seventh Imam.

This is just one of the many ways that Sunnis and Shiites are divided. Outsiders think of the followers of Islam as one large homogeneous block. No doubt Muslims look at Christendom in the same way. In reality, there are endless divisions and movements within Islam, and they are often at loggerheads with each other.

Today more than 10 percent of Muslims are Shiites. Most of them live in Iran, but there are also some in Iraq, Bahrain, Afghanistan, and elsewhere. Almost all of them live in the Middle East with the exception of Azerbaijan, where Shiites comprise the majority of the population.

9. A significant distinction between the Sunni and Shia is the important idea of *ijtihad,* or independent reasoning. According to Shiites, *ijtihad* is still acceptable.

10. There are additional, more minor differences between these two large seg-

ments of Islam. For example, Shiites believe that a secret interpretation of the Koran, a hidden esoteric understanding, has been transmitted by Muhammed to Ali, the infallible interpreter.

THE SPREAD OF ISLAM

UPON THE DEATH OF Husayn, the Shiites selected his oldest son, Hasan, as caliph, but at the same time, General Muawiya (661–680) proclaimed himself caliph in Damascus. The civil war lasted 12 years. Ultimately Hasan accepted Muawiya as caliph and moved to Medina to live a carefree life on a government pension. There is talk that he had 60 to 90 wives and hundreds of concubines. Nevertheless, various Shiite groups consider him among the Imamates.

THE UMAYYAD DYNASTY

Muawiya was the founder of the Umayyad dynasty, which lasted from 661 to 750. Damascus became the new capital, and Muawiya settled the matter of succession once for all by naming his son Yazid as the next caliph and demanded of everyone an oath of allegiance to him. Muawiya originated not only a new dynasty, but a centralized monarchy. He surrounded himself with all the trappings of royalty, acquired slaves, and enjoyed his harem. It was a far cry from the simple Bedouin structure typical of the Arab homeland. Gradually, four social groups developed within Arab culture:

• The ruling Arab garrison

• People linked to an Arab family. These converts did not fit into the

Arab tribal structure. Even though they were converts to Islam, they did not enjoy all the privileges of the ruling elite. They needed Arab sponsorship to advance in life. Dissatisfied, this group was in the forefront of opposition to the regime.

- Jews and Christians, the so-called People of the Book, were second-class citizens with limited civil rights, but more or less free to live according to their own laws as long as they paid a special tax. Syria was still largely Christian and provided a seasoned bureaucracy, which was invaluable for the fast-growing Islamic Empire.

- Slaves were at the bottom of society.

The unexpected death of Yazid, son of Muawiya, was the signal for another war of succession. The Umayyads were victorious. Once the ruling group was firmly established, more people were willing to embrace Islam. A contributing factor to the growth of Islam was the sale and dispersion of prisoners of war into Muslim households, where they learned Arabic and became Muslims. For a while this was the primary method of recruiting new believers. The government did not promote the conversion of Jews and Christians because it had no desire to lose the money gained from the tax paid by non-Muslims. In Central Asia the government made conversion to Islam more difficult by requiring circumcision, the knowledge of at least one *Sura,* and some ritual fulfillment. In Syria the bulk of the population remained Christian till the thirteenth century. In spite of these precautions, the Arab elite was slowly supplanted by a new emerging group of non-Arab Muslims.

In 698, Carthage in North Africa fell to Islam. Within 100 years the Muslim conquest stretched from Spain to India, and the military expansion continued till it was stopped in 732 by Charles Martel at Tours, only 100 miles from Paris. Given the situation, triumphalism is not surprising. Caliph Abd-al-Malik erected the Dome of the Rock in Jerusalem, a shrine over the rock from which Muhammed is said to have ascended to heaven. Jerusalem, associated with the mystic journey of Muhammed, became the third holiest city of Islam after Mecca and Medina. The same caliph built the extraordinary Umayyad Mosque in Damascus, one of the largest of Islam.

Stopped in the West by Charles Martel, war now raged in Central Asia. In the battle of the river Talas, Turco-Arab forces defeated the Chinese army of the T'ang dynasty in 751. Several historians agree that "this historic day determined the fate of Central Asia. Instead of becoming Chinese, as the general trend of earlier events seemed to presage, it was to turn Muslim."[107] Gradually the Umayyad Empire crumbled. Muslim Spain seceded, and one of the new rulers, Abdulrahman II (912–961), took the title of caliph. The disintegration did not wait for the colonial powers now blamed for every evil in the Middle East. Egypt was lost to a radical Shiite movement, and semi-autonomous rulers and warlords sprang up all over the Middle East. Bujid mercenaries ruled Iraq and Western Iran. The Seljuk Turks occupied Baghdad in 1055.

Radicals rewrite history and paint a picture of a united, peaceful Muslim community, the *umma,* divided only by the advent of Europeans who came with the motto "divide and conquer." This is a distortion of historic reality. Present-day inter-Muslim antagonisms have deep roots in ancient history.

The Umayyads beat the Chinese army but could not save their own dynasty. For ten years tribal and regional wars shook the empire till the Abbasids emerged. They killed every member of the Umayyad family except Abdel Rahman, who fled to North Africa and established a new Umayyad dynasty in Cordoba (Spain) in 756.

THE ABBASID DYNASTY

The Abbasid dynasty, named after Abbas, an uncle of Muhammed, lasted from 750 till 1258. In 763 the capital of the empire was moved to Baghdad, which became the largest city in the world outside of China. The eastward shift of the capital had unexpected consequences in the western reaches of the empire. Spain became independent under an Umayyad dynasty.

Under the Abbasid, most civil servants were Christians. The government had no choice but to use experienced Christians who had been well trained in the days of the Byzantine Empire. Under the Abbasids, foreigners entered the army and intermarriage became common between Arabs and non-Arabs. A child born of a slave in a Muslim household became a free Muslim. This greatly added to the number of Muslims. Occasional bloody Shia revolts were brutally suppressed. Best known of the Abbasid rulers is Harun al-Rashid (786–809), who may have sent a white elephant to Charlemagne. The *Thousand and One Nights* stories convey an idea, however exaggerated, of the luxury of the Abbasid court. Less known, but more talented, was al-Mansur (712–775). Influenced by Persian court ceremonial, the caliph wore royal robes and a crown. Court ritual became ever more complex. The ruler was veiled

from his audience and called the shadow of God. Meanwhile, the empire disintegrated under the twofold onslaught of the infiltration of Turkish tribes (c. 1000) and internal dissention due to theological disputes. Spain, Morocco, Tunis, and Egypt declared independence from the empire. At one point there were three simultaneous caliphs—in Baghdad, Cairo, and Cordoba. Baghdad was the new seat of power, but the rivalry with Damascus continued. Internal strife and disarray to the point of chaos was the order of the day.

One of the extremely violent movements, the Qarmations, accepted Ismaili Shiite teachings but added extra dimensions, such as holding property and women in common. They defeated the armies of the caliph and even plundered the holy city of Mecca. They disappeared from history around 1050, but not before inspiring the later Assassins.

THE SELJUK DYNASTY

Under the leadership of Tughril Beg (990–1063), founder of the new Seljuk Dynasty, the Turks ravaged Iran and, in 1055, captured Baghdad. They took control of the empire and ended the Abbasid caliphate. But Seljuk control was short-lived. The Mongols arrived and swept everything before them. Baghdad fell in 1255. The Mongols also settled the fate of the Hashshashin or Assassins, a subsect of the Ismailis. Best known, although perhaps legendary, is the "Old Man of the Mountain" and his paradise. Regardless of apocryphal stories, it is undeniable that assassins (perhaps high on hashish—a word at the root of 'assassin') carried out political murders. These early terrorists called themselves *fedayeen,* a word that has come back into prominence recently.

The Crusades are often mentioned in the contemporary Arab press and literature, but at the time they occurred, they provoked little interest in the Arab world. The Crusades were an aberration, not part of true Christian principles or biblical dogma. On the other hand, Islamic jihad is frequently mentioned in the Koran.

The crusaders invaded only a tiny fraction of the vast Islamic Empire. They occupied Jerusalem for less than 100 years and were finally expelled by Saladin in 1187. Although portrayed today as just another example of Western imperialism, the Crusades were actually a European response to Arab advances and conquests.

THE OTTOMAN EMPIRE

The Byzantine Empire lost the battle of Manzikert in 1071 and the victorious Seljuk Turkish forces moved on to the Bosphorus. But squeezed between Byzantium on the west and the Mongols on the east, the Seljuk Empire could not survive. It ended when the Mongol forces of Ghengis Khan overcame their kingdom. Out of the ensuing chaotic situation the Ottoman Empire emerged under the leadership of Osman (1258–1326). He and his men—the Osmanli—saw themselves as *ghazies,* or warriors dedicated to fight the infidels. They succeeded brilliantly. Over time the Ottoman Empire controlled Bulgaria, Hungary, Serbia, Bosnia, Greece, and other parts of Europe. Byzantium fell to Mehmed the Conqueror in 1453.

The most remarkable of the Ottoman sultans was Suleiman the Magnificent (1529–1566). He led 13 major military campaigns over a 40-year period. With 20 nationalities in his realm, the population under him was equal to the populations of France, England, and Germany. Most

of the Balkan was under his control and he advanced to the walls of Vienna, which he failed to conquer. The next 26 sultans presided over the slowly disintegrating Ottoman Empire. The reasons for this decay were mostly internal. The sultans had an overweening sense of superiority and felt no need to learn from anyone. Affairs of state were left in the hands of a vizier. All too often the harem ruled the sultan. Slowly, the rest of Europe responded to Ottoman aggression and recovered more and more territory while the Muslim world remained frozen in immobility. For centuries any independent interpretation of the Koran was outlawed. Islamic jurists refined points of law, but there was no overall review or reformation. All too often the *ulema* were subservient to the sultan. Under Mehmed the Conqueror (1451–1481), the learned doctors of the law agreed that fratricide was a perfectly legal means for eliminating wars of succession. Under political pressure, Islamic law was re-interpreted. In India, Akbar the Great (1556–1605) was honored by the *ulema* as "interpreter of Islam," even though he was illiterate.

In spite of occasional haphazard attempts at reform, medieval thinking dominated life across the Ottoman Empire. In World War I the empire sided with the Central Powers. Out of the defeat and debacle modern Turkey emerged, thanks to Kemal Ataturk, the father of the nation. The caliphate was abolished—an almost unthinkable event—and the last sultan dispatched into exile. In 1923 a republic was proclaimed and modern Turkey was born. The victorious Allies carved up the Ottoman Empire and took control of the Middle East. With the end of colonialism after World War II, new possibilities emerged when countries with an overwhelming Islamic population became independent. This included Indonesia (1945), Syria, Lebanon, Jordan (1946), Pakistan (1947), and countries in West Africa (1960). New leaders fanned the fires of nationalism, the best-known among them being Nasser of Egypt, Sukarno of Indonesia, Bourguiba of Tunisia, and Ali Bhutto of Pakistan. But there was no Islamic unity, no sense of common purpose. Nor have the new independent Islamic nations of the Middle East (Jordan and Saudi Arabia among them) enjoyed peace. Wars have not only been fought against Israel, but Iraq and Iran have fought each other and civil war has taken place in Lebanon and Yemen. The creation of Israel by "the West" was resented bitterly by Muslims. The West makes a convenient scapegoat for the difficulties of the Arab world, and may sometimes have contributed to the problems—but the underlying causes of decades and even centuries of stagnation have deeper roots. One result of all this tumult has been the birth of radical Islamic movements that are not representative of the rest of Islam and have done untold harm to the vast majority of Muslims.

ISLAMIC TERRORISM

AN ALARMING DECLINE

The combination of these two words should be an oxymoron, a connection never established. The reality is different. Thinking Muslims—let alone non-Muslims—cannot help but wonder: What exactly happened to the Islamic world? Why the decline after the golden age and centuries of preeminence? How could the glorious Ottoman Empire collapse? It was the arrival of General Bonaparte in Egypt in 1798 that shattered the last illusions. France, the oldest ally of the Ottoman Empire, had turned against her. In a scant three weeks, French armies landed in Egypt and entered Cairo. Bonaparte's easy victory over the flamboyant Mamelukes stunned the Muslim world. The Russian advance in the Caucasus, the British conquest of India and Malaysia, the Dutch presence in Indonesia, and the French and British control over vast areas of Africa all underlined the total collapse of the Muslim world. Who should be blamed? What should be blamed? How could one explain the lethargy of the Muslim world, the centuries of stagnation, the industrial and technological backwardness?

A CALL FOR REFORM

More and more Muslim scholars deplored the illiteracy of the masses, especially of the women, and the prevalence of popular superstitions. Some would-be reformers said they discovered some principles of democracy in the Koran. At one point Muhammed is told to "take counsel with them in the conduct of affairs," and elsewhere believers are admonished to "conduct their affairs by mutual consent,"[108] but the context is not about democracy.

Some scholars took a koranic admonition to heart: "Allah does not change a people's lot unless they change what is in their hearts"[109] Reform movements have hoped to propel Islam more into the modern world. Some have looked for moral and religious renewal. Others have looked to cultural change and education as a way out. Liberal movements have emerged that have relied on *ijtihad*—personal reasoning—and rejected the medieval interpretations of Islam. Reformers have called for a return to the early principles of Islam, when personal viewpoints were more acceptable and rigid orthodoxy had not yet been established. Instead of adhering to a literal interpretation of the Koran, some have embraced the ethical content and advocated gender equality, an openness to modern culture, and a reliance on a natural sense of right and wrong. Some have even promoted democratic principles and opposed Islam as a political movement. They have opposed jihad and proposed tolerance. Their calls have gone largely unheeded. It would be hard, not to say impossible, for many Muslims to accept modern principles and to demonstrate that somehow they echo koranic teaching and the early days of Islam. The voices of reformers have typically been ignored; strident voices are heard more readily.

In India, Sayyid Abmed Khan (1817–1898) pioneered modern education for Muslims and India. He was the founder of the Anglo Oriental College and the father of the intellectual and political Muslim class in India. His interpretation of the Koran hoped to reconcile Islam with contemporary civilization.

AN URGING TO RETURN TO THE PAST

Other would-be reformers took the exact opposite approach—they rejected accommodation with the prevailing culture and all innovation and preached a return to the "good days" of the past. One of the first significant reform movements along this line was initiated by Abd al-Wahhab (1703–1792), a radical Muslim Puritan. He revived some of the teachings of Ibn Taymiya (1263–1328), a conservative scholar of the Hanbali school who opposed the cult of the saints and prophets (popular at the time) and all *bid'a,* or inventions, and

all legal and philosophical developments of Islam. Abd al-Wahhab also denounced the worship of saints (still popular) and pilgrimages to their tombs, and rejected tobacco, music, and fine apparel. Even the observance of Muhammed's birthday was condemned. Books were burned. An adulteress stoned. Wahhabi opposed both Sunni and Shia Muslims. Whoever disagreed with this severe approach was treated like an apostate and killed. Karbala, the great pilgrim center of Shiites, was sacked in 1802 and the shrine of Husayn laid waste and looted. Even the tomb of Muhammed was opened and the jewels within distributed to the soldiers or sold.

Eventually an alliance was agreed upon between Wahhabi and Ibn-Saud, chief of the Nadj in central Saudi Arabia. Any area conquered by the king would follow strict Wahhabi rules. Ultimately this led to the formal foundation of the Kingdom of Saudi Arabia in 1932. The Wahhabi movement has remained a pillar of the throne, and Wahhabi thinking controls Saudi Arabia. The *sharia* is the law of the land. A somewhat uneasy alliance is maintained between the royal Saudi family and the Wahhabi *ulema.* The country remains staunchly conservative, but not sufficiently enough for the extremists among the Wahhabi. They condemn the political power structure and deplore the lack of loyalty to Islamic precepts within the royal family. Many Wahhabi believe that Saudi Arabia—not to mention other Muslim countries even less religious—has strayed, and the only answer is violent jihad. Directly or indirectly, the Wahhabi movement has inspired al-Qaida and similar terrorist organizations.

The Wahhabi movement is sometimes called Salafism, which literally means "early generations." The word refers to the early companions of Muhammed and the first three generations of Muslims "when purity prevailed." According to an ancient tradition preserved by Bukhari, Muhammed said, "The people of my generation are the best, then those who follow them, then those who follow the latter."[110] History paints a different picture. The first generations were hardly suitable models. Yet Salafi is a clarion call to return to ancient values. For Salafis, both Sufis and Shiites are heretical. Only a most literal understanding of the Koran and the *hadith* are needed. They ignore the four traditional schools of interpretation. Some draw a distinction between Salafi and Wahhabi, others do not. They might disagree to some extent about the nature of the Saudi Arabian government and the necessity of armed jihad. Those who believe that the Saudi government has moved away from Islamic purity have the option to remain passive and to avoid discord in the community. They rely on a koranic text admonishing Muslims to obey those in authority, and if there is a quarrel, to "refer it to God and the Messenger." Others oppose the government vehemently, accept the idea of violent jihad, and become Islamists, Jihadists, Qtubi, or embrace al-Qaida.

THE SHAPING OF TODAY'S MINDSET

Mawdoudi (1903–1989) of Pakistan proposed the concept of a modern Islamic state based on Islamic law, the *sharia,* and saw jihad as a supreme tool of Islamic revolution. Toynbee observes that "to apply the notion of the division between church and state to Islam would run counter to the whole Islamic concept of religion."[111] Mawdoudi suggested a gradual implementation of Islamic law for fear of alienating the middle class. He was the founder of Jamaat-e-Islami, an Islamic party that has had a major influence on radical Islamic movements.

In Syria, Rashid Rida (1865–1935) denounced the excess of the Mawlawi sufis, protested the unthinking perpetuation of past modes of thinking, and advocated *ijtihad* in his interpretation of the Koran. He influenced Hassan al-Banna (1906–1949) of Egypt, an earnest young man who joined a Sufi order at 12 and became a full member at 16. He advocated moral reform as essential to the renewal of Islamic society. In 1928 al-Banna founded the Muslim Brotherhood that is at the root of almost all contemporary Islamic terrorist movements. al-Banna was convinced that the only way to stop the decline of Islamic civilization relative to the West was a return to an unadulterated Islam. He opposed all forms of modernism and rejected Western ideas and culture, and denounced Westernization and secularism relentlessly. Initially the Brotherhood promoted only social activism, but in the 1930s Mawdoudi's ideas traveled from Pakistan to Egypt, and the Brotherhood moved from moral to political action. Assassinations were organized and volunteers sent to fight in Palestine against Israel. When a member of the Brotherhood assassinated the prime minister of Egypt, the group was officially dissolved and banned. A government agent killed al Banna. Although the Brotherhood is still banned in Egypt, unofficially, they are tolerated. In government elections, their candidates run as independents. In the elections of 2005, they secured 88 seats in the 454-member parliament. This might include protest votes in opposition to the ruling regime, and the exact strength of the Brotherhood is difficult to determine.

But the goal of the Brotherhood remains unchanged: the reestablishment of an Islamic caliphate and of Islamic nations ruled by Islamic law. Some Arab nations pay lip service to this idea, but the political reality is different.

The French encouraged Arab Christians in Syria to study in Paris, where they were infected with the virus of nationalism. When these Arab Christians returned to the Middle East, they founded the Baath movement that still rules Syria and Iraq. The dual purpose is the renewal of the Arab world and a new union of all Arabs. Hans Kung describes it as a mixture of French socialism and German nationalism.[112] Ironically the Baath party, created to unite Muslims, split because of disagreements between Syria and Iraq. Unity remains elusive. Nevertheless, the Salafists are determined to pursue their goal and expect that ultimately, the whole world will live under the umbrella of Islam as defined by the Salafists. They too emerged out of the Muslim Brotherhood. For them, the Koran is the only valid constitution. In both North Africa and Europe they have produced many splinter groups and cannot maintain unity among themselves, although they are still basically like-minded. Pipes describes them as "revolutionary in outlook, extremist in behavior, totalitarian in ambition."[113] They would like to enforce *sharia* on a territorial basis, not on a personal level. This would require non-Muslims living in Muslim nations to live under Islamic law, which would be an intolerable situation for all non-Muslims. Efforts to impose this viewpoint have been made in Northern Nigeria and created considerable tension. Under *sharia* law, the penalty for apostasy is severe and ranges from ostracism to execution. Under Islamic law, those who convert from

Islam are threatened by death. In Islamic countries, apostasy is seen as treason to the state. The fate of "apostates" is illustrated by Salman Rushdie, whose *Satanic Verses* led to a *fatwa* or religious opinion by Iran's Ayatollah Khomeini, who wanted Rushdie put to death. The contrast with the freedom of religion in the West is so great that it is difficult for most people to imagine—let alone understand—what it means to live under Islamic law.

Recent newspaper reports have highlighted the killing of Christians in Egypt, where perhaps 10 percent of the population are Copts. Christians have recently been killed in Indonesia as well. Several Muslim countries, including Saudi Arabia and Turkey, do not allow missionaries. Anyone critical of Muhammed is killed.

Mawdoudi's thinking also made a deep impression on Sayyed Qtub (1906–1996), a radical Islamist who inspired al-Qaida along the way. Qtub memorized the Koran at age ten. While in the United States, he had negative experiences and was more convinced than ever of the problem of Western decadence. Upon his return to Egypt he joined the Muslim Brotherhood and became more and more radical. He rejected the gradual implementation of change and insisted on an abrupt break with the past and the immediate implementation of his political program. His extremism attracted many young people in search of an ideal. After the assassination of al-Banna, Qtub took his place and filled the leadership vacuum. After the attempted assassination of Nasser in 1954, Qtub was imprisoned for ten years. While in prison, he wrote extensively and laid the foundation of jihadist ideology. Briefly set free after ten years in prison, he was re-arrested, condemned, and executed by hanging.

His basic premise was that both contemporary society and states were infidels that needed to be eliminated. His writings have inspired extremists, and some of the tactics used by al-Qaida can be traced to Qtub.

SPLINTER GROUPS AND HEZBOLLAH

As usual there are splinter groups, such as Takfir wal-Hirja, which was founded by Shukri Mustafa (1942–1978), another member of the Muslim Brotherhood. He was imprisoned with Qtub and became a radical disciple, but founded his own group after his release from prison. His spiritual roots can be traced to Wahhabism, the Muslim Brotherhood, and Qtub. Shukri Mustafa suggested that change be brought about in stages, beginning with a withdrawal from all the population because of corruption and decadence and followed by steps taken to cleanse the land. Modern education and science needed to be rejected. Nothing was necessary except the Koran. For Mustafa, it was permissible to kill fellow Muslims who were not pure enough. Takfir gunmen have killed Muslim worshippers in the Sudan while at prayer in a mosque. They accept the Shiite rule of dissimulation and can go undercover for the sake of the movement. They can even shave their beards, drink alcohol, and go into topless bars. The fact they work in small, hidden cells makes detection extremely difficult.

One fairly new movement is Hezbollah ("party of God"), which came into being as a response to the invasion of Lebanon by Israel in 1982. In 1992 Hassan Nasrallah—a student of Shiite theology—became the general secretary of Hezbollah with the goal of establishing a Shiite Muslim fundamentalistic state modeled on Iran. They, like Hamas, sponsor extensive social service networks and fund schools, orphanages, mosques, and health clinics. Like most jihadist movements, Hamas is rooted in the Muslim Brotherhood and was born in Egypt. The word *Hamas* is an acronym for Arab words meaning "Islamic Resistance Movement." *Hamas* happens to mean "zeal," and the acronym is appropriate because the Hamas combine Islamic fundamentalism with Palestinian nationalism. In 1987 Amed Yassin founded Hamas as the political arm of the Brotherhood in the West Bank and Gaza. They were involved in the intifada or Palestinian uprising against Israel.

FUTURE GENERATIONS OF TERRORISTS

Ideals painted in bright colors are always attractive to young people. What *Time* magazine called "the Generation Jihad"[114] defines many young Muslims who are restive, rootless, and in search of absolutes. *Time* refers specifically to young Muslims who feel alienated by the European society in which they grew up. In France, almost 25 percent of these youths identified with Salafism, regardless of the violence associated with the movement. Some young Arabs and other Islamic believers in Europe have become embittered by the lack of economic opportunity. Extremists have exploited the situation, and fanatics have been born. Religion is not the primary issue, but it furnishes a convenient ideology that inspires and motivates. In the process, religion is debased and misused. Islamic jihad both individualistic and suicidal, has virtually nothing in common with jihad as it has been practiced in the past and is not part of Islam as historically understood. Islam as such is not a threat to the West, but an ill-conceived militant Islam is a threat to all; "there is, indeed no comparable danger in the world today."[115]

ISLAM AND THE ARTS

When the Arabs exploded out of the Arabian Peninsula, they entered a highly civilized area and inherited the rich cultural development of both the Byzantine and Persian Empires. Almost unavoidably, Islamic art was born.

Although the Koran does not explicitly prohibit the imitation of living things in art, the painting of human beings is explicitly forbidden in the *hadith*. It was feared that somehow this might lead to idolatry. Some Islamic scholars had the idea that creating a statue or a painting was almost an act of defiance, as if man were setting himself up to compete with God the Creator. It is also true that Muhammed, the ultimate pattern, had no pictures in his house. The conclusion on this matter seemed self-evident.

Given the artistic atmosphere of Syria, Iraq, and Persia, Arab conquerors could not remain indifferent to all forms of art, and three forms in particular developed significantly: architecture, calligraphy and illumination of manuscripts, and the arts of small objects such as ceramics, glass, ivory, woodwork, textiles, and metals.

Architecture focused on mosques. At first mosques were patterned after the simple house of Muhammed, but over time, changes were made that were influenced by traditional cultures. One of the most remarkable examples of early Islamic architecture is the Dome of the Rock in Jerusalem. It is one of the earliest surviving Islamic monuments. Erected by Abd-al-Malik (646–704), it was a shrine to house the rock from which Muhammed is said to have ascended on his mystic journey to heaven. The dome is over 100 feet high and sits atop an octagonal building. The gilded gold of the dome scintillates in brilliant sunshine. Jerusalem, in competition with Mecca, became a place of pilgrimage and the third most holy city of Islam after Mecca and Medina.

When the Umayyad made Damascus the new capital of the Islamic Empire, it seemed imperative to build a mosque worthy of the greatness of the caliphate. The Umayyad Mosque—or Great Mosque—took the place of the Church of St. John the Baptist, so named because the church featured a chapel with the relic of the head of the forerunner. The relic is now enshrined inside of the mosque [the hand of John the Baptist is said to be in Istanbul]. The Great Mosque features three minarets, the most famous being the Minaret of Jesus. Tradition holds that it is here that Jesus will return to fight the Antichrist. Another minaret features an astronomical clock.

It was under Caliph al-Walid (706–714) that The Great Mosque was built. Even though 12,000 workmen were involved in the construction, it took almost ten years to complete the task. There are three splendid structures in the courtyard, including a fountain in the center. The interior, almost 450 feet long, is divided by two tiers of white marble columns that create three aisles, perhaps inspired by the typical Christian basilica. The carpets, the mosaics, the enameled tiles, and the *mihrab*—which indicates the direction of Mecca—are adorned with gold, silver, and precious stones—all combined to create not only a sanctuary but a symbol of political power. As usual, koranic schools and tombs surround the Great Mosque. The most important is the mausoleum of Saladin, the famous Arab hero who defeated the Crusaders.

Over the centuries, Islam has spanned cultures from Spain to Southeast Asia, and different architectural styles have merged or influenced each other. The British brought Moroccan/Spanish architecture all the way to Malaysia, where it is known as the Moorish style. With the addition of Indian elements, the famous Taj Mahal was built in Agra. The Taj is one of the best-known monuments in the world and the high point of Mogul or Indo-Muslim art and architecture. Shah Jehan built the Taj in memory of his wife. It stands in a garden and is reflected in a long, narrow pool of water. It took 20,000 workers 22 years to build the Taj Mahal, a building that confirms that the ruling passion of the Shah was magnificence. The builders used almost 1,000 pounds of gold and 5,000 gems. Four slender minarets, detached from the main structure, frame the tomb dominated by a lofty dome. The idea of a double dome had previously been used in the mausoleum of Humayun. The idea is simple, but effective. The inner dome is a hemispheric ceiling centered over the tomb at a normal height. This allowed the architect to raise the outer dome to great heights without causing the interior "harmony" to be disturbed. Artists were brought in from Italy to teach the art of inlaying marble, and others created mosaics of precious stones. Two identical buildings flank the Taj, and koranic inscriptions in magnificent calligraphy adorn the buildings.

Stonecutters, sculptors, and inlay artists came from faraway Baghdad and even Constantinople. Upon completion of the mausoleum, Shah Jehan ordered the hands of the craftsmen to be cut off to ensure that no one else could ever use their talent.

In India, Aibak (1150–1210) erected the Qutab Minar, a daring construction of a 240-foot-tall tower. The tower expressed the triumph of Islam. Stones from 27 Jain and Hindu temples were incorporated into the structure. The first and third tiers are star shaped, the second level features circular projections, and the fourth level is circular. A fifth tier was added later.

Suleiman the Magnificent was an ambitious builder and found in Sinan the perfect architect to express his dreams in stone and mortar. Sinan was a Greek Christian, perhaps never even trained as an architect. At one point he was a Janissary. He designed hundreds of mosques and adjacent buildings, such as schools, hospitals, inns, baths, and tombs. The Suleimaniya is one of the finest mosques of the Ottoman Empire. The building was completed in seven years. The center of the dome is 154 feet above the floor. Semidomes and arches flank the dome. Huge porphyry columns support arcades, and granite, marble, and porphyry abound. Stained glass windows add touches of color and filter the light. The inscription over the entrance reads "O God who opens all doors, open the door of felicity."

Calligraphy, as an art form, reached new heights in the Islamic world. As Muhammed's proclamation was written down, it became visual. Writing was an almost sacred art. Arabic is written from right to left, and vowels are not necessarily transcribed. The alphabet consists of 18 letters, but if the marks and accents (used to indicate vowels) are added, the total reaches 29. In the cursive script, the letters are joined together. Splendid samples of Arabic writing are seen in the Dome of the Rock. A koranic text was used to create a magnificent decorative inscription that is over 800 feet long and circles the Dome. The letters stand out brightly against the dark blue background of the tiles. The square Kufic alphabet was used (named after the city of Kufa in southern Iraq). Till the tenth century, the Koran was always transcribed in the Kufic alphabet, each angular letter standing alone. Later, several cursive scripts were developed. Calligraphy is frequently used to decorate the walls of mosques.

Decorative arts had a unique advantage in Islamic culture. They were free from the limits imposed by reality, which meant artists could pursue ideal forms and patterns. Most famous perhaps are the arabesques representing a unique combination of geometric forms. From an artistic standpoint they can be interpreted as endless patterns, extending even beyond the visible and therefore a reminder of the invisible world. Complex but harmonious designs represented both order and unity.

A seemingly reliable tradition relates that Muhammed protected an icon of Mary from destruction when the idols of the Kaaba were eliminated. Although there is no formal condemnation of painting in the Koran, the *hadith* is uncompromising on the subject. It was therefore scandalous that Bellini of Venice was invited to the Ottoman Court to paint the portrait of Mehmed the Conqueror (1479). Most everything painted by Bellini in Istanbul was removed as "indecent" by Mehmed's successor. Only the portrait escaped destruction. It is all the more surprising that miniature painting became the rage at the Mogul court of India. Akbar (1542–1605) requested that 100 painters illustrate the story of the adventures of Hamza-nana, whose legendary feats went back to the days of Harun al Rashid. Fifteen years later, 12 volumes had been produced that included 1,000 illustrations. Other books, including the famous Shah-nama, were also illustrated.

Carpets were necessary in every mosque. The designs were determined by the function. Many carpets featured a niche, a reminder of the *quibla,* or the direction of Mecca. Often carpet designs included a lamp and flowering branches. This imagery is based on *Sura* 24, entitled "Light," where we read that God is the light of the heavens and the earth: "His light may be compared to a niche that enshrines a lamp."

Other weavers created magnificent textiles. A fine quality of cotton is called *muslin,* a name derived from the city of Mosul in Iraq, a major textile center. The silk fabric called *damask* was originally produced in Damascus. The same is obviously true of the Damascus blade, which denotes steel of the finest quality.

Mosaics were allowed under the Umayyads (661–750), who, like the later Moguls, had few religious scruples. A Byzantine emperor sent qualified workers to adorn the mosque in Medina and their work was "furtively tolerated." The Umayyads even liked frescoes and pictured the human body.

Pottery may have traveled to the Middle East from China via the Silk Route in the days of the T'ang dynasty (618–906). In the ancient Islamic realm, pottery was produced in Samarra, or what is now Iraq. Blue porcelains of the Ming dynasty found new artistic expression in Iznik, Turkey, a city that became renown for artistic pottery.

POINTS OF CONTACT

Muslims and Evangelicals are both concerned about global poverty and Africa. Both groups oppose the domination of public and international discourse by secular ideas. Both believe that religious figures and values should be treated with respect in the media; neither like the glorification of casual sex in popular entertainment."[116]

That statement is true, but it is so broad that it becomes almost meaningless, and it applies equally well to other religious groups. It should be clear by now that the differences between Christianity and Islam cannot and should not be minimized. Nevertheless, it remains equally true that there are significant points of contact and agreement. Muhammed told his followers to "be courteous when you argue with the People of the Book." This is a good admonition—not always followed—that invites reciprocity. Christians should be prepared to answer questions and explain the hope we have and do it with "gentleness and respect."[117] Christians are ambassadors and therefore necessarily diplomatic. Christians are witnesses, not prosecuting attorneys. Witnesses relate what they have experienced. According to the words of Christ, it is the Spirit who will bear witness to him and convict the world of sin and guilt.[118] We can only present the facts of our experience and share information, but without the Spirit, who internalizes the facts and convicts, new life will not blossom. We present the external evidence, the Spirit provides the internal evidence.

SOME ISLAMIC BIBLE INTERPRETATIONS

THE KORAN CONTAINS A great amount of material taken from the Bible. It is not surprising that there should be numerous points of contact between Christianity and Islam. Perhaps the most obvious one is Abraham, who for Christians is a hero of faith and for Muslims is a recipient of truth. From the Islamic perspective it is Ishmael, not Isaac, who plays a central role in God's plan—one largely ignored by Christians. Abraham prayed for Ishmael and God promised to bless him.[119] The culmination of the story is told in Genesis 21. God renewed the promise of a great posterity to Ishmael, but in the very same context we are reminded that the covenant is with Isaac.[120] Some Muslim commentators make the point that Ishmael came into the household of Abraham long before Isaac, and as the firstborn, he was entitled to the birthright and a double portion. But the son of a slave woman had no equal standing with the son of the wife, and the Bible is quite clear on the issue (Genesis 20).

Some Muslim scholars believe that God has shifted Himself away from Israel. They quote Matthew 21:43, where Jesus, speaking to Jews, said, "The kingdom of God will be taken away from you and given to a people who will produce its fruit." The idea of a shift away from the Jews is a tacit admission by Muslims that the Jews were the chosen people—through Isaac, not Ishmael. In the same context, Muslim authors write that Jesus referred to Israel as "the stone the builders rejected," and that it is this very stone that will grind everything to powder.[121] They see it as a fit description of the victories of the early Islamic movement. The context makes it clear that the stone is Christ, an interpretation confirmed by Acts 4:11. In a way, it is surprising that Muslim scholars advance an argument that is based on a text that is supposedly corrupt.

The idea that Muhammed was the long-awaited prophet announced by Moses[122] is hardly credible because it was stated explicitly that this prophet would be from among the nation.

Is Muhammed the fulfillment of the promise made by Christ concerning the *paraklete* or Comforter? This idea was already examined on page 25. There is not a shred of evidence that the biblical text has been altered. In what sense can it be said of Muhammed that he (the person, not the teaching) will be with you forever, dwell with you, and remind you of all that Christ has said?[123] None of those apply to Muhammed.

Muslim scholars have pointed to other Old Testament texts that they believe are references to Muhammed, including Isaiah 42, but verses 2-3, for instance, are hardly an appropriate description of the character and action of Muhammed. Other references, such as Isaiah 60:1ff, are even more farfetched, and the thought that Isaiah 60:7 refers to the Kaaba in Mecca is hardly a correct understanding of that text.

There are some interesting texts in the Old Testament that deal with Arabia or mention Arabic tribes such as Kedar, and these might be more neutral areas of conversation that, ultimately, point to the authority of Scripture. But a purely intellectual debate like that, which has already continued for centuries, will probably settle nothing.

A CHRISTIAN APPROACH

FROM A MUCH MORE practical and personal perspective there is the issue of sin and guilt. The Koran states unequivocally that "your unintentional mistakes shall be forgiven, but not your deliberate errors."[124] The same distinction is made by Moses,[125] and the same conclusion is drawn. Is it not true that everyone at some point has committed

a "deliberate error"? Elsewhere we read, "If God punished men for their sins, not a creature would be left alive. He reprieves them all till a time ordained; when their time arrives, not for one hour shall they stay behind: nor can they go before it."[126] Not a creature would be left alive; sin is universal. It is a message strongly emphasized throughout the Bible. Man is alienated from God, has sinned, has literally "missed the mark," and has fallen short of God's glory. How can a holy God forgive sin? We are told that "good deeds make amends for sin" (*Sura* 11), but how are the deeds measured and balanced? Can deeds that proceed from an imperfect person be truly and absolutely good? Besides, our obligation to God always exceeds our achievement, no matter how great it might be.

The more Islam insists on the holiness of Allah—one of the chief characteristics of God—the greater the problem of building a bridge between frail, sinful humans and the eternal God. Islam does not offer the assurance of forgiveness. That is precisely why Christ came into the world: to die, to atone, to be a mediator. Since the Koran often mentions Jesus (called *Isa*) and since there is some ambiguity about his death in the Koran, it would not be out of place to talk about the death of Christ and the meaning of the cross in terms of obtaining forgiveness and salvation. Instead of sharing abstract theological propositions, why not share the personal experience, the new life that has become ours? Hear the great promise of God:

Sing to the LORD a new song,
  his praise to the end of the earth....
Let the desert and its towns raise their voices;
  let the settlements where **Kedar** lives rejoice....
Let them give glory to the LORD.
  ISAIAH 42:10-12

SHINTOISM *and* BUDDHISM

Once there was a prince named Sattva. One day he and his two elder brothers went to a forest to play. There they saw a famished tigress which was evidently tempted to devour her own seven cubs to satisfy her hunger.

The elder brothers ran away in fear, but Sattva climbed up a cliff and threw himself over it to the tigress in order to save the lives of the baby tigers.

Prince Sattva did this charitable act spontaneously, but within his mind he was thinking: "This body is changing and impermanent; I have loved the body with no thought of throwing it away, but now I make it an offering to the tigress so that I may gain Enlightenment." This thought of Prince Sattva shows the true determination to gain Enlightenment.

A BUDDHIST FABLE

SHINTOISM *and* BUDDHISM

PEOPLE HAVE LIVED IN Japan for thousands of years, but not until the beginning of the Christian era did Japan emerge from the twilight of myth and legend to enter history. Most Japanese ancestors came from Siberia via Korea. A few came from Southeast Asia and the Polynesian Islands. The mysterious Ainu of uncertain ancestry settled in the north.

If the early history of Japan is wrapped in obscurity, mythology flourishes. We are told that heaven and earth formed a chaotic mass or appeared like an egg. The clearer part was separated to become heaven; the grosser elements settled down to become earth. From a reed-shoot somewhere between heaven and earth or from the midst of a void, deities were produced spontaneously. Finally, seven generations of gods appeared. The last couple was called Izanagi (the Male-who-invites) and his younger sister Izanami (the Female-who-invites). They stood on a floating bridge connecting heaven and earth and stirred the brine with a jeweled spear. When the spear was withdrawn, drops fell and created the island of Onogoro. Izagani and Izanami came down to Onogoro and decided to create more islands and children. They walked around a heavenly pillar; one came around from the left, and the other from the right. When they met on the other side of the pillar, the goddess spoke first. This was a serious error of proper decorum and

she gave birth to a "leech-child" that they set adrift. After they observed the ritual correctly they gave birth to 14 islands and 35 deities. The birth of the fire-god damaged the mother, and the father cut off the god's head in anger. The drops of blood gave birth to eight more gods. Izanagi was deeply distressed by the death of her son and went down to the underworld to search for him. Izanami followed and rescued her from hell, but he became impure by contact with the underworld and had to cleanse himself. As he washed his left eye, the goddess Amaterasu was born, the goddess of the sun. From his right eye came the goddess of the moon, and when he washed his nose, Susanoo, the god of the sea, appeared. Izanagi ordered his elder daughter, Amaterasu, to rule the plain of heaven and gave her a necklace of jewels. Amaterasu gave birth to eight children. The oldest male became the ancestor of the emperors of Japan, who are the direct descendents of the sun goddess.

Susanoo, the god of the sea, occasionally went on a rampage. He broke a hole into the top of a weaving hall and dropped a flayed horse through it. Amaterasu, the sun goddess, was terrified. She hid in a cave and plunged the world into darkness. The other gods gave orders to make a mirror and hung a string of 500 jewels on a sacred tree. They used offerings and liturgies and had one deity cavort in front of the cave. The sun goddess, wondering about the noise of laughter, was lured out of her hiding place. She saw the mirror and was curious about the reflection. As she moved forward for a closer look, the god of force seized her hand and dragged her out of the cave. A rope was placed in front of the cave to prevent her return to the grotto. Her brother Susanoo, the prankster, was banished for his bad behavior.

Susanoo met a man whose daughters had been devoured by an eight-headed snake. The god got the snake drunk and cut the monster to pieces. In the tail he found a sword that he presented to the sun goddess. The mirror, the string of jewels, and the sword have become emblems of Imperial power.

The Ise shrine, dedicated to Amaterasu, is the most important in Japan and houses the sacred mirror. Like all Shinto shrines, Ise faces east, toward the rising sun.

One of the direct descendants of Amaterasu, the sun goddess, was Emperor Jimmu, founder of the Imperial line, who, according to Japanese legends, ascended the throne in 660 B.C., but this is contradicted by the facts of history. The first historical references to Japan appear in Chinese documents of the first century, but it is only in the fourth century that the Yamato clan emerged as the dominant political power in the western part of Japan. They even controlled a small area of what is now South Korea. In 712, at the request of Empress Gemmyo, Ono Yasumaro created the *Kojiki,* the first collection of ancient myths. The purpose of the *Kojiki*[1] was to settle the imperial genealogy once for all and to strengthen royal authority. In 720 a committee of scholars compiled another collection, the *Nihongi,*[2] to strengthen the dynastic claims of the Yamato—also known

as the Sun Line—after their illustrious ancestor, the sun goddess. The *Nihongi* clearly affirms the sacred genealogy of the ruler. We are told that, fighting an enemy, the emperor exclaimed, "I am the descendant of the sun-goddess, let us follow her rays and trample them down." The emperor is called "the God incarnate, the Emperor Yamato-neko who rules the world."[3] In the same document there are several references to the kingdoms of Korea, usually reporting the offering of tribute. This indicates the close connection that existed between these two countries.

AN OVERVIEW OF SHINTO

KEY BASICS

The myths found in these ancient collections are part and parcel of Shinto, at the time a primitive polytheistic religion. The origin of Shinto is unknown. There is no founder, there are no sacred books, there is no precise dogma. *Shinto* means "the way of the gods." Shinto is a simple worship of the forces of nature, venerated under the name *kami,* which is usually translated "god," but the *kami* are neither omnipotent nor omniscient. They are beings of a higher plane, a life-energy, but are devoid of the attributes normally associated with God. Even Amaterasu asked advice of other gods and goddesses and used messengers to obtain information. Any object of reverence can be a *kami,* including plants, rocks, birds, beasts, exceptional people, and of course, the forces of nature. Specialized *kami* overlook human activities and may even dwell in man-made objects. Some *kami* are deified ancestors or great figures of the past.

A *kami* can be anything that inspires awe or appears mysterious, anything out of the ordinary—even exceptional evil. *Kami* can do good or evil, but none are absolutely wicked. There are eight million *kami*. Given their number, the presence of a *kami* affects every aspect of life. The *kami* are endowed with a certain energy or force (*tama*) that can be violent or peaceful. This power supports life, dwells in humans, and departs at death. It is thought that this life force enters the sacred object stored in the sanctuary (*honden*) of the Shinto shrine. It is this *tama* that is invoked in prayer.

According to Sokyo Ono, Japanese people themselves do not have a clear idea regarding the *kami* because "it is impossible to make explicit that which by its very nature is vague."[4] Along the same line, Littleton writes that "there are very few people, Japanese or foreign, who understand Shinto thoroughly."[5] Nevertheless, Shinto permeates Japanese society and every aspect of life.

Sacred mountains, such as Mt. Fuji, and sacred rocks and caves are the abodes of the *kami*. Shinto shrines are in evidence everywhere. It is easy enough to recognize them thanks to the *torii*, or sacred gateway, usually painted vermilion. The *torii* consists of two pillars, slightly slanted toward each other, with a straight cross beam and a curved lintel. Often there is more than one *torii* standing before the main sanctuary. Also in front of the sanctuary is an ablution basin, essential for ritual cleansing, or the rinsing of the hands and mouth. Ritual purity is paramount; it is a central aspect of Shinto ritual and deeply rooted in mythology. Izanagi had been polluted by contact with the underworld and cleansed himself in a stream. In the process the solar deity Amaterasu came into being. Disease and death create ceremonial impurity. A sacred pine branch is used in purification rites.

Then there is the myth of Susanoo, who, after rampaging through the palace of his sister Amaterasu, is compelled to make recompense. He not only offers a sword to Amaterasu, but his beard is cut and his nails are pulled. After wrongdoing, it is essential to restore proper relationships through offerings of compensation. This is yet another form of purification.

KEY PRACTICES

When the worshipper approaches the sanctuary he is usually greeted by a pair of stone lions guarding the *haiden,* or hall of worship, where priests conduct the rituals and individuals make their offerings. A large wooden box stands in front of the *haiden* for those who give monetary offerings. The priests and their families eat any offerings of fruits and vegetables. Worshippers announce their presence to the deity by clapping their hands and tugging on a heavy bell rope hanging from the eaves. Normally laymen cannot enter the interior of the shrine. The main sanctuary, or *honden,* houses the sacred object in which the spirit of the *kami* is believed to reside. Only the chief priest is allowed in the *honden*. The hidden symbol is often a mirror, a wooden image, or a sword. A wand with strips of paper folded in a zigzag fashion hangs before the door of the inner chamber.

Usually more than one deity is enshrined, each one with a special function. The Kasuga Shrine in Nara, one of the most famous Shinto shrines, was erected in 710. The central sanctuary or *honden* enshrines four major deities. Others are housed in subordinate shrines on the temple grounds.

The Kasuga Shrine features five auxiliary shrines and 56 subordinate ones. Some 1,800 metal lanterns hang in the walkways painted in bright vermilion. Hanging lanterns and stone lanterns usually surround the shrine. They are gifts from devotees. Kasuga holds 1,000 ritual events a year to entertain and please the *kami*.[6] The setting of a Shinto shrine is invariably in a beautiful wooded area. Since animals are seen as divine messengers, their statues adorn the grounds. The fox spirit is feared because it brings calamities that can be avoided only through proper ritual. The same is true of evil ghosts. Colorful banners symbolize the presence of the *kami*, and at the same time are offerings to the *kami*. Some banners are purely ornamental.

Shinto does not have a weekly religious service. People visit shrines at their convenience. Some may visit a shrine on the first and fifteenth of each month. A few traditional dates are significant to most believers. Special festivals are observed for girls at age three and for boys at age five. There is also an adult day. Spring and autumn festivals circle the year along with many more festivals. Particularly important is New Year's Day. The rites and festivals have a strong sensory appeal.[7]

At home, daily morning and evening offerings of a few grains of rice, vegetables, or rice wine honor the *kami* who, in return, extend their blessing. Neglect makes them unhappy. On a special shelf are memorial tablets or soul representatives. They carry the names of ancestors who are revered and worshipped. After 33 years the dead ancestor merges into the collective body of all the other household ancestors. The *kami* is like the embodiment of the family's vital force. The spirit of the dead—released from physical limitations—becomes once again part of the universal life force. The purpose of life is to realize the ideals of ancestors, to fulfill the hope of the ancestral *kami,* and to prepare the next generation accordingly.

KEY BELIEFS

Shinto rests on the assumption that people can be happy if they worship properly and maintain *wa,* or harmony in relationships. Chinese Daoism and the concept of yin and yang, the harmony of the two basic forces of nature, was widely known and accepted in the seventh century.

Man and the world in which he lives are seen as inherently good. It is evil spirits that cause evil, but in Shinto thinking, there is no absolute good or evil. Nothing, not even killing, is considered unconditionally evil. Everything depends on the specific situation. The concept of sin in the biblical sense is weak, not to say absent. Man has a divine nature (like a clear mirror) but it is necessary to remove the accumulated dust (on the surface of the universe) through purification in order to rediscover it. Whatever disturbs social harmony or peaceful development is seen as evil. The greatest virtue is sincerity, a true heart. It is this *magokoro,* this bright pure mind, that makes all other virtues and communion with the *kami* possible. This made it easy for Shinto to adopt the Confucian moral code when Confucianism was introduced in Japan in the fifth century.

The most important aspect of Shinto is not to disturb existing harmony. Salvation is simply to live in harmony with the world. Believers honor *musuhi,* the creative and harmonizing power of the *kami.* Prayer is for help in *this* life. The goddess of food, literally "she who possesses mochi" (or rice-cake), is worshipped in Ise, and after the sun goddess, she occupies the most important shrine.

It is difficult to reconstruct Shinto as it might have been at the beginning of Japanese history because in the course of time, it was deeply influenced by both Buddhism and Confucianism and spiritualized. For instance, the mirror that played such an important role in the original myth is now seen as an important symbol because it reflects everything as it is and is an image of the pure mind of the *kami*. As a ceremonial object, it continues to be associated with the sun goddess.

Ancient elements of shamanism are also noticeable in Shinto. Charms are worn for healing and protection. There are five auspicious colors: white, yellow, red, blue, and purple. *Ema* are small prayer tablets. Luck plays an important role in daily life, and offerings are helpful to obtaining good luck.

Shinto priests read prayers in classical Japanese that is no longer understood. Each word, each gesture, each movement, the details of each ceremony are prescribed in age-old ritual codes. The proper ritual observed in all shrines is found in the *Saishi kitei,* published by the National Organization of Shrines.

Shinto has dominated Japanese thinking throughout history. In the early days the primary social group was the clan. The head of the clan was in charge of worshiping the guardian deity, the *kami*. The *kami* of the Imperial Household and perhaps those of a few powerful clans could be considered national deities. Most *kami* have only local significance.

After the arrival of Buddhism in Japan, Shinto had no choice but to develop theoretically and, in the process, it underwent considerable change. It is necessary to revisit Shinto across the history of Japan to observe the many changes that have taken place.

AN OVERVIEW OF BUDDHISM

THE BEGINNING

India, where Buddhism originated, did not maintain a strong Buddhist tradition. In China Buddhism was widespread, but even before the coming of Communism, most Buddhist sects, except for Zen, had disappeared. Only in Japan did many traditional sects continue to flourish. Buddhism is an integral part of Japanese history. Currently about 200 Buddhist sects coexist in Japan.

Buddhism came to Japan in 552. The king of Paekche in Korea sent a letter to the court of Yamato requesting help against his enemies and, at the same time, recommended Buddhism: "This doctrine is among all doctrines the most excellent. But it is hard to explain and hard to understand." Buddhism was presented as the religion of the civilized world because it came to Korea from China, which was considered the center of culture. The ruler of Paekche sent bronze statues of Buddha along with sutras, sacred Buddhist writings, to Japan. Emperor Kimmei (539–571) shared the letter with his court. The Mononobe clan and military leaders opposed an alliance with Paekche and the acceptance of Buddhism. No troops were sent to Korea, and in 562 the Japanese were forced out of Korea.

The Nakatomi clan in charge of ritual also rejected the acceptance of Buddhism. They were committed to Shinto. But the Soga clan accepted the idea that Buddhism was the choice of most civilized nations and was prepared to accept the new religion. Each clan had a hidden agenda. Both the Mononobe and the Nakatomi derived their power from blood ties to the royal family, which was hallowed by Shinto. They would almost automatically oppose Buddhism. Proper lineage and connection to the royal family was everything. On the other hand, the power of the Soga clan was based on service to the court, not family connection. The Soga welcomed Buddhism as a new and different source of authority that could easily coexist with Shinto. For many, Buddha was just another *kami*. Because opinions were divided, the emperor framed a diplomatic answer: "Never from former days until now have we had the opportunity of listening to so wonderful a doctrine. We are unable, however, to decide of ourselves." In spite of misgivings, he allowed the powerful Soga clan to erect a temple for the statue of Buddha.

When an epidemic broke out afterward, it was attributed to the anger of the national deities, the *kami*, who were said to be upset by the intrusion of Buddhism. The statue of Buddha was cast into a canal and the temple burned down. But the epidemic continued and became worse. This was now interpreted as an expression of the anger of Buddha. The Soga were allowed to remain Buddhist, and additional Buddhist monks came from Korea.

Emperor Yomei died during the pestilence (587) and a war of succession broke out. The victory of the Soga clan at the battle of Shigisen decided the future of Buddhism in Japan. Umaka, head of the Soga clan, determined that Sujun (588–592) should be the new emperor, but had him assassinated when he showed signs of increasing independence. Umaka now appointed Suiko (593–628), his daughter, as empress and nominated prince Shotoku (574–622) as regent. It was Shotoku who implanted Buddhism permanently into Japan.

Originally from India, Buddhism infiltrated China in the first and second centuries and triumphed from the fourth to the eighth. In 384 a Chinese monk brought Buddhism to Paekche in Korea, and from there it came to Japan. By the time Buddhism entered Japan it was already 1,000 years old and had developed a complex theology and a colorful ritual. Buddhism proposed answers to the problems of suffering and death. No such answers were available in Shinto. But regardless of the original teaching of Buddha, "the classical forms of Japanese Buddhism emphasize in one way or another a this-wordly attitude"[8] diametrically opposed to Buddha's teaching.

According to tradition, Siddharta Gautama, the founder of Buddhism, lived from 563 to 483 B.C. There is considerable uncertainty regarding the exact dates. Some scholars favor 490 to 410 B.C. We do know that he was born in Kapilavastu, near the border of Nepal. His father, Suddhodana, belonged to the Sakya clan, and Gautama is sometimes called Sakyamuni, or the sage of the Sakyas. He was raised in luxury as befits a young prince. Married at 16, he lived in a palace his father had built for him. Tradition relates that a hermit predicted that the child would either grow up to subjugate the world or, were he to forsake court life, to become a Buddha, an enlightened one.

Suddhodana tried to shelter his son, Gautama, from negative experiences, but on one of the son's his excursions outside of the palace he encountered an old man, a sick man, a dead man, and a begging monk. For the first time the young prince became aware of the reality of suffering and death. Shortly after the birth of his son Rahula, the prince, at age 29, left his family to seek answers to the problems of human existence. He was tempted by the devil, who offered him the whole world if only he rejoined his family, but the prince turned his steps to the south with a begging bowl in his hand. For six years he followed the most rigorous asceticism but failed to obtain the answer to his quest—how to end the relentless cycle of rebirth that he accepted as a given. He concluded that neither austerity nor self-indulgence led to salvation and opted for a more balanced approach, a middle way. Artists often portray Gautama as having a skeletal appearance when he imposed the most severe asceticism upon himself. At age 35, after prolonged meditation, he found enlightenment under a fig tree, now known as the bo tree (Wisdom Tree) and became the Buddha, the Enlightened One. Tradition informs us that he remained silent for 49 days before he preached his first sermon not far from Banares in a Deerpark at Sanath. Tradition calls the sermon "The Turning of the Wheel"* because it "set the wheel of Dharma in motion."[9] The five followers that had stayed with him throughout the years, became the original members of the Buddhist order. They spread the message far and wide, and the Buddha himself became an itinerant preacher and spread his new insight till he died 45 years later. Unfortunately there is a gap of 150 years between the spoken word of the Buddha and the earliest written records of what he said.

Not surprisingly the four holiest sites of Buddhism are those where the Buddha was born, where he was enlightened, where he delivered his first sermon, and where he died.

THE BELIEFS

Buddha claimed to have discovered a fourfold basic truth:

The first truth is the noble truth of pain: birth is pain, old age is pain, death is pain. Suffering is part of the very nature of life.

The second truth deals with the cause of suffering. Buddha taught that it comes from cravings or desires, especially those rooted in the physical body. The problem is the will to live, the desire for individual existence. This desire, he taught, promotes suffering and leads to rebirth. Desire arises from ignorance.[10]

The third truth was a logical conclusion. If selfish craving is at the root of the problem of pain, the solution is to eradicate all desire. When passions die, the problem of pain is solved. Be not attached to existence or nonexistence, not to anything inside or outside, not to good things nor to bad things, neither to right nor wrong.[11] To eliminate all desire is tantamount to the extinction of the personality.

The fourth truth points out how all desire can be eliminated. It is achieved by following the eightfold path that leads to the extinction of desire and the end of suffering. The eight steps on this path include right views, right intentions, right speech, right actions, right livelihood, right efforts, right mindfulness, and right concentration or meditation.

Buddhism teaches that all humans have an innate affinity for enlightenment. The original pure nature of man is defiled by worldly desires, and those desires are not part of the essence of man. Even those

---

* The wheel is a symbol of Buddhism. The eight spokes of the wheel represent the Noble Eightfold Path.

reborn as beasts or demons never lose their original "Buddha-nature," one that defies definition.

Buddha accepted some of the basic beliefs of Hinduism, such as reincarnation and the idea of *karma,* and the law of cause and effect. This inescapable law means that rebirth is conditioned by our own actions. It is easier for people to accept their position in life, their fate, if it is the result of an immutable law of cause and effect determined by the actions of past existences.

Buddha took over the idea of reincarnation from Hinduism, but paradoxically, denied the transmigration of the soul, the idea that the soul passes from one body into another after death. For Buddha, there is no soul. To advocate rebirth without transmigration of the soul is a difficult position in terms of logic. Buddha rejects the idea of a soul living in a body. There is no such thing as an ego, a self. It's an illusion. What, then, is transmitted from one life to the next? What lives on is not some invisible part (a soul), but the *karma,* the result of everything that has happened before. The *karma* is an unchangeable law that continues to operate. The new being appears by the force of the *karma.* This is difficult to understand. The immutable law of *karma* means that there *must* be consequences. The force of this law will therefore produce a new being. Could it be said that the immutable law of gravity must continue to function and if no body is available, the law of gravity will produce something so that it can continue to function?

The self is said to be an illusion, like everything else in life. It is an illusion to distinguish between existence and nonexistence, between good and bad, between right and wrong. Everything is only a succession of causes. A thing in itself does not exist; nevertheless, this nonexisting thing has a connection with causes. It is in this sense that one might say about a thing that 1) it does not exist, but that 2) it is not nonexistent. It is a paradoxical statement and typical of the abstract speculations that abound in the original Buddhism. It's a small wonder that later developments fundamentally changed Buddhist teaching. After all, someone might ask, "If everything is an illusion, can it truly be said that an illusion exists? Are the desires that have to be eliminated real?"

In a book published in 1997 and distributed free of charge to promote Buddhism we find the following simplifications, all of which reason from effect back to cause:

Effect: Why are you an orphan in this life? Cause: Because you had killed birds in your previous life.

Effect: Why do you not have children in this life? Cause: Because you plucked and destroyed all kinds of flowers in your previous life.

Effect: Why are you born a horse or an ox in this life? Cause: Because you had not paid your debts in your previous life.

Effect: Why are you born as a pig or a dog in this life? Cause: Because you had cheated and harmed others in your previous life.

Effect: Why are you intelligent and wise presently? Cause: Because you had been a vegetarian and recited Buddha's name in your previous life.[12]

The list could be endless. It is a far cry from Buddha's attempt to give a philosophical underpinning to his thoughts about reincarnation and justice.

According to Buddhism, it is possible to be reborn as an animal. We are told of an elephant with six tusks that was seeking Buddhahood. He saved a hunter's life, but the ungrateful hunter returned to kill the elephant for the sake of his tusks. The hunter, knowing that the elephant was seeking Buddhahood, disguised himself in the robe of a Buddhist monk, caught the elephant off guard, and shot him with a poisoned arrow. The dying elephant had compassion on the hunter and sheltered him in its limbs to protect him from the fury of revengeful elephants.[13] The story takes for granted that somehow the hunter and the elephant are able to communicate on an intimate level and are aware of each other's disposition. It is also assumed that the elephant (and by extension, all other animals) has a consciousness that allows him to pursue Buddhahood. It is difficult to know how the animal can accumulate merit to be reborn as a human. Even if born into a wicked beast, a demon, or into hell, man still retains a buddha-nature.[14]

According to Buddha, once the cycle of rebirth ends, nirvana is reached. The nature of nirvana is difficult to define. Literally it means "blowing out," but whether one who has reached nirvana actually exists is one of the four questions Buddha refused to answer.

Popular Buddhism has simpler answers and imagines a "Pure Land of the West," where people live in serenity and work on the *karma* of their past lives.

After the death of Buddha, his disciples tried to reconstruct what they had heard and commit it to writing. Comments and interpretations made by learned monks were added to the collection. Significant Buddhist writings number into the thousands. One of the most important collections is the *Tripitaka,* written on palm leaves in the Pali language. It goes back to the first century. The sacred books are said to contain the words of Buddha, but "it is impossible to be sure where history ends and embroidery begins."[15] The *Tripitaka* is roughly 11 times the size of the Christian Bible and has given rise to endless interpretations.

"Popular Buddhism probably never corresponded very closely to the abstract, impersonal vision of the universe which scholars attribute [on rather slender grounds] to Buddha himself."[16] The annihilation of all desire would logically lead to total indifference to all fellow humans. In the Buddhist personality, detached from everything and everybody, the desire for the good of others and for social justice would be eradicated. No wonder Buddhism has been fundamentally altered over time. The changes have been so profound that linkage of today's Buddhism with the ancient teachings of Buddha is slender at best.

Through the ages, Buddhism experienced innumerable splits into many different schools of thought. Already the Second Buddhist Council in 383 B.C. produced a schism. Later, two basic schools of thought emerged: Theravada or Southern Buddhism, and Mahayana or Northern Buddhism. Theravada Buddhism is often called Hinayana Buddhism (literally, "the small vehicle"), a disrespectful title used by the Buddhist majority, who believe that the teachings are far too difficult for the masses. Southern Buddhism dominates in Thailand, Sri Lanka, and Burma. In Thailand, as well as everywhere else, Buddhism has split into many sects. King Mongkut (1851–1868) studied Pali so he could read the sacred books in the original language and discover the truth. He reached the conclusion that all ordinations in Siam

(Thailand) had been invalid. He adopted stricter rules—such as having the monk robe cover both shoulders rather than one. The reformed sect, called Thammayutika, stressed learning and launched village schools that taught mathematics and science. A new civic sense developed and helped unify Thailand.[17] Later the king of Thailand compromised and went back to the former rules for ordination and consequently healed the split.

In most countries it was Mahayana Buddhism that reigned supreme—such as in Korea, China, Mongolia, Tibet, and Japan. Here, too, sects multiplied. One of the most important differences between these two major schools of thought is how they view the person of Sakyamuni. Buddha himself had next to nothing to say about God and was perhaps an atheist. Nevertheless, Mahayana Buddhists have deified him. For them, Buddha is God. He is eternal. He knows the thoughts and feelings of all men. Sometimes he appears in history. According to Buddhist sources, he has no set form and can therefore appear as an incarnation of evil or as a woman, in a brothel or in a gambling house. Regardless of his appearance, it is always dictated by compassion. In Mahayana Buddhism the emphasis falls on mercy…and that hardly goes hand in hand with the extinction of all desire.

At first Buddhism was a religion of monks. They had to wear old garments, obtain their food through begging, "their home is where night finds them as under a tree or on a rock," and they used only a special medicine made from urine.[18] Such demands were far too difficult for the masses. Buddha himself established the *Sangha,* the Buddhist order. New recruits had to adhere to the three-refuge formula:

I take refuge in the Buddha
I take refuge in the Doctrine
I take refuge in the Order

Buddha had a rather low opinion of women. He thought that the mind of a woman is easily disturbed and misled. "She yields to her desires and surrenders more easily to jealousy than man."[19] Buddha finally agreed—reluctantly—that an order for nuns could be established. By the time Buddhism reached China, at the beginning of the modern era, 250 monastic rules for males had been developed and 500 for women. It is an eloquent commentary on the position of women. By the time Buddhism reached Japan, it had constructed any number of sophisticated theories and easily triumphed over the simple nature worship of Shinto.

Few *kami* had a nationwide following, and the emperor of Japan saw Buddhism as a unifying force for the different clans. Buddhism was disseminated from the top and initially embraced by the aristocracy. Buddhist art and ritual dazzled them. There was nothing similar in Shinto. Accommodations were made to Shintoism, and the *kami* were accepted and re-interpreted as manifestations of the Buddha.

THE HISTORY

THE NARA ERA

It was under Prince Shotoku (593–622) that Buddhism was made into the state religion of Japan. He ruled the land for 30 years as a regent for his aunt and mother-in-law. He has been called the Prince Charming of Japanese history and been endowed with every virtue. He was said to be able to listen to ten people simultaneously. Modern historians question many of the actions attributed to him. In 607 he erected the Horyu-ji Temple in Nara, on his own residence. An inscription at the temple explains that Emperor Yomei (585–587) wished to have a statue of the Buddha of healing because the emperor fell sick at the very beginning of his reign. He died before the project could be carried out, but his sister, Empress Suiko (593–628), and crown prince Shotoku fulfilled Yomei's wish. Unfortunately the Horyu-ji Temple burned down in 670. It took 40 years to meticulously rebuild the complex, and the wooden buildings there are the oldest in Japan.

In 710, Nara became the capital and cradle of Japanese culture. Shotoku was heavily influenced by the T'ang culture of China, but there were two major departures from the Chinese model. First, in China, the "mandate of heaven" could be withdrawn from the emperor. Not so in Japan. In China, a new dynasty could gain the throne. But in Japan, the present emperor is a direct descendant of the early Yamato rulers. A change of dynasty is inconceivable because of the divine origin of the royal family. Second, in China, advancement was based on passing a series of tests. But in Japan, promotion was based not on merit or knowledge, but on lineage, or on clan or family connections.

Prince Shotoku used Buddhism to help unify Japanese society and to centralize administration. Monks acquired high positions in government, but Shotoku, impressed with all things Chinese, imported Confucian learning. At the same time, Shinto continued to be part of official state functions.

Shotoku maintained excellent diplomatic relations with China and Korea. He imported Korean artists for his many building projects, and it is perhaps true that the best Buddhist architecture is found in Japan. Most famous is the Horyu-ji Temple. Black and white guardians, frightful in their intensity, were carved in front of the gate in 711. They are symbols of light and darkness. A five-story pagoda, 105 feet high, gently tapers toward the top. The five stories symbolize the five elements—water, fire, earth, metal, and wood—that, according to Buddhism, constitute the universe. The Kondo, or Golden Hall, is the central building and houses the principal object of worship: the triad of Buddha (in the center), Yukishi (on Buddha's right), and Amida (on Buddha's left). The four heavenly generals stand at the four corners. Originally the walls of the Kondo were decorated with paintings representing the Pure Land of Amida. The Horyu-ji Temple is based on a Korean model that followed a Chinese pattern derived from a structure of Indian origin. The Lecture Hall, the Bell House, and the Sutra Hall are all part of the complex, along with the hall of Prince Shotoku's soul—a soul that, according to Buddha, does not exist.

In 645, the Soga clan fell from power and was put to the sword. The Nakatomi clan took control. They ushered in reforms designed to strengthen the political power of the sovereign. At the apex stood eight principal ministries with 7,000 officials. The country was divided into 66 provinces. Private ownership of agricultural land was abolished and came under imperial administration. A new tax register was created for better population control and the tax code was revised. Officials were appointed by the court and drawn from aristocratic families. In Nara they were educated in the Confucian tradition, which stressed the centrality of the emperor along with moral precepts.

It was during this era that a disastrous military campaign ended the Korean adventure. Henceforth a defensive policy was embraced, and Korea was not invaded for the next nine centuries.

The Kofuku-ji Temple [20] was founded in 669 by the Fujiwara family and moved to Nara 40 years later. The temple was the headquarters of the Hosso sect, one of the six schools of Buddhism in vogue at that time. The Hosso sect, although quite small, has survived. The Hosso taught an idealistic Buddhism originally imported from India. They believed that everyone came into the world with one of five different dispositions, including one that is beyond salvation, an idea quite unacceptable in Japan.

The five-story pagoda of the Kofuku-ji Temple is the second highest in Japan. Across history wooden temple buildings burned down again and again, but they were always rebuilt meticulously. The octagonal hall of the Kofuku-ji temple is station number nine on the pilgrimage road of 33 Buddhist temples. The treasure house features a superb collection of Buddhist art, including the Yakushi triad. Yakushi-Nyorai is the Buddha of healing, who is said to help stop epidemics. He is often depicted with a flask in his hand. Gakko, *bodhisattva* of the moon, and Nikko, *bodhisattva* of the sun, flank Yakushi Buddha. A *bodhisattva* is an exceptional being, someone who could have escaped the endless cycle of reincarnation but chose not to enter nirvana in order to help others attain enlightenment. This is a paradoxical concept from the standpoint of Buddhism. Once someone reaches the state where all desire is eliminated, why would this person "desire" to help others?

Bodhisattvas are extremely popular, and some have compared them to Catholic saints. People pray to them and, in some fashion, the merit accumulated by the *bodhisattva* can be transferred to the worshipper. They are often represented with multiple heads and arms as an indication of their power to help.

The Kofuku-ji Temple features 12 heavenly generals sculptured in relief on wooden boards and four heavenly kings carved in wood, which are protective deities that guard Buddha. Why guards are needed is not immediately apparent. There are four, one for each cardinal direction, and they are easy to recognize. The king of the south is equipped with an umbrella, the king of the east holds a musical instrument, the king of the north carries a pagoda, the king of the west is accompanied by a dragon. The temple also houses the statues of the eight supernatural guardians of Buddhism. The statues were made using the dry-lacquer technique. A core of clay is wrapped with layers of hemp soaked in lacquer. Everything is then covered with a lacquer surface that is sculptured. One of the eight guardians is Ashura, who is elegantly represented as facing all directions and equipped with six arms. The temple also houses dry-lacquer sculptures of several of the ten great disciples of Buddha as well as fierce gate guardians—muscular figures breathing menace with fiery eyes of crystal. The statuary collection is extraordinary. Similar groupings are also found in most other Buddhist temples, although they are not necessarily of the same artistic quality.

It is intriguing that some of the sculpture shows traces of Greek influence. It all goes back to Alexander the Great. When he invaded India, the artistic legacy of Greece was introduced and left permanent marks. From India some aspects of Grecian sculpture spread to China via the Silk Route and reached Japan via Korea. It is often noticeable in the folds of the robe of Buddha.

In 685 the Yamato government issued a decree ordering the establishment of Buddhist family altars in every household. Later, Emperor Shomu (724–752) ordered the construction of a national system of monasteries. Todai-ji was the chief temple of the system and occupied 16 city blocks. It housed the Buddha Vairocana. A distinction was made between

- the historic Buddha of the past, who had lived in India

- the Maitreya or future Buddha, who would come to purify the world

- the Vairocana or present cosmic Buddha, who illuminates the world

Buddha was now seen as an abstract force, an impersonal god, the reality behind everything. "Buddha has always existed in the world which is without beginning or end."[21]

Emperor Shomu undertook the construction of a colossal bronze statue of Buddha, which was cast in eight stages over a three-year period and completed in 749. The creation of this gigantic bronze statue, almost 50 feet high, was a remarkable technical achievement. Monks from India and China came to the dedication of the statue and of the Great Buddha Hall. The Todai-ji became one of the chief temples and a center for rituals for the peace of the nation.

The oldest structure of the Todai-ji is the Hokke-do, or the Lotus Hall. Sixteen statues crowd the main image of Buddha. As usual, he is depicted with long earlobes, elongated by the heavy earrings he had worn in his earlier life as a prince. The small bulge on the top of his head symbolizes his superior wisdom. For the first 500 years there were no statues or images of Buddha, but most Buddhist temples now feature a large number of statues, including Buddha, divine guardians and generals, bodhisattvas, apsara (musical angels), goddesses, demons, disciples, and judges of the underworld.[22] The rich heavenly pantheon offers wonderful opportunities for artistic expression.

In the eighth century, Tantric Buddhism entered Tibet. It is an esoteric form of Buddhism. "The uncontested predominance of Esoteric Buddhism, however, resulted in an extreme degeneration of Buddhism in Tibet."[23] Tibetan Buddhism is known as Vajrayana Buddhism, or diamond vehicle Buddhism. There are four principal and four minor schools of Buddhism in Tibet. The Kagyu school, founded in the eleventh century, prefers oral teaching and experience and pays only minimal attention to textual study. This school also developed visualization techniques. Tsonkhapa (1357–1419) created a synthesis of the different schools of thought, and the Geluk school was born. The meditation techniques of all the previous schools were integrated along with the teachings of the highest tantra yoga.

Traditional Buddhists were called the Red Caps; the Reformed Buddhists were the Yellow Caps. In the fifteenth century, a monk renowned for his virtues was thought of as an incarnation of a bodhisattva and received the title of Dalai Lama. The title and the office have come down to our own day. The Dalai Lama traditionally follows Geluk practices.

Many traditional Buddhists in Tibet believe that the correct ritual can secure the help of the bodhisattva toward enlightenment. The ritual might involve the position of the fingers, mantras repeated in a special tone of voice, or demand efforts to visualize the shape of the *bodhisattva* that is invoked. This is merely preparatory, and further knowledge is said to come in stages. Tibetan superstition ascribes magical powers to certain initiated individuals, and some schools of thought say that desires are extinguished by fulfilling them. This has paved the way for sensual enjoyment as a religious experience.

Tibetan Lamaism refers to the *lamas,* or superior ones, worshipped as incarnations of their predecessors. Historically Tibet had an enormous number of monasteries, and far too many young people became monks. At one point there was a monastery with almost 100,000 lamas. The country suffered because of the presence of so many economically unproductive monks. This was an important contributing factor to the decline of Tibet.

In Japan, the great scandal of the eighth century was the love affair between Empress Shotoku and a Buddhist priest. She had abdicated in favor of Emperor Junnin, but when he was assassinated, she once again ascended the throne. It appears that she fell in love with a monk, Kokyo, whom she promoted as her chief minister. The Fujiwara stepped in and the priest was banished and the empress lost the throne. The affair created a permanent distrust of ambitious monks and women on the throne.

In Japan's early history, the royal residence was moved upon the death of an emperor because of the ritual impurity associated with death. But the cost of doing this was enormous, and eventually the idea was abandoned. This led to Nara being selected as a permanent capital. But during this time, half the government income was spent on Buddhist temples, statues, and

works of art. Emperor Kammu (781–806) felt that he had no choice but to establish a new capital to escape the overpowering influence of Buddhism. At first the capital was moved to Nagaoka; then in 794, Kyoto was chosen.

The Heian Era

The Heian era lasted from 794 to 1185. Kyoto became a major metropolitan center and remained the capital for more than a 1,000 years. The Kyoto city plan followed a Chinese model. The main north-south road was almost 280 feet wide, a width more appropriate for the larger Chinese cities.

Various Schools of Buddhism

To diminish the political influence of Buddhism, Nara-based monasteries were not allowed to move to the new capital. Inevitably the monasteries regained power. Emperor Kammu himself established temples at the eastern and western edges of the city. He had been told that they were essential for the protection of the city. Kukai, also known as Kobo Daishi (774–835), had persuaded the emperor that sutras or sacred writings of the Shingon ("True Word") sect were vital to the preservation of the state. The Shingon sect relied heavily on ritual and mysticism. They taught that it was possible to achieve union with the cosmic Buddha by careful observance of Shingon teaching. The idea that buddhahood, or enlightenment, could be achieved in *this* life was a totally new concept. According to Shingon teaching, there was no need to wait for nirvana at the end of countless incarnations. Union with Buddha could be achieved by reciting mantras (sacred incantations) and practicing mudras (sacred gestures).

Kukai taught that all other schools of Buddhism, all heresies, even Confucianism and all other religions were only offshoots of Shingon, the Absolute Truth. Shinto was easily absorbed, and it was assumed that all the *kami* were manifestations of the cosmic Buddha. The *kami* were also subject to the law of karma, unable to escape the cycle of cause and effect. Even destructive *kami* were incorporated into the system. They were seen as supernatural beings waiting for enlightenment. This mixture of Buddhism and Shinto was called Twofold Shinto. In many instances Buddhist priests took over Shinto shrines. Buddhist scriptures were read in front of *kami,* and Buddhist statues were placed in Shinto shrines.

In the Toji Temple the exact position of every statue in the main hall was arranged by Kukai himself according to a *mandala*—a magic circle diagram—described in an esoteric text. The Vairocana or cosmic Buddha is usually at the center of the *mandala.*

It was in 805 that Saicho (767–822), upon returning from China, introduced Tendai Buddhism, based on the Lotus Sutra. It was thought that this sutra is the last sermon preached by Gautama Buddha just before his death. In reality it was composed long after his death and reflects the later development of Mahayana Buddhism. The headquarters of the Tendai sect was established on Mount Hiei, and the monastery became a huge Buddhist center with 3,000 buildings and 20,000 monks. Many were fighting monks who were frequently involved in internal political and military struggles. They were finally defeated by Nobunaga in 1571 and the buildings burned down.

If Shingon hoped to meet emotional needs, Tendai was more intellectual. The basic idea in Tendai Buddhism is that everything can attain enlightenment because it is intrinsic in all things. Objects of nature can become Buddhas, or enlightened—even a blade of grass or a tree. This thought created an easy bridge to Shinto, which was always respectful of nature. For most people the abstract speculations of Tendai were difficult to follow. For the masses it was enough to recite five words summarizing the basic teaching. Every group had a different formula, a shortcut to felicity. The formula was used like a mantra.

Between these two schools, the earlier Hinayana Buddhism of the Nara period was eliminated. Tendai Buddhism was favored by the aristocrats, and in spite of the best efforts of Emperor Kammu, Buddhism became once again a powerful force in the life of the nation.

Various Changes in Power

During the Heian period, important political changes took place. Estates became hereditary and important clans came to control vast areas of the country. Theoretically the crown retained the rights of ownership, but the actual shares in the produce of the land went to the landowners. The power of the emperor was limited. His most important role was to function as a chief priest for Shinto.

A strong military push was made to eliminate the "barbarians" in the north, and successful wars routed the Ainus. The title of *shogun* was given to the military commander. Literally this means "barbarian-subduing general." The word *shogun* entered the vocabulary.

The Nakatomi clan changed their name to Fujiwara and retained power for centuries. It was customary for imperial princes to marry Fujiwara ladies. Between 724 and

1900, 54 of the 76 emperors were born to Fujiwara mothers. Once the child was born, the emperor was persuaded to retire and a Fujiwara regent was installed. Once the child was old enough to rule, the regent took the title of *kampuku,* or spokesman, and retained effective control. Meanwhile the retired or cloistered emperor tried to influence events from behind the scenes. At times there were several cloistered emperors and politics became murky. Everything was done in the name of the emperor, but the real power was with the Fujiwara clan. The emperor had the position; the Fujiwara had the power. The emperor was respected, but his edicts were ignored. The Fujiwara estates were larger than those of any other family or religious group. Because many wealthy landowners paid no taxes at all, the government, short on revenue, could not afford to maintain a national army. To protect themselves from lawlessness, the landowners formed their own militia. They came to be known as samurai, or men who serve.

The aristocrats came to occupy magnificent palaces. The Boydo-in, a summer residence in Uji, is a masterpiece of Japanese architecture. Most famous is the Phoenix Hall (so named because of the two golden birds on the roof), which was completed in 1053. It is the only building out of more than 30 that is still intact. It was Fujiwara Michinaga who laid the foundation of the villa. Four of his daughters were imperial consorts.

This was an age of clan warfare. Most famous are the battles between the Taira under Yoshitsune (1159–1189) and the Minamoto under Yoritomo (1147–1199). Their leader received the military title of *shogun,* which he invested with new meaning and made hereditary.

One of the cloistered emperors used the Taira clan to dislodge the Fujiwara, who lost a final battle in 1185, in which the Taira finally triumphed. This signaled the end of the Heian period. The Taira exterminated most of the Minamoto but spared the oldest son (Minamoto Yorimoto) and kept him hostage in Kamakura among his relatives. Yorimoto married into the family and gathered dissatisfied men to create another army. After five years of warfare, the Minamoto regained control.

In spite of all this turbulence, this was a period of intense artistic production. For centuries Chinese characters had been used to write Japanese, but around 900 a phonetic system was developed to write Japanese. More women were encouraged to write; one of the first and most famous was Lady Murasaki, who produced the first complete novel in world history in about 1004, *The Tale of Genji.* In the book Lady Murasaki relates the loves and psychological development of the Prince Genji, and the story inspired paintings and monuments.

When the Taira were defeated the emperor hoped to regain control, but was frustrated by Yoritomo. The victorious general installed a military regime in Kamakura that became the new administrative center of the country. When Yoritomo fell off his horse and died at age 52, his widow, Hoso Masako, took over, and now the Hojo family controlled Kamakura and acted as regents for the shogun. At one point Hojo Masako retired to a Buddhist nunnery and became the "nun-shogun." She controlled the shogunate from behind the scenes. The political structure became opaque. In Kyoto the emperor and the cloistered emperor(s) and the *kampuku* (regent) vied for control, and in Kamakura (the real seat of power), the Hojo family controlled the shogun.

Occasionally an emperor tried to reassert imperial authority. For example, in 1221 Emperor Go-Toba (1180–1239) made an attempt to assert himself, but was defeated and exiled.

The Kamakura Era

One of the most important events of the Kamakura era (1192–1333) was the Mongol invasion. In 1274 Kublai Khan launched an armada of 300 large and 450 small vessels with 15,000 Mongols and Chinese, 8,000 Koreans, and 7,000 sailors. After small initial success, a storm destroyed the fleet and forced Kublai Khan to abandon the invasion. Japanese resistance had been stronger than anticipated. A few years later, in 1281, the Mongols launched a second invasion. Meanwhile, the Japanese had created a defensive line, but this time it was a typhoon that delivered Japan. Some 100,000 men drowned or were killed as they re-embarked. It was a spectacular deliverance for the Japanese, who believed more than ever that their land was divinely protected. They called the divine wind *kamikaze,* a word that received new significance in World War II. The unexpected deliverance led to a revival of both Shinto and Buddhism.

Pure Land Buddhism

The civil wars and the Mongol invasion fuelled dire predictions that in spite of the protection of the 11-faced *bodhisattva* Avalokiteshvara, nothing could prevent the decline of Buddhism. In reality, the chaotic situation gave new impetus to Buddhism. Previously confined to the aristocracy, Buddhism now became a reli-

gion for the masses but in simplified form. Honen (1133–1212) introduced Pure Land Buddhism from China. He taught that salvation is possible through the merits of Buddha Amida. Buddha had manifested himself as a *bodhisattva* and vowed that he would never be complete till all people, with sincere faith, entered the Pure Land. To reach this goal it is enough to repeat a simple prayer called the *nembutsu:* "Praise to the Buddha Amida." It was simple, it was for everyone, and it guaranteed salvation, or rebirth in the Pure Land. It mattered not whether one's disposition was good or evil. Even sinners, as sinners, are eligible for rebirth in the Pure Land if they invoke Amidabha sincerely. In the Pure Land there is no suffering. Clothing, food "and all beautiful things appear when those who live there wish for them." Jewel-laden trees adorn the landscape, and holy teaching fills the air.[24]

It was tempting to dismiss discipline and to rely on the merits of Amidabha, although Honen stressed the importance of benevolence. Honen wrote, "if one who eats fish should be reborn into the Pure Land, a cormorant would certainly be the one. If one who does not eat fish should be reborn into the Pure Land, a monkey would indeed be the one. Whether or not one eats fish does not count, but it is the one who invokes Amidabha that is bound to be reborn in the Pure Land."[25] Personal efforts—such as practicing asceticism— could not merit salvation. Only through faith in Amida could the Pure Land be reached. Not even meditation or the cultivation of virtue could help. The invocation of Amidabha was enough.

It seems that at some remote period of time Buddha appeared as King Amidaba, but then gave up kingship to become a monk. Eons later, always in search of enlightenment, he made 48 vows and promised that upon attaining buddhahood he would create the Pure Land and open it to all. Anyone repeating his name ten times in sincere faith was eligible for the Pure Land. Since Buddha had accumulated virtue through eons of time, he could freely offer the Pure Land to all believers. To obtain enlightenment, it is enough to rely on the power of Amida. When Buddha appears to those who recite his name, Avalokiteshvara (the *bodhisattva* of compassion) and Mahasthama-prapta (the *bodhisattva* of wisdom) will always accompany him.[26]

It is understood that Amidabha's vows proceeded from his merciful concern toward all living things. This is a far cry from the detachment demanded by Buddha—the indifference to all things and the extinction of all desire.

Some of the old prejudices against women are reflected in *The Sutra of the Master of Healing*, where we are told that "this Buddhaland is eternally pure, it has no women...in all aspects it is equal to the Western Paradise." If a woman wholeheartedly cherishes the name of the Buddha of Medicine, she shall never again become a woman in the next rebirth.[27] The same sutra informs us that to ensure good health it is enough to recite this brief sutra 49 times, to light 49 candles for 49 days, and to free 49 animals. In many Chinese markets, caged birds are offered for sale for this purpose, enabling the new owner to set them free and to accumulate merit. (How many birds are trained to return to the seller?)

The Pure Land sect became immensely popular. By the end of the seventeenth century, this sect had more than 6,000 temples.

Buddhist texts were transmitted from India to China and reached Japan via Korea. The translation of Buddhist Indian texts into Chinese presented an enormous challenge. The Chinese language did not seem to have the necessary terminology to communicate the sophisticated abstract thoughts characteristic of original Buddhism. Initially translators used roughly equivalent Daoist terms already familiar in China. Some readers might have assumed that there was not all that much difference between Buddhism and Daoism. It helped the original acceptance of Buddhism in China. Gradually, better translations of the Buddhist texts were produced, but in the process, Buddhism changed and took on a Chinese face. Finally 1,440 scriptures had been made available in Chinese in 5,586 volumes. By the time Buddhism reached Japan via Korea, additional adaptations to local cultures had been made. Buddhism was received in each country "according to the character of the recipients."[28] That was also true in Tibet, where Buddhists routinely ate meat because the severe climate made such a diet mandatory. Modifications and adaptations were part of the transmission. As Buddhist sources inform us, it took a hundred years for the Japanese to "digest and remodel the imported religion so as to make it completely their own"[29] and to develop a truly Japanese Buddhism. It is true that Buddhism in Japan is fundamentally different from Buddhism in Thailand—in many instances, they are diametrically opposite in the most fundamental aspects. Instead of nirvana or extinction we find the Pure Land, and instead of severe asceticism to reach enlightenment we find the recital of a simple formula.

Whereas Honen recommended endless repetitions of the *nembutsu*, his most famous disciple, Shinran (1173–1262), founder of the True Pure Land sect, believed that one single heartfelt invocation was enough. The immense Buddha statue in Kamakura, the Daibutsu, gives solid expression to this conviction. In Kamakura, shogun Yoritomo agreed with one of his court attendants to erect a great image of the Buddha. The statue of Buddha Amida—Lord of the Western Pure Land—was erected in 1252, and at 43 feet tall, it towers over the area. Exactly 656 curls crown the Buddha's head, each one winding clockwise. He features all the typical characteristics of Buddha statues, including the long earlobes, reminders of his royal descent. The fleshy excrescence on the head symbolizes wisdom. "There are webs between the fingers symbolizing fulfillment."[30] The pose is one of meditation, his legs crossed in front and his body slightly inclined.

In the debate over which was the most important sutra, the Buddhist monk Nichiren concluded that the most important was Saddharmapundarika, the Lotus of the True Law, which is better known as the Lotus Sutra. Merit could be earned by reading or copying the sutra. Nichiren (1222–1282) based his teaching exclusively on this text and taught his followers a different formula: "Glory to the Sutra of the Lotus of the Supreme Law."

According to Nichiren, the transmission of this sacred text, the Lotus Sutra, depended on blood relationship. Not surprisingly, perhaps he believed himself to be the reincarnation of *bodhisattva* Jogyo, to whom this sutra had been entrusted. Nichiren also stressed the importance of faith as the sole requisite of salvation. He was remarkably intolerant and condemned all other Buddhist sects, not to mention all non-Buddhists. Several modern Buddhist movements trace their spiritual ancestry to Nichiren, including one of the best known, the Soka Gakkai, which came into being in the 1930s and has sometimes been accused of brainwashing followers. In Japan, this group is involved in political activities (more on this soon).

The victory in the aforementioned Mongol invasion (i.e., the fact that the Japanese retained most of their defensive positions) had taken place on Japanese territory, and that made it impossible for the government to apportion property as rewards to the victorious army. In addition, the best administrative positions went to the Hojo family, regardless of merit or ability. In spite of the retreat of the Mongols, there was widespread dissatisfaction with the government.

Emperor Go-Daigo (1288–1339), who had an energetic personality, attempted to gain full authority over Japan. He attacked the *bakufu*—or military government of Kamakura, but was defeated and exiled. He found a way to return, rallied his followers, and led them to victory. The Hojo regency was destroyed. The Ashikaga clan, which had been a close ally of the emperor and led the fight, now turned against Go-Daigo, who had no choice but to flee once more. He took the royal regalia with him to set up a government in exile, known as the southern court. The northern court promptly appointed Ashikaga as shogun, and civil war raged for decades. The Ashikaga clan never managed to control the other major warrior families. They delegated authority to local constables who gradually extended their power and became territorial lords or *daimyos*. The conflict ended in 1392 with a sensible compromise, but the central government had been fatally weakened and for the next

100 years, anarchy prevailed and hundreds of *daimyos* fought against each other. These events did not prevent shogun Yoshimitsu Ashikaga from building the Kinkakuji, or Golden Pavilion, in 1397. He retired at age 38 to enter the priesthood. Three years later he began the construction of the villa in the Kyoto area. The formal name of the pavilion is Rokuonji, the name of the place where Buddha preached for the first time. Upon the death of Yoshimitsu the building became a Zen temple "of the Shokokuji sect of the Rinzai-shu."[31] The Golden Pavilion was built over a pond to symbolize harmony between heaven and earth, and the entire building was covered with gold leaf.

Zen Buddhism

During the Kamakura era yet another Buddhism sect, Zen Buddhism, was introduced from China by the monk Eisai (1141–1215) and promoted by Dogen (1200–1253). *Zen* means "meditation." Eisai promoted the Rinzai teaching, which is a call to self-realization and is presented as the essence of Buddhism. Buddha, by contrast, denied the very existence of the self and his focus was on extinction of desire, not self-fulfillment through illumination. Zen is criticized by followers of the Pure Land sect as "nothing other than a Buddhism colored by the Chinese way of thinking."[32] Zen Buddhism claims insight into the essential nature of the cosmos and a full realization of our true nature, thanks to a state of higher consciousness. The new insight into the true nature of the self "leads to the realization that there is no fixed entity commonly referred to as oneself. There is only boundless, infinite, unobstructed space."[33] Admittedly this is "based on assumptions that cannot be proved by intellectual argument,"[34] but that is not surprising, since Zen is irrational and hopes to escape the bondage of logic. It requires no intellectual effort. According to Carl Jung, Zen attempts the "complete destruction of the rational intellect."[35] For Zen, only experience is meaningful, although one should think that this experience has to be interpreted with the help of logic.

In Zen Buddhism, the focus of meditation should be the question, Who am I? and to find the answer "not to think is the best thinking."[36] But since there are instincts, habits, and intellectual judgments that arise "from somewhere," clarification is necessary.[37]

In the Chinese Buddhist tradition there is no single authoritative interpretation of the many sacred texts. There was disagreement about the merits of individual sutras. There were as many opinions as scholars. Zen escaped the problem by rejecting the significance of the written word. If and since one cannot rely on an authoritative text, the voice of the master becomes most important, as does the consensus of the community. This explains, in part, the strong zen discipline and the authoritarianism of zen masters.

Hundreds of books have been written to explain Zen when it is actually beyond explanation and defies both logic and definition. Only Dogen relied on scriptural authority. Later he taught that only a priest can be a true Buddhist and formulated strict rules covering every aspect of life—even minor activities. Dogen agreed with the Pure Land sects that enlightenment is impossible through one's own effort and can be obtained only through faith. In this he opposed the Chinese view that illumination is the result of personal effort. In the words of Carl Jung, "it is still extremely hazy how such an enlightenment comes and of what it consists."[38]

There are three major Zen sects. The Obaku sect was founded when Yinyuan Longqi, a Chinese monk, came to Japan in 1654. The Rinzai sect, which claims 2.5 million adherents, and the Soto group, with approximately seven million followers, each have a distinct methodology. All three sects agree that rationality must be rejected. Zen has a nonlogical character. There are a hundred answers to the question "What is the essence of Zen Buddhism?" including the following:

> I am tired, having been sitting for a long time.
> Today and tomorrow
> The wind blows and the sun heats
> Frost comes upon clouds
> In the daytime I see mountains.[39]

Ideally, Zen teaching is transmitted from the heart of the master to that of the initiated without relying on speech or writing. It is a matter of intuition.

Dogen taught that enlightenment is not a matter of the mind, but of the body. It is best to do away with all mental deliberation and simply go on sitting. Indeed, sitting in meditation is the gateway to bliss—rather than walking, standing, or reclining. Incense burning, adoration, reciting the *nembutsu*, confession, sutra reading—all these are in vain. Simply sit and meditate, for reasoning is pointless. Intuition is said to prevail over reason.

Illumination, or *satori*, is reached through spiritual and physical discipline. The sitting is tightly regulated, with either the cross-legged lotus posture or the half-crossed posture (right foot on the left groin), with the legs and backbone forming a 90-degree angle, the eyes slightly open (so that an area only three feet ahead can be seen), the tongue touching the upper jaw, etc.[40] Meanwhile, sutras are quoted to bolster zen presentations.[41]

The utter simplicity of Zen and the discipline required of keeping body and mind under control—sitting in a meditative stance—had a strong appeal to the military. Most soldiers were not familiar with the sutras anyway, and learned instead to rely on instant Zen by the use of *koans*, or paradoxical statements intended to shock the mind out of routine patterns of thought. The *koans* present insoluble problems intended to cleanse the mind from the desire to speculate and investigate theological questions. One popular *koan* questions, "What is the sound of one hand clapping?" Apparently the *koan* is resolved "whenever we enter the great death experience. The answer itself comes to us instead of us answering it. It is really the voice of heaven or revelation."[42] If we fail to find the answer to the *koan*, it is because we have not experienced this great death.

That Zen originated in Buddhism is beyond question. Author Daisetz Teitaro Suzuki admits that the main ideas are derived from Buddhism.[43] It is a branch of Mahayana Buddhism, which includes the Four Noble Truths (about suffering) and the eightfold path. *Bodhisattvas* are venerated in Zen temples along with Buddha. We are told that "Buddhist teachings as propounded in the sutras and *sastras* are treated by Zen as mere waste paper," but we are also informed that monks listen to the reading of a sutra before the meal. And when they eat, the monks also "think of those departed spirits and other beings who are living in this and other worlds, and each [monk] taking out about seven grains of rice from his portion offers them to the unseen."[44]

Zen is different in the West than in the East because teachers adapt their training to the needs of the students.[45] In the West, the Buddhist aspect is minimized. According to Zen there is no God to worship, no ritual to observe. Adepts no longer rely on ritual and pay no attention to Buddhist statues. Zen stressed simplicity. It strongly influenced Japanese culture, especially in architecture, painting, poetry (haiku), flower arrangement, and the tea ceremony.

Zen rock gardens have become world famous, especially Ryoan-ji. The building, originally a country villa, was erected in 1450 and only later dedicated as a Zen temple. The rock garden goes back to 1499. It measures 90 feet by 30 feet. It contains three groupings of rocks, and it is impossible to see all 15 rocks simultaneously. The walls surrounding the garden are made of clay boiled in oil. It is up to each visitor to discover the meaning of the garden. Do the rocks represent islands (continents) and the raked gravel the sea (or rivers)? Is the visitor looking at a tiger carrying cubs across the water, do the rocks spell out the character for heart? All interpretation is necessarily subjective; each person has to find a unique meaning.

In 1546 Otomo Sorin became a Christian and was baptized at age 48. It has been suggested that the stones in his "zen" garden are in the shape of a cross.

The typical Zen-inspired painting is black and white with powerful brush strokes devoid of nonessential details. Perhaps the greatest Zen painter was Sesshu (1420–1477), who, in spite of the turbulent times, managed to visit China. He created impressionistic paintings and favored the monochrome simplicity of Zen.

Further Fragmentation

The Onin Wars (1467–1477) ignited because of a ferocious quarrel between two regional barons. In the process, Kyoto was devastated more than once. No strong leader emerged to take control, to fill the political vacuum. Internal strife prevailed for decades. Religious groups, warrior monks, samurai, *daimyos,* and powerful clans all fought each other. The first major peasant rebellion erupted in 1428. A severe famine in 1457 killed hundreds of thousands of people.

Warriors were more loyal to their local commanders than to distant shoguns. It was the *daimyo* who administered various regions, collected taxes, built towns and castles, and maintained bridges and irrigation canals. By 1467 there were 260 *daimyos*—an extraordinary fragmentation of the country. The time had come for men such as Nobunaga, Hideyoshi, and Ieyasu to unify the country and, in the process, inaugurate the Tokugawa era. These three personalities dominated during the sixteenth century. All three were deified. That same century saw the final defeat of the Ainu in the north. But a new group of "barbarians" arrived from the south when a ship was blown off course and three Portuguese sailors reached Japan in 1543. Other Portuguese followed and, a few years later, Spaniards also reached Japan. With the Europeans came the first missionaries and harquebuses, the early version of a portable gun.

The Momoyama Period

This period (1568–1600) was dominated by two personalities: Oda Nobunaga and Toyotomi Hideyoshi.

Oda Nobunaga

Oda Nobunaga (1534–1582) was a brilliant and ruthless military commander. When *daimyo* Yoshimoto left the Pacific coast of Japan to march to the capital to gain control, the only remaining obstacle was the small army of Nobunaga, which was hugely outnumbered. Nobunaga took advantage of a thunderstorm to surprise his larger enemy and gained an unexpected victory. Yoshimoto was killed in battle. Till the very end of his life, Nobunaga fought three major military clans and two powerful religious institutions, including the militant Tendai monks of Mount Hiei. Periodically these well-armed monks descended from their mountain stronghold to invade Kyoto. To prevent attacks by the enemy, they carried portable shrines. The monks did not hesitate to attack other Buddhist sects, and they ransacked Kyoto. Nobunaga surrounded Enryakuji, the monastery on Mount Hiei, and set fire to the brush surrounding the buildings. Whoever tried to escape was killed. Thousands of men, women, and children were burned alive.

It took Nobunaga ten years to conquer the headquarters and temples of the Jodo Shinshu sect in Osaka. Nobunaga was so relentless he did not even hesitate to execute members of his own family. In his battles, he was one of the first to use firearms, which were introduced by the Portuguese. Clan after clan was subdued, and Nobunaga became the consummate warlord. He acted with ruthless efficiency. He built strong castles and used them as administrative centers. Then Akechi, one of Nobunaga's top generals, killed Nobunaga in 1582. By the time of his death, Nobunaga had gained control of one-third of the nation. Hideyoshi immediately destroyed Akechi and his army and emerged as the new leader.

Toyotomi Hideyoshi

Toyotomi Hideyoshi (1536–1598) was of humble origin and orphaned at age seven. He left home at 15 and joined the army of one of the many *daimyos*. Later he transferred his allegiance to Lord Oda Nobunaga and rapidly became one of his chief deputies and leading generals. Hideyoshi's military career was remarkable—he commanded large armies of more than 250,000 men and used the latest innovation, muskets. By 1590 he was lord of all Japan. After 120 years of fragmentation, Japan was finally unified. A combination of brilliant military strategy and the skillful use of muskets and artillery guaranteed Hideyoshi's victories. Even the best armor of the most courageous men could not stop bullets. With short and powerful military campaigns, Hideyoshi conquered and unified Japan in eight years. He used both speed and daring to achieve victories. He also had a talent for diplomacy and the art of conciliation. Hideyoshi was lenient to the defeated and often allowed them to retain their possessions. Many *daimyos* submitted without a fight because of Hideyoshi's humane attitude. Ieyasu, a potential rival, was allowed to retain control of his five provinces. With an eye toward protecting the mantle of succession, Hideyoshi became the guardian and supporter of Samboshi, a grandson of Oda Nobunaga. Hideyoshi also adopted Nobunaga's fourth son and presided over his funeral rites. Oda's heirs thus entered the service of Hideyoshi.

Hideyoshi rebuilt Kyoto, which had been devastated by civil wars. He restored the Toji Temple to conciliate and control the Shingon sect, which was ever ready to meddle in politics. He moved the Nishi Hongan-ji Temple to its present location to secure the good will of the Pure Land sect, which controlled large areas of Japan. The Nanzen-ji center of the Rinzai Zen sect, in ruins for 200 years, was restored with help from Hideyoshi. He established excellent relationships with all the important religious groups.

Francis Xavier, a Franciscan Jesuit missionary, had been well received by Nobunaga in 1549 as a counterweight to the Buddhists. The Jesuits introduced Japan to Arabian horses, which were far superior to the small Mongol species. They also brought clocks, new weaving techniques, and other inventions. It is possible that by 1571 there were already 30,000 Christians and, ten years later, perhaps 50,000 with some 200 churches. Samboshi, the son of Nobunaga, became a Christian. Some *daimyos* were converted and in 1582 several were sent to Rome in the first diplomatic mission to Europe. When they returned eight years later, the climate of tolerance had changed. In 1592 Hideyoshi announced that "Japan is the land of the gods" and called Christianity a "pernicious doctrine." But it seems that the edict was really aimed at the zealots who were determined to destroy local temples. Some Christians acted as brokers in gold and silver, thanks to their connection with the Portuguese, and developed an almost independent base in Nagasaki. The expulsion order was not enforced, but the warning should have been heard. In spite of the letter of the edict, land was offered to the Franciscans in 1593.

One of the most significant edicts dealt with the possession of weapons. Peasants were no longer allowed to own swords or any other weapons. Supposedly these weapons were collected to melt them down to make nails and spikes for the construction of a huge Buddha. The edict established a clear class distinction between the samurai, who carried weapons, and the peasants, who did not. There were also edicts that prohibited farmers from abandoning full-time cultivation and soldiers from re-entering village society. These regulations contributed to the rigid social structure that developed during the Tokugawa era. There was little social mobility. Status and residence could not be changed. Everything was carefully regulated, from seating arrangements to hairstyles, from who could ride on horseback or use litters. Permission was needed to travel on the few approved routes. Even or especially *daimyos* needed approval before they could form marriage relationships. Alliances between lords also needed government consent. The castles of the *daimyos* were leveled, and Hideyoshi's control became absolute. The emperor was honored, but powerless. His palace was relatively modest, but the setting very attractive. Hideyoshi received the highest court honors: He was named Great Minister of State and proclaimed *kampaku,* or regent, in 1585.

Hideyoshi was the most prolific builder in Japanese history.[46] Kyoto was rebuilt, and temples were restored. Tens of thousands worked on his official Kyoto headquarters. The construction of Osaka Castle began in 1583.[47] The strongest fortress in Japan was completed in three years because 30,000 laborers worked around the clock. Two hundred ships a day ferried the blocks used for the base of the fortress. Two moats and walls 120 feet high surrounded the central keep. Enough food and ammunition could be stored in the castle for a garrison of 90,000 to continue fighting for years. Many stones in the castle walls have markings that indicate work areas assigned to feudal lords.

Today Osaka Castle contains an interesting collection of treasures that belonged to the Toyotomi family.[48] Even in those troubled times, magnificent swords were produced, both long swords and shorter ones for self-defense. Gold plated, close-fitting armor was crowned with gold-leaf helmets. The ongoing clan wars did not stop artistic creativity. Quivers with arabesque designs in lacquer, tea bowls and teakettles, incense burners, intricately designed containers, ornate boxes of various sizes, magnificent paintings on long scrolls, elegant cosmetics including ornamental hairpins, and more had an artistic touch.

Toward the end of his life, Hideyoshi may have suffered from megalomania. He requested tribute from Korea and Taiwan. In a letter to Manila, he wrote that he anticipated an easy conquest of China. As a first step, he invaded Korea in 1592 with an army of more than 150,000 and a back-up force of 100,000 more, not to mention sailors. They met little resistance. Only the Korean navy, under the brilliant admiral Yi-Sun-Shin and his armored fleet, the famous turtle ships, gained significant victories and helped to cut off Hideyoshi's supply lines. The Japanese army reached Seoul in three weeks. The Koreans were unprepared for this onslaught. Korean guerrillas harassed the army, and the Chinese crossed the Yalu River to intervene. Gradually Hideyoshi's armies were driven back by the combined Korean and Chinese forces. Still, in the process, Korea was devastated. Since at least one of Hideyoshi's generals was a Christian, it was perhaps Korea's first contact with Christianity. The gradual retreat of the Japanese was followed by five years of negotiations. In 1597, a new army landed with instruction to kill men, women, and children. But within a year, Hideyoshi died, and hostilities ended.

Hideyoshi had adopted a nephew whom he appointed to be his successor. Later, suspected of disloyalty, the nephew was exiled and ordered to take his own life. It could be because a concubine finally gave Hideyoshi an heir. Nothing can excuse Hideyoshi's savage destruction of his entire family, which was perhaps due to a degree of madness. His reaction to an incident in 1596 was equally strange. A Spanish ship, the San Felipe, was wrecked on the coast of Japan. The authorities confiscated the cargo. The captain and his Franciscan countrymen hoped to recover the cargo of gold and silver. The ensuing controversy ended when Hideyoshi arrested several Franciscans and 17 Japanese Christians and sent them to Nagasaki to be crucified. Perhaps Hideyoshi was concerned about the rapid growth of Christianity, since by this time several hundred thousand Japanese had embraced Christianity. Actually the Japanese were interested in using the Christians to help establish a connection with Spain via the Philippines as a counterweight to the Portuguese and to break the latter's commercial monopoly.

Hideyoshi appointed his infant son to the post of *kampaku*, or regent of Japan, under the guardianship of a five-man regency council—all former adversaries—among them Tokugawa Ieyasu.

They swore a solemn oath of loyalty, but Ieyasu promptly disregarded the claims of the heir. The battle of Sekigahara in 1600 pitted Ieyasu against Hideyoshi loyalists and resulted in a decisive victory by Ieyasu. It took almost 15 years before Osaka Castle fell and Toyotomi Hideyori, the son and appointed heir, committed suicide. The last remnant of the Hideyoshi faction was wiped out.

Immediately upon the death of Hideyoshi, Emperor Go-Yozei declared him a divinity of the first rank with the title Most Bright God of Our Bountiful Country.[49]

Did Toyotomi Hideyoshi have religious convictions? At some point in the course of the second invasion of Korea, toward the end of his life, he wrote that god is the root and source of all existence. Buddhism in India, Confucianism in China, and Shinto in Japan speak of this god.[50] Perhaps Hideyoshi envisioned an ultimate reality, god, behind all fleeting appearances. He used religion for political purposes and was too cautious to give voice to personal convictions.

The relatively brief Momoyama Period brought lasting change that deeply impacted Japan for centuries under the Tokugawa. Perhaps incessant warfare and the brutal regime of Oda Nobunaga contributed to the lack of religious fervor. It is not without significance that the focus was on castles and palaces rather than shrines and temples. There was "a growing indifference to traditional religion among the ruling classes."[51] As well, contact with a few Europeans created a new awareness of the outside world and almost automatically led to a new self-evaluation.

The Tokugawa Period

The new Tokugawa era (1603–1853) began with Tukugawa Ieyasu (1542–1616),

followed by 14 shoguns, till at last Yoshinobu resigned his post in 1867. The government set up its headquarters in Edo (now Tokyo).

Contact between Shinto and neo-Confucianism deepened. The Tokugawa era encouraged the development of Confucianism and neo-Confucianism at the expense of Buddhism and Christianity. But there was a significant difference between the traditions of Japan and China. The parent-child relationship, filial piety, was primary in China, but in Japan the samurai focused more on the ruler-minister relationship with a commitment of absolute loyalty that, in the end, led to the emperor cult.[52]

Ieyasu had barely been named shogun when he built Nijo Castle to serve as Kyoto headquarters and residence. It was one of the first castles to be surrounded by inner and outer moats, draw bridges, and high towers. Ieyasu took the unprecedented step of inviting the emperor to visit the castle, located not far from the Imperial Palace. The emperor complied 20 years later, long after Ieyasu's death.

Once Ieyasu had overcome the last remnants of Hiyori followers, he was firmly entrenched. His revenue equaled 2,500,000 *koku* of rice, or 12,500,000 million bushels. It was estimated that one koku of rice, or five bushels, was sufficient to feed one man for one year. The disparity between rich and poor was enormous, and there was little social mobility. The Confucian societal structure was rigid. The samurai class was the most honorable, followed by the peasant class because they were essential producers, then came the artisans who created finished products and, at the bottom of society, the tradesmen, who did not seem to produce anything tangible. Subclasses were engaged in ritually unclean activities such as tanning. At least throughout this long period of time the country was at peace, although peasant uprisings occurred about once a month. Minute aspects of everyone's lives were regulated. Peasants were not allowed to drink tea or sake and were told when to rise, what to eat, and where to plant bamboo. Even high-ranking samurai could not escape detailed regulations. They were allowed 13 kind of silks. Merchant families were encouraged to serve modest meals that were carefully defined. Perhaps these rules and regulations were not strictly enforced or frequently evaded, but they depict a heavy-handed administration and left little wiggle room.

Contact between samurai and peasants was not permitted, and for the peasants, no contact was permitted with townsmen. Court etiquette was equally strict; even the length of the kimono was determined. Religious disputes and the affairs of the powerful Buddhist monasteries were left in the hands of the clergy, but the management and taxation of the vast temple holdings came under government control. The royal family was under strict supervision and not allowed to leave the palace grounds. The function of the emperor was strictly ceremonial; he was to be the link between heaven and earth (as Confucians saw the matter) or to function as the Shinto high priest, or the link between his divine ancestors and his people. Ritual kept him fully occupied. The *daimyos* were not allowed to move troops outside their own domains. Alliances among them were not permitted. They were limited to a single castle and a specific number of samurai.

Most of the modern cities began as castle-towns. The beginning of urbanization took place from 1580 to 1610. The samurai lived close to castles for defense purposes and as tradesmen were needed and servants required, small cities developed and gave birth to the modern cities that dot the landscape of Japan.

Ieyasu embraced Buddhism inclusive of Shinto and adopted the Confucian code of ethics. Shortly before his death he made arrangements to have himself deified. The Toshogu Shrine built in 1651 honors the shogun. A large number of stone and bronze lanterns, donated by feudal lords, flank the long approach to the ornate gate.

Under Iemitsu (1623–1651), every *daimyo* was compelled to maintain a residence in Edo, where his family stayed permanently to guarantee good behavior. The feudal lord himself had to reside in Edo every other year. In addition to the cost of the dual residence, the journeys to Edo, complete with retainers, were prohibitive. Some *daimyos* arrived with a retinue of 1,000 persons. These huge expenses severely limited the financial flexibility of the *daimyos,* even of the wealthiest.

Economic and Political Development

During this era there was a resurgence of interest in Confucianism, very much in line with the conservative attitudes of the Tokugawa regime. Confucian scholarship was treated as a separate branch of learning. By the end of the seventeenth century, every self-respecting *daimyo* had a Confucian adviser dealing with questions of ethics and historical precedent. Confucius had advocated a complex system of reciprocal duties in step with feudalism, and Confucian ethics supported samurai thinking. The concept of the "Confucian gentleman" did not allow them to participate in commerce or industry.[53] Because the samurai became restless in times of peace, Ieyasu sent 3,000 to conquer the islands now known as Okinawa—ostensibly because they had refused to assist Japan in the invasion of Korea. From then on, Okinawa paid tribute to both China and Japan. Over time the samurai transformed themselves from fierce warriors into competent civil administrators. The samurai occupied a high social position, but their income was inadequate, and as "gentlemen," they could not debase themselves to earn extra income. Unfortunately for the samurai, stipends were denominated in rice and the price of rice increased but little in the seventeenth and eighteenth centuries, whereas prices of other goods rose. The samurai became increasingly impoverished. The fact that some *daimyos* reduced the stipend was hardly helpful.

The shogun controlled about one-fourth of the territory, the so-called "heavenly domain." The rest of the country was ruled by the more than 150 *daimyos* or feudal lords, whose domain, the *han,* ranged from very small to vast areas. The *han* enjoyed relative independence, except in matters of religion and war. Occasionally they had to help maintain or develop the infrastructure (roads, bridges, canals). By and large matters of taxation (between 30 and 40 percent) remained in the hands of the local *daimyo.* When the lord had to reside in Edo, managers had to be appointed and the administrative machinery became cumbersome. Nevertheless, throughout the long Tokugawa era, bureaucracy worked remarkably well.

In spite of the Confucian prejudice against merchants, they gained more and more importance as a market economy developed. By 1720 the city of Edo, with one million people, featured as many merchants as samurai. Edo, the future Tokyo,

had become one of the largest cities of the world, followed by Osaka, which had half as many residents.

The first few shoguns favored foreign trade, but this was carefully regulated, and it was no longer exclusively in the hands of foreigners. Japanese individuals were given licenses to trade and ships carried Japanese wares to Siam (Thailand), the Philippines, and elsewhere. Thousands of Japanese settled in foreign ports across southeast Asia. In the first 30 years of the seventeenth century, more than 300 ships received the vermilion seal and were licensed to trade. All this ended rather abruptly because of internal political developments partly related to Christians.

Will Adams, a British subject, arrived in Japan in 1600. He was a pilot and gunner and became an adviser to Ieyasu. The Dutch also became present. The two Protestant countries, the Dutch and British, were at war with Spain and Portugal. Echoes of the conflict reached Japan. Unfortunately the Christians in Japan had sided with Hideyori (son of Hideyoshi) and fought against Ieyasu at Osaka Castle. It should not have come as a great surprise that in 1614 an edict of the Tokugawa shogunate called for the expulsion of all missionaries. Some went to Macau, while others decided to stay and keep a low profile in the hopes that everything would eventually return to normal. That never happened. After 1618, Christians were seriously persecuted. In 1622, 51 Christians were executed at Nagasaki, and two years later, another 50 burned alive at Edo. All in all, between 3,000 and 4,000 were killed. In 1633, 30 missionaries were executed, and by 1637, only five were left at liberty. Then came the great Shimabara uprising in 1637, when 35,000 insurgents rose up against the local *daimyo* and accused them of brutal treatment and impossible taxes. The insurgents were largely Christian and were joined by *ronin,* or masterless samurai whose lords had been dispossessed. The rebellion was centered on the Shimabara Peninsula, easily defended and subdued only with enormous difficulty. The shogun even asked the Dutch for help, and they shelled the rebels from the sea. Finally the defenders were overpowered and massacred. The remaining Christians were hunted down.[54] Although the majority was either killed or abjured, many went underground and emerged again in 1865, maintaining their faith secretly for two centuries.

Ieyasu was keenly aware of the possibility of another unfriendly coalition in which Christians might be a possible catalyst. The Christian concept of personal conscience was considered subversive in a society where harmony with the clan and unconditional obedience to superiors were viewed as prime virtues. Thus contact with Portugal was made illegal. Japanese were no longer allowed to leave the country, and those who had stayed away for more than five years were unable to return. Catholics were not allowed to enter Japan. The building of oceangoing vessels was interdicted. In 1614 an edict ordered all Japanese to register as members of a Buddhist sect. This did not automatically affect Shintoists since, for the most part, these two religions co-existed peacefully, but temple validation was required for marriage, employment, and travel.

International trade was severely restricted. Only the Dutch were allowed to trade, and their visits were limited to Deshima, a tiny man-made island in the harbor of Nagasaki. Because the island was artificial, the legal fiction could be maintained that international trade was not carried out in Japan. Limited trade continued with Korea via Tsushima Island and with China by way of the Ryukyu Islands (Okinawa). For all practical purposes, Japan was a closed country. Initially motivated by political reasons, the seclusion was propelled by Confucian principles till isolation was complete by 1639. Korea, strongly Confucian, followed a similar path and came to be called the Hermit Kingdom. As a result of this seclusion, the countries missed out on the enormous technological advances being made elsewhere and the industrial revolution that changed Western Europe.

Gradually, Dutch books were translated into Japanese and new ideas began percolating through society. After 1720, foreign books were no longer banned. Poetry enjoyed a renaissance thanks to Basho, who created the classical haiku 17-syllable poem. Increasing wealth and urbanization, along with less religious fervor, combined to create a new atmosphere and gave rise to the "floating world"—entertainment areas complete with restaurants, theaters, and prostitutes. Kabuki theater, a mixture of pantomime and dance, flourished. After 1629, only male actors appeared on the scene. Woodprints of kabuki stars became popular. They were mass-produced and available to everyone. Artists produced netuske, little toggles often highly ornamented, used to attach a little *inro* or medicine box to the sash, or perhaps to connect a pipe and tobacco pouch. Some painters achieved world renown, notably Kitagawa Utamaro (1754–1806) and his series of *Ten Physiognomic Types of Women.* Hiroshige (1797–1858) gained fame with his series of the *Tokaido Road, Mount Fuji,* and *Moon and Hares,* to name only a few. His works were exhibited at the Exposition Universelle in Paris in 1878. Harunobi painted a charming *Couple under Umbrella in the Snow,* and Eishi (1756–1829) selected geishas as subjects. Most of the themes were nonreligious, another indirect indication that religion had lost influence in Japan.

In the late eighteenth century, crop failures and famine resulted from natural disasters. One million peasants may have died between 1780 and 1786. Floods followed the famine, and a gigantic fire erupted in Edo and reduced 183,000 homes to ashes. In the 1830s some 400 peasant uprisings and urban riots took place—more than in the entire seventeenth century. Most of the rebellions were only local; nevertheless, this was a clear indication that change was mandatory, even before the arrival of Commodore Perry. Perhaps these events stimulated renewed interest in religion.

A revival of Shinto was largely due to Motoori Norinaga (1730–1801) and, to a lesser degree, his disciple, Hirata Atsutante (1776–1843). Norinaga was, above all, a linguist who spent 30 years in the study of the ancient Kojiki Shinto text to rediscover the true Japanese nature of the material. He contrasted Japanese/Shinto sensitivity with Chinese/Confucian rigidity. Norinaga emphasized the "mystical power-of-becoming" and spontaneity, and interest in life here and now over against the renunciation of Buddhism.

Although the Tokugawa era may appear static, a more careful analysis indicates that it was marked by momentous changes. Buddhist thinking had lost flexibility. Intellectuals turned to Confucianism, and the emphasis shifted to study. Literacy increased dramatically. Unfortunately, forward thinking was difficult for Confucianists. They could only paint the future in the colors of the legendary golden age of the past.

The growth of the money economy, increasing urbanization, an improved communication system, the impoverishment of the samurai class, the new wealth of merchants, the rise of a new artistic culture, and the propagation of new religious sects are only some of the high points of the Tokugawa era. It has been suggested that living conditions for most Japanese families in the middle of the nineteenth century were roughly equivalent to those of England just prior to the Industrial Revolution.[55]

The Growth of New Sects

If traditional religions seemed to have lost their hold, new religious movements proliferated. They recruited the bulk of their believers from localities where famine had prevailed or where pre-industrialization had created economic dislocation.

Kurozumi Sect

One new religious leader was Kurozumi Munetada (1780–1850), a Shinto priest. At age 20 he made up his mind to become a living *kami.* He carries the title of "divine founder" of the sect. In 1814 he experienced a "divine union" with the goddess Amaterasu Omikami while contemplating the rising sun. He taught that Amaterasu, the Universal Spirit, is made visible in the sun, reinforcing the divine presence that resides in all humans. The central tenet of the new Kurozumi sect was faith in the sun goddess, the pivotal creation deity that guaranteed eternal bliss and relieved people of evil here and now. Worshiping Amaterasu promised peace and prosperity and offered believers cures from disease, long life, many children, bountiful harvests, and success in trade and business.

The worship of Amaterasu, purification ceremonies, and pilgrimage are clear indications of the Shinto roots of the movement. There are also elements of Buddhism in the search for emptiness of self, will, and thought. According to the founder, "perfect pursuit of the Buddhist Way is actually the same as pursuing the Way of the Great *Kami*."[56] He used neo-Confucian vocabulary and echoes of Chinese Daoism appear here and there. The message is simple: Leave behind all evil thoughts and drop off self-concern to return instantly to the divine condition in which we originated. Because Munetada had already become a *kami* within his lifetime, it is not surprising that many acts of healing have been attributed to him.

Tenrikyo Sect

The Tenrikyo sect ("Teaching of Divine Reason") was founded by Nakayama Miki in 1838 when, at the age of 13, she discovered by divine revelation that she was possessed by a deity called Tenri O no Mikoto, self-identified as the "true and original god who descended from heaven to save mankind." Released from her trance, Nakayama abandoned her family and began to preach Tenri's "divine wisdom." Tenrikyo is Shinto with Buddhist admixtures. The purpose is to attain the "joyous life" through ethical conduct and positive social action, and there are three levels of understanding of the one and only God. The headquarters of the sect, in the Nara area, is thought to be the central point of creation. Some adherents do not think of Tenrikyo as a religion, but rather as a theory about the universe. For some it is quite normal to accept both Christianity and Tenrikyo because both are monotheistic. The relationship with Buddhist groups is more negative because there is considerable rivalry between Soka Gakkai and other sects. Nakayama promised a new moral order that would free people from the miseries fostered by incompetent officials and unfair economic factors. Faith was presented as powerful to cleanse human beings of the "eight dusts" producing selfishness, which would be replaced by a new ethic of selflessness and mutual aid. Tenrikyo was presented as the sole means of escape from earthly sorrow.

Singaku Sect

The Singaku sect ("Heart Learning") was another fairly widespread movement. Ishida Baigan (1685–1744) founded it and gave his first public lecture in 1729. Although of peasant extraction, he managed to move into a different class when he was only 11 years old. He was apprenticed to a Kyoto merchant. A few years later he returned to his native village and, at 23, began to preach Shinto. He was not successful. He continued to study and, at age 40, experienced enlightenment. Three years later he lectured privately and finally opened a lecture hall. His focus was on meditation and charity. He practiced asceticism to "throw away the self." Although his emphasis was religious, his teaching had its greatest impact in the sphere of economics.[57] Along with Shinto, he offered an amalgam of ideas culled from Zen Buddhism, Daoism, and Confucianism and adapted them to the needs of the people of his own time. Intense personal piety and ethical rigor were combined. "Knowing heaven, at least for Baigan, means that one's own heart is united with the heart of heaven and earth. He tells us that heaven and earth create all things and all things are in their hearts united with heaven and earth."[58] His life demonstrated that class barriers could be overcome; he started out a peasant, became a merchant, and went on to become a teacher. He denied the existence of intrinsic differences between all humans and instinctively opposed the rigid class structure of society. His group and others were forerunners of the economic development that has been characteristic of Japan. He helped prepare the ground for the enormous changes of the Meiji Restoration.

Konkokyo Sect

A farmer, Kawate Binjiro (1814–1883), founded the Konkokyo sect in 1859. To him the universe is the body of the Parent God. By listening and understanding, the body can become an agent for the divine. He rejected asceticism and stressed mutual aid. The focus is definitely on this world and the expectation of becoming a living god. The sect is registered by the government as one of the new Shinto sects. There are relatively few followers today.

The same period saw scholars known as *kinnoka,* or "imperial loyalists," who draw ideas from Confucianism regarding the centrality of the Imperial House. This was another factor that helped prepare the Meiji Restoration.

The Transition Period

After the opening of China to international trade and increased shipping across the Pacific Ocean, Japan was unable to maintain her isolation. The arrival in Tokyo Bay of Commodore Matthew C. Perry with four steamships—promptly dubbed "black ships"—was a pivotal event. It was illegal for foreign ships to enter the bay, but the shogun was unable to prevent the "visit" of Commodore Perry. He came with protestations of friendship contained in a diplomatic letter from President Fillmore of the United States. Several issues demanded attention, including the fate of shipwrecked sailors and the provision of whaling ships (which needed coal, wood, and food). The letter suggested a normal commercial relationship between Japan and the United States. Perry promised to return six months later to obtain an answer. It was the responsibility of the shogun to protect the realm, but he could not possibly repel the foreigners with the weapons at his disposal. He had no choice but to sign the Treaty of Kanagawa with the United States. Two cities could now receive ships from the United States— Shimoda and Hakokade. A consulate was established at Shimoda. Another treaty was signed in 1858, the crowning achievement of Townsend Harris, the first American consul. Several ports were opened to foreign trade the following year, including Yokohama and Nagasaki. Treaties with the British, the Russians, and the Dutch followed in quick succession. In 1859, a Catholic priest accepted the appointment as interpreter of the French consulate in Tokyo, and in the same year representatives of three Protestant churches reached Japan. The official reason for their presence was to serve the foreign community within the country. The Russian Orthodox Church also appeared, noticeably in the person of Nicolai, chaplain to the Russian consulate. By the time of his death, 30,000 Japanese had discovered Christ through this Russian Orthodox missionary.[59]

The Treaty of Shimoda had been signed without consultation with the emperor. The court refused to ratify the treaties. The prestige of the shogunate was shattered. When foreigners arrived in Japan, they were attacked by those who wanted to expel the "barbarians." A British citizen, Charles Richardson, was killed on the Tokaido highway by retainers of the

Satsuma-based *daimyo*. When he refused to pay compensation, the British bombarded Kagoshima. The shelling (which took place in 1867) exposed once again the impotency of the shogunate.

A new shogun hoped to shore up his prestige by marrying Princess Kazu, sister of the emperor, but the fate of the shogunate was sealed. A visit of the shogun to the court in Kyoto, the first since 1634, was fruitless. A campaign was launched to expel all foreigners. The slogan *son no, sonno-joi,* "revere the emperor, expel the barbarian" was heard around the nation. It was widely believed—and not without justification— that the treaties that had been signed with foreigners had been done under duress. They were revised 25 years later.

In 1868, troops under the command of Saigo Takamori proclaimed the restoration of the Imperial rule, and Emperor Komei placed his 14-year-old son Mutsuhito on the throne. He took the name of Meiji (1867–1912). The shogun's resignation was accepted and a proclamation abolished the office. Tokugawa lands were confiscated.

The capital was then moved to Tokyo, or "eastern capital," at the beginning of the modern era.

The Modern Era
Changes of Mind-Set
The Meiji era was marked by a deliberate break with the past and a firm step in the direction of modernization. Japan had become painfully aware of her technological lag and was determined to catch up and compete with the West. The new slogan was "Eastern ethics (values based on Confucianism) and Western science."

One of the first steps was the proclamation of a Charter Oath, sworn by the monarch to the *kami:*

1. All matters of state shall be decided by public discussion;

2. all classes high and low shall unite to promote the economy and welfare of the nation;

3. all officials and the common people shall be allowed to fulfill their aspirations;

4. base customs of the past shall be abandoned, and all actions shall be in line with the principles of international justice; and

5. knowledge shall be sought throughout the world.

Almost immediately Japanese individuals were sent abroad to study everything from military science to technology. Ten years later, hundreds of Japanese were studying in North America and Europe. Even the emperor left his palace and traveled. He took more than 100 trips to survey his country. Not that transportation was easy—in 1872 there were only 18 miles of train tracks; by 1914 there were 6,900 miles.

In 1870 commoners were permitted to take surnames. A year later the decimal system was adopted and the yen was established as a monetary standard to replace the almost 1,600 kinds of paper notes. The Gregorian calendar was accepted. In 1871 it became legal for commoners and samurai to intermarry. By 1875, more than 500 foreign advisors had moved into the country.

Samurai were no longer required to wear swords, and within a few years it was forbidden to wear them in public. This was not what traditionalists had anticipated when they restored the power of the emperor. They had opposed the shogun because he had failed to repel the Western powers. A major rebellion was launched in Satsuma with 22,000 samurai led by Saigo

Takamori (1827–1877), the very man who had led the fight against the shogun. Their hope was to restore the traditional order. Saigo, who has been called the last of the samurai, was defeated six months later and committed suicide. The old Confucian-based social order was dismantled. The samurai in particular were dismayed when universal conscription became law in 1872. Exceptions included family heads, heirs, and anyone who could pay 270 yen. Farmers responded with 30 uprisings. The samurai suffered a devastating loss of status, and even the generous stipend of the government could not appease their anger or obliterate their shame. Most of the 273 *daimyos* were pensioned. By this time, the old order was irrevocably lost. Japan was the first non-Western state to adopt a constitutional form of government in 1889.

Confucianism had always stressed education, but the system in Japan was outmoded. Under the Meiji restoration, many of the more prominent educators were Christians.[60] By 1890 a new educational philosophy had been developed with a focus on Japan's uniqueness and Confucian morality.

At the beginning of the twentieth century, Christians made a notable contribution to the foundation of socialist and trade union movements in an effort to solve the grave social problems caused by rapid industrialization. Many of the founding members of the Social Democratic Party (1901) were active Christians. In 1912 a Christian, Suzuki Bunji, founded the Friendship Association, which developed into the Japan Federation of Labor.

To jumpstart the technological revolution demanded capital, which was not readily available. The government nationalized and developed industries and sold them to independent operators. Industrialization was impossible without government leadership and economic support. It was the beginning of the great *zaibatsu* or business conglomerates such as Mitsubishi, Sumimoto, and Mitsui. Firms were connected through personal and historic relationships (the family and the clan), common ownership, and goals. Different companies often had interlocking boards of directors, and a shared pool of capital and technology.

Changes in International Relations

At the time it seemed that every great European power had colonies. Japan, in search of greatness, cast an eye on Taiwan and Korea. From a Japanese viewpoint, Korea was like a dagger pointing at the heart of Japan. In 1879 Okinawa had been incorporated into Japan, and the nation was keen to expand its influence into Korea. In 1894 Korea suffered from a massive peasant uprising. One of the demands in the uprising was the expulsion of all foreigners and the end of modernization. The government was unable to yield to these demands and called upon China for help to suppress the rebels. In accordance with previous agreements, the Chinese had no choice but to notify the Japanese, who promptly landed at Inchon. Once the Tonghak armies of Korea were defeated, the Chinese and Japanese armies faced each other. Japan was victorious in the Sino-Japanese war (1894–1895), which led to the treaty of Shimonoseke. China was forced to recognize the absolute independence of Korea and yielded Taiwan to Japan. Over the course of the war the Japanese had conquered Port Arthur, but thanks to European interference, they were forced to evacuate the city. Tens of thousands had died in the conquest of Port Arthur and the Japanese bitterly resented being forced to evacuate. This became one reason for Japan's war against Russia (1904–1905). Both Russia and Japan were wanting to extend their influence over Korea. In the Russo-Japanese war, both sides suffered huge losses. Theodore Roosevelt helped to mediate a peace accord. The Treaty of Portsmouth made Korea a Japanese protectorate. A few years later, in 1910, Korea became a Japanese colony, but resistance in Korea continued unabated. The Japanese economic exploitation of Korea helped Japan in the war effort against the Allies in World War II. The assumed Japanese superiority (because of advanced modernization) bred a Japanese contempt of Koreans, and during this time, between 100,000 to 150,000 Korean women were forced into the unenviable position of being "comfort women."

In 1923, the great Kanto earthquake struck Japan. Some 100,000 people died, and 60 percent of all the homes in Tokyo were destroyed along with every factory between Tokyo and Yokohama.

Changes on the Religious Front

In 1924 alone almost 100 new religious sects had their start, with many more in the years that followed. These sects garnered millions of followers. Charismatic leaders appealed to the socially and economically disadvantaged and promised help here and now as well as utopia on earth in the near future. One of the more significant sects was the Soka Gakkai movement.

Makiguchi Tsunesaburo (1871–1944) become a convert to the Nichiren type of Buddhism and in 1937 created an organization that became the forerunner of the Soka Gakkai movement. During World War II the followers in this movement refused to fasten Shinto amulets to the doorposts of their movement headquarters and to participate in government-sponsored Shinto rites. This gained national notoriety for the group. The founder was imprisoned in 1943 and although the group's sacred formula was recited 2,000 times a day, he died in prison one year later. Toda, his disciple, was freed in 1945 and in 1946 became the founder of the reorganized Soka Gakkai sect with 5,000 members. The emphasis now fell on the prophetic personality of Nichiren and his interpretation of the Lotus Sutra, the veneration of his mandalas, and the formula *Namu myoho ren ge-kyo.* Recitation of these words guaranteed success and good luck here and now. The members thought of good and evil as relative and determined by circumstances. Even killing can be a good work, especially if the victim is an enemy of Soka Gakkai. To be enlightened simply means to live a pleasant life from morning till night. This teaching is so far removed from the original form of Buddhism that Buddha himself would not have recognized it. Nevertheless, it is enormously popular. And why not? The promise of material well-being, the lack of firm moral requirements, and the simplicity of needing only to recite a formula all make Soka Gakkai attractive. A touch of mysticism is provided when hundreds or thousands of voices chant the sacred formula over and over again till mass hysteria ensues. In 1964 the Soka Gakkai movement became affiliated with the Clean Government Party, which has since become politically active and successful. The movement embraced an aggressive outreach technique that is totally at variance with the usual Buddhist approach. People who are suffering bereavement are visited by members and told that an even harsher future awaits them unless they join the movement. It is assumed that the experience of suffering makes people more likely to want to join the Soka Gakkai fold.

After World War II, other new religious movements took root in Japan. Some are anti-Semitic, and others have identified with the Jewish people at least culturally. Some of these groups see Japan as the Garden of Eden and Abraham, Moses, and Jesus as Japanese, and others claim to be descendants of the famous so-called ten lost tribes of Israel. These small movements are noteworthy only because they are bizarre.

Ikura Teshima (1910–1973) founded one of the larger new groups. He was baptized in a Protestant church, spoke in tongues, and had intense religious experiences. His followers consider themselves Christians but obey Jewish laws, perhaps in imitation of some of the early Jewish Christians. They believe that they are the descendants of one of the Jewish tribes and are fierce Zionists. Pilgrimages to Israel are part of their religion. They indulge in a few special rituals such as walking barefoot on hot coals and standing under waterfalls. They claim to accept Christ as Savior yet they also embrace elements of Shinto. Many of the teachings of Christianity are rejected as aspects of Western thinking that are unfit for Japan, including the teaching about Christ's substitutionary atonement.

The Aum Shinrikyo group is very small and the only reason for mentioning this doomsday cult is the notoriety it gained in 1995 when it used sarin gas to kill people in the Tokyo subways. The founder, Shoko, believed that bad karma could be removed by suffering. He embraced an eclectic Buddhism. In the year 2000 the group changed its name to *Aleph,* the first letter of the Hebrew alphabet.

Throughout Japanese history, Shinto had been connected with the political state.[61] From 1868 to 1945, Shinto enjoyed an exceptionally privileged status. The government even created a Bureau of Shinto. One purpose of State Shinto was to enhance a sense of national identity and to reinforce loyalty to the emperor. Individual rights were seen as a gift of the emperor, not as something inherent. State Shinto was viewed as an expression of patriotism rather than a religion. At the head stood the emperor, the high priest of Shinto. Shinto priests became state employees, and Shinto was stripped of its Buddhist elements. Already in 1876 as many as 87,000 Buddhist temples were closed and 56,000 monks and 5,000 nuns returned to lay life. Buddhism was, after all, a foreign religion, and the patriotic reaction that flourished with the Meiji restoration was unfavorable to Buddhism. At the end of World War II, State Shinto was disestablished. At the time of the Meiji restoration changes had been made that affected Shinto: Hereditary priesthood had been abolished, and anyone could now become a Shinto priest, be married, and perhaps have a second occupation.

Shinto continues to have a high profile in Japan today. Imperial functions such as marriage or coronation are carried out according to Shinto ritual. Popular Shinto features innumerable festivals, some of which involve the entire nation, and others that are only local. The construction of a building demands a ceremony to purify the land, and another celebration takes place when the building is completed. Most of the events of Japanese life are punctuated by Shinto ritual.

Changes on the Military Front

In 1931 some Japanese military officers deliberately created an incident (the Mukden Incident), in which a section of railroad was blown up. They blamed the Chinese for it, and moved to place Manchuria under Japanese control. The League of Nations disapproved of the occupation of Manchuria, and Japan left the League in 1933. War with China started through another relatively small incident at the Marco Polo Bridge (Beijing) in 1937. One year later, Japan controlled the largest cities and major ports of China. Japan also linked itself into an alliance with Germany and Italy, and after Japan's bombing of Pearl Harbor in 1941, the United States went to war against Japan. By late summer of 1945, much of Japan lay in ruins, and two large cities had experienced the horror of the atomic bomb. Emperor Hirohito (1926–1989) told his countrymen they must "bear the unbearable." On New Year's Day, 1946, the emperor disavowed his divinity. A peace treaty was finally signed in 1951 in San Francisco.

Since that time, Japan has risen from the ashes like the proverbial phoenix and become one of the major economic powers of the world.

POINTS OF CONTACT

SHINTO

From a Christian perspective, Shinto's emphasis on ritual impurity and the necessity of purification is significant. Defilement creates separation from the *kami*. Unfortunately Shinto's concept of sin is superficial; nevertheless, the restoration of a proper relationship with the deity cannot take place without cleansing and compensation. The holiness of God, the serious nature of sin, and how to bridge the gap between God (holy) and man (impure) might be good starting points for a conversation.

Shinto sees all of creation as footprints of the gods. Shintoism is intimately connected with nature, with the world here and now. But the world is no longer an ideal place. Man was expelled from the Garden of Eden and excluded from the garden till Christ rose from the grave, making possible the beginning of a new creation that will culminate in a new heaven and earth.[62] Even the most beautiful flower arrangements are only a pale image of the glory to come. Christians are waiting in anticipation of the liberation of creation from bondage and decay.[63] We recognize our ecological responsibility and join the Japanese in the love of creation so often expressed in the book of Psalms.

CONFUCIANISM

Confucian ethics permeate Japanese thinking. The inadequacy of the ethical principles in Confucianism is reviewed under China—Confucianism and Daoism on pages 107-124.

Respect of old age and ancestors finds an echo in biblical genealogies beginning with Christ Himself (Matthew 1)...as long as it does not become ancestor worship. Confucianism's focus on the family is certainly in line with Christian viewpoints. But Confucian ancestor worship can become an almost intolerable burden with its intense focus on the past. The burden of laws, regulations, and ceremonies is lifted only when the grace of God has been experienced.

One of the major obstacles to sharing Christianity will be its claims of being the only way to heaven, for Japan is steeped in a syncretistic culture where people are simultaneously Buddhist, Shintoist, and Confucian. Perhaps Paul, the great missionary, can serve as a model. He was sufficiently flexible to become all things to all men so that by all possible means he might gain some.[64]

Robert Bellah produced an excellent study on the Tokugawa era with special emphasis on religion and concluded that Buddhism, Shintoism, and Confucianism, the traditional religions of Japan, were of a "magical type" with little ethical content.[65] In these religions, there is never a tension between nature and deity, an abyss between holy demands and personal shortcomings, nor a consciousness of sin and one's need of salvation.

BUDDHISM

IT IS ENOUGH TO recite the (magic) formula *namu-Amida-Butsu* for all sin to be cleared away. In this context the word *faith* has to be redefined because it is no more than an intellectual agreement to a certain proposition, the dogma concerning the vows and merits of Amidabha. It is not faith working by love in the New Testament sense. Nevertheless, it is significant that Buddhists realize the need for a mediator, the insufficiency of all human efforts to obtain salvation (however defined), and the need for faith (although limited in concept) and reliance on someone else. It is understood that the vows of Amidabha proceeded from a merciful concern for all living things. It is true that God loved the world and in his mercy sent Christ, the mediator, who cannot be understood apart from his death and resurrection.

In Buddhism the idea of atonement and redemption are missing. Sin and evil are minimized or perhaps seen as unimportant. The concept of righteousness or divine holiness is dormant at best. At any rate, there are significant points of contact with Christian teaching.

It is significant that Buddhists have moved so far away from the original Buddhist teaching ("eliminate all desire") that the idea of a mediator (*bodhisattva*) whose merits can save (Amida Buddha) dominates the Pure Land religion. If for Buddhists the concept of faith has a different meaning, it furnishes at least a starting point in conversation.

One always has to inquire what exactly is meant when someone claims to be Buddhist because there are so many varieties of Buddhism. The majority of Buddhists, by far, are committed to Mahayana Buddhism, which is complete with mediators. It expresses a deep need and underscores the impossibility to gain the Pure Land by meritorious works. But it takes more than a simple formula like the *nembutsu* to enter eternal felicity.

If a Hinayana Buddhist seriously tries to eliminate all desire by following the eightfold path, he or she will discover the limits of the human will, the inevitable moral failure, and face the problem of sin. Without a mediator (as envisioned in Mahayana Buddhism), there is no bridge to nirvana—not that it matters all that much since it would seem that eternal bliss is virtually identical with extinction. There must be a better hope, a more positive expectation.

Buddhism's denial of the personality is an interesting contrast with Christianity—in the latter, the individual is highly valued because each person is said to be created in the image of God and redeemed by God to a new spiritual life—not extinction. Christianity teaches that it is better to suffer than to extinguish love, and the greatest example is found in the person of Christ.

Piers Vitebsky makes the astute observation that "the forms of Buddhism adopted by converts in Western countries are almost nowhere to be found in Asia, where Buddhism is always entwined in the cult of gods and spirits."[66] This is certainly true of Zen Buddhism in search of *satori,* or enlightenment. But does not a viewpoint—any viewpoint—require an intellectual understanding? Can such be reduced to vague feelings that are shapeless and unstable? If *satori* defies all concepts, as adepts of Zen tell us repeatedly, how can Daisetz Teitaro Suzuki state that we need "years of earnest study to the understanding of its primary principles" in order to have a fair grasp of Zen?[67] How can it be studied if it cannot be presented rationally?

Paul speaks of a transformation that takes place through the renewing of the *mind,* of a new self renewed in *knowledge* in the image of Christ, and prays for his beloved Philippians that their love may increase in *knowledge and depth of insight.*[68] The Christian has not abdicated reason but has experienced renewal, gained a new perspective (reason, philosophy), enjoys deeper emotions (feelings, mysticism) and empowered by God can do what he was unable to do previously (will, ethics).

A FINAL WORD

IT HAS BEEN SAID that Japanese have a "nonrational orientation." This simply means that theirs is a different approach, not an inferior one. A famous piece of Japanese syllogism goes like this:

> When the wind blows it becomes dusty. If it becomes dusty it becomes injurious to the eyes. If it become injurious to the eyes, many people become blind and there would be many *shamisen* players (an ancient stringed instrument). If many *shamisen* players come, then here is a great demand for shamisens (instruments). Then the cats are killed to make the strings of the musical instrument, and when the cats are killed the rats increase. When the rats increase, the boxes are chewed and become articles in great demand. THEREFEORE, when the wind blows, the box makers become prosperous.

This type of thinking is remote from Western logic, but it is something to keep in mind when we approach Japanese people with our irrefutable arguments for Christianity. There is a good reason why Japanese people can be simultaneously Buddhist, Shintoist, and Confucianist. The problems of people are seldom intellectual. Rather, the practical, real issues are matters of guilt and forgiveness (the past), how to live successfully (the present), and life after death (the future). Christianity offers unique answers for every one of these.

CONFUCIANISM
and DAOISM

Once upon a time, I, Chung Tzu, dreamt that I was a butterfly, fluttering hither and thither, to all intents and purposes a butterfly. I was conscious only of my happiness as a butterfly, unaware that I was Tzu. Soon I awakened, and there I was, veritably myself again. Now I do not know whether I was then a man dreaming I was a butterfly, or whether I am now a butterfly, dreaming I am a man. Between a man and a butterfly there is necessarily a distinction. The transition is called the transformation of material things.

CHUANG TZU, DAOIST

CONFUCIANISM *and* DAOISM

THE EAST AND SOUTH China Seas, the Gobi Desert, and mountain ranges separate China from the rest of the world. Only the northern steppe is wide open—otherwise the geographic isolation would be complete. Invaders were usually "northern barbarians." Nevertheless, China always maintained contact with countries to the west. Trade with Central Asia followed the tortuous Silk Route, which was hazardous at the best of times. Indian embassies appeared at the Han court in A.D. 89. In A.D. 97 a Chinese delegation reached Rome. The occasional maritime expedition established connections with Indonesia and other countries.

The Chinese Bronze Age began around 2100 B.C. Magnificent pieces of bronze were created for ritual purposes or used as food vessels, musical instruments, and weapons. Jade, more ancient than bronze, was believed to link humans to the gods and to eliminate evil. A flat jade disk, called *bi,* was used in sacrificial ceremonies. The corpses of wealthy aristocrats were covered with jade. Small jade pieces were linked by gold or silver thread to cover the deceased from head to toe.

THE SHANG AND THE ZHOU

THE VERIFIABLE HISTORY OF China begins at around 1550 B.C. with the Shang Dynasty, which lasted 500 years. The ancient tomb of Lady Fu (c. 1200 B.C.) was discovered in 1976. This royal consort was buried with 2,000 artifacts, including 468 pieces of bronze and 750 of jade. Her tomb illustrates the magnificence of the Shang Dynasty. Some of the largest bronze vessels from the Shang era weigh as much as 1,500 pounds.

Ritual vessels often featured monster faces, perhaps to ward off evil. The purpose of ritual and sacrifice was to please powerful deities, to obtain their blessings, and to avoid calamities. State officials—not priests—offered animals, wine, and flowers to ancestors. The Shang Dynasty inherited the custom of burying people alongside the dead. Large retinues of people have been discovered in the tombs, including guards, concubines, servants, and charioteers. Most of the victims were probably slaves. Offerings of dozens of oxen were not unusual. Sacrifices were offered to the gods of heaven, the gods of earth, and human ghosts.

In the sixth century B.C., burial customs changed. Humans were no longer entombed with the dead. Wood or clay replicas, small statuettes, or even paintings were used to accompany the deceased into the world of the dead. They were furnished with all the necessities of life, even replicas of pigpens and wells and whatever else might be needed in the afterlife.

People believed that humans had two souls—a *hun* soul and a *po* soul. The nature of the soul is not clearly defined. The lower *po* soul descends with the body into the grave. The spiritual *hun* soul ascends and survives as a ghost, and has to be sustained by sacrifices. A neglected soul might become demonic and cause crop failure or illness. The dead needed the living to receive offerings, and the living needed the dead for protection. It was an arrangement of reciprocity that was later echoed in Confucianism. Ancestor worship was deeply embedded in the culture and became an integral part of both Confucianism and Daoism. The boundaries between the living and the dead were fluid.

Society was religious. People worshipped Shang Di, the Lord on High, later replaced by T'ien or heaven. Folk religion included nature worship like the Snake Spirit, the Wind, the Queen Mother of the West and the King Father of the East and veneration of the planets, rocks, and stones. Although transformed to some degree, nature worship was also incorporated into Daoism and Confucianism.

The art of writing developed around the thirteenth century B.C.. Simple questions about agriculture or war were carved on turtle shells or on the shoulder blade bones of oxen or deer. Shallow pits were bored on the underside of the bones to facilitate cracking. A heated bronze tool was then applied, and the resulting cracks were interpreted. Using "oracle bones" was a method of communicating with ancestors. Heaven's intentions could also be discovered by anything out of the ordinary, such as a solar eclipse or damage caused by locusts.

The shamans, the diviners, were the elite of Shang society along with scribes and the heads of illustrious families. Society was rigid. Peasants continued to live in semi-subterranean dwelling pits or caves. Around 1200 B.C. the spoked wheel and the chariot appeared and changed the nature of warfare dramatically. Power was defined by 1) the number of chariots owned and determined by the rank of the person; 2) the possession of ritual bronze vessels; and 3) a connection to the royal family.

King Wu, ruler of the seminomadic Zhou, defeated the Shang and inaugurated the rule of the Western Zhou (c. 1050–770 B.C.). By and large they adopted and perpetuated Shang culture. They had few leaders of outstanding ability and there was little innovation. To assure control over the Shang, Zhou rulers appointed family members to run vassal states and to receive tribute. The nobility made their position hereditary and eroded royal authority. The Zhou emperor carried the title Son of Heaven. He alone had the right to offer sacrifices to Shang-Di. Through sacrifice and complex ritual he played a vital role in the maintenance of cosmic order. Rituals of a lesser order were related to the sun, the moon, and the spirits of earth and sky. The cult of heaven ended in 1912 when China became a republic.

For Confucius, "heaven" is both the natural order and a supreme but impersonal moral force underlying the universe. He said, "Heaven is the author of the virtue that is in me." He also said, "When you have offended against heaven, there is nowhere you can turn to in your prayers."[1] For him there is a bond, a cosmic harmony between man and heaven, and it is our responsibility to discover the will of heaven.

The decline of the Western Zhou under King Li (878–828 B.C.) was accelerated by invasions by the steppe people. The Zhou also faced increasing competition from other principalities that developed in the central plain of China. Finally, internal divisions weakened the kingdom and ended the rule of the Western Zhou. In 770 B.C. the capital was transferred to Ch'eng-chou, close to modern-day Luoyang. It was the beginning of the Eastern Zhou Empire, which lasted till 221 B.C. This time span is divided into two distinct periods: The first one, from 770 to 476, is known as the Spring and Autumn period. It was the title of the official annals of the kingdom of Lu for that period. The second time segment, from 476 to 221, carries the self-explanatory name of the Warring States. The fragmentation of the realm was extraordinary. The existence of 170 states has been recorded, although there were only seven major contestants. Some dukedoms may have been as small as 11 square miles. Alliances were formed and broken in rapid succession. The fifth and sixth centuries B.C. "saw a sudden spurt in the process of disintegration of feudalism, with as yet no emergence of a new administrative machinery to take it place."[2]

CONFUCIUS

WHO HE WAS

In the midst of this chaotic era, Confucius emerged. He has influenced the thoughts, ethics, and politics of China more than anyone else. *Confucius* is the Latin rendering of K'ung Fu-tzu or Master K'ung. He was born near modern Qufu in the province of Shandong. Little is known about him. Even the traditional dates of his life, 551–479 B.C., are uncertain. Traditions about Confucius, even those accepted by serious scholars, "are of questionable accu-

racy."[3] We know next to nothing about Confucius once legends and myths have been eliminated. It is difficult, perhaps impossible, to disentangle fact and fancy. It was centuries after the death of Confucius that Szema Ch'ien (145–85? B.C.) produced the earliest biography.

Confucius was perhaps the son of a secondary wife or concubine.[4] We know that he had an elder brother and a niece. Perhaps the best interpretation of various traditions is that Confucius belonged to the impoverished, low-level aristocracy. His father was a military official, and he died when Confucius was three years old. His mother died when he was in his teens. He was married at 19 and had a son and at least one daughter. If he followed the normal pattern, he entered school at age ten and for the next nine years studied music, poetry, archery, ritual, calligraphy, and arithmetic. If so, the teaching was not wasted. Confucius was fond of singing and played a stringed instrument. He saw music as a civilizing influence, an expression of the harmony of the universe.

In one of his few autobiographical statements, Confucius said, "At fifteen I set my heart on learning; at thirty I took my stand [or: planted my feet firmly upon the ground]; at forty I came to be free from doubts [or: no longer suffered from perplexities]; at fifty I understood the Decree of Heaven; at sixty my ear was atuned [or: I heard with docile ear]; at seventy I followed my heart's desire without overstepping the line."[5]

Confucius was passionate about learning. "Even when walking in the company of two other men, I am bound to be able to learn from them. The good points of the one I copy; the bad points of the other I correct in myself."[6] When somebody inquired about him, the master suggested that the answer might have been, "He is the sort of man who forgets to eat when he tries to solve a problem that has been driving him to distraction."[7]

Perhaps Confucius's artistic temperament made him fastidious. When fish or meat were not fresh, or neatly cut, he would not eat. Nor did he eat unless the proper sauce was available. When the mat was not laid out properly, he would not sit down. He specified that a gentleman should avoid using dark purple- and maroon-colored silk for lapels and cuffs. His own informal fur coat was long but with a short right sleeve. He had a night robe that was half as long again as he was tall. The detailed list of what he considered the appropriate dress code and correct behavior goes on and on.[8]

Much has been written about the Confucian work ethic, and one might almost assume that it is at the heart of his teaching. This is not the case. In fact, the true gentleman does not work—at least not with his hands. He does not take up the "minor arts." The artisan "masters his trade by staying in his workshop; the gentleman perfects his way through learning."[9]

For that matter, such a work ethic is not uniquely Confucian. The Greek poet Hesiod (c. 800 B.C.) suggested that "gods and men are angry with the man who lives idly" and the apostle Paul, in line with Jewish culture, wrote, "If a man will not work, he shall not eat."[10]

Confucius was a man with a sense of mission. When a gatekeeper asked, "Where have you come from?" a disciple called Tzu-lu answered, "From the Kung family." The gatekeeper commented, "Is that the Kung who keeps working towards a goal the realization of which he knows to be hope-

less?"[11] The master persisted regardless of obstacles.

Confucius was not an originator. "The Master said, I transmit but do not innovate; I am truthful in what I say and devoted to antiquity."[12] It is a correct self-evaluation. Traditional values, as old as Chinese history, are deeply embedded in Confucian teaching, including ancestor worship. Confucius looked back to the early Zhou Dynasty as the golden age of Chinese history. Few historians would agree.

WHAT HE TAUGHT

As an educator, Confucius hoped to form gentlemen who would play a decisive role in the government of the nation. He taught his disciples the art and philosophy of government. Whereas the top echelons of Chinese society monopolized learning, Confucius accepted students from all walks of life as long as they were intelligent and eager to learn. This was a significant departure from the norm. However, H.G. Creel believes that "it is possible that all of Confucius' disciples were men of some aristocratic lineage, though a number of them were in depressed circumstances."[13] Confucius was unwilling to teach those who were intellectually limited. "When I have pointed out one corner of a square to anyone and he does not come back with the other three, I will not point it out to him a second time."[14] He endeavored to create an aristocracy of virtue and ability, but could not suggest a system that would compel the government to employ the most capable. All too often government decisions were based on a person's lineage, and not his capacity.

Confucius assumed that some people, the very best, were born with innate knowledge. The majority had to study hard to attain knowledge.[15] This idea of "innate genius" has often been criticized. For the most part Confucius refrained from abstract speculation about it. He never explained how one went about to acquire knowledge or how one could distinguish true and false knowledge. The teacher did not set down clear, specific standards.

The Analects mention 22 of Confucius's disciples by name. Nine became officials of some importance. Although tradition says Confucius had a very large number of students, he probably never had more than 70 disciples whom he trained for political careers.

Ethics are at the heart of Confucian teaching. The small man understands what is profitable, the gentleman understands what is moral, and he is always on the side of what is moral.[16]

Confucius envisioned a cosmic moral order sometimes called the *tao* (the way), a way of life, perhaps not clearly defined but inspiring a sense of reverence. It gave his teaching a religious dimension. The *tao* is superior to law because it never changes, whereas the law varies from country to country. With tao, gentlemen from different states are all able to follow the same principles. They are not motivated by selfishness but guided by the principle of *li*, which is sometimes translated "ritual," but the English word does not convey the full meaning of *li*. It is an echo of the cosmic order. The ritual expresses propriety. It imparts a certain rhythm, a certain order to life. *Li* is a standard of conduct, the appropriate action in every situation, the correct behavior at all times. There is a pattern and therefore no need for improvisation. Unfortunately, *li* can easily degenerate into discussions about the "appropriate" length of a sleeve and invite external conformity

and legalism. For Confucius the ritual is not performed "for its own sake, but in order to enter into a special relationship with the object of the ritual."[17] Through *li* one can be in harmony with the cosmic order, the *tao*. Everyone has to be related properly within the hierarchical order that has been established.

A key element of Confucian teaching was *ren,* perhaps best translated "humaneness." "It is the supreme virtue, and the most fundamental principle advocated by Confucius."[18] *Ren* is manifested in reciprocity. "Our obligation towards others should be in proportion to the benefit we have received from them."[19] Hence what has been called the silver rule: "Do not impose on others what you yourself do not desire. The Master said, 'love your fellow man,'"[20] but this obligation to love decreases by degrees as it extends outward and away from the family and the clan. This was one of the key differences between Confucius and Mo-Tsu, who advocated universal altruism.

Did Confucius ever have the opportunity to put his precepts into practice? It seems that at one point he occupied a minor post but was usually not consulted. Perhaps he merely received a title without commensurate authority. He certainly would not have stayed very long in such a false situation. Perhaps it is a sound tradition that Confucius was the chief magistrate of Chung-tu (a small town 28 miles west of the capital), where "he pursued his policy of sex segregation so vigorously that men and women walked on opposite sides of the street." He also "hammered at honesty so assiduously that objects lost on the street were not picked up."[21]

Confucius was not accepted as counselor in his home state of Lu. He finally left Lu in 497 B.C. (in his mid-fifties) and stayed away 14 years. He wandered from state to state hoping to serve at court and to meet a leader with moral concerns and willing to put Confucius's theories into practice. But he searched in vain. He finally returned to Lu, where he lived and taught the last few years of his life.

Confucius stressed correct interaction in five basic relationships: those between prince and minister, father and son, husband and wife, older and younger brother, and friend to friend. The most important, he said, is the father/son relationship. It is at the root of all the others. Perhaps Confucius had the idea of reciprocity in mind, but in practice the father was the absolute ruler just like the emperor. In the small circle of the family, children assimilated attitudes of obedience and cooperation that made it possible for them to eventually become useful officials. The family and the state followed a similar pattern—one of orderly subordination to authority. These relationships are strictly hierarchical, with the key words being *respect* and *obedience*.

Under the Han Dynasty, a concept known as the "three bonds" became popular. According to Han Fei Tzu, "the minister serves the king, the son serves the father, and the wife serves the husband." The three bonds, "based on dominance/ subservience, underscore the hierarchical relationship as an inviolable principle for maintaining social order."[22]

According to Wu-Chi, "Master K'ung excels all the other teachers of men, Christ and Buddha not excepted."[23] Nevertheless, he is compelled to admit that Confucius put men above women, the aged over the young, and the literate elite above the unlettered. Wu-Chi concludes, "I deplored his intolerant attitude towards women and

serfs; I revolted against his priggishness at court."[24] For Confucius, women were difficult to deal with. "If you let them get too close, they become insolent. If you keep then at a distance, they complain."[25] The idea that a widow should not remarry created considerable hardship because many girls were betrothed at age three to five years and frequently the "husband-to-be" died in infancy. The girl was then condemned to lifelong widowhood. Women were not seen as individuals, but as part and parcel of the family, as "entities" part of the hierarchical structure. Early on girls submitted to the father, and later to the husband. And if their husband died, then they deferred to the oldest son.

In the Daxue, or "Great Learning," which was originally a chapter in the *Liji* ("Book of Rites"), we are told by Confucius:

> Wishing to order well their states, they first regulated their families,
>
> Wishing to regulate their families, they first cultivated their persons,
>
> Wishing to cultivate their persons, they first rectified their hearts,
>
> Wishing to rectify their hearts, they first sought to be sincere in their thoughts,
>
> Wishing to be sincere in their thoughts, they first extended to the utmost their knowledge.

What did Confucius mean by "regulated their families"? In China, the family and the extended family have always been central. The family "has been the incubator of morality and a microcosm of the state. From one point of view, Confucianism might be defined as the philosophy of the Chinese family system."[26] Even death does not break the family ties because in many ways, the dead ancestors are still in control. Filial piety finds in ancestor worship the focal point.

As long as the parents are alive the dutiful son should not go far afield in his travels, and should comply with the rites related to serving them. And when they die, he should comply with the rites related to burying them and making sacrifices to them.[27] The funeral of a parent should be carried out with meticulous care, complete with sacrifices to remote ancestors. For three years after the death of the father the son should make no changes to his father's ways and suspend all ordinary activities.[28] And why not mourn three years? Did his parents for the same length of time not nurse the child?

The typical Confucian family had a small shrine that contained a wooden tablet with the names and the dates of birth and death of the three previous generations. The ancestral spirits are thought to reside in the tablets. Twice a day an offering is placed before the ancestral tablets and the "spiritual essence" is consumed. The family eats the "leftover" food. After a few generations, the tablets are taken to larger ancestral halls for the extended family.

Confucius praised one of his disciples for making offerings to ancestral spirits and gods with the utmost devotion.[29] But he was reticent on speculative issues. When someone asked how one should serve spirits, Confucius said, "Till you have learned to serve man, how can you serve ghosts?" In answer to a question about the dead, he said, "You do not understand even life. How can you understand death?" He suggested that the better part of wisdom is to keep a respectful distance from the gods and spirits while showing them reverence.[30]

One of Confucius's disciples complained that one couldn't get the master's views on human nature and the way of heaven. He refused to speak about prodigies, force, disorders, and gods.[31] There were a hundred schools of thought at this time, with Confucianism, Daoism, Mohism, and legalism offering different responses to contemporary problems. For Confucius, whose prime concern was social harmony, the answer to the reigning chaos was one that did not involve brutal force. The small circle of the family could mirror the cosmic harmony and become the starting point of renewal.

Shortly after Confucius's death, his followers split into eight distinct schools, and within one year of his death the disciples had erected a temple at Qufu where Confucius was buried. The purpose of the temple was not to serve as a meeting place for worshippers. Confucian temples were used for annual ceremonies, especially to observe the birthday of the sage.

It would be difficult to exaggerate the importance of Confucius. He has been called the supreme editor (not the author) of Chinese culture.[32] His influence spread across Korea (which was even more Confucian than China), Japan, Taiwan, Vietnam, and as far as Malaysia. "At the broadest level the Confucian ethos pervading many Asian societies stresses the values of authority, hierarchy, the subordination of the individual's rights and interests, the importance of consensus, the avoidance of confrontation, 'saving face,' and, in general, the supremacy of the state over society and of society over the individual."[33]

THE SACRED TEXTS

Was Confucius the author of the Analects? According to H.G. Creel we have no convincing evidence that he wrote or even edited anything at all—not even the Ana-lects. Perhaps so, but the Analects certainly reflect his thinking. It is obvious that some of the sayings have been divorced from their original setting. It is reasonable to assume that Confucius's disciples edited the Ana-lects. Some scholars take a rather dim view of the Analects. For Huston Smith the col-lection is "patently didactic, so pedestrian that they often appear commonplace."[34]

Several books have wrongly been attrib-uted to Confucius. For example, the *I Ching,* of which the original text is ear-lier than Confucius. The ten appendices or "wings" date from various periods all later than Confucius. And he probably had nothing to do with the *Liki* ("Book of Rites") or the *Shu-ching,* or "Book of History."

Confucian scholars seem to think that Confucius probably rearranged the pieces of the *Shih-ching* or "Book of Poetry," and Lin-Yut'ang deems it possible that Con-fucius "wrote the bare skeleton of events" related in the *Ch'un-ch'iu* or "Chronicles of Spring and Autumn."

THE SCHOOLS OF THOUGHT

There was a time when Mo Tzu (c. 480–390) was as famous as Confucius. We know next to nothing about him. The key charac-teristic of his teaching, called *Mohism,* was universal love or benevolence, over against the "graded love" of Confucianism, with a strong preference for one's own relatives. Mo Tzu believed that family selfishness was the principal cause of quarrels and advo-cated universal altruism. Hans Kung agrees with Mo Tzu that "in Confucianism, the love of others remains oriented entirely to natural feeling and to familial and national ties."[35] According to Confucius, "barbarian tribes with their rulers are inferior to the

Chinese states without them (rulers)."[36] Thus he had no reservation about the Chinese dominating barbarian tribes and imposing the Chinese way of life on them. Mo Tzu, however, advocated universal love, but his voice was silenced—perhaps because his teaching opposed class distinc-tions. Mo Tzu's teaching, like Confucius,' was basically this-worldly, in search of the benefit of the greatest number. He main-tained a utilitarian viewpoint and taught that benefit and harm are the standards by which to judge good and evil.

Mencius (372–289) popularized the teachings of Confucius and guaranteed his triumph. He is called "the second sage." He visited several states but failed to obtain an influential position at any court. In an era called the Age of Warring States, to denounce war as a crime was not well received.

Confucius was ambiguous about human nature. The sage admitted that he had never met anyone who really cared for good-ness, and he had given up all hope of ever meeting a good person. He wondered if anyone had ever managed to do good with his whole might for as long as a single day. He observed, "I have yet to meet the man who is as fond of virtue as he is of a beauty in women." He said he had no hopes of meeting a good man.[37]

Master Meng or Mencius had firm con-victions on this issue. He taught that man is fundamentally good but corrupted by bad government. "There is no man who is not good, as there is no water which does not flow downwards." The fault is not due to the original endowment, but something has happened to lead man's heart astray. The remedy is simple. "The principles of self-cultivation consist in nothing but trying to look for the lost heart." He taught that humaneness (*ren*), righteousness, propriety (*li*), and wisdom are part of man's essential nature, part of his inheritance from birth. Man is distracted by the influence of external forces, the inroads of daily activities.[38] It is our responsibility to recover our natural goodness. Mencius was thoroughly convinced of the perfectibility of man through the system of Confucian ethics.

Hsun Tzu (c. 298–238) believed that human nature is evil and that goodness has to be acquired. Virtue is the result of training, whereas vice is spontaneous. Correction is possible through the strict application of draconian laws. Desires should be guided by the rules of propriety and character molded by rites and music. His brilliant disciple Han Fei (d. 233 B.C.) embraced legalism. Since it is the responsibility of the state to control chaos, the state must be all-powerful. Hsun Tzu agreed with Mencius that a failing sovereign could be forced to abdicate. The sovereign is like a boat and people are like water. Water can carry the boat and, at the same time, can overturn it.

Confucius had stressed *jen,* or humaneness; Mencius had emphasized *yi,* or righteousness; and Hsun Tzu had focused on *li,* or ritual. These three have remained the cardinal virtues of Confucianism.

The Qin Dynasty— the Legalist School

At first the legalistic school was dominant, especially during the Qin Dynasty (221–206 B.C.). The Qin fought the northern barbarians for a century and, in the process, gained considerable military expertise. They used this to defeat the Eastern Zhou in 256 B.C. In a ten-year period, King Zheng destroyed the six major power centers in the country, and by 221 B.C., he completed the conquest of China. The king took the title of Qin Shi-huang, or "Imperial Sovereign of Qin." He was the first emperor of China and founder of the short-lived Qin Dynasty. The name of China is derived from the name Qin.

The triumph of the army placed the military in absolute control, with the emperor at the helm. The emperor embraced the legalistic school of Confucianism and divided the country into 36 military districts, which were later increased to 48. Soldiers were organized into squads of five. If any one of the five was killed in battle, the other four were beheaded. All weapons were confiscated (unless held by the Imperial army) and recast into 12 gigantic bronze statues placed in front of the Imperial Palace. Hereditary lords were eliminated and aristocracy abolished. There was only one source of power, one authority. For each district the emperor appointed a civil governor, a military commander, and an Imperial inspector, all of whom checked upon each other and reported to Qin Shi-huang. For chancellor Li Si the purpose of government was to strengthen and enrich the state, not to serve the people. The interest of the state was always paramount. Confucian legalists deemed people stupid, idle, greedy, treacherous, and in need of strict supervision. Control was exercised through the enforcement of draconian laws and rewards and punishment. The people were not trained toward virtue through moral example, as Confucius himself had advocated. The Legalist theory is simple: If light offenses are punished heavily, heavy offenses will not come. If penalties are heavy and rewards few, then the ruler loves his people. A wise man creates laws, but they control a foolish man. Contrary to Confucianism, filial piety was considered one of the ten evils and care for the old nothing but a parasitic function. Confucius would not have recognized the teaching that claimed to honor him. Rites and music were seen as signs of dissipation. Totalitarianism was absolute. "He who accomplishes a great work, does not take counsel with the multitude."[39]

Learning was despised. Legalists adopted an anticultural program and said there was no need for literature or books. In 213 B.C. all books (except those dealing with medicine, agriculture, or divination) were burned. When 460 scholars dared to oppose Imperial ideology, they were buried alive.

The emperor standardized weights and measures and adopted a single coinage for the realm. It was a round copper with a square hole in the center. The shape survived for centuries. The uniform coinage facilitated both commerce and tax collection. Chinese characters were also standardized.

To protect the realm against external enemies, existing pieces of wall were connected and those of the conquered nations demolished. This was the beginning of the famous Great Wall of China. What is seen today was built later, under the Ming dynasty. Qin Shi-huang conscripted hundreds of thousands of workers to erect palaces, build highways, and dig canals. A vast road network crisscrossed the new empire and was used by Qin Shi-huang to conduct inspection tours. The construction of his mausoleum (begun in his lifetime) involved more than 700,000 workers, and prisoners of war were assigned to construction projects. Tens of thousands were buried alive upon completion of a specific job to maintain utmost secrecy about the project. Of the estimated 20 million people in the empire at the time, fully ten percent were engaged in construction work.

Qin Shi-huang's posthumous fame is assured ever since the discovery of the terra-cotta army (1974) by villagers who were digging a well. The first pit contained 6,000 soldiers and 40 chariots. The second pit was filled with archers, charioteers, cavalry, and infantry. Other pits were home to the headquarters of the army. Qin Shi-huang had conquered six states to the east and because he was concerned they might rise up in an attempt to defeat the empire, the terra-cotta army faced east, arrayed in battle formation. Molds were used to create this immense army. On average, soldiers were six feet tall and made with solid legs, but hollow torsos, heads, and arms. Ears, noses and hair were added after the two parts of each head had been molded together. In this fashion everyone presented an individualized appearance, including the horses. This was an early form of mass production. In 1980, archaeologists discovered yet another large pit with two sets of bronze horses and chariots.

Qin Shi-huang took several journeys to sacred mountains in search of the elixir of immortality, an important component of Daoism. The emperor died while traveling in search of a Daoist magician. Li Si kept Qin Shi-huang's death secret, and his will was set aside. Prince Fusu, the legitimate successor, committed suicide. Li Si appointed Huhai, a weak character who was easily manipulated, as emperor. External enemies and internal uprisings occurred. Liu Pang—a minor official— joined the insurgents, rose in the ranks, defeated the Qin army, eliminated his ally, and killed Emperor Huhai. The year 206

B.C. ended the Qin Dynasty. Liu Pang, the new emperor, inherited a unified and highly centralized state.

The Han Dynasty—
Official Confucianism

Under the Han Dynasty (221 B.C.–A.D. 24) Confucianism became the official state ideology. Sacrifices were offered to Confucius, to his ancestors, his family members, his disciples, the four associates, the 12 philosophers, and others. It was in the days of Emperor Wu (141–87 B.C.) that Confucianism triumphed. Ssuma-Ch'ien (c. 145–90 B.C.) was the great historian of the Han court and the father of Chinese history. The details we have about the life of Confucius—factual and legendary—come from Ssuma-Ch'ien. He was castrated when he fell afoul of Imperial pleasure for writing an unwelcome memorandum.

The emperor adopted the Hsun Tzu branch of Confucianism, which contained strong elements of Legalism. It was a convenient perspective for authoritarian leaders, and Emperor Wu maintained the centralization of power in his person. Civil service examinations were based on the Confucian classics, and, in theory, only those who were successful entered the bureaucracy. In reality, private connections trumped national interests. Tradition, local customs, and personal favors determined everything that was done—not rationality or legal structure.

The effectiveness of the country's bureaucracy was hampered by the Confucian rejection of specialization as an appropriate quality of the educated gentleman.[40] A Confucian saying, "The gentlemen is no vassal,"[41] discouraged specialization.

Confucianism strongly supported learning, especially the study of the classics.

The Grand Academy, an Imperial university, was founded in 124 B.C. Even foreign students were enrolled, especially Japanese. The university occupied 2,140 buildings and 1,850 rooms. A special bureau was established in A.D. 29 for the care and preservation of paintings.

Emperor Wu inaugurated a system of "leveling" in which the government bought grain in periods of abundance and made it available in times of scarcity—and in the process made a handsome profit. In the year A.D. 11, the Yellow River shifted and silt filled up the river channels, causing major flooding. Historians record more than 1,600 floods and 1,400 famines in China prior to 1911.

It was in this era that *The Art of War,* a classic treaty on warfare, was written. The work is attributed to Sun Tzu, but the real author remains unknown. He wrote that all warfare is based on deception: "When capable of attacking, feign incapacity; when active in moving troops, feign inactivity… appear where you are not expected."[42]

Incessant warfare stimulated the invention of new weapons, such as the sword and the crossbow. Molds were used for casting iron. From the northern barbarians the Chinese learned to ride—rather than drive—horses, which mandated the adoption of trousers. The sundial is one of the many technological achievements of the Han Dynasty. Steel was produced from the second century B.C. onward. The Chinese used the water wheel and the wheelbarrow centuries before they appeared in Europe. An ingenious odometer was designed by Ma Jun. A moving axle would drive a set of gears that moved wooden figures to beat a drum about every 550 yards. Zhang Heng invented a seismograph in A.D. 132, and a two-person draw-loom was used to create brocade. The person on the upper level determined the design. Only two inches could be produced in a single day. Most of China's silk was produced in large state workshops. Silk was one of the most important export commodities. It was in this time that the ox-drawn plow appeared, and that pedals were used to operate chains of buckets to raise water from one level to the next. Ideas traveled in both directions on the Silk Route—east-west and west-east. Trade flourished by land and by sea. Writing as an art form arose at the beginning of the Han Dynasty.

As for beliefs, religious thoughts, popular superstition, and official state worship were all fused together. It was believed that everything in the universe was made of one single vital energy or substance called *qi*. Yin (female) and yang (male) were seen as two complementary (not antagonistic) forces, both manifestations of *qi*. These ancient beliefs underlie feng-shui and other contemporary aspects of Chinese thinking.

The energetic Emperor Wu came to a point where he decided to end China's appeasement of its northern invaders. He refused to send gifts—a euphemism for tribute. To achieve his goal, he used a combination of diplomacy and forceful military action. Hundreds of thousands were involved in the conquest of Central Asia and the opening of the Silk Route. Wu managed to secure control of Korea, and the empire expanded more as he launched eight major campaigns. We can get an idea of the scale of the army battles when we consider that out of 140,000 horses involved in one war, only 30,000 returned.

The cost of war required new revenues. Everyone paid taxes in coin. License fees were levied on boats and carriages, and a special tax was imposed on merchants. Punishments were converted to fines to help enrich the state treasury. State monopolies regulated salt, wine, and iron and generated more revenue.

Gradually the administrative apparatus of China changed. By 108 B.C. there were 84 commanderies and 18 small kingdoms. The smaller areas were easier to control, but the spirit of regionalism reasserted itself. After the death of Emperor Wu, plots multiplied. The key players were advisors, empresses, eunuchs, and adventurers. Power was in the hands of generals who fought each other and, at the same time, tried to put down peasant rebellions that were inspired by religious mysticism. Toward the end of the Han Dynasty the Yellow Turbans, a Daoist sect, staged an uprising. They had a formidable army of 360,000 and occupied large sections of the country. Nine months later they were crushed, but the Han Empire collapsed. The instability of the empire seemed like a failure of Confucian ethics, and the popularity of Confucianism entered a long period of decline.

DAOISM

THE TEACHINGS OF DAOISM are attributed to Lao-Tzu, which means "The Old Master." Some Daoists claim three "spiritual ancestors": Lao-Tzu, the (legendary) Yellow Emperor, and the celestial Master Zhang. The focus of philosophical Daoism is to be in harmony with the *tao*, the impersonal law of the universe. Popular Daoism has absorbed many elements of traditional folk religion.

If we know little about Confucius, we know even less about Lao-Tzu (604–531 B.C.), who is often depicted riding an ox. Tradition informs us that he was roughly contemporary with Confucius. Many have questioned his very existence. At best he is a shadowy figure. One of the better traditions makes him a royal archivist who left court life to retire to a life of solitude. Legend has it that Lao-Tzu walked off toward the West through a mountain pass never to be seen again. But before he disappeared, a gatekeeper convinced him to leave a scroll behind, the *Tao Te Ching,* of which Lao-Tzu is the putative author. It is "among the most obscure books in the world."[43] It is probably a compilation of fragments from the sixth to the fourth centuries.

Daoism has no founder or starting date. "The more one knows about Taoism, however, the more difficult it is to define it."[44] Chuang Tzu (369–286 B.C.) opined that it is impossible to reach absolute truth because speech, by its very nature, cannot express the absolute. One cannot develop a standard by which to determine what is absolutely right. He concluded that one should simply transcend all differences and unite with the *tao.*

Under the Han Dynasty, Daoism (as well as Confucianism!) came into its own and Lao-Tzu was deified. It is believed that he was an incarnation of the Supreme Purity, one of the highest Daoist gods.

It is imperative to distinguish philosophical Daoism from religious Daoism. The latter was for the masses and boiled down to a search for immortality on earth through divination, astrology, and magic.

PHILOSOPHICAL DAOISM

Philosophical Daoism held that the *tao* is the operating principle of the universe. The *tao* is the law of development and change. It seems that the Absolute (the *tao*) had a sudden desire to know itself and divided itself from nonexistence into existence, a cataclysmic event leading to an endless chain of cause and effect. The *tao* "sublimates" into *qi,* the vital energy of the universe and forms the Three Purities, the highest gods. They are emanations of the *tao.* This may not be very clear or logical, which is exactly why it is difficult to explain Daoism.

Tao means "way" or "pathway." It is a mysterious process where "being and nonbeing give birth to one another" even though they are one and the same. Once they arise, they differ in name and complete each other, like long and short.[45] The *tao* is the void out of which all reality emerges, and it precedes the birth of the universe. The *tao* gave birth to one, one gave birth to two, two gave birth to three, and three gave birth to ten thousand things. They shouldered yin and embraced yang, blending *qi* to establish harmony.[46] The *tao* is beyond words and defies definition. It is invisible and inaudible. It is an emptiness, a silence, a dark enigma that can be experienced through meditation. The secret is "sitting with a blank mind." The *tao* is

> Looked at but never seen,
> it takes the name *invisible.*
> Listened to but never heard,
> it takes the name *ethereal.*
> Held tight but never felt,
> it takes the name *gossamer....*
> this is called *formless form*
> or *nothing's image,*
> *called spectral confusion....*
> something you meet without seeing a front
> and follow without seeing a back.
> — *Tao Te Ching*

The *tao* is characterized by spontaneity. Man, instead of living in harmony with the *tao*, impedes the spontaneous flow. The goal of the Daoist is to become one with the *tao* and to be in harmony with the order of nature. The *tao* is self-balancing and cyclical. Daoism intersects with the yin-yang concept, but everything is always in a state of flux and only a specialist can determine what is happening at a particular moment in time. Enter religious Daoism and the interpretations of the priest or shaman.

The secret is not to interfere, to do nothing, to allow everything to evolve naturally. "A sage does nothing and so ruins nothing.... when you never strive you never go wrong.... whatever you try to improve you actually ruin."[47] Action only hinders the *tao*. Dwell in nonbeing, absorb the *qi*, and attain physical immortality. Give up learning, give up all distinctions between good and evil, and be natural.[48] One of the greatest expositors of Daoism, Chuang Tzu, insisted that the true sage rejects all distinctions. There are no absolutes. "How much difference is there between yes and no? And is there a difference between lovely and ugly?"[49] In *The Great Supreme,* Chuang Tzu observes that "living in accord with the Tao, joy and sorrow touch me not." The suppression of desire is like an echo of Buddhism, but the resemblance is superficial, the context is different. The idea is not to interfere with the unfolding of natural needs, and that includes food, shelter, and sex. The desires for wealth and power are said not to be natural.

The role of man is to be receptive to the *tao*, to remain passive. Vital energy comes from being in the right place at the right time and in the right frame of mind. A modern slogan might be "Go with the flow." "When man practices doing nothing, he helps all beings do what they must do."[50] Both Lao-Tzu and his greatest disciple, Chuang Tzu, believed that the world would be better off without any ruler, law, or morality. "A leader is best when people barely know that he exists."[51] "When a gentleman is unavoidably compelled to take charge of the government of the empire, there is nothing better than inaction."[52] The goal of the Daoist sage is to withdraw into the life of a hermit and to contemplate the universe; he is not a man of social or political achievements. Nevertheless, Daoists launched many attempted revolutions across the history of China.

Aside from the *tao* a large body of literature has developed over the centuries. The *Tao-tsang,* or Taoist canon, includes 1,226 volumes. The principal books are alleged to be divine revelations made to Taoist adepts in a state of trance. None bears the name of the author or the date of composition; many are written in a coded, esoteric language that can be understood only by the initiated. T'ao Hung-chin (456–536) listed more than 400 Daoist deities organized by rank.

The correct Daoist attitude is called *wu-wei,* a creative quietude. In order not to squander the life force, a person is to avoid friction and conflict. To cultivate *wu-wei* is to "inhabit the furthest peripheries of emptiness and abide in the tranquil Center."[53] Do not stand in the way of the *tao*, the natural, spontaneous operation of the law of the universe. It is a logical conclusion to believe that nature is superior to civilization. Do not impede the flow of water by building a dam, do not interfere with the natural rhythm of nature. Rather, maintain natural spontaneity. Do nothing, and everything gets done. Since nature acts with complete spontaneity, we should do likewise…wherever it may lead.

RELIGIOUS DAOISM

Religious Daoism moves on a totally different level. One principal deity and focus of worship is the Jade Emperor, who was born before heaven and earth were separated and stands at the apex of the divine hierarchy. He is usually depicted as sitting on a throne with strings of pearls hanging from the brim of his hat. Other high deities are the Three Pure Ones and the Four Heavenly Ministers. They "assist the Jade Emperor in ruling the universe."[54] The Yellow Emperor, a legendary ancestor of the Chinese people, is a popular deity credited with the invention of writing, the calendar, music, mathematics, and the arts of healing.

Guan Yin is the most popular deity and is worshipped by both Daoists and Buddhists. The latter see her as a *bodhisattva.* Sometimes depicted as a man but more commonly as a young woman, Guan Yin delivers individuals from misfortune. These gods govern hundreds of spirits, including those in charge of wind, rain, thunder, lightning, water, and fire. The Five Kings of Hell govern the underworld. Some believe that there are 36 hells and ten judges. The influence of Buddhism is most noticeable when it comes to Daoist views of life after death.

Inspired by Daoism and motivated by a desire to establish spiritual purity in the expectation of a messianic age (the return of Lao-Tzu?), the Yellow Turbans rose against the Han government. Daoist messianism flared up again and again and inspired several armed rebellions. The Yellow Turbans were defeated and out of the ashes rose the first Daoist organization under the leadership of Zhang Daoling, the Heavenly Master (A.D. 126–144). We are told that Lao-Tzu appeared to this hermit in a mountain cave and complained of the lack of respect for truth. Zhang became the Heavenly Master with the mission to destroy all demonic structures and to return everyone to true orthodoxy. The new sect opposed the bloody sacrifices that were offered to the spirits of the dead and substituted them with vegetables. A novelty was the confession of sins to priests who wrote down the details and offered the document to heaven (on mountaintops) to the earth (by burial) or to the rivers (by drowning). They thought of the celestial hierarchy as a mirror image of the earthly existence, complete with a heavy bureaucracy.

The search for physical immortality continued in spite of the daily reminder of the reality of physical death. The belief in physical immortality was sustained by the Eight Immortals said to be living in bliss somewhere beyond the boundaries of China. Several expeditions were sent out to remote islands to find the Immortals, but without success. Special halls are dedicated to them and in Ch'ian they have their own temple. The Immortals are said to move about in the celestial realm, dwell in grottos, wander across the earth, and fly among the stars.

The individual Daoist is encouraged to increase his *qi* through morning and evening scripture recitation. In the evening the yang declines and the yin grows, but the proper balance is restored through the recitation of prayers.

"The belief evolved that the Taoist adepts only appeared to die, that what was buried in the tomb was not his true body, but only a resemblance."[55] Some Daoists taught an "inner alchemy," a transformation of the heart and mind through yoga and meditation. The secret of meditation was to visualize an inner light and to focus the mind on the inner organs or on the gods residing there. It was believed that breathing techniques and appropriate diets facilitated the vital flow of *qi*.

Zhang organized his followers into 24 parishes. Trained male and female priests officiated. For services rendered, the sect levied a tax of five pecks of rice. To this day the group is known as Five-Peck Daoists.

Many Daoist sects came into existence, but they all embraced the same basic teachings and their differences were relatively unimportant, related only to practice and ritual. Daoism addresses the individual and is a salvation religion promising redemption to anyone who will allow the *tao* to control his life. It is a mixture of folk religion that sometimes degenerates into crass superstition, magic, and alchemy. The most essential ingredients for alchemy were cinnabar and gold, but more was involved than mere chemistry. The alchemist had to undergo extensive rites of purification.

Daoism is known for its colorful rituals. Daoist priests expel demons through complex rituals. Priests play important roles at funerals. They prepare the necessary forms for the underworld bureaucracy. Sometimes written memorials are burned to convey messages and requests to the gods. Personal salvation comes through religious practices carried out by priests—practices such as prayer, reading sacred texts, and ritual dance. Priests perform purification rites that can last for days. Rituals surrounding the lunar new year are best known for their dragon dances and firecrackers, which are intended to chase away the demons. The end of the new year celebration is signaled by the Lantern Festival.

Some of the priests have dual functions—they are both priests and shamans (or spirit-mediums) who are experts in fortune-telling and interpreters of good or bad omens. They create talismans, an involved process that demands ritual purification and a serious intention on the part of the priest for the talismans to be effective.

Daoism had a profound impact on Chinese culture. Traditional Chinese medicine owes much to Daoism (including acupuncture), along with *t'ai chi* (a movement technique*)*, the martial arts, and feng shui, not to mention a significant influence on the arts. Daoism is especially noticeable in paintings, where majestic scenery usually eclipses tiny human figures. The pursuit of alchemy stimulated science and led to the accidental discovery of gunpowder.

On the popular level, the effort to increase the *qi* or vital flow of energy took many different forms. Some thought that *qi* was like a breath, a vapor that could be captured through proper breathing techniques. Some professional Daoists would burn talismans and place the ashes in warm water. They would then drink the draught and, in this fashion, tap into cosmic energy. There are 36 grottos scattered across China where one can tap into the energy of the universe. There are also 72 "blessed sites" most suitable for worship. Daoists venerate sacred mountains because they are the dwelling places of deities and immortals. The most sacred is Mount Tai (in the Shandong Province). Mount Hua (Shaanxi Province) has been the home of famous recluses. Mount Qingcheng (Sichuan Province) is the place where the celestial master taught the *tao*.

Since the *tao* embraces everything, earth, sky, and humanity are part of one whole living organism complete with "veins of the dragon." Where such veins or channels converge, good luck and *qi* abound. Specialists practice feng shui ("wind and water") and determine the location of propitious places. Feng shui is a mixture of geography, architecture, ethics, and Daoist principles. It is a system of geomancy or mechanical divination done to find the correct spot for a city, a grave, a house, or a business. The communists derided feng shui as a feudal superstition, but it is once again guiding the design of buildings "from government offices to state banks in mainland China."[56] Currently feng shui masters enjoy great popularity, and the government takes a hands-off approach to them.

Over the centuries, Daoism split into many different schools. Only two have survived: the Quanzhen ("Totally True") sect or Complete Perfection, and the Zhengyi ("Exact One") sect, or Orthodox Unity. Both believe in the *tao,* deities, and the Eight Immortals, and multiple heavens and hells. The differences between the sects are minimal and relate to vegetarianism, the marriage of priests, and other like issues.

Today the center of Daoism is in Taiwan. Most famous is the Lungshan Temple, where both Buddhist and Daoist deities are worshiped. In China, the White Cloud Temple is the headquarters of one of the two official Daoist sects. The magnificent temple has splendid statues of the Four Heavenly Emperors—one is Gouchen, representing the constellations surrounding the polar star, and another is Ziwei, emperor of the north pole star.

The sacred text of the Tao Te Ching is open to innumerable interpretations. For example, the following is the entire text of chapter 12:

The five colors will blind eyes
The five tones deafen ears
The five tastes blur tongues
Fast horses and breathtaking
   hunts make the minds wild
   and crazy
Things rare and expensive make
   people lose their way.

That's why a sage tends to the
   belly,
   not the eye,
Always ignores *that* and chooses
   this.

Commentary: "Colors" have legitimate functions in the arts but are easily perverted into sensuous distractions. The chase or "hunt" represents livelihood from the perspective of effort and struggle. The original, normal function has been distorted into ambition. People "lose their way" when they are motivated by desire. It has also been suggested that it is better to seek inner alchemy or inner transformation than external remedies. The "sage tends to the belly," or the middle, the center, and listens to the intuitive mind. They are inner-directed and ignore the "eye" or external matters. Others think that the "eye" refers to subjective vision. Ignore "that" and make intelligent choices.

That many other interpretations are possible should be obvious. People are still writing commentaries on the text and seldom agree with one another.

DAOISM ALONGSIDE BUDDHISM AND CONFUCIANISM

For a while the three great religions— Confucianism, Daoism, and Buddhism— coalesced, in line with an old Chinese saying, "The three teachings flow into one." On Mount Hengshan, one of the five mythical mountains in China, is the Hanging

Monastery, which is supported by thin stilts and hugs the side of the mountain. It goes back to the sixth century. Confucius, Buddha, and Lao-Tzu are worshipped there in one single cave. That there were overlapping areas between these religions is hardly surprising because both Confucianism and Daoism have deep roots in traditional Chinese thinking. But there are also substantial differences. Daoism advocates a natural order; Buddhism insists on renouncing the world and all desire. Daoists hope for physical immortality; Buddhists hope to escape from life and reach nirvana. Confucianism emphasizes respect for the rules of society; Daoism addresses the behavior of the individual. Buddhism deals with the problem of suffering and meeting the needs of the common people, and has a strong focus on the hereafter. Daoism is interested in the here and now. Buddhism is artistic and philosophical, Daoism is mystical and idealistic, and Confucianism is ethical and pragmatic.

There are points of contact between the three. The breathing techniques of Daoists are in line with yoga. The eightfold path of Buddhism is in sync with the Confucian emphasis on ethics and humaneness. The Buddhist idea that karma predetermines life finds an echo in the Confucian idea that each person has prescribed relationships. Buddhist speculations about being and nonbeing have affinity with Daoist ideas of the *tao* emerging out of the void. For centuries people were Daoist in private life and hygiene, Confucian in ethics and public life, and Buddhist at death.

There were also large areas of disagreement. Daoists objected to the many Confucian rules of behavior because they made spontaneity impossible. It seemed to Daoists that such codes were against natural behavior. The idea of monkhood is diametrically opposed to Confucian family ethics. If there is no offspring, who will honor the ancestors?

The demise of the Han Dynasty was followed by several hundred years of war. A new, powerful aristocracy emerged and played an important political role in the country. In north China, 16 kingdoms succeeded each other between 304 and 439. The Northern Wei (386–535), who came from the region of Mongolia, were not part of the Chinese Han but belonged to the Tuoba Xianbei. They managed to unify north China and in the process were modified by Chinese influence. They followed a legalist policy and used heavy-handed state intervention to control the population. Hundreds of thousands of people were deported. The Wei were great patrons of Buddhism. In A.D. 493 the capital was moved from Datong to Luoyang, where more than 1,000 Buddhist temples were built. The city is famous for the Longman Grottoes, one of the most important cave temples in China with almost 100,000 statues. More than 10,000 monastic establishments dotted the country.

The Sui (581–618) took advantage of the dismemberment of the Wei state and managed to unify the empire. They maintained the basic institutions they had inherited.

BUDDHISM

BUDDHISM INFILTRATED CHINA IN the first and second centuries, following the commercial routes through central Asia. Buddhism, unlike Confucianism, was not concerned with ritual pollution and became a "merchant religion." The oldest Buddhist temple in China is found in Luoyong, the old capital city. The original structure of the White Horse Temple goes back to A.D. 68. Buddhism triumphed in China from the fourth to eighth centuries. Wenli, the first emperor of the Sui Dynasty, used Buddhism to legitimize his right to rule.

The translation of Buddhist Indian texts into Chinese was a challenge. There are literally thousands of sacred texts, and only a few could be selected for translation. Translators used Daoist technical terms, the only ones available. To some it might have seemed that Daoism and Buddhism were almost indistinguishable and that Buddhism was a variation of Daoism. This greatly facilitated the acceptance of this alien religion. Later, more texts from India were brought to China, and better translations of the Buddhist works were produced. These translation efforts extended over a millennium. In the process, adaptations were made, and interpolations and Chinese literary ornaments were added. In the end, Chinese Buddhism came to differ in many ways from Indian Buddhism.[57] In part, the differences are due to the Buddhist teaching that it "should be preached in consonance with the spiritual, moral, and intellectual level of the audience."[58]

It was the Mahayana form of Buddhism that entered China. This form was less rigid than Hinayana Buddhism and offering salvation through *bodhisattvas*. Mahayana Buddhism was more acceptable in China and was never given to abstract theories to the same measure as in India. The idea of compassion and of devoting one's life to others—rather than extinguishing all desire and entering nirvana—was more in line with Chinese thinking. The eightfold path of Buddhism could be aligned with the Confucian emphasis on ethics. The ideas of reincarnation and karma helped to understand the miseries of the present. They explained why, for so many people, life was almost unbearable. Finally, the easy form of the Pure Land Buddhism that ultimately prevailed—the simple invocation of Amidhaba—was very attractive.

The Ch'an sect, better known by its Japanese name of Zen, traces its roots back to an Indian master, Bodhidarma (c. 520). But it was Huineng (638–713), a monk, who was the actual founder of the Zen school. He promoted the appealing idea of instant illumination without years of asceticism. The reasoning was simple: If there is only nothingness, it can surely be realized in an instant. The only problem is that the idea of nothingness is not in accord with the experience of our five senses. Another obstacle to the acceptance of nothingness is reason. Therefore, rationality has to be undermined. This can be achieved with the help of a *koan*, a statement that subverts reality. The *koan* is not an apparent paradox that might be reconciled on further thought, but rather, it remains totally irrational. In this fashion the listener is shocked into a new awareness of the insufficiency of reason and can receive illumination and accept the irrational. Harvey Cox observed that the parables of Jesus contained unexpected twists and surprising inversions that undercut the audience's expectations and overturned social and religious conventions, but because they were rooted in reality and did not require the abdication of reason, they did not subvert reality in the same way as the *koans*.[59]

Daoists were attracted by the positive image of the Western Paradise promised by Pure Land Buddhism, a concrete place much easier to imagine than the formless *tao.* The Buddhist emphasis on knowledge was in line with Confucian thinking. For both Buddha and Confucius, ignorance—not sin—is the great evil. As for differences, in Mahayana Buddhism, salvation is acquired through the mediation of a *bodhisattva.* In Confucianism, everything depends on self-effort. The *bodhisattvas* invited faith, and the Confucians pursued knowledge.

The reliance on a *bodhisattva* is contrary to the Theravada or Hinayana school of Buddhism. They cherish the dying words of Buddha, "strive for your salvation with diligence." In Hinayana Buddhism there is no room for dependence on someone else for salvation. Reliance is on the teaching, not the teacher, and on meaning, not a formula. Reliance is on "definite meaning," not provisional understanding, and on transcendent wisdom, not mere knowledge. Theravada and Mahayana Buddhism also differ in their interpretation of karma. According to the former, it is an unbreakable law of cause and effect. Mahayana Buddhism accepts the idea that good karma can be transferred to someone else's credit. *Bodhisattvas* (and especially the Buddha himself) had accumulated such a huge treasure of good karma that, filled with compassion, they were eager to make the transfer.[60] In like manner the Catholic Church draws on the treasure of the superabundance of good works performed by saints and the infinite merits of Christ to dispense indulgences.

If the *tao* of the Daoists could not be defined, neither could the nirvana of Buddhism. Some Buddhist theories must have seemed strange, especially the idea that there is no soul, that the self does not exist. Ancient traditions spoke of two souls. Again, the idea of monkhood was opposed

to traditional religion because ancestor worship depends on progeny. People used to amulets were ready to accept the relics of Buddha and of Buddhist saints or *arhats,* the chief disciples of the historic Buddha who have attained nirvana. Innumerable relics were venerated. The bones of a finger of Buddha were a precious relic lost for hundreds of years but rediscovered in 1987. The bones are now in the Famen pagoda west of Xi'an.

Daoists had peopled heaven and earth with innumerable gods so that the idea of the celestial beings of Buddhism was easily acceptable, especially of the Four Heavenly Emperors. Each one had a special characteristic. The king of the south held an umbrella, the king of the east a musical instrument, the king of the north carried a pagoda, and the king of the west came complete with a dragon.

Ideas of heaven and hell were vague in Daoism and absent in Confucianism. Buddhism offered detailed answers that were quickly absorbed by Daoism. Daoism had no information about life after death, and Buddhism filled the void. *Bodhisattvas* were extremely popular, especially Avalokiteshvara, a male figure venerated in China as a female figure, Guan-yin, the goddess of mercy.

THE T'ANG DYNASTY

The Sui were succeeded by the T'ang Dynasty (618–907), one of the greatest in the long course of Chinese history. General Li Yuan was a Sui official related to the royal family. He joined a rebellion and captured the capital. In 618 he proclaimed the new T'ang Dynasty, which was named after his fiefdom. He installed a puppet prince but soon took over and reigned from 618 to 626. The empire was divided into 300 prefectures and 1,500 counties that were all under the direct control of a central administration. Every able-bodied male received 100 *mu* of land, of which 80 reverted to the government's if the "owner" retired. Meanwhile the peasants paid taxes and performed labor for the government. Because of defective registration, taxes were no longer based on families, but on the land. Almost half of the government's revenue came from the salt monopoly.

Although Buddhism had triumphed and by 694 ceased to be treated as a foreign religion, Confucian classics continued to furnish the sole contents for state examination and consequently access to government positions.

The early T'ang rulers were Confucian Legalists, none more so than Empress Wu (690–704), but civil service examinations were open to all in an effort to break the power of the clans. Under the T'ang, China was one of the richest, most powerful, and most technologically advanced nations of the world. For a while, T'ang armies were invincible and China became "the strongest and largest empire on earth."[61] Emperor Taizong (626–649) inaugurated the golden age of the T'ang Dynasty. He forced the abdication of his father, murdered his two brothers and their ten sons, and took control. In spite of such an inauspicious beginning, he inaugurated an era of good government. He was passionate about calligraphy and appointed some ministers solely on the basis of their fine handwriting. Poems from 2,200 poets of that time have survived to today. Maritime expeditions (relatively rare in Chinese history) went all the way to Palembang in Sumatra (Indonesia) and to Champa on the east coast of Vietnam. In 630 Turkish tribes were crushed and for 120 years Central Asia came under Chinese control. Tibet was pacified in 641 when a Chinese princess married the king of Tibet. Korea was subjugated in 668 after several unsuccessful attempts. Eventually the T'ang Empire spanned from Korea to Iran.

The aristocracy had always been the main component of the army, but now for the first time peasants were also included. However, because the cavalry had to provide their own horses, peasants were practically excluded from serving in that capacity. The horse became a status symbol. Imperial stables sheltered 40,000, and the empire was home to 700,000. The government established stud farms, and cross-breeding the horses in China from other regions helped produce taller horses than the original Mongolian ponies.

The T'ang conquests led to an influx of foreigners into China. Chang'an, the capital city with one million people, was both cosmopolitan and dynamic and one of the largest cities in the world. It was the gateway of the Silk Road. Visitors included Syrians, Arabs, Persians, and Tibetans. Ships sailed to India and the Persian Gulf. Embassies from other countries made regular appearances in China. The elite welcomed everything from Central Asia and the Middle East. The dances and music of Central Asia became fads. At one point there were 20,000 musicians connected with the palace.

Muslim merchants introduced Islam to China. The first mosque was built in the capital. One of the oldest is the Niujie Qingzhen So Mosque in Beijing, built in 995. This mosque is quite different from the typical structure (dome and minaret) because of the stylistic adaptations made with China in mind. The mosque looks almost like a Chinese temple and blends into the Chinese landscape. Under the T'ang Dynasty, religious toleration prevailed...at least for a while. Nestorian missionaries from Persia arrived in 635, as recorded on the famous Nestorian stele now in the Xi'an Forest of Stone Tablets Museum. The Nestorian monk Alopen came to Chang-an and was free to preach the gospel and to build churches.

Among the great public works of the T'angs were major canals. The first really big canal, 130 feet wide, connected Luoyang and Beijing. Great efforts were made to improve communications between the two capitals, Luoyang and Chang'an, which were separated by 250 miles.

One remarkable achievement was the creation of the T'ang law code, promulgated in 637 complete with 502 articles. It was accepted by the Ming Dynasty and provided the basis for the Qing Code that remained in force until 1905.

In 751 the Chinese suffered a major defeat at the Battle of Talas at the Talas River. T'ang power in Central Asia was destroyed by the armies of Islam. It was a battle with large historic consequences that determined the future of Central Asia. "Instead of becoming Chinese, as the general trend of earlier events seemed the presage, it was to turn Muslim."[62] A Chinese victory would have had serious consequences for Kyrgyzstan, Tajikistan, Uzbekistan, and Turkmenistan (as these countries are known today).

Under the T'ang Dynasty, eunuchs rose to power. Initially they were only used to supervise harems, but in time they gained more and more influence. They became buyers of supplies and messengers and, in this capacity, had access to the entire palace.

An unusual interlude is the story of Lady Yang, a famous Chinese beauty who played an important role in Chinese history. Yang Gufei became an Imperial concubine and Emperor Xuanzong was so infatuated with her that he granted important posts to her relatives, including An Lushan, a barbarian general who was half Sogdian and half Turkish. The barbarians were favored because they were remote from the intrigues within the court. By 750 An Lushan controlled the northeastern region of China and had 106,000 troops under his command. A year later he was made governor of a second military district and controlled 200,000 troops, or half the regular T'ang forces. He coveted the post of prime minister and when he failed to receive the appointment, An Lushan, now in sole control of three military regions, launched a military rebellion. In 755 he marched to Luoyang and proclaimed a new dynasty. The capital fell to the rebels. Eight years of civil war followed. The army refused to fight for the emperor unless his paramour, Lady Yang, were executed—a dramatic situation that has inspired novels and plays. The emperor abdicated in favor of his son. In 757 An Lushan was assassinated by his son, and anarchy prevailed. Local governors took control. Bandits ravaged the country. The rebellion of An Lushan had been suppressed with the help of mercenaries, and now military expenses absorbed a large percentage of state revenue, with much of it distributed to the Uighurs, a Turkic people from Central Asia. As a reward for their service, they were allowed to plunder Luoyang for three days. Increasingly the government became dependent upon foreign mercenaries. The T'ang court lost its authority and, after the An-Lushan rebellion, was never the same.

The emperor became the plaything of warlords. Even the Tibetans managed to briefly occupy Chang'an in 763!

Buddhist sects had grown enormously over this time, and now the state faced unexpected problems. Innumerable fictitious ordinations robbed the state of income, diminished the labor force, and weakened the army because monks were exempt from service. There was even a shortage of metal suitable for coinage. So much metal had been used to create huge cult images that there was a shortage of bronze. Buddhist monasteries owned large land holdings, escaped taxation, and became bankers. These abuses unleashed a fierce persecution of Buddhists under Emperor Wu Tsung. Some 40,000 temples large and small were destroyed, and 250,000 priests and nuns were forced back into lay life and became taxable. The loss of 4,600 Buddhist monasteries was such a severe blow that Buddhism never really recovered.

The end of the T'ang Dynasty signaled another period of chaos. The breakup of the empire produced five dynasties in the northern area and nine kingdoms in the south. The dismemberment was facilitated by the fact that commissioners in charge of the military districts had considerable autonomy and the central government had yielded power to the regions.

THE FIVE DYNASTIES AND TEN KINGDOMS

It should almost be expected that Vietnam would shake off the Chinese yoke and from then on remain independent. In the northeast, the Khitan Empire (946–1125) controlled its own territory, followed by the Jurchen Empire (1115–1227), which annexed large areas of north China. In order to secure their territory, the Chinese gave up 16 prefectures south of the Great Wall and thereby destroyed the traditional defense system. This gave the Khitans access to China. Fortunately for China, the Khitans failed to take advantage of the weakness of their neighbor and were slowly assimilated.

General Zhao Kuangyi launched the new Northern Sung Dynasty (960–1126) and reigned from 976 to 997. It took the general 20 years to unify all of China, not including the Khitans. Civil officials took over from the military and filled administrative positions. They qualified through civil service examinations based on Confucian texts. Study began at age five and went on for 30 years. The top grade or *jinshi* opened the door to 200 positions available each year. Next to the Temple of Confucius in Beijing is a collection of 198 steles with the names of 51,624 scholars who qualified for the *jinshi* between 1416 and 1904. In 1044, examinations for lesser positions were for the first time administered on the provincial level in the official schools. Although merchants and artisans were excluded, there were still too many candidates for the limited number of available positions. Some sources mention 400,000 candidates. To prevent fraud, examination papers were copied by clerks and numbered. For three days students sat in separate cubicles to take the tests. Being hired to even a low government position was an enormous asset because ultimately the entire family would benefit, and perhaps the clan.

Kaifeng, the capital, was located on the Grand Canal, a practical but indefensible location. The city soon reached a population of one million people, the equivalent of the total number of inhabitants in

England at that time. In 1163 the city had a synagogue for Jews from Iran.

Wang Anshi (1021–1086), an economist, statesman, and poet, tried to implement revolutionary reforms. Many large estates had escaped taxation and an unfair burden fell on the peasants. Wang Anshi tried to protect the small farmers from exploitation. He advocated "green crop money" for the planting season at the reasonable interest rate of 20 percent—reasonable by the standards of that day. Conservatives fiercely opposed Wang Anshi and made sure that the system failed. They insisted that a proper paper trail was essential. Papers had to be filled out for loan applications, the needs of the borrowers had to be investigated, collateral had to be approved, and inevitably the bureaucracy mushroomed to the point that the system was doomed to failure.

Wang Anshi created a peasant militia to help reduce the number of professional soldiers needed and save money in the process. He fixed commodity prices and regulated labor. When he tried to include practical knowledge into government tests, he aroused strong opposition. The Confucian idea of a gentleman was not compatible with specialized or practical knowledge. In the end, the status quo was re-established. Wang Anshi's reforms were not implemented; privilege was too deeply entrenched.

A Jurchen tribal chief then claimed the title of emperor and inaugurated the Jin Dynasty (1115–1234). An alliance was sought with the Sung Dynasty (1120) to crush the Khitans, but managed to subdue them without help from the Sung. The Jurchen now turned against their former allies, the Sung. In 1126 they captured Kaifeng. The military history of the Sung

is one of retreat or retrenchment. Huizong (1101–1125), the last king of the Northern Sung, had a taste for luxury. He was a musician and a patron of the arts. He collected paintings and owned close to 6,400 of them. He became a Jurchen prisoner and died in captivity.

The ninth son of Huizong was not in Kaifeng when the capital fell and fled south to perpetuate the Sung rule. The Southern Sung (1127–1279) became a vassal state of the Jurchen and paid a heavy tribute in silk and silver.

In spite of the turbulent times it was an era of significant technological progress. Movable type is mentioned in 1086—long before Gutenberg—but appeared even earlier in Korea. An astronomical clock graced Kaifeng (c. 1090). Treadmills turned paddle wheels. Gunpowder saw new applications; a flamethrower was developed, operated by a pump. Grenades were created. Mortars were used in warfare. Warships were equipped with catapults. Watertight compartments in ships were large enough to hold several hundred persons. Some ships sported four decks, several masts, a dozen sails, and could carry 500 men. In comparison with Europe, the China of the eleventh and twelfth centuries was ahead in many ways. Even sporadic epidemics did not stem progress. The one in 1232 killed a million people.

In 1214 the Southern Sung stopped paying tribute to the Jurchen when the latter were pinned down by the Mongols. The Sung formed an alliance with the Mongols against the Jurchen, but the Mongols were victorious without help from the Sung. By the time the Sung understood the threat posed by the Mongols and reacted, it was too late and the empire was lost.

NEO-CONFUCIANISM

IN THE MIDDLE OF the political chaos, and given the void created by the decimation of Buddhism, Neo-Confucianism developed in the eleventh and twelfth centuries. Confucian scholars developed theories regarding the origin of the universe and about human nature. Although they borrowed much from both Buddhism and Daoism, they condemned both for seeking to escape from the world and refusing to shoulder social responsibilities. Confucianism developed an overarching concept of the universe and life—a total, integrating worldview. They discovered "the basic identity of the natural order and the human order, of the moral and the cosmic."[63]

Confucian thinkers established parallels between the cosmos and humanity. Since all things exist because of *qi,* there had to be a correspondence between the universe and man. Initially the *qi* is without form, but then it contracts and heaven (yang) and earth (yin) come into existence. Since the *qi* has two forms, void and solid, humans also have two inclinations, good and bad. How the *qi* came into being or why it contracted were speculative questions usually avoided by Confucian scholars.

Confucianism remained stagnant for about 1,000 years, till Chu Hsi (1130–1200) came along and infused new life into the system. He was the great synthesizer and a prolific author. He based his teaching on a combination of 1) the *I Ching,* 2) the Analects, 3) the works of Mencius, and 4) the "Great Learning," and 5) the Doctrine of the Mean, the last two taken from the *Liki* or the Book of Rites. The *Liki* mentions 300 principles and 3,000 rules of conduct and offers advice on many topics: Do not roll rice into a ball, do not leave rice on the table, do not let your soup run out of your mouth. Do not smack your lips, do not leave a bone dry, do not throw bones to a dog, and do not persist in trying to get a particular piece of meat. Do not turn rice about to let it cool off, and do not get porridge with chopsticks. Do not gulp up your soup, do not stir your soup about, do not pick your teeth, and do not add sauce to your soup. Bite off boiled meat with your teeth, but do not bite off cured meet with your teeth.

Chu Hsi's commentaries on these books were eventually integrated into the curriculum of the civil service examinations, making his philosophy the new state orthodoxy for the next six centuries. His doctrine of sagehood stressed the interrelatedness of the world and man. He defined *li* as the passive, organizing principle, and *qi* as the dynamic one. *Li* is immaterial; *qi* is concrete. *Li* is the same in all humans, but *qi* appears in different densities. If it is murky it needs cleansing by extending knowledge of *li.* To restore the original good nature, one must investigate things and practice self-cultivation.

For Chu Hsi, human beings represented the summit of the universe because they participated in the "Great Ultimate" and possessed a nature that had come through the interaction of yin and yang and the five agents of metal, wood, water, fire, and earth. Basic moral principles were embedded in human nature, including humaneness, righteousness, propriety, and wisdom. It was our responsibility to develop these principles and to live harmoniously. The influence of Daoism and Buddhism on Confucian thinking is illustrated in the words penned by Chu Hsi:

> We need not talk about empty and far-away things; if we would know the reality of Tao we must seek it within our own nature.
>
> Each one has within him the principle of right, and what we call Tao, the road along which we ought to walk.
>
> The means by which we all may day by day banish human desire and return to Divine Law lie within our reach, and to use them is our duty.
>
> The one thing we must realize is that we must use our earnest effort and master it, get rid of its excesses, and restore the Mean.
>
> Virtue is the practice of moral law.
>
> Virtue is what is received into the heart. Before serving one's parents and following one's elder brother, already to possess a perfectly filial and fraternal mind: this is what is termed virtue."[64]

Neo-Confucianists tried to construct a system of philosophy that had been missing in Confucianism. They were particularly interested in the human condition and used thoughtful analysis to understand the personality. The special focus was on the emotions. Scholars spoke of six types of mind and basically agreed that fundamental goodness is the basic character of the original mind. Somehow the mind is ensnared by greed. This is the condition of the ordinary man, but not the original condition. It is the "flow" of the human mind. The pure human mind comes first; the original mind is correct but was corrupted later. As long as a fairly superficial view of sin and guilt prevail (deviation from propriety), not even the subtlest analysis provided radical transformation and renewal or pointed to effective transcendence.

THE YUAN OR MONGOL DYNASTY

The Yuan or Mongol Dynasty (1279–1368). Ghengis Khan (c. 1167–1227), whose real name was Temujin, was orphaned at age 12. His mother was a Nestorian Christian. When his father was poisoned, the clan thought Temujin too young to rule. For years he lived in poverty. He killed his half-brother in a dispute over the spoils of a hunt. Captured in a raid, he managed to escape. He became involved in innumerable adventures and grew in stature. By the age of 25 he had united the Mongol tribes into a single federation, which was no small achievement. Tribes that resisted were annihilated. At a meeting in 1206 he was enthroned as the Mongol emperor and received the title of Ghengis Khan, or Universal Ruler. It was an empty title, however, and the right to rule had to be earned. At age 35 he began to fight for supremacy. He took control of an ever-growing empire. Some battles were ferocious and lasted as long as three days, but Ghengis Khan always triumphed. He destroyed the Jurchen and sacked Beijing (1215). The capital burned for one whole month. A few years later he added Korea to his Chinese conquest. In spite of the fact that he was illiterate, he had excellent diplomatic and political skills.

Ghengis Khan, famous for his ferocity, introduced a concept previously unknown in Asia: the principle of equality before the law. He was tolerant of all religions. Buddhist and Daoist monks, Nestorian priests, and Muslim imams were neither subject to land or trade taxes, nor any kind of requisition.[65] He paid close attention to shamanistic predictions. He sponsored the reconstruction of the Daoist Temple of the White Cloud and rebuilt the Buddhist Temple of the White Pagoda, both in Beijing. Arniko, a brilliant Nepalese architect, served the dynasty for 45 years. The Khan's favors were distributed without regard to race or rank. Appointments were based on ability. The opportunity for promotion was open to everyone. His lifestyle remained simple, except for his indulgence of food and drink toward the end of his life.

Ghengis Khan invited a famous Daoist, Ch'iu Ch'ang-chuen, to join him in Afghanistan. Ch'ang-chuen was age 71 at this time, and he and 18 disciples set out from China on the long journey. They reached Ghengis Khan, but the Daoist master was unable to communicate the secret of longevity. Nevertheless, he was highly honored and the Daoist Ch'uan Chen sect became popular.

The Southern Sung saw the devastation of Beijing and enjoyed watching barbarians (the Mongols) slaughtering other barbarians (the Jurchen). Once they recognized the awesome power of the Mongols and the formidable destruction of Beijing, they reacted and attacked the Mongols—with disastrous consequences to themselves (1234). The Mongols were better armed and had more horses. They never rode the same horse two days in a row. Their archers were the best. Force of circumstances had compelled them to learn the art of siege warfare. The Mongols triumphed over the Sung, but it was left to Kublai Khan to complete the subjugation of the Southern Sung.

Ghengis Khan's empire stretched from Korea to Hungary. Upon his death, 40 virgins decked with jewels and rich ornaments were sacrificed to the Khan's spirit. The empire was divided into four regions, one for each of the sons of his favorite wife.

Kublai Khan, a descendant of Ghengis Khan, continued the war against the Southern Sung. The siege of the twin cities of Siangyang and Fancheng lasted five years, but the Mongol advance was unstoppable. In 1276, Hangchow, the Sung capital, fell to the Mongols.

Kublai Khan proclaimed himself first emperor of the Yuan Dynasty in 1271. A dynastic alliance by way of marriage appeased Korea. Kublai demanded homage from Japan, but was repulsed. In 1281 the Mongol armada sailed toward Japan, but was destroyed by a typhoon. The campaign against Japan was abandoned. Kublai then sent an ambassador to Java, asking for her submission. When the envoy was mistreated, Kublai sent an army to subjugate the country. Success was limited, and the expedition failed.

Kublai had only a rudimentary knowledge of spoken Chinese and was totally illiterate when it came to written Chinese. Although the Yuan Dynasty based promotions on merit, regardless of class or race, non-Chinese individuals occupied most key positions. The small number of Mongols could all too easily have been overwhelmed by the innumerable Chinese, if not militarily, certainly administratively.

The Mongols improved communication in China. The Grand Canal was extended to Beijing thanks to the labor of three million people. The Mongols established an excellent postal network with 50,000 horses (some suggest 200,000 horses) placed at 1,400 relay stations. They also used oxen, mules, and 6,000 boats to help facilitate communication. Under ideal conditions, riders covered 250 miles in a single day.

Kublai Khan maintained a delicate balance between the Chinese civilization and the nomadic culture of the Mongols. Intermarriage between Mongols and Chinese was forbidden. When the conquest of China was completed in 1279, the population was divided into four groups: First came the Mongols, and second came their allies, such as the Tibetans. These two groups were tax exempt. Next came the former subjects of the Jin Empire, such as the Jurchen and Khitans. Last were the people who had been part of the Southern Sung state.

THE POLOS

Kublai opposed the government's civil service examinations for prospective workers. He was not anxious to use Chinese advisors. He deliberately attracted people from Tibet, Persia, and the Golden Horde (a Mongol state that includes modern Kazakhstan). Two Venetians, Niceolo and Maffeo Polo (the father and uncle of Marco Polo), met Kublai Khan, who requested "100 wise men learned in the law of Christ." The Polos traveled to Rome to fulfill this request, but the timing was unfortunate. After the death of Pope Clement IV in 1268 there was a vacancy that lasted several years, till Gregory X was finally elected. It was precisely at that juncture that the Polos arrived in Rome and thus were unable to achieve anything.

Still, it is surprising that the request went unfulfilled. The legends of Prester John, which told of a Christian king and nation that existed somewhere in the Orient, had circulated in the West, and that alone might

have induced a king to react favorably to Kublai Khan's request. Many in the West had hoped to form an alliance with Prester John in the East to help oppose Islam. In 1253, William of Rubruck was dispatched by the Pope and Louis IX to seek an alliance with the Mongols against the Muslims. When Marco Polo stopped at Sarai, headquarters of the Golden Horde, he heard about the visit of Rubruck. There is a historical base, then, for the Prester John legends. The Kerayit people, probably Turks or Mongols, are thought to have been converted to Nestorianism around the year 1000. Supposedly the clan was lost in the steppe and saved by an apparition of Saint Sergius. At any rate, word reached the Nestorian patriarch of Baghdad and it seems that 200,000 Kerayits were baptized. In the twelfth century they still bore Christian names, and that may be the source of the legends of Prester John.[66]

Marco Polo (1254–1324) observed that there were three Nestorian churches in Kanchow and more churches in other cities. The Ongut, another Turkish tribe, had also embraced Christianity. Their princes frequently intermarried with the Ghengis Khan family, which explains the connection between the Mongols and Christianity. There were also many Christians among the Uighurs. Mention should be made of the occasional Christian envoy to China, such as Giovanni dal Piano dei Carpini (c. 1182–1252), a Franciscan. There were other such Europeans who followed the Silk Road and reached China.

In 1307 Pope Clement V appointed Montecorvino archbishop of Beijing. He received help from three Franciscans. The most famous Catholic missionary was the Franciscan Odorico da Pordenone, who commented on the many Nestorian churches in Azerbaijan and reached Canton via India. He stayed in Beijing for two or three years before returning to Europe. Pope Urban V also appointed an archbishop of Beijing, but the Mongol Dynasty had just been overthrown and the Ming were hostile to foreign religions. Christians now labored under a distinct disadvantage because they were seen as close associates of the Mongols.

A Temple of Confucius was built in Beijing in 1302. During this time, Daoist, Buddhist, and Confucian shrines and temples were all equally honored. Religious tolerance prevailed throughout the empire although Chabi, wife of Kublai Khan, was an ardent Buddhist. Later Kublai also embraced Buddhism. His four principal wives each had a household of 10,000 attendants, and Kublai used from 30 to 40 new concubines each year.

Some of Kublai's advisors became extremely unpopular and paid with their lives. An intense battle arose between Daoists and Buddhists to gain the upper hand in the new empire. Daoists claimed that Lao-Tzu had gone through 81 incarnations, and one of them was as the Buddha. But Lao-Tzu offered a simple Buddhism that was nothing but a corrupted form of Daoism. The Buddhists responded by claiming that Buddha had lived long before Lao-Tzu and that both Confucius and Lao-Tzu had been disciples of Buddha.

The occasional anti-Muslim legislation was politically motivated, and the same is true of Buddhist and Daoist control systems. The latter sold charms at enormous profits, and Kublai appointed a Daoist "pope" to determine the authenticity of certain books.

LAMAISM

THE CONQUEST OF TIBET in 1281 had the unexpected consequence of bringing great prominence to the Tibetan form of Buddhism known as Lamaism. Kublai had sent for Phags-pa (1239–1280), a Tibetan lama, both to guarantee Tibetan vassalage and to convert the Mongols. To the great delight of Kublai Khan, the Tibetan guru created an alphabet of 41 letters, which he presented in 1269 as a way of writing Mongolian. It appeared ideally suited to the language, and Kublai promulgated an edict regarding the script. He hoped that the new official script would help unify the realm, but regardless of official efforts, it was never accepted.

TANTRISM

PHAGS-PA BECAME A CLOSE adviser to Kublai Khan, and Buddhists continued to exercise inordinate influence over the empire. Tibet imported an esoteric Buddhism known as Tantrism. Buddhism entered Tibet in the eighth century when images of the Buddha were first seen in the country. In the eleventh century four sects evolved, including the lineage that gave birth to the Dalai Lama. The fifth Dalai Lama took control as both the secular and religious leader of Tibet.

The followers of Tantric Buddhism claimed that it is the most advanced form of Buddhism. The meanings of the tantras are deliberately veiled. They can be understood only with the help of a guru. There are four classes of tantra, and within each class there are subdivisions. The highest tantra prescribes meat because at this point one is "able to transform the five meats into purified substances through the power of meditation."[67]

It was openly admitted that some of the Tantric teaching could not be traced back to Buddha. People were told that the truth was unveiled after the Buddha became a principal deity. Tantrism teaches that there is a difference between the explicit reading of sutras and the implicit reading. This has to be determined on the basis of reason. In the end, reason controls scripture. In addition, Tibetan Buddhism enjoys four subtle distinctions: There is a difference between 1) the empty, 2) the great empty, 3) the very empty, and 4) the complete empty.

The good news proclaimed by Tantrism is the idea that nirvana can be reached in a single lifetime, and that it is not absolutely necessary to go through countless incarnations. Help of celestial *bodhisattvas* such as Avalokiteshvara—known as Chenrezik in Tibet—is indispensable. To move forward to the place of enlightenment, it is essential to engage the body in 1) sound, 2) sight, and 3) motion. The sound explains the sacred mantras (such as *Om Mani Padme Hum,* or "Hail to the Jewel in the Lotus") repeated incessantly in a special tone of voice and called "an acoustic trigger." The motion is linked to the mudras or symbolic gestures, especially of the hands and fingers. The sight is provided by the mandalas, usually a colorful and intricate geometric design showing four entrances. At the center is the dwelling of a god.

Concentration and incantation help to expedite one's union with the deity. Because sexual union is said to be a foretaste of merging with the deity, there is—

from a Western perspective—a remarkable emphasis on sex. We are told that the best opportunity to generate the experience of clear light is during sexual climax, when the "vital elements" are "melted" and, through the power of meditation, their flow is reversed upward. But even at this supreme moment of mystic union, when one apprehends the divine form of a deity, one is at the same time clearly aware of its empty nature.[68] The ultimate purpose of existence is said to be to achieve a favorable birth in our next life.[69]

Kublai was the first Chinese ruler to designate his own successor. Upon his death in 1294, a quick succession of emperors tried to seize and maintain power. Internal dissension and rebellions led to the collapse of the empire. The combined rule of eight successors to Kublai Khan lasted only 26 years. The ongoing struggles among Mongol factions encouraged uprisings and rebellions.

There were at least four groups up in arms during this time. The most daring and clever was Chu Yuan-chang. He was of humble origin, the son of a landless farm laborer, and he had starved and begged as a boy. He learned literacy from a Buddhist priest. The young man was astute and used diplomacy to his advantage. He took advantage of several religious movements that waited for the coming of the Maitreya Buddha, a Buddhist messiah. The most famous secret society was the Red Turbans, a powerful group in revolt against the "foreign government" of the Mongols. Yuan-chang was able to eliminate his rivals and took advantage of the civil strive among Mongols to advance his cause. He defeated all other claimants to the throne and proclaimed the new Ming Dynasty (1368–1644) in Nanjing.

THE MING DYNASTY

Yuan-chang became the first Ming emperor and adopted the name *Hongwu* (1368–1398). He completed the conquest of China by 1387. Hongwu was dictatorial and ruthless. When he found out his prime minister was plotting against him, he had the prime minister beheaded along with his family and everyone even remotely connected to him. Waves of other political purges claimed some 100,000 lives. Hongwu never learned the art of delegation, perhaps because he wanted to retain absolute control.

The Emperors

Ming means "radiance," but the Ming Dynasty was not noteworthy for its brilliance. With few exceptions, the emperors were mediocre. Emperor Yongle (1403–1424) was a compulsive builder. The Imperial Palace in Beijing is representative of the best of Chinese architecture. The new palace, now known as The Forbidden City, was surrounded by walls 33 feet high and had corner towers and magnificent gates. The moat surrounding the palace is 170 feet wide. Thanks to a million workmen and 100,000 artisans, the construction of the Imperial Palace complex was completed in three years.

The Forbidden City is divided into several courts, each one featuring a main building along a single axis. The overall plan reflects cosmic harmony. Minor halls flank the main buildings. There are living quarters, pavilions, ornamental lakes, and audience halls. The Hall of Supreme Harmony was the center of the emperor's activities. It was the place for formal ceremonies, Imperial exams, grand receptions, and the appointment of army commanders. There were other important buildings, including the Hall of Middle Harmony, the Hall of Preserving Harmony, and the palaces of Heavenly Purity, Earthly Tranquility, and Gathering Excellence. Then there was the Hall of Mental Cultivation, several pavilions, the stone-carved balustrades, the Imperial garden, the gates, the bronze lion, and huge bronze vats (in case of fire). The palace was indeed a city, and entrance was forbidden to all commoners. The complex was home to 24 emperors of the Ming and Qing dynasties, and the last king was expelled in 1924. The Meridian Gate, the main gate, faces the famous Tiananmen Square (Place of Heavenly Peace).

From this palace, Emperor Yongle launched his extraordinary maritime expeditions under the leadership of Cheng Ho, a Muslim eunuch and one of the greatest navigators in world history. Admiral Cheng Ho (1371–1433) set out with 62 large treasure ships and 225 smaller ones. He sailed with 27,000 men (including five astrologers) and made landfall in Indonesia, Malacca (a great maritime center in Malaysia), and Sri Lanka. On average, each voyage lasted 20 months. To this day, there are temples in southeast Asia that are dedicated to Admiral Ho. He reached the coast of Africa and returned with ostriches, zebras, lions, and a giraffe that astonished everyone and was painted by Shen Du, the court painter. Admiral Ho also painted and authored books.

From the throne hall, Emperor Yongle launched six maritime expeditions. Each one involved at least 20,000 men. The missions were diplomatic, military, commercial, and highly prestigious. The seventh expedition, under Xuande (1426–1435), Yongle's successor, was the last one—perhaps because of insufficient resources, or because Confucian scholars were opposed to trade and foreign contacts.

The emperor lived in royal splendor, but his subjects lived in abject poverty unless there was an exceptionally good harvest. Under the Ming Dynasty the food supply improved, especially after the introduction of maize, sweet potatoes, and peanuts from the New World. Ceremonies and rituals were the full-time occupation of the emperor.

The Confucian Temple of Heaven was built in 1420 and is the most important Confucian temple. In line with the ancient Chinese idea of a round heaven and a square earth, the temple is circular in shape and stands in a square court. Everything was perfectly in line with yin and yang or even and odd numbers. Harmony between heaven and earth was maintained through the emperor, who is like a hyphen, the link between heaven and earth, connecting with heaven through ritual and sacrifice and relating to the people through government. On the day of the winter solstice the Emperor ascended the heavenly altar to pray and offer sacrifice. The worship ceremonies took place on the Circular Mound Altar, a three-tiered stone terrace. The purpose of the sacrifice was not redemptive or for purposes of expiation, but only to pay homage. Upon completion of the sacrifice, memorial tablets were enshrined in a special building. At the conclusion of the worship ceremonies, tablets for the sun, the moon, stars, wind, thunder, rain, and clouds were enshrined in the East Side Hall and West Side Hall. Confucian ancestor worship did not exclude the worship of natural objects like the stars, planets, rocks, or stones.

A stove for the burning of the offerings was made of glazed bricks and featured a calf on top. There were a number of iron stoves in which to burn sacrifices offered to the ancestors of emperors and the gods of the sun, moon, and stars. Heaven or providence is impersonal; secondary spirits move freely among mortals.

The Empire

Repeated attacks and the advance of the Mongols mandated a new line of defense, an inner wall that was built under the Ming rulers. This wall, the Great Wall of China, is more than 3,000 miles long. Sentries signaled from beacon towers with fire by night and smoke by day. In spite of the wall, the army—which had come to depend more and more on mercenaries—could not protect the north against incursions from the steppe. The wall was as illusory as the Maginot Line built by the French army in the 1930s. The Great Wall never stopped invasions from the north. In the southwest, ethnic groups in search of independence created considerable unrest. And the coast was unprotected and not safe from enterprising pirates.

The administration of the palace complex and the machinery of government fell increasingly into the hands of eunuchs. At one point, 70,000 were in government service, of which 10,000 served in the capital. They controlled the secret police, had files on government officials, and had become the tax collectors. Emperor Yongle had forbidden eunuchs to learn how to read and they had been banned from politics, but 50 years later, they controlled everything. The antagonism between them and the leading government families was intense.

Under the Ming Dynasty, households were registered either as military or civilian. The former, about two million households, paid fewer taxes or none at all, but they provided the manpower for the army.

Wang Yangming (1472–1529), a philosopher, official, and thinker, dominated neo-Confucian thinking for a century. He postulated an innate moral knowledge that only needed rediscovery because it had been contaminated by egotism. The secret to intuitive knowledge was meditation. This, he said, would generate self-knowledge, and moral action would inevitably follow. Tired of academic discussions and theories, Wang Yangming advocated the unity of knowledge and action. He was certain that correct knowledge would almost automatically produce appropriate action.

He also organized more than 25 military campaigns and helped to repress several rebellions.

Hideyoshi (1536–1598) of Japan dreamed of the conquest of China and invaded Korea in 1592. The Korean military was unprepared and the Japanese had the advantage of muskets. Eventually, Seoul was occupied. However, Chinese intervention, guerilla resistance, and naval defeats forced the Japanese to retreat. A second invasion ended when Hideyoshi died, and the Chinese resistance almost bankrupted the nation. China was no longer in a strong position to fend off the Jurchen, who were infiltrating the northeast.

In 1598, under Emperor Wanli, Matteo Ricci (1552–1610) reached Beijing via Macao, where the Portuguese had obtained a foothold. He was well received because of his scientific knowledge. He studied Chinese and the Confucian classics and gained the respect of scholars. In addition, the Jesuit missionaries were men of science. They made significant contributions in mathematics, astronomy, and cartography. Converts helped to translate 7,000 books. A cathedral was erected in Beijing in 1650 and rebuilt in 1904. It stands on the former residence of Matteo Ricci. By and large the Jesuits were tolerated and they enjoyed success in their endeavors. In 1692 an edict of toleration was issued. The adaptations made by Ricci to Chinese traditions generated long and bitter controversies among the missionaries. An appeal was made to Rome to settle the issue, which was known as the Rites Controversy. The pope sided with those who opposed accommodation. The emperor ruled that only those missionaries who did not refuse to honor Confucius could stay in the kingdom. In spite of these difficulties, Christians still numbered about 200,000 by 1750.[70]

Imperial porcelain factories flourished under the Ming Dynasty. Areas with the necessary minerals and an abundant supply of wood for fuel became home to hundreds of thousands of craftsmen. Ceramics became a state monopoly, and jade remained a great favorite. With the exception of the royal crown, gold was not as highly valued as in other countries. The technique of building up layers of lacquer had been developed during the Sung Dynasty, and lacquer carving flourished during the Ming Dynasty. Artistic creations evoked great interest outside of China, but initially private trade was discouraged. Business with Japan could be transacted only at Ning-po, while Foochow was set aside for trade with the Philippines. Canton became the center of trade relations with Southeast Asia. Ultimately, the commercial isolation of China was the direct result of Confucian teaching.

Silk, which was much in demand, required the mass cultivation of mulberry trees so silkworms could be fed. The worms had to eat 100 pounds of mulberry leaves in order to produce 15 pounds of cocoons that ultimately yielded one pound of raw silk.

A popular insurrection and the military might of the Jurchen—who now called themselves Manchus—spelled the end of the Ming Dynasty. The Manchus had helped the Ming stop the Japanese invasion of Korea, but soon—and in spite of the Great Wall—the Manchus occupied cities such as Datong. The Chinese temporarily cooperated with the Manchus to defeat local insurgents, but once calm was restored, the Manchus stayed and behaved savagely. Beijing fell to the Manchus in 1644. The last Ming emperor strangled himself behind the Imperial Palace.

THE QING DYNASTY

Resistance continued in the south and was led by Koxinga, who finally fled to Taiwan with 900 ships and 25,000 men. He defeated the Dutch, who had taken the place of the Spanish in Taiwan. Koxinga and his son held out till 1683, when the Manchus annexed Taiwan. It took the Manchus 40 years to eliminate all opposition and to pacify the island. The Manchus numbered only one million and in order not to be absorbed, forbade mixed marriages and enforced strict segregation.

The first four emperors of the Qing Dynasty ruled for a total of 151 years. Emperor Kangxi (1662–1722) was a patron of the arts. He adopted Chinese culture and sponsored Chinese classical studies. In 1669 a treaty was signed with Russia to help secure the northern frontier. For the first time, China accepted the principle of diplomatic equality with another nation. Toward the turn of the century, the British were allowed a foothold in Canton.

In 1744, Chienlung (1736–1796) converted a palace into a Lamaist temple. This was a brilliant stroke of diplomacy. The complex is called the Lamasery of Harmony and Peace, and there are 1,134 rooms in the temple. The architecture is a combination of Manchu, Chinese, Mongolian, and Tibetan designs. The Evil-Dispatching Ceremony is held once a year, in which lamas wear exotic clothes and masks and perform religious dances.

Under Chienlung, the empire reached an enormous size and enjoyed significant influence in Nepal, Siam (Thailand), Vietnam, Korea, and other border regions. Not everyone welcomed the somewhat foreign, tantric interpretation of Buddhism. The simple idea of the happy Buddha—present or future—remained popular.

Art reached new heights, but artists—especially writers—had to be exceptionally careful because of severe censorship. The perception of the slightest criticism of the Manchu government provoked severe punishment. The easy tolerance of Christianity by Kangxi—who had been cured of malaria by Jesuits—came to an end. Christianity was branded a heterodox sect and banished in 1724. Only a handful of Jesuits were allowed to stay in China. In 1784 the first ship from the United States arrived in China and the first Protestant missionary followed. Robert Morrison of the London Mission Society arrived in 1807. He compiled the first Chinese-English dictionary and made significant contributions to education, orphanages, hospitals, and health. The missionaries were great institution builders. Growth was slow but steady. Around the turn of the twentieth century there were 2,800 missionaries and 85,000 Protestant Christians. The Catholic Church had 850 nuns and priests and 700,000 converts. A few years later, in 1906, there were 3,500 Protestant missionaries and 180,000 converts.

The death of Chienlung signaled the decline of the dynasty. Huge expenditures, pervasive corruption, and dynamic population growth created enormous problems. Peasant rebellions, often more religious than political, flared up again and again. The secret White Lotus sect fought the central government for eight years. The sect combined the worship of the eternal mother with the messianic expectation of the Maitrea Buddha.

The Taiping Rebellion broke out in 1851 and ended in 1864. It was anti-Manchu, inspired by a religious amalgam and messianic hope. The leader was the charismatic Hung Hsiu-Xiuquan, who claimed to be the younger brother of Jesus Christ. Initial success and the capture of Nanjing, which was held for 11 years, were followed by defeat. Everything unraveled because of military pressure and inefficient administration. Some 20 million victims later, the rebellion was stamped out.

Tea had arrived in Europe in 1640 and had become a national habit in England. The British had to pay for the tea with silver. Nothing else was acceptable to Chienlung.

The drain on Britain's silver was offset by the British importation of opium into China. This was a simple way to balance the books—offsetting purchase of tea for export to England by importing opium. Though opium was officially outlawed in China, the British imported it in ever-growing quantities from India. Smuggling became endemic, and China experienced a growing trade deficit and large quantities of silver left the country.

There were other issues as well, especially the treatment of foreigners in China who fell afoul of Chinese law. England was not willing to have her citizens subject to Chinese law. In one incident the Chinese government seized 20,000 cases of opium in Canton—each chest usually contained 150 pounds. This precipitated the First Opium War in 1839. By 1842 the Chinese had no option but to sign the Treaty of Nanjing. Hong Kong was ceded to Britain, and several Chinese ports were opened to trade. Other Western powers demanded similar privileges.

The supposedly illegal search by Chinese authorities of a ship sailing under the British flag precipitated the Second Opium War and led to the Treaty of Tianjin in 1859. Eleven more ports opened their doors to international trade, and missionary activity was officially sanctioned. The enforcement of the terms of this treaty provoked the last opium war and the occupation of Beijing. The Summer Palace was destroyed but subsequently rebuilt by Empress Cixi. She diverted funds designated for the Imperial fleet and used them to build the palace.

In spite of wars and uprisings, life at court remained unchanged. The emperor, confined to his palaces, was out of touch with reality. Power was in the hands of Empress Cixi. When Emperor Hsien Feng died childless in 1861, Cixi, his concubine, assumed the regency. When at age four Guangxu was chosen as the new emperor, Cixi adopted him as her son so that she could continue on as regent. The young emperor came of age in 1887 and tried to assert himself two years later. He was convinced that only the adoption of Western technology and ideas could save the empire. In 1898 the Hundred Days' Reform was proclaimed, and edicts came fast and furious from the throne in favor of reform. The movement was squashed when Cixi accused the emperor of conspiracy and confined him to his palace. The emperor was sequestered, and the conservatives triumphed. The emperor became a virtual prisoner, and Cixi retained absolute control for decades She was astute and decisive, she patronized corrupt eunuchs and misused public funds.

Anglo-French gunboat diplomacy led to concessions and treaties signed under duress, but these were "marginal disasters" compared to the rebellion in the northwest (1862–1877), Muslim uprisings in the southwest (1855–1873), the Nian movement (1853–1868), and the Taiping wars (1851–1864).

The Sino-Japanese War of 1894 erupted when Japanese and Chinese forces confronted each other in Korea. The Chinese navy was destroyed, and the admiral committed suicide. The Chinese army was also defeated. This accelerated the disintegration of China.

In 1898, Britain established stronger spheres of influence in China by getting a 99-year lease to Hong Kong's New Territories. This included exclusive rights to railroad construction and mineral resources.

Cixi led the forces of reaction. The violently antiforeign Boxer Uprising began in 1900. Cixi sided with the Boxers, who believed that magic would protect them against bullets. Cixi declared war on all foreigners. When Allied forces entered Beijing in 1901, she fled to Huaqing.

> By Imperial edict and in line with her conservative leanings, Cixi placed Confucius on the level of the gods: In view of the supreme excellence of the great sage Confucius, whose virtues equal Heaven and Earth, and make him worthy of the adoration of a myriad ages, it is the desire of her Imperial majesty the Empress Dowager Zhu Hsi, etc., that the great Sage shall in future be accorded the same ritual sacrificial Ceremonies of worship accorded Heaven and Earth, when sacrifice is paid by the Emperor.[71]

On her deathbed, Cixi selected the three-year-old nephew of Emperor Guangxu as the next and last ruler of the Qing Dynasty. P'u Yi was later known under his Imperial name of Hsuan Tung (1909–1911). On October 10, 1911, China became a republic.

MODERN PERIOD

Sun Yat-sen (1866–1925) is honored by both Nationalists and Communists as the Father of the Republic. He attended a Christian missionary school then went on to medical school. Burdened by the growing problems in China, he quit his medical practice to devote his attention to helping bring about change. In the attempt to bring about change, he turned to revolution rather than reform and founded a secret society. A plot to overthrow the Chinese government failed, and Sun Yat-sen fled to Japan.

Sun Yat-sen was one of the earliest Western-trained intellectuals in China. It was an army revolt that finally sparked the revolution, which occurred while Sun Yat-sen was out of the country. Cities and provinces declared their independence of the central government. Sun Yat-sen later returned to China and accepted the post of provisional president of the Republic of China. In a face-saving agreement, the emperor and Sun Yat-sen both resigned in 1912. Yuan Shikai became president. He believed that only dictatorship could save the country. Upon his death in 1916, warlords took control of the country for the next 12 years.

The New Culture Movement (1915–1923) aimed at the destruction of what was left of Confucian culture. In the early years of the new republic, "most of the young intellectuals…viewed [Confucianism] as a great obstacle to the transformation of China into a modern state" and believed that unless Confucianism was discarded, "social and political progress based upon 'science and democracy' would be impossible."[72] It was pointed out that Confucianism was a product of the feudal society, so its ethics were unsuitable for modern society.

A small group of Communists met in Shanghai in 1921 and founded a new party. Mao Tsedong was in attendance, but not presiding (although pictures depicting this event were made to show Mao in a leadership position). His control of the Communist party didn't occur until 1945. Mao had only a secondary-school education, but he supplemented that by reading voraciously. There was a brief period of cooperation between Communists and Nationalists, but their ideological differences could not be bridged. The next few decades were chaotic, with struggles between warlords, rampant inflation, and fighting between Communists and Nationalists or against the Japanese.

Chiang Kai-shek, who was Sun Yat-sen's successor, received his military training in both Russia and Japan. In 1928 he established the Nationalist government in Nanjing. A few years later the Nationalists controlled most of China, but the Communists survived and, in the end, the Nationalists lost the civil war. In 1949 Chiang Kai-shek and two million people fled to Taiwan. And on October 1 of 1949, the People's Republic of China was proclaimed by Mao Tsedong from the Gate of Heavenly Peace.

Orthodox Communists believed that the urban proletariat should be the vanguard of the revolution, but Mao believed that the peasants should and would fill this role. He strongly disagreed with the communist adviser from Russia on this issue. After several uprisings failed with no military victory in sight, Mao retreated and led the famous Long March of 5,000 miles to escape the armies of Chiang Kai-shek. Some 86,000 people started the journey, but only 20,000 to 30,000 reached Yan'an.

When Mao took control of the government, he initiated a phase of consolidation (1949–1952). This was followed by the Soviet phase (1953–1958) and a five-year plan. Some 20,000 trainees and 10,000 technicians received instruction in the USSR. Large "agricultural collectives" were established in China. Everything became the business of the state. The land belonged to the collectives—i.e., the state. Peasants became wage earners. Everything was turned over to the commune in return for food, clothing, shelter, medical care, and burial. Men and women were forced to live separately. Their children were taken away and placed under state care.

In the hard years of 1959–1962, as many as 30 million may have died in famines. Mao was unwilling to listen to instructions from Moscow and developed a divergent form of Communism. Links with the USSR were severed. Mao now initiated the Great Leap Forward. It was a dismal failure. To regain the initiative, he launched the Cultural Revolution.

An interparty struggle developed between Mao and Liu, who controlled the party. Mao used the Red Guards as a counterweight. Millions were sent to the countryside "to learn from peasants." The army finally suppressed the Red Guards and the party was purged. Mao died in 1976.

China has undergone dramatic changes over the last few decades, and it is too early to get a broad historical perspective of what has taken place. The story is told that someone once asked Mao Tsedong what he thought of the French Revolution of 1789. He answered that it was too early to tell. The last 100 years of Chinese history have been turbulent, and changes have been cataclysmic. It is still too early to tell what these changes mean in the long run in terms of history.

Communism and Religion

Communism looks upon all religions as mere superstitions. Once the Communists took control of China, the persecution of the Christian church was a foregone conclusion. In 1952 Communists forced all missionaries to leave and hoped to eradicate "all traces of what they deemed foreign imperialism."[73] An effort was made to separate the Roman Catholic Church from the Holy See in Rome by appointing bishops without approval from the Vatican (1958). The Vatican has not recognized the Chinese Catholic Patriotic Association or the seminaries they have sponsored. There are five regional seminaries and one was opened in Beijing fairly recently (with a contribution of $9.2 million from the government). Meanwhile the Roman Catholic Church flourishes underground.

Protestants were forced to join the Three-Self Patriotic Movement, the name of which stands for self-support, self-government, and self-propagation. The concept was originally promoted by missionaries, but was later reinterpreted in line with Communist theory and antiforeign rhetoric. All churches and congregations in China are now registered with the government and are subject to its control. Believers who find this unacceptable and refuse to practice their faith in government-registered churches are subject to persecution.[74] Although the Chinese legal system forbids any and all independent associations, underground churches are still growing rapidly. Some observers estimate that there are 30 million Christians in China, of which about half belong to underground churches. Other estimates are much higher. In Beijing alone the number of unauthorized churches has reportedly grown from 200 in 1996 to over 1,000 today. Under the present circumstances, all statistics are unreliable.

There are occasional erratic swings of the pendulum in the Communist attitude toward religion. In the years following the failed Great Leap Forward, some freedom was granted in the countryside and led to a revival of religious practices "that were believed to have been definitely eliminated by communist indoctrination."[75]

Since the late 1970s, organized religions have once again been tolerated, but only as long as they stay under the strict supervision of the state. The case of the Falun Gong is illustrative. The rise of the Falun Gong is only the latest and perhaps most visible indication of a resurgent spiritualism in China. Traditional religions, mystical movements, and cults have attracted millions of followers in recent years. The Falun Gong sect—which is marked by elements of Buddhism, Taoism, and Qigong (physical and breathing exercises)—mounted illegal mass demonstrations in 30 cities around the country in 1999. The government immediately mobilized all its resources to crush the movement. "The challenge of Falun Gong, if not overcome, could spell the end to the Communists' religious monopoly."[76] The Chinese government claims that Falun Gong is an evil cult. Such accusations could be leveled by the Chinese government against most religious organizations. It is not because of a peculiar doctrine a group might teach, but because of the effectiveness of an organization that the regime may feel threatened. A decentralized network of local groups is a form of organization that has often been used by peasant rebels in the past and by the Chinese Communist party in the 1920s and 1930s.

Confucianism and Communism

How have Communists dealt with the legacy of Confucianism? At times the sage was denounced furiously. By 1969 a campaign against Confucius was underway and, in 1974, "the systematic criticism reached unprecedented dimensions."[77] The opening statement of the Analects, "Is it not a joy to have friends come from afar"[78] was interpreted to means that "this clique draws to them counter-revolutionary accomplices and wants to expand their counter-revolutionary organization."[79] The same booklet, published in 1974, characterized Confucius's teaching as nothing but chaff without a single grain of wheat. The condemnation of Confucius coincided with the influence of the so-called Gang of Four. After the fall of this group, things changed. The party decided to appeal to a sense of patriotism and tried to instill pride in the ancient Chinese culture. In 1980 a commentary on the same Analect text claimed that "friends" meant "disciples" and presented a dissertation on education. Sometimes it was easy for the party to simply reinterpret the sayings of Confucius. Thus, "to answer hatred with goodness" should undoubtedly be restricted to party-members.

What passes as Confucianism in China today is little more than an ethical code of conduct devoid of a transcendental dimension or anything that would constitute religion. This was an easy transition to make because the supernatural dimension of Confucianism has always been weak. There was only an underlying belief in a moral heaven to which Confucius appealed from time to time. According to a visitor's guide to Taiwan, "the teachings of Confucius are not a religion. Rather, they are a guide to appropriate personal behavior and good government, and they stress the virtues of self-discipline and generosity."

People have been surprised at the ease with which Communism has triumphed in China in spite of the fact that Buddhism, Confucianism, and Daoism have all been entrenched in the country for centuries. Perhaps the transition was easy because there are parallels between Confucianism and Communism. For example:

1. For Confucius, the emperor stood at the apex of the entire structure, sole mediator between heaven and earth. In a similar fashion, Mao stood at the head of the state, the Great Helmsman, towering over everyone in solitary splendor.

2. Imperial edicts were beyond discussion; Mao's dicta brooked no contradiction.

3. The Confucian classics were basic. Mao's Little Red Book, at times almost the only one available, was "like a magic amulet."[80]

4. The common people lived in abject poverty, ignored by the elite. Under Mao the common people did not benefit more than absolutely necessary, and the top party members were the new elite.

5. An enormous bureaucracy carried out the affairs of state. The same is true under Communism. Bureaucrats had to pass tests to receive the coveted positions. The new test is party affiliation and loyalty.

6. Under the Imperial system there was no room for a loyal opposition. This inspired the formation of secret societies. Similarly, the Communist regime does not tolerate dissent. Those who disagree form underground organizations.

7. Hierarchical principles dominate in both Confucianism and Communism.

The list could easily be lengthened. The Chinese tradition was not a bulwark against Communism.

The Future of Confucianism

Since 1984 the People's Republic of China has celebrated the official birthday of Confucius (September 28). Confucianism still retains a certain amount of diffused influence that is almost elusive.[81] What is the future of Confucianism in China? That Confucianism cannot possibly be restored to its original form is beyond argument, nor is it desirable for that to happen. The emperor is no more, the ritualistic Imperial sacrifice will not be restored, and the old rigid class structures are irrevocably doomed to oblivion.

Are there elements of Confucianism that retain validity? The press has embraced the idea of "Confucian ethics." Can and should such a system be "extracted" from the overall teaching and be presented as the essence of Confucianism? What about a *Reader's Digest* version of Confucianism called *The Best of Confucius?* Are these ethics superior to other concepts even though the concept of sin is absent and

self-perfection is equated with ceremonial and ritual propriety?[82] Is the silver rule superior to the golden rule? The ethics of Confucius are similar to those proposed by Aristotle (384–322 B.C.), whose comments about the superior man could almost have been authored by Confucius—but not by a Christian. (Aristotle: "The grand objects of the superior man's ambitions are honors, but only if it is offered by distinguished persons...he has a better memory for benefits conferred than benefits received...he never hurries [or so people think] and has a deep voice and a deliberate way of speaking.")[83] Is it because of the prestige attached to the name of Confucius that some would like to maintain Confucianism as a viable alternative? Could it be due to strong nationalistic feelings or a justifiable pride in the ancient culture of China? Confucian ethics have had no perceptible effect on economic or social improvement across history and have failed to lay the proper foundation for progress and discovery. The utter unsuitability of Confucianism within the context of modern capitalism has been depicted by Max Weber in his book *The Religion of China* (1951).

Confucianism (and Daoism) sees the cosmic order as fixed and organized for the happiness of man. The wise person will adjust to the world, to its orders and conventions. Change should not be initiated. Confucianism "became a relentless canonization of tradition."[84] Wu Tien-wei agrees and observes that for the true believer "to change the situation is futile."[85] For Confucianism, faith means that "moral man is to conform himself to his life circumstances; he does not desire anything outside his position."[86] The Confucian acceptance of the world "as given" stands in sharp contrast to the Protestant rejection of the world; it is the difference between "rational adjustment" and "rational mastery," between adaptation and transformation.

Much has been written about the Confucian emphasis on the family. But the hierarchical structure in Confucianism is not desirable. The position of women across Chinese history speaks for itself. The kinship concept of Confucianism discourages both individualism and independence, and the cohesion of the family unit was largely based on the ancestor cult.[87]

POINTS OF CONTACT

CONFUCIANISM

It would perhaps be unusual to meet someone who is a traditional Confucian… at least on an exclusive basis. The fact that Confucianism is in search of wisdom allows an easy connection with the biblical book of Proverbs. Confucian ethics also offer a transition to the Sermon on the Mount. To honor one's parents is one of the Ten Commandments (Exodus 20:12), and could open the door for a Christian to initiate a conversation regarding ancestor worship. Without reviving the ancient Rites Controversy, it is important to distinguish between worship and respect or honor. Most evangelicals hold to conservative values, a territory where Confucians should feel at home.

DAOISM

Some of the same observations apply to Daoism, even more so in view of the strong emphasis on *wu-wei*, or floating along, moving only when pressure is exerted. This noninterference prevents innovation and encourages an almost limitless passivity. The sage withdraws into the life of a hermit and contemplates the universe; he is not a person of social or political achievements.[88] On the other hand, the true Daoist is at one with the *tao* and therefore irresistible. He cannot be raised or humbled, he is the highest of all creatures.[89] If the intellectual aspect is not convincing, popular Daoism hardly merits serious consideration. For an outsider Daoism seems like an extraordinary collection of superstitions. The emphasis on longevity continues. The orientation is this-worldly, and Buddhism fills the void as far as life after death is concerned.

Meditation is a point of contact with Daoism (Genesis 24:63; Luke 10:39,42). The Psalms celebrate the works of God in creation and history (Psalm 1:1; 77:12; 143:5; cf. Psalms 8; 19; 103; 107). God's works and activity culminate in his coming, or the incarnation. The Daoist's interest in physical immortality (breathing techniques, diets, the elixir of life) is an opportunity to share about the quality of the Christian life both physical and spiritual, temporal and eternal. There is a difference between harmony with an impersonal *tao* and walking in conscious fellowship with a personal God.

BUDDHISM

There are easy points of contact between the Eightfold Path of Buddhism and the Bible's Sermon on the Mount. The Mahayana Buddhist emphasis on compassion has superficial parallels with the idea of Christian love, and Jesus stressed the lengths to which such love ought to go: "A disciple was to love others not just as he loved himself, but in the same measure as Christ had loved him, with selfless self-sacrifice even unto death."[90]

Buddhism seeks salvation through a *bodhisattva,* a mediator, and so does Christianity. The Buddhist idea that one can escape karma and receive someone else's accumulated merits is consistent with the biblical idea of atonement through substitution, or redemption through Christ. Questions about the nature of the sin that has to be forgiven and about ethics can be raised. If all is an illusion, are not value judgments about good and evil also "unreal"?

It is not out of place for a Christian to address the contradictions inherent in Buddhism. The soul does not exist, nor does the self, yet transmigration and reincarnation are maintained. Tantric Buddhism, especially the Prasangika view, speaks of phenomena as empty...but they do exist.

They do not exist in and of themselves inherently. They possess the characteristics of existing, but are dependent on other factors, causes, and conditions. Also, Buddhist ethics lead to an "ultimate reality" that simply "is" (if anything can be said to exist)—a nirvana that is neither good nor evil. Is emptiness the supreme value? Is it a value at all? In what sense? Can emptiness serve as a foundation for ethics? Is this the best hope for mankind?

It is a breath of fresh air to turn to the Scriptures and to be assured that "truth is seen in him" (1 John 2:8), the truth in the sense "in which the real differs from the unreal, the substance from the shadow."[91] In Hebrew the word translated "truth" designates something solid, rock-like, permanent, unshakable, eternal. So let us speak the truth in love and proclaim Christ, who is the way, the truth, and the life.

HINDUISM, JAINISM, and SIKHISM

*Set thy heart on me alone, and give me thy under-
standing: thou shalt in truth live in me hereafter. But if
thou art unable to set thy mind on me, then seek to reach
me by the practice of Yoga concentration. If thou art not
able to practice concentration, consecrate all thy work
to me. By mere doing actions in my service thou shalt
attain perfection. And if even this thou art not able to
do, then take refuge in devotion to me and surrender to
me the fruit of all thy work—with the selfless devotion
of a humble heart. For concentration is better than mere
practice, and meditation is better than concentration; but
higher than meditation is the surrender in love of the fruit
of one's actions, for on surrender follows peace.*

BAGHAVAD GITA 12:8-12

HINDUISM, JAINISM, *and* SIKHISM

THE SHAPE OF INDIA is like a huge inverted triangle reaching from the Himalayas to the Indian Ocean. The Himalayas are a formidable barrier in the north, 200 miles wide and 1,500 miles long. The Indus and the Ganga (or Ganges) rivers run through the Himalayas and empty into the Indian Ocean. Great civilizations have always developed around major rivers such as the Nile in Egypt, the Euphrates and Tigris in Mesopotamia, and the Yangtze and the Yellow Rivers in China. India has been no exception.

SOCIAL AND RELIGIOUS DEVELOPMENT OF ANCIENT INDIA

THE INDUS VALLEY, THROUGH which the Indus and Ganges flow, is the cradle of civilization in India. It goes back to 2,500 B.C. and lasted a thousand years. The earliest beginnings go further back, but are impossible to trace.

The first surprise is that while this civilization in the Indus Valley covered a very large area, both the pottery styles and weights and measures were the same throughout the area. This makes it logical to assume there was a centralized administration. The crops raised here included wheat, barley, and peas. The horse was known, but does not seem to have played

a major role. For transportation, the people used a two-wheeled oxcart.

The other surprise is the urban character of this culture. City planning was detailed right down to the size of the bricks. The two major cities are Mohenjo-daro and Harappa, which are 400 miles apart.

Mohenjo-daro ("mound of the dead") is laid out in a grid pattern and was probably home to no less than 30,000 people. Some streets were as much as 33 feet wide. A remarkable underground drainage system with large sewers kept the streets sanitary. Some houses were two and even three stories high, complete with wells and bathrooms connected by a system of drains to sewers running beneath the main streets. Construction was of mud-baked bricks but occasionally sun-dried bricks were used, as in Mesopotamia. Because stone was not used, archaeological finds are meager. Nevertheless, more than 100 ancient sites have been identified. We know that there were frequent commercial contacts with Sumer (Mesopotamia). The seals and beads are similar, and there is other evidence of extensive contacts between these two old civilizations.

In Mohenjo-daro a large bath eight feet deep, 23 feet wide, and 39 feet long has been discovered. It was made watertight with bitumen. The surrounding rooms seem to indicate it was used for ritual washings. The largest building in Mohenjo-daro was 230 feet long and 78 feet wide. It was perhaps an administrative or priestly center. We don't know much about the religion of the people, but we do have a few clues. Bodies were buried with copper mirrors, cosmetics, and pots of food intended to serve the dead in the voyage to the afterlife. Skeletal evidence suggests different types of people lived here, including people from the Mediterranean and Mongol regions.

A large quantity of seals, made of soapstone, has been unearthed—over 4,000 seals and tablets to date. The seals are beautifully executed and depict fish, birds, elongated water buffaloes, sheep, goats, pigs, elephants, and crocodiles. The most popular seal features a bull with one horn; the second horn is concealed by the first.

Some seals may portray Siva (or a prototype of Siva) as lord of the beasts. These seals show a three-faced figure sitting cross-legged and surrounded by a tiger and an elephant. A few phallic emblems have been found at Harappa, also pointing to Siva worship. The presence of figurines indicates that the mother-goddess was also worshipped.

The brief inscriptions that appear on seals have not been deciphered. There are never more than 27 symbols, and usually there are less than ten. The artistic creations are remarkable.

How did this ancient civilization develop? Perhaps the Sumerians played a minor role, but it was an impetus at best and the specific development was in accordance with the people's own rhythm.[1] More puzzling is the question why the civilization declined. In Mohenjo-daro the later seals are made from clay instead of soapstone and the pottery is clumsy. City planning had seemingly been abandoned. Strangely enough, archaeologists have not found evidence of such a decline at Harappa. Eight times destroyed by floods it was always recreated, brick for brick, each house in exactly the same location—and the dimension of the bricks never changed.

The Indus Valley civilization came to an abrupt end c. 1500 B.C. Historians once assumed this was due to invasions by the Indo-Europeans, but this theory has been abandoned. No one knows what precipitated the decline. Could it be a climate change? Was there a flood due to erosion caused by loggers denuding the hills in search of firewood? Was it dwindling water resources or an earthquake triggering a flood, or a combination of factors? The best theory might be a change in the course of the Indus River, which had nourished this civilization and made irrigation possible. Only the city of Lothal survived, complete with a long wharf controlled by a sluice gate. It seems that the city was rebuilt three times.

Some features of this grand civilization were transmitted to subsequent generations, including perhaps the worship of Siva, who is not mentioned in the Rig Veda. We have to wait for the decipherment of the language before we can know more.

THE ARYANS
Their Background

In ancient times, for centuries invaders entered India through the Khyber Pass in the northwest part of the country. For long periods of time, wave upon wave of Indo-European migrants entered the Indus Valley. These waves were not really invasions, but rather, migrations that began around 1500 B.C. and continued for about 600 years. These people called themselves Aryans, meaning "noble." Their original home was somewhere between the Caspian and the

Black Seas and the Russian steppes. From there they spread out in different directions. Some moved toward Greece, Rome, and Germany, and others went to Media and Persia, or modern Iran. The words *Aryan* and *Iran* have a common origin. These Indo-Europeans included several ethnic groups, among them the Mitanni, whose kings and gods had Indo-European names; the Kassites, who established a loose hegemony over Mesopotamia in 1525 B.C.; and the Sogdians, the Bactrians, and the Hittites (who appear in the Bible) with their large kingdom in what is now Turkey. They were all part of the Indo-European migration. In a peace treaty signed about 1400 B.C. between the king of Mitanni and the king of the Hittites, the witness of the gods Indra and Varuna was invoked. These gods played significant roles in the Vedas, the sacred books of India. This is a clear indication that these gods came to India with the Aryans.

The word *Aryan* is not a racial term and does not designate a Caucasian of non-Jewish descent. The myth of a homogeneous pure Aryan race—not to mention the superiority of that race—is just that: a myth, which was exploited by Hitler with horrible results. Even today there are still small groups in the United States and elsewhere calling themselves the Aryan Nation. But *Aryan* is a linguistic term! These people spoke Sanskrit and probably included several ethnic groups who all spoke the same language.

We know next to nothing about the Aryans. They left no cities, no monuments or statues, no seals or images, no temples. They had no written language, but they did have a rich oral tradition written down much later and known as the Vedic tradition. Their own legends portray them as drinking, gambling, and fighting like Homeric heroes. They lived a nomadic existence on the high plateau of Persia and became fierce warriors. They adopted patterns and learned crafts from the peoples whom they subjugated and accepted many elements of other superior civilizations. The urban civilization of the Indus Valley was certainly more advanced. The Aryans became cattle breeders and agriculturists, and by 500 B.C. they were plowing with eight oxen as a team.

Their Caste System

The Indo-European newcomers disliked the darker color of the indigenous people, a mixture of Dravidians and Harappans. The Aryans developed a system called *varna,* in which people were differentiated by color. This, in turn, developed into the caste system. Four distinct castes emerged: the *Brahmins* or priests, an intellectual aristocracy; the *Kshatriyas,* or rulers and warrior nobility; the *Vaisyas,* the common people such as farmers, workers, and merchants; and finally the *Sudras,* who were servants engaged in menial work.

Only the first three castes included Indo-Europeans. The *Sudras* were the indigenous people. Regardless of the initial intention, castes came to determine every aspect of social life. Once the lines were drawn, the system was rigid especially because one's caste was hereditary.

Cattle were important to this civilization. "The farmer prayed for increase of cattle; the warrior expected cattle as booty; the priest was rewarded for his services with cattle."[2]

The Laws of Manu may have been composed around the beginning of our era, but they embody older traditions. We read that "in order to protect the universe

He, the most resplendent one, assigned separate (duties and) occupations to those who sprang from his mouth (Brahmins), arms (Kshatriya), thighs (Vaisya) and feet (Sudra)."[3] There are thousands of rules for each class. For example, "He who does not (worship) standing in the morning, nor sitting in the evening, shall be excluded just like a Sudra, from all the duties and rights of an Aryan."[4] The details in these laws are extraordinary and cover minute aspects of everyday life. There is a distinct set of rules for each caste that governs food, marriage, and occupation. A Brahmin's meal will procure long life "if he eats facing east; fame, if he turns south, prosperity if he turns west and truthfulness if he faces east."[5] It was a given that a child would follow the vocation of the family into which he was born. This is part of *dharma.*[6] *Dharma* is the cosmic rhythm, the social order and moral law, the all-embracing traditional order. As Will Durant observes, "to be a Hindu meant not so much to accept a creed as to take a place in the caste system, and to accept the *dharma* or duties attaching to that place by ancient tradition and regulation."[7]

The *jati* or occupational classifications are not as rigid as those that govern the choice of a marriage partner. Today discrimination based on caste may be illegal, but it remains a significant factor in the choices people make, especially in marriage.

Across the centuries adjustments have been made, but the fundamental system or concept has remained intact. The small evolutionary stages of development from the four original groups to the contemporary multiplicity of castes are shrouded in obscurity. Today there are 3,000 castes, which are largely based on occupation (*jati*). In an effort to elevate the status of and confer some dignity on the untouchables, Ghandi called them *harijans,* or children of God.

For reason of ritual purity it was quite impossible for a Brahmin to travel outside of India. Contact with foreigners was virtually impossible for the upper classes. This concept of "pollution" inhibited trade.

Apart from color prejudice, the Aryans realized that they would always be in a minority position regardless of their military triumphs. To keep their identity intact, it was essential for them to remain aloof from the indigenous people. Those who belonged to the top three castes, Indo-Europeans all, underwent a special initiation rite, were invested with the sacred thread, and were called twice-born. The Brahmins were exempt from taxes.

It was only when ritual was invested with magic power that priests or Brahmins gained preeminence and became the top caste. Previously the warriors, or *Kshatriyas,* had occupied the most exalted rank.

In a bizarre way the caste system may have taught tolerance. If a member of another caste was isolated or exluded, he was not automatically despised. His food could not be enjoyed, but the different eating habits of the castes could perhaps teach acceptance and tolerance. Social contact was forbidden. Caste boundaries were inflexible and it was impossible to rise to a higher level. The caste system blocked the upward mobility of people and no doubt much talent want unrecognized and unused as a result.

It has been suggested that the concept of caste may have been an integrating factor in Indian society. Outsiders with different customs did not become part of a melting pot but rather, lived side by side with others and occupied a well-defined place in society.

But after everything that is conceivably positive has been said about the caste system, it cannot be denied that the system had a negative influence on personal and social development. The Bhagavad Gita takes the caste system for granted. "The four orders arose from me, in justice to their natures and their works," and again, "The works of Brahmins, Kshatriyas, Vaisyas and Sudras are different, in harmony with the three powers of their born nature."[8]

Their Religion
The Vedic Religion

The Indo-Europeans brought the Vedic religion with them when they came to India. Some indigenous deities (such as Siva) were incorporated into the region's worship system. Indo-European culture gradually merged with the Indus Valley civilization and produced a new level of sophistication.

The Vedas represent an early stage of Indian religion. We find no evidence of temples or images. The Vedas describe a sacrificial religion with a multiplicity of gods. Some Vedic hymns express a spirit of philosophical inquiry. Rightly celebrated is the creation hymn (a title, not part of the original), which is short enough to reproduce it in its entirety.

1. Then [in the beginning] was not no-existent [something that did not yet exist, but had a latent potentiality of existence] nor existent: there was no realm of air, no sky beyond it.

   What covered in? And where? And what gave shelter? Was water there, unfathomed depth of water?

2. Death was not then, nor was there aught immortal: no sign was there, the day's and night's divider.

That One Thin [the primordial substance out of which everything developed], breathless, breathed by its own nature: Apart from it was nothing whatsoever.

3. Darkness there was: at first concealed in darkness this All was indiscriminate chaos. All that existed then was void and formless: by the great power of Warmth [the principle explaining movement, life and thought] was born that Unit.

4. Thereafter rose Desire in the beginning, Desire, the primal seed and germ of Spirit. Sages who searched with their heart's thought discovered the existent's kinship in the non-existent.

5. Transversely was their severing line extended [a line drawn by the ancient seer to separate the lower and the upper world and so produce duality out of unity]: what was above it then, and what below it?

   There were begetters, there were mighty forces, free action here and energy up yonder.

6. Who verily knows and who can here declare it, whence it was born and whence came this creation?

   The Gods are later than this world's production. Who knows then whence it first came into being?

7. He, the first origin of this creation, whether he formed it all or did not form it, whose eye controls this world in highest heaven, he verily knows it, or perhaps he knows not.[9]

The hymns were believed to be the result of revelations received by intuition by *rishis* or seers, as a sort of cosmic vibration turned into verbal forms by the recipients. The Vedic religion involved the worship of the forces of nature, such as the rain, the wind, and the thunder. They were gradually personified. Surya, the sun god, is addressed in a hymn in the following words: "His bright rays bear him up aloft, the God who knoweth all that lives, Surya, that all may look on him.... Surya, God among the Gods, the light that is most excellent."[10] One of the most important gods in the vedic pantheon is Indra, a mighty warrior who, with his thunderbolt (the lightning), breaks up the clouds and brings the rain. He is a powerful dragon-slayer, a god who rides his chariot and is armed with mighty arrows. He is the image of the perfect warrior. Indra is also a god who enjoys feasting, drinking, gambling, and dancing, making him a faithful echo of his worshippers, the conquering Aryans.[11]

In the Rig Veda more hymns are addressed to Indra and Agni than any other gods. Indra is said to live on Mount Meru, the center of the earth. In the post-vedic period Indra fell from the front rank of the gods and was given a lower status. He is inferior to the holy triad of Brahman, Vishnu, and Siva.[12]

Savitar is the "sustainer of the heaven, lord of the whole world's life, the Sage, he puts on his golden-colored mail.... Savitar has stretched out his arms to cherish life, producing with his rays and lulling all that moves."[13] He is the principle of motion, which causes the sun to shine and the wind to circulate. "Send us this day, God Savitar, prosperity with progeny, drive thou the evil dream away."[14] It is a familiar request, as is the following addressed to Varuna:

1. Let me not yet, King Varuna, enter into the house of clay: Have mercy, spare me, Mighty Lord.

2. When, Thunderer! I move along tremulous like a wind-blown skin, have mercy, spare me, Mighty Lord.

3. O Bright and Powerful God, through want of strength I erred and went astray: Have mercy, spare me, Mighty Lord....

4. O Varuna, whatever the offence may be which we as men commit against the heavenly host, when through our want of thought we violate thy laws, punish us not, O God, for that iniquity.[15]

Agni, the fire god, has many shapes. He lives in heaven and on earth. On earth, flames issue from his mouth to lick up the *ghee* (butter oil) offered by the priests. On earth he is the mouth of the gods, the fire on the sacred altar lifting the sacrifice to heaven. He is the link between the gods and men. On earth he is the guest of every hearth and protector of every home. In the end it is Agni who accepts the body as an offering through the flames of the funeral pyre. Agni also dwells in heaven. In the form of lightning he carries messages between heaven and earth. He is also the flame at the heart of the sun.

Soma, a plant, was an essential part of the sacrifice. It was the drink of the gods, a symbol of immortality. Soma was born from the churning of the sea, one of the few occasions when the gods and demons cooperated. The line separating demons from the gods is not very clear.[16]

The hymns of the Rig Veda were transmitted orally and committed to writing at approximately 1000 B.C. The word *Veda* means knowledge, especially sacred knowledge. The most important of the Vedic collection is the Rig Veda, with 1,028 hymns. Some of the hymns go back to 1300 B.C.

Faithful oral transmission continued for hundreds of years till the text was finalized in its present form around 600 B.C.[17] Greater and lesser gods appear, but no monotheism. The word *henotheism* has been coined to indicate that at the moment of prayer the worshipper is focused on one deity to the exclusion of all others and attributes supreme power to the god he faces, but this focus might be turned to another god altogether at another time.

> They call him Indra, Mitra, Varuna, Agni, and he is heavenly nobly-winged Garutman [the celestial bird of the sun]. To what is One, sages give many a title: they call it Agni, Yama, Martarisvan [all these names, says the poet, are names of one and the same Divine Being, the One Supreme Spirit under various manifestations].[18]

At this point the Rig Veda anticipates the later development found in the Upanishads. The same note is heard elsewhere: "One All is Lord of what is fixed and moving, that walks, that flies, this multiform creation."[19]

Aside from the hymns of praise in the Rig Veda there are also the hymns for priestly chanting in the Sama Veda, the technical instruction regarding liturgy and sacrifices in the Yaju Veda, and finally, much later, a book filled with mantras, spells, and blessings and curses called the Atharva Veda. A mantra is a formula transmitted from the guru to the pupil to evoke the presence of a particular deity. The student has to keep it secret and say it silently as a part of his prayers. Somehow spiritual consequences were thought to flow from the recitation of mantras.[20]

The sacred syllable *om* is the supreme sound, "the Word of Eternity,"[21] the syllable from which all creation arises. It "goes back to late Vedic times. Many ritual specialists came to believe that the power of the Vedic hymns resided not so much in their specific content but in the very sounds that they communicated. Many Hindus even today believe that sound and vibration are at the very core of what makes up the universe. The sounds of different syllables become the various powers that make up the world around us.

Grammarians claim that

> AU is the broadest and most rounded utterance the voice can make; the "M" is the most narrow and closed. In the process of pronouncing the syllable, the whole range of articulate sound is (at least in theory) encompassed. Since all sounds are to be found in OM, it follows that all words are included and, if all words are included, then all truth and wisdom, and in particular the words of the Vedas, are included as well. For that reason, OM is used at the beginning of sacrifices, meditation, prayers, and before performing yoga. Chanting OM as a mantra is believed to bring about mental and emotional calm, to overcome obstacles, and to enhance understanding.[22]

Brahmanism

Vedic worship was simple. Food and drinks were offered to the gods on a square altar. The square is considered the perfect shape because the circle implies motion (Buddhists, by the way, prefer the circle). Brahmanism was the result of a long evolution. Philosophical questions were raised—although occasionally anticipated in the Rig Veda. Who is the greatest god? Who is the real Creator? Perhaps the gods are only the manifestations of an eternal self-existent cosmic being, the Brahman.

Slowly the priests developed complex rituals and insisted that the slightest deviation from these rituals might create cosmic disorder. Even the number of bricks used to build an altar was fixed, and not one brick could be out of line. The priests determined exactly how much *ghee* or clarified butter should be poured into the fire, how much soma juice was necessary, and which position of the hands was appropriate. They taught that touching the sacrificial goat in the wrong spot could ruin everything. The sacrifice was now supposed to be a reenactment of cosmic acts to prevent chaos. In this fashion the leading role of the aristocracy was usurped by the priests, who had the power to bestow divinity through the magic of ritual. The priests or Brahmins came to amass more and more power. "In the ritual texts, it is the sacrifice itself—not the devas [the gods]—that is the central concern. The sacrifice can bring immortality and even divine status."[23] The rituals associated with the sacrifice gradually increased in complexity, and some required more than a dozen priests. The rules became so complicated that only accredited specialists could perform the rituals.

Asceticism also gained ground as a method to discover truth outside of the Vedic texts. The Vedas continued to be revered as the most sacred literature of India, but interpretation moved from the literal to the spiritual. A whole new literature developed, the Upanishads. Here, sacrifices are rejected as people search for enlightenment, perhaps through esoteric knowledge. This is neatly summed up in the following text:

> Thinking sacrifice and merit is
> the chiefest thing,

Naught better do they know—
deluded!

Having had enjoyment on the top of the heaven won by good works

They re-enter this world, or a lower.[24]

Several of the Bible's Old Testament prophets voice a similar sentiment. The stress is no longer on the correct performance of ritual, but on the proper disposition. It is significant that this more thoughtful literature appeared somewhere between 600 and 400 B.C. Karl Jaspers, the Swiss philosopher, called this era the axial period in world history. The sixth century B.C. saw "a tidal wave of revolt against the priestcraft of the ancient world. This wave shattered the power of the old religions, though their cults continued to exist as backwaters for centuries."[25] A deepening spirituality was sweeping across the entire world. The great Jewish prophets, Isaiah at the beginning of the period and Jeremiah toward the end, were active in Judea. In Greece Anaximander and Heraclitus proclaimed their philosophies; in China, Confucius the Sage and perhaps Lao Tzu the mystic emerged; and in India, Mahavira and Buddha hoped to reform Hinduism.

Upanishads means "sitting close or opposite to" a teacher to understand the meaning of secret teaching. Important ideas were developed and later dominated Hinduism. The new insight is that all is Brahman, that he is the one spiritual reality behind all phenomena and appearances. All else is delusion, error, or *maya* (illusion). The religious man seeks release from the wheel of life that he may fade into the world soul. Brahman (not to be confused with the god Brahma) is the one mind behind the many.

The almost sacred formula is *tat tvam asi,* or "You [the individual] are that [the universal essence]." The Upanishads proclaim the unity of the Brahman and the *atman,* the oneness of the Absolute and of the self. They are one and the same. Monism is at the heart of the Upanishads. There is only one all-embracing reality, one ultimate substance, the Brahman. The many Vedic deities are seen as "refractions of the One." It is remarkable that "some of the Upanishads see Brahman as a personal Lord."[26] Definitions are impossible because Brahman is beyond all thought and imagination.

Currently there is a gap between the *atman* (the self) and the Brahman—a gap that can be bridged through knowledge and self-discipline. Even in this life it is possible to experience union with the Brahman, although the Absolute remains undefined. Union is achieved through ecstasy, meditation, and asceticism. The ultimate goal is the merging of the soul into Brahman, like the merging of a drop of water into the ocean. What prevents the union is karma, an obstruction that prevents people from reaching Brahman. Karma is the cosmic law of sowing and reaping, of cause and effect. It is not a law made by man or god. The gods themselves are subject to karma. Clearly they cannot help. Karma is impersonal and impartial. The soul carries accumulated karma from incarnation to incarnation till finally the correct knowledge, disciplined behavior, and good deeds have the preponderance over evil. Once the fruit of the evil karma has come to fruition and no new evil karma has accumulated, nothing stands in the way of union with Brahman—without ritual or priests.

Although at first sight the Upanishads seem to extinguish the role of the priests, the Upanishads were quickly accepted and integrated into the existing brahmanic system. The priests suggested that the message of the Upanishads was only for ascetics and only control the end of life—once all the other responsibilities toward family and priests had been fulfilled. Life, according to the priests, was organized into four distinct segments: 1) the student, at the home of his teacher, studies the Vedas. The student must honor the guru as if he were his father. 2) At about age 25, the student returns to the parental home to marry and set up a household. His role is to earn wealth, enjoy his wife, and follow the practice of *dharma,* the moral law or cosmic order. 3) The third stage demands an inner detachment from all things. In this state of mind the student may continue to live with his family, ideally in a secluded place. 4) Finally the student accepts the role of a homeless wanderer, totally detached from everything terrestrial and liberated from ordinary life. In the words of Sharma, "learn the principles of morality and vocation in the first twenty-five years of your life, earn wealth and enjoy sensuous pleasures in the next twenty-five years. Thereafter lead a virtuous life in a hermitage for another twenty-five years, and then seek liberation."[27]

Inextricably linked with the idea of karma is the concept of reincarnation. The idea that souls are reborn in a new body after death, be it human or animal, became popular after 600 B.C. and is a cardinal tenet of Hinduism. But how is it possible to improve karma when one is incarnate in an animal, since improvement comes through self-knowledge? Is this possible on an animal level? The answer offered by Hindus is that new series of increasingly complex bodies are formed until at last a human one is attained. Up to that point, the growth is automatic. Once graduated into a human body, this automatic ascent ends. With freedom comes responsibility, and the law of cause and effect operates once again. "The mechanism that ties these new acquisitions together is the law of karma." [28] The specific form of reincarnation is determined by karma—the law of cause and effect. What is done in this life determines the next. Both karma and reincarnation help to explain the present. The well-being of the wicked simply means that they live off "karma capital" acquired at some point in the past. The suffering of the present time is nothing but the karmic fruit of a prior life. How can I complain about my terrible situation when it is due to the law of karma, my past bad behavior? Even heaven and hell are temporary stages. Ultimately, all will be absorbed into Brahman and individuality will be extinguished. For Hindus, nirvana is this merging into the Brahman. The final state cannot be "adequately described within the constraints of human language." [29] No one knows how long it might take to be reincarnated after death.

Two famous epics, the Mahabharata and the Ramayana, belong to the ancient Indo-Aryan tradition. Supposedly they relate events that took place between 1000 and 700 B.C., but their present form is from the fifth century A.D.

The Mahabharata has been called the longest poem in the world because the original Sanskrit version is supposed to have had 100,000 verses. It tells the story of the struggle between the Kauravas and the Pandavas, descendants of two brothers, one blind and therefore unfit to rule. Jealousies and intrigues at court forced the Pandavas into exile, where they formed alliances with kings and Krishna (an incarnation of Vishnu). They expected to take possession of their kingdom and were disappointed when it was equally divided. In a dice game the Pandavas lost everything and returned to exile for 12 years. The final battle between the two contestants lasted 18 days. Thousands were killed, and only the Pandavas survived. The Bhagavad Gita was inserted into the Mahabharata at some point in the first four centuries of our era.

The Ramayana has only 24,000 couplets and relates the story of Rama, the seventh incarnation of Vishnu. The poem legitimized hereditary kingship. Just before the coronation of Rama, his stepmother intrigues successfully to have him exiled for 14 years. Sita, his wife, accompanies him voluntarily. Ravana, the demon king of Sri Lanka, hears about the beauty of Sita and abducts her in his aerial chariot while Rama is in pursuit of a magical gazelle. The search for Sita begins and, with the help of an army of monkeys, a bridge is raised between the mainland and Sri Lanka. The ten-headed Ravana was killed and Sita reclaimed. The monkey chief was Hanuman, worshipped today as a god. Once reunited, Sita had to prove her chastity. She mounted a funeral pyre, and the fire failed to consume her.

Both the Mahabharata and the Ramayana show a constant interchange between the gods and the central characters. The final editing of these poems corresponds to the emergence of Hinduism.

Hinduism

In response to the challenge of Buddhism and Jainism to both Vedism and Brahmanism, Hinduism was more clearly formulated. Hinduism is the most distinguishing feature of India, but difficult to define. "No single approach is able to enunciate its basic concept and philosophy...it is a mixture of sects, cults and doctrines which have had a profound effect on Indian culture."[30] There is no founder, and no single set of beliefs. Different and even contradictory views of God are embraced. Some Hindus do not believe in any god but claim to be Hindus and are accepted as such. For many Hinduism is a way of life. "A Hindu may be identified as one who does not deny being one."[31] According to the same Hindu author, it is an "ethnic religion"[32] because it always involves caste. There is no missionary activity. In spite of the lack of definition, some basic ideas are shared by most Hindus: 1) the high regard for the Vedas, 2) the belief in karma and, consequently, in 3) reincarnation and 4) the caste system. Some think of Hinduism in terms of the three essential elements of yoga or self-training, *puja* or worship, and sacrifice.

Centuries elapsed between the creation of the Vedic writings and the formation of Hinduism as we know it. In the course of time, some deities changed their function. Some gained popularity at the expense of others. Brahmin priests became the sole mediators between the gods and men, and the deities became increasingly remote. Only the two great epics narrowed the gap. The need for devotion to the gods promoted the desire for images, which appeared on the scene in the fifth century B.C. Finally a new triad emerged: Brahma, Vishnu, and Siva. Through time, Brahma has never enjoyed the popularity of Vishnu and Siva.

Vishnu is the source and the protector of the universe and works for the welfare of the world. Whenever the world is threatened by evil, Vishnu appears. There have been ten incarnations or avatars of Vishnu to save the world.

Vishnu is blue in color, clothed in yellow, and has at least four hands. He is depicted as holding a wheel, a conch shell, a mace, and a lotus. The wheel represents the universal mind, the powers of creation and destruction. The conch shell symbolizes the origin of things through its connection with water. The mace is a symbol of authority. And the lotus, which has six petals, represents control over the six seasons. Vishnu's open upraised palm is a *mudra,* a gesture expressing reassurance.

Vishnu has taken on the attributes of several other deities. His avatars (incarnations) include 1) a fish, 2) a tortoise, 3) a boar, 4) Narashima, a man-lion, 5) a dwarf, 6) Parashurama, a warrior hero, 7) Rama, and 8) Krishna. The last incarnation was 9) Buddha. One is yet to come, 10) Kalkin, who will ride a white horse and annihilate the wicked—a messianic idea perhaps borrowed from Buddhism or Christianity. When his work is done he will be reabsorbed into Vishnu…and a new cycle will begin. Time does not move from a beginning (creation) toward an end (the new creation), but is cyclical, moving in everlasting cycles without beginning or end.

Vishnu took the form of a fish (*matsya*) to warn Manu of the flood, which destroyed mankind. Only Manu survived because he built a boat, landed on a mountain peak, and gave birth to the human race. When the earth was submerged, a demon took control till Vishnu as a boar (*varaha*) set the earth free. The tortoise (*kurma*) is connected with the episode of the "churning of the sea." A snake was used as a rope, and gods and demons cooperated and churned the sea of milk to produce the liquid of immortality. When the mountain used as a churning stick threatened to collapse, Vishnu became a tortoise to stabilize the mountain, and the gods continued to churn. As a boar, Vishnu descended into the bottom of the ocean to rescue the earth. As half-man, half-lion (Narashima), Vishnu fought a demon. By accepting Buddha as an avatar of Vishnu, Buddhism was effectively incorporated into Hinduism. "Buddhism as a mass religion did in some sense turn to Hindu belief."[33]

Krishna is the most significant of the ten incarnations and this avatar is surrounded by countless myths. He is portrayed as a mighty hero and dragon slayer, and the sound of his flute attracts countless maidens. The Mahabharata makes him an adviser of the Pandavas and, in the middle of the battle, the famous Bhagavad Gita is introduced. It is a philosophical conversation between Arjuna, the charioteer, and Krishna. In the Gita, Arjuna becomes the soul of man, and Krishna the charioteer of the soul.[34]

Arjuna faces his kinsmen in both lines of battle and is unwilling to kill the members of his own clan. He is told, "think thou also of thy duty and do not waver," a duty that is in line with God's eternal plan. Salvation comes not through ritual, sacrifice, or knowledge, but rather, the first step is obedience to duty. "Do your duty, even if it be humble, rather than another's even if it be great."[35]

Only he who surrenders all desires is free from all ties, who "neither rejoices nor sorrows if fortune is good or ill, his is a serene wisdom." The necessity to abandon all desire is stressed again and again. "Kill the desire, the powerful enemy of the soul." Expect nothing; rely on nothing. Without vain hope such a man "is the master of his soul, he surrenders all he has, only his body works: he is free from sin. In the end he is one with God and goes unto God."[36] But

the final truth of the Gita is that the central value is *bhakti,* or devotion to God.

The path is not easy, and meditation (yoga) is one way. "Let him find a place that is pure and a seat that is restful, neither too high nor too low, with sacred grass and a skin and a cloth thereon." On that seat practice yoga for the purification of the soul "with upright body, head and neck, which rest still and move not; with inner gaze which is not restless, but rests still between the eyebrows."[37]

Karma Yoga or action-discipline is another path toward *moksii,* or liberation from the cycle of birth and rebirth. The action has to be dispassionate to prevent the occurrence of negative karma. Focus must be on the deed, with indifference toward success or failure. If killing is involved, it should be without passion, hatred, or malice.

The better path is devotion, or *bhakti-yoga.* "The greatest of all Yogis is he who with all his soul has faith, and he who with all his soul loves me." Again, "only by love can men see me, and know me, and come unto me" and "he who loves me shall not perish."[38]

If the total absence of desire is not achieved in this life, then, upon reincarnation, "he begins his new life with the wisdom of the former life; and he begins to strive again, ever onwards toward perfection."[39]

Finally the point is made repeatedly that all is *maya*—appearance, illusion, and even death. "The wise grieve not for those who live; and they grieve not for those who die—for life and death shall pass away...the unreal (physical life and death) never is: the Real (the soul) never is not."[40] The soul is eternal and never ceases to exist. The Gita, the crown jewel of sacred literature, teaches a full-fledged theism. Instead of knowledge as the path to God, *bhakti,* or loving devotion, is the key—a devotion that is centered on one supreme person, God. *Bhakti* love is the bond of union between man and God.

The consort of Vishnu is Lakshmi, the popular goddess of wealth and fortune. She is usually portrayed with four arms with gold coins dropping from her hands. Not surprisingly she is usually painted in bright, golden colors. She was born from the churning of the ocean.

A deity of great significance is Siva, who was perhaps already worshipped in the days of the Indus Valley civilization. If so, that would make him one of the few non-Aryan gods. His conveyance is *nandi,* a bull. Siva represents destructive forces, but creation and destruction are said to be indissolubly connected, and Siva is usually represented as a phallic symbol, which represents pro-creation. The image of the dancing Siva is very popular. He dances to the cosmic tune of formation, preservation, destruction, and release—that is, reintegration into the Absolute. He is poised inside a *mandala* surrounded by a ring of cosmic fire. One leg crushes the back of an evil dwarf of darkness, and the other leg, which is raised, launches the universe on yet another cycle. We are now in the fourth and last age or cycle, the most degenerate one. This age lasts for 432,000 earth years and, according to tradition, started in 3102 B.C.[41] It is Siva's activity that is the source of movement in the universe—both of good and evil, and of bliss and misery. Everything is cyclical and moves in endless repetition.

Siva's consort is Parvati, who has many different names, including Uma (gracious), Bhairavi (terrible), Kali (black), and Durga (inaccessible)—all different aspects of the same goddess. As Uma she practices asceticism, as Durga she uses her eight arms to destroy demons and takes frightful shapes, and as Kali she is terrifying. Kali is frequently represented with a necklace made of skulls.

Among the most popular gods is Ganesha, who is easily identified by his elephant head. His vehicle is the rat. He stood guard when his mother bathed and refused to give access to Siva, who retaliated by cutting off his head. When Siva saw the distress of his consort Parvati, he promised to replace the head with that of the first creature he encountered, which happened to be an elephant. An image of Ganesha is found in virtually every household because he is said to remove obstacles and grant wisdom.

Hanuman, the monkey god and great friend of Rama, is revered throughout India. The monkey face sits atop a strong human body. In the Ramayana, his loyalty and inventiveness is beyond question.

The followers of Vishnu, by far the largest group of Hindus, are called Vaishnavites. They are easily recognized by the vertical lines on their forehead. The red dot is a reminder of the radiance of Lakshmi, a consort of Vishnu. One Vaishnavite school maintains the identity of the soul even in the bliss of union with god, a truly monotheistic position.[42]

The followers of Siva, more than 200 million, are called Shaivaites (or Saivas) and are distinguished by two or three horizontal lines on their forehead. An additional dot indicates that in the opinion of that person, the god he worships is the supreme godhead. No one knows how many gods are worshipped in India, but devotees fall in a few basic categories.

Monism teaches that all things are one in their innermost essence. The goal of salvation is to escape the cycle of rebirth and to merge into the one absolute reality. Brahman—not to be confused with Brahma, one of the gods—teaches that everything that exists is an aspect of Brahman and, to some, the many gods are only different expressions of this one reality. The return of the soul to oneness is compared to a drop absorbed in the ocean. The result is a peculiar combination of being and nonbeing that defies all description. According to Ramanuja, "You are that" only means that Brahman and you are inseparable (not identical).

Henotheism is perhaps practiced (unconsciously) by many who worship preeminently one of the many gods, be it Vishnu or Siva, Ganesha or Hanuman. The worship is not exclusive. The reality of other deities is accepted. There are no doubt monotheists whose primary guide would be the Gita, whose teaching regarding loving God and the love of God presupposes a personal God.

The structure of Hindu temples is pretty much the same throughout India. They are designed for individual and not congregational worship. There is no seating. People come to view the image of the god. Some devotees visit the temple of their choice daily. The deity is housed in the innermost sanctuary with enough floor space for devotees to walk around the statue, a practice that is mandatory after prayers. The deity is treated like a person and properly awakened, bathed, fed (later the food is given to worshippers), and dressed. For the most part the gods are easy to identify—either by their color or the objects held in their hands (for instance, Krishna is blue and plays the flute). The gods are honored with gifts of flowers and fruit. As far as the image of the deity is concerned, the divine spirit remains in the icon as long as the devotees wish.[43]

A spire sits atop the innermost temple room, except in the south, where a richly ornate spire adorns the entrance porch that leads to the main hall. A vestibule connects the main hall with the innermost sanctuary. The square rooms are an echo of the (square) cosmos. Upon entering the temple, worshippers ring a bell suspended from the ceiling. Devotees then approach the priests, who apply the *tilak* (red or yellow paste) to the center of the forehead. The *tilak* is a symbol of the search for the opening of the third eye.

Small shrines are found in many homes, and pilgrimages to sacred temples, cities, mountains, rivers, and trees are not uncommon. There are literally thousands of places that claim a special status and become centers of pilgrimage.

The Laws of Manu proclaim, "He who does not (worship) standing in the morning, nor sitting in the evening, shall be excluded, just like a Sudra (lowest class), from all the duties and rights of an Aryan...let him stand during the morning twilight, muttering *Savitri* until the sun appears but (let him recite it), seated, in the evening until the constellations can be seen distinctly."[44] The *Savitri* is the golden text, the holiest mantra: "May we attain that excellent glory of Savitar, the God: So may he may stimulate our prayers."[45] Savitar is a solar deity. Even as the sun awakens the world, so Savitar awakens the spirit of man. This brief prayer is recited daily, every morning and evening.

Jainism

Mahavira, the founder of Jainism, was roughly contemporary with Buddha. Legends surround him just as they do Buddha.

Prior to his birth his mother saw 14 apparitions of favorable omens in her dreams, including an elephant, a bull, the moon, and other objects. The embryo was transferred from one womb to another. The night he was born even the demons rained gold, silver pearls, and diamonds on the palace. Mahavira was born a prince, married Yasoda, and had a daughter. At age 30 he left everything behind for 12 years of asceticism and then reached illumination and became a Jina, a hero, an overcomer of evil and misery. He preached for 30 years and finally died of self-imposed starvation at age 72. Except for fasting unto death, all other methods of voluntarily chosen death are forbidden, even in case of incurable diseases.

Jains believe that Mahavira was preceded by 24 Tirthankaras, or saints who have reached perfection, whose ideas Mahavira simply articulated. He was the last of the 24 saints who were named *jina,* or conqueror, because they broke the karma chain. *Jina* is the name for the "supreme souls who are totally free from all attachment, etc. that defile the soul."[46] Mahavira accepted the traditional teaching concerning the cycle of birth and rebirth determined by karma.

Salvation, the escape from karma, is possible through penance and disciplined conduct. Mahavira's view of karma is unusual. It exists in the form of fine material particles, atoms of a special type, attracted toward and bound with the soul. The karma makes an impression upon the soul and leaves a trace. Upon death the karma continues to exist there (in conjunction with the soul) but remains inactive till the next birth or one of the following ones. On the principle that you must reap what you have sown, the karmas are dissociated from the soul only when they have yielded their fruits completely. Everything has to come to fruition.

Good deeds do not cancel the law of the karma, and it is important not to accumulate new traces of karma so that the soul can finally find release from the cycle of incarnations. How can this be achieved? Through purification. It is conceded that impure states have not started at some point in time but are beginningless. Soul and karma were bound together from time immemorial. This leads inevitably to the conclusion that there are those who are not capable of attaining liberation.[47]

Mahavira taught that everything in the universe, material or otherwise, has an indestructible soul. This includes trees, rocks, and running water. There are different types of souls—some are "gross earthbound souls."[48] The soul needs cleansing, and that purification can be achieved through extreme asceticism—even to the point of voluntary suicide, which may be the only way to escape the endless cycle of rebirth. The soul is indestructible and once it is liberated and no longer reincarnated, it reaches its full potential and attains godhood.[49] Every soul is omniscient "but due to defilements it loses this knowledge; through emancipation its original omniscience is regained."[50] At the same time, all individuality is lost because all liberated souls are absolutely alike.[51] The worship of this "god" is not to please him, but to purify one's self. Jains are atheists regardless of the usage of the word *god* or *gods.* For Jains, the universe is infinite and was not created by a deity. Prayer is directed to *arihantes* who serve as examples because they have reached illumination and will not be reincarnated.

To the Jains, the doctrine of nonviolence is central and is carried to an extraordinary extreme. From the Jain perspective it is easy to understand the ban on eating by night because of the fear they might eat flying insects.[52] One significant sect of Jains refused to wear clothes in order to avoid the accidental killing of insects. This meticulous concern for everything living made it impossible for Jains to be farmers, for there are too many insects whose deaths cannot be avoided while farming. Even the mere act of walking can cause the death of an ant, and ideally the devotee uses a feather duster and sweeps the path before him to avoid this possibility. This can hardly be expected of the average layman, and therefore the ideal is monkhood, the only path to salvation. Because farming was out of the question, the best occupation for Jains was trade and commerce or handling financial transactions. Combined with the Jains' austere approach to life, wealth was easily and almost inevitably generated.

Jains belong to one of four groups: monks, nuns, laymen, or laywomen. Everyone has to take at least the five vows: nonviolence, truthfulness, nonstealing, chastity, and nonpossession—i.e., detachment. Abstinence from meat is a given, but the avoidance of onions, potatoes, garlic, and other such vegetables because they grow underground is perhaps unexpected.

Jainism challenged the ritualism of Brahmanism and indicated a new road to escape rebirth. It was a threat to the established religion because salvation could be attained without priest or sacrifice. Since both Jainism and Buddhism share the same cultural background of Hinduism, there are obvious points of contact. There are also some basic differences. Buddha denied the permanence and even the existence of the soul. According to Buddha, the soul too, along with everything else, is only *maya,* or illusion. Man is only bodily events, perceptions, feelings, dispositions, and states of consciousness.

Like so many other religions, Jainism has established categories and classifications. For instance, there are four main birth-types: human existence, animal existence, celestial existence, and infernal existence.[53] There are six obligatory duties, and 14 stages of spiritual development.[54] The teachings that had originally been transmitted orally were finally committed to writing in the third century B.C. while the final version was edited around the fifth century A.D.

Buddhism

Buddha launched the other great protest movement at about the same time as Mahavira. It was an age of intellectual ferment—the age of Socrates and Plato, Confucius and Lao-Tsu, Mahavira and Buddha. Buddha's princely education did not keep him from observing sickness (a diseased man, stricken with fever), old age (a toothless man, bent over), death (a corpse wrapped in cloth), and finally, a holy beggar (a monk, serenely begging). He left the royal palace and followed a regime of extreme asceticism in an attempt to find answers to the riddles of life. But his body and mind deteriorated, and he sought a middle way. He almost died in these fruitless efforts, but a village girl fed him and he revived.

Legends about Buddha's life abound. At Gaya he vowed not to rise till he had found enlightenment. After 49 days of sitting in yogic meditation under a banyan tree, he achieved illumination and became the Buddha. He remained silent for another 49 days, then preached his first sermon in a deer park, not far from Banares, and spoke in the vernacular. He proclaimed a middle path, rejecting both extreme asceticism and self-indulgence. He came away with the knowledge that life is suffering, and suffering is caused by desire. Suffering is eliminated when desire is extinguished, and desire can be eliminated by following the Eightfold Path, including right speech, right conduct, and right effort.

Buddha professed no knowledge regarding gods, worship, offerings, prayers, priests, or rituals. Later the Mahayana school of Buddhism deified him. The salvation he proposed was devoid of ritual and relied only upon self-effort. It excluded priests and was open to all, regardless of caste. For Buddha, salvation is the cessation of being…although (and paradoxically) that is not necessarily the same as the extinction of being. Buddha refused to speculate on the difference. He was in search of nirvana, literally a "blowing out." Definition is impossible; the final state cannot "be adequately described within the constraints of human language."[55]

The teachings of Buddha were transmitted orally, including his famous first sermon at the deer park. It was only much later that the sayings of Buddha were collected and documented. One such collection is the Dhammapada, consisting of 423 verses in Pali, although the earliest oral and written accounts are in Sanskrit. The Dhammapada originated in Sri Lanka, where Buddhism arrived in the third century B.C. These are supposedly utterances from the Buddha on 305 different occasions. The text is organized by topics and divided into 26 chapters. In a number of passages the text is uncertain and some of the textual problems "are likely to remain unsolved."[56]

Theoretically it is true that Buddhism did not limit the offer of salvation, but for all practical purposes it was impossible for the untrained to follow the intricacies of Buddhist speculation. It was the simplified version of a totally different Buddhism that became popular, complete with *bodhisattvas,* or saviors, and a real paradise.

Initially there were no representations of Buddha. Around the beginning of our era, temples and images appeared, and there were different styles. Mathura used local sandstone to create a smiling Buddha whose robe was draped to leave the right shoulder bare, but Buddha himself appeared in a full-bodied form. Further west a Greco-Buddhist style developed, influenced by statues of Apollo. Here the Buddha is youthful, with wavy hair and a monastic robe that covers both shoulders and has the classical folds of a Roman toga. The same style can be found as far away as Korea and Japan. The Buddha statue came with 32 signs, including the *ushnisha,* the cranial bump symbolic of wisdom or omniscience (disguised by the topknot), and the *urna,* the curl of hair between the eyebrows, a symbol of Buddha's renunciation. Sri Lanka represented Buddha with a serious face and a heavy build.

The Hellenistic Influence

Thanks to Alexander the Great and his brief conquest of India, artistic elements from Greece were combined with those of India to create a unique style. And later, more than just art was affected. At the beginning of our era, Iranian and Hellenistic influences modified Buddhism even more. New elements were incorporated and the appeal of Buddhism was broadened to make it a religion of universal salvation. Previous incarnations and a savior to come, the Maitreya Buddha, completed the picture. Relics became popular. Mahayana Buddhism evolved. Adepts of Mahayana claim that the (secret) teaching goes back to the Buddha himself.

Originally Buddhism required self-effort, but in Mahayana Buddhism the devotee can expect the help of divine powers. At first Buddhism emphasized wisdom and said that ignorance, not sin, is the great evil. Now the stress falls on compassion, in stark contrast with the idea of eliminating all desire. Initially the demands of Buddhism were such that only monks had a realistic chance of reaching enlightenment, but now the door is open to all. At first the ideal person was the *arhat*, the saint who had reached nirvana with the help of Buddha, who alone had reached nirvana without help. But that raised a question: Was not the desire to attain nirvana ultimately selfish? Was it not better to put off the idea of personal extinction and stay in the world to help others? Did not Buddha stay in the world after his enlightenment?

The new ideal is the *bodhisattva*, one who has attained enlightenment and stands at the threshold of nirvana but due to compassion does not escape but decides to help others achieve enlightenment. It has sometimes been suggested that this idea was due to the impact of Christianity.[57]

According to some traditions, Buddha died because he was so polite that he accepted a piece of pork even though he knew full well that it was spoiled. Upon his death he requested that his body be cremated and the remains enshrined in a series of *stupas* (funerary mounds) that would serve as focal points for worship and meditation. Soon the *stupas* were embellished with carved railings and gateways and evolved into full-fledged pagodas in China, Japan, and Korea.

Although Buddha accepted the notions of karma, reincarnation, and transmigration, he maintained that in transmigration nothing passes from one life to the next because everything is soulless.[58] Contrary to Hinduism, Buddha did not believe in the existence of an eternal soul.

The three cornerstones of Mahayana Buddhism are 1) the person of the Buddha, 2) the teaching of the Buddha, and 3) the Buddhist order. Members of the order had to be over 20 years of age and vow to observe ten precepts. Other Buddhists are committed only to the first five. No food after noon, sleeping on a mat, and other rules guide the order.

The Tantric Influence

Tantric Buddhism replaces asceticism with total self-indulgence and sensual pleasure. Liberation is reached through enjoyment. Since the world could not subsist without the reproductive principle, eroticism and sensuality are part of the process of reaching nirvana. Initiates may use forbidden practices to break taboos and rise beyond the bounds of morality. The breaking of a taboo is seen as a ritual denial of caste distinctions. The door is wide open to every conceivable abuse in the pursuit to achieve "liberation." By contrast, in the Bible, the apostle Paul denounces those who might conclude, "Let us do evil that good may result."[59]

One key person to embrace Buddhism was King Bimbisara of the Magadha Empire in ancient India. Bimbisara gained political preeminence when he controlled Kashi (Banaras) and Kosala (east of Banaras) through warfare and marriage alliances. He was assassinated by his son,

Ajatashatru, a fate shared by at least five kings of Mathura. When Buddha died his relics came under the control of Mathura, and the capital, Rajagriha, hosted the first Buddhist council.

INTERNAL AND FOREIGN POWERS IN ANCIENT INDIA

In 327 b.c. Alexander the Great appeared in India. From the standpoint of Indian history, his incursion was only a footnote. It has been said that Alexander's great achievement was not invading India, but getting there, for by this time, his armies had covered 15,000 miles. After a hard-fought battle, Alexander defeated Poros of the Punjab and installed him as a vassal. Now he faced Nana, who had inherited the large kingdom of Maghada. Nana had assembled an army of 200,000 infantry, 20,000 cavalry, innumerable chariots, and thousands of war elephants. Although the numbers were surely exaggerated, still, a substantial army faced Alexander and his men, who were homesick, weary, and perhaps intimidated. They would go no further, and forced Alexander to go back. The last of Alexander's generals left India in 317 b.c. Only small garrisons stayed behind, but this was enough for Hellenistic ideas to percolate throughout the Indus Valley and impact the arts.

Chandragupta Maurya (321–c. 298 b.c.) defeated the Nandas and came to occupy the capital of the kingdom. This began the Mauryan Dynasty, and Chandragupta reigned for 24 years. He is credited with having an enormous army and driving out the last Greek garrisons. In 305 he defeated Seleucus Nicator (358[?]–281 b.c.), who

had inherited part of Alexander's Empire and established the Seleucid dynasty. Though Nicator had been defeated, he maintained a friendly relationship with Chandragupta. A treaty yielded parts of Afghanistan and areas of modern Pakistan to Chandragupta, who furnished 500 elephants to Nicator. The Mauryan Empire "was probably the most extensive ever forged by an Indian dynasty."[60] As Chandragupta drew near the end of his life, he became an ardent follower of Jainism, left his throne, and deliberately ended his life by starvation.

Chandragupta was followed by Bindusura, but it was Ashoka (c. 268–233 b.c.) who was by far the most prominent king of the Mauryan Dynasty. His empire extended from Afghanistan (northwest) to Assam (northeast) and from the Himalayas in the north to Mysore in the south. A military victory in Orissa came at a considerable loss of life. The carnage changed Ashoka's outlook. He foreswore violence and embraced certain Buddhist principles. These were proclaimed in long inscriptions on cliff faces or hemispheric granite rocks or high sandstone pillars. These 30-foot-high pillars, scattered across the empire, were made from tan-colored sandstone. The pillars were crowned by four lions that pointed to the four cardinal directions—perhaps an indication of Persian influence. In the inscriptions Ashoka advocated *dhamma,* a sense of duty of good conduct and decency. *Dhamma* should not be automatically equated with Buddhism. Although *dhamma* was distinctly Buddhist, it had also became fairly traditional in India and the word itself is not enough to determine the nature of the religious beliefs of the king.

The idea that Ashoka became a Buddhist monk is legendary. In fact, it is difficult to know to what degree one may speak of a "conversion" to Buddhism. For one thing, it was perfectly normal for people in ancient India to combine different religious viewpoints. None were held exclusively. Perhaps it is significant that the inscriptions never mentioned Buddha or the Eightfold Path, an essential ingredient of Buddhism. Perhaps Ashoka used Buddhist ideas as a unifying factor in his kingdom. We have insufficient information for reaching definite conclusions. In line with Buddhism and Jainism, Ashoka opposed animal sacrifices and abstained from meat, but uniformity was not imposed. He banned animal sacrifices in the capital and regulated the slaughter of animals for food. Generally speaking, tolerance prevailed. On the other hand, Ashoka did not disband or reduce the army nor abolish the death penalty.

Buddhism's influence brought changes to funeral rites in India. Bodies were now cremated. Ashoka opened seven of the eight stupas that had been erected over the relics of the Buddha and redistributed the relics across his kingdom. A special style of Buddhist architecture also began to emerge.

Buddhist clergy met in Patalipura and settled the Pali canon. Pali was derived from Sanskrit and was popular in the days of Buddha. It became the sacred language of much of Buddhist scripture. Missionaries were sent to Sri Lanka, Thailand, and elsewhere, and Indian culture penetrated Indonesia and Cambodia. Grandiose Buddhist structures still dot the landscape in countries adjacent to India. Most famous are the temples of Angkor. Most of them are dedicated to Hindu deities, but King Jayavarman VII adopted Mahayana Buddhism and built the city of Angkor Thom. One of the temples is the Bayon, second only to the Angkor Wat. The bas-reliefs incorporate over 11,000 figures. There are vivid sculptures of the Cambodian navy defeating Champa, complete with people who were drowning and devoured by crocodiles. Other reliefs depict cock fighting, a seller using fraudulent scales, a kong-fu scene, chess players, sumo wrestlers, and Chinese acrobats. Angkor Thom, also built by Jayavarman VII, features a 600-foot-wide moat and walls 24 feet high and 30 feet wide.

Borobodur, another Mahayana monument, was built between 780 and 860 in Central Java, Indonesia. It is one of the great monuments of civilization. The temple features more than 500 statues of Buddha. Around the base, 160 panels illustrate Buddha's discourse on cause and effect. On another level the life of Buddha is carved on 1,240 bas-reliefs—from his pre-existing state to his first sermon, complete with all the legendary materials. Laid end to end, the carvings cover almost 3,300 yards. The temple is built like a pyramid, and the three lower terraces are square while the top three are circular. Borobodur was part of a large temple complex, and some of the ruins—including those of Mendut and Pawon—are still standing.

In India itself, Buddhism had only a temporary impact. With the death of Ashoka began a period of decline. Fifty years after the demise of Ashoka, the empire collapsed and became politically fragmented. The last occupant of the throne was killed by his own general. In the aftermath the Sunga Dynasty (185–73 B.C.) took control of the central and eastern parts of India. With the Sunga came a strong reaction against Buddhism. For example, the horse sacrifice was reinstituted. Ruler followed ruler in quick succession. The south became detached from the empire and foreigners controlled areas of the northwest. In the following centuries, Indian history "plummets once again to a murky obscurity."[61] Though there was much instability in India, we do know that the Roman emperor Augustus (31 B.C.–A.D. 14) received an Indian embassy. Trade flourished with exports of teak, sandalwood, ivory tusks, jasper, carnelian, onyx, pearls, pepper, and indigo.

It is possible that Christianity entered India in the first century by way of trading ships from the West.[62] St. Thomas is said to have arrived in Malabar in the year A.D. 52 and traveled east till he reached the Madras area, where he preached and was martyred in A.D. 68. "The Syrian church survives in strength in the region of Malabar and may well have been founded in the first century A.D."[63] In view of the active trade between the Middle East and India, it would be surprising if Christians had not arrived in India in the first century.

One of the more interesting personalities to emerge in this period is King Kanishka of the Kushan Empire. The Kushans were probably descendents of a Mongolian tribe. The Yueh-chih people of China were forced into this vast area because of the pressure exerted by the Huns. Kanishka was both a poet and an excellent military leader and under his rule, the empire stretched from the border of Afghanistan through northern India, to Varanasi. His only defeat was at the hands of the Chalukyas, when Kanishka tried to expand the empire toward the south of India. The king is celebrated by Buddhists as a key personality along with Ashoka and Harsha, but this may be due to the fact that he presided over the Fourth Buddhist Council. It was then that Mahayana and Hinayana split.

It is said that Buddhism spread through Central Asia thanks to Kanishka. In reality it was an age of syncretism and Zoroastrian and Indian deities were honored along with Buddha and Greek gods. Kushan was also in a unique geographic position to facilitate trade of goods and ideas between east and west. It was at about this time that different artistic schools emerged—the Ghandara school with Greco-Buddhist sculpture, and the Mathura school with Hindu art. Unfortunately we cannot be certain about the exact dates of Kanishka's rule, but it was anywhere between A.D. 125 and 225, and most scholars are inclined to accept the early date.

THE CLASSICAL PERIOD OF INDIA

THE GUPTA ERA (A.D. 320–467) has sometimes been called the classical period of Indian history. The first ruler was Chandragupta I (A.D. c. 320–335), who is not to be confused with a ruler of the same name under the Mauryan Dynasty who ruled 650 years earlier. Chandragupta created an alliance via marriage with the powerful Licchavi tribe to the northeast. The kingdom greatly expanded under Sumudragupta (c. 335–375), who called himself the Conqueror of the Four Quarters of the Earth. His conquests, however, were superficial. Usually the kings he defeated were reinstated and their armies withdrawn. There was no annexation of new lands, and no permanent occupation. The basic structures of the conquered lands were left intact. As long as Sumudragupta's supremacy was acknowledged, he was satisfied with a nominal submission from other lands.

Chandragupta II (376–c. 415) was a great patron of the arts. Sanskrit saw a remarkable and unexpected revival. This was no doubt an indication of the strong resurgence of Brahmanism and of the influence of the Brahmin priesthood. A collection of fables called the *Panchatantra* later inspired *The Book of One Thousand and One Nights* and perhaps storytellers Jean de La Fontaine and Giovanni Boccachio. Among the more remarkable compositions are plays by Kalidasa, who has been called the Sanskrit Shakespeare. Unfortunately, few of the plays have survived.

Nalanda, a university located southeast of Patna, became a center for the study of Buddhist texts and is often spoken of as the oldest university in the world. A Chinese traveler, Hieun-Tsang, visited Nalanda in 630 and mentions the meditation and lecture halls, numerous stupas, and the library. The center was lavishly endowed by the Pallava Dynasty.

Gupta civilization reached a high point during this era. Aryabhatta (c. 499) calculated the length of the solar year with remarkable precision (at 365.35 days). The decimal system was perfected when the zero was invented. The medical arts had progressed to the point that cataracts were removed from people's eyes. A medical treatise was found that described surgical instruments, caesarian sections, and guidelines for reconnecting a severed ear, a nose, or fingers.

During the Gupta era, divorce in the higher classes became almost impossible. Ordinary people were usually monogamous. Only kings, chiefs, and the rich were polygamous. In law, women were treated as minors. They could take up a religious life but could not officiate as priests. Widows could not remarry (even if they were widowed in childhood). Some had to sleep on the ground, eat one meal a day, and never attend family festivals.

Agriculture flourished. Wheat and barley grew in the north, rice and millet elsewhere. Peasants used shallow wooden ploughs pulled by oxen, used sickles to harvest, and oxen for threshing. The winnowing was effected by simply tossing the crop in the wind.

The Gupta worshipped Vishnu, but this did not prevent them from offering Vedic sacrifices or sponsoring Buddhist establishments, although Buddhist monasteries were usually located far from the population centers.

The peak of the Gupta Empire was reached under Kumaragupta (c. 415–455)—who performed the horse sacrifice—and his successor, Skandagupta (c. 455–470). The latter repulsed an invasion of the White Huns who came down from Kabul and invaded the Gupta Empire. Later a secondary Hun chief settled in Ghandara (c. 520) and the local population was massacred ruthlessly. The chief persecuted Buddhists and destroyed monasteries and the splendid artworks of the Greco-Buddhist civilization that had developed. It was the end of the Gupta.

THE POST-CLASSICAL PERIOD OF INDIA

THE PALLAVA KINGDOM BECAME the next dominant power. They were in the southeast part of India, and their center was west of Madras. Their origin is uncertain, and the dynastic founder was Simhavarman (c. 550). The high point of the kingdom was reached between 600 and 650. It was the last dynasty to patronize Buddhism. It was during this era that an extraordinary bas-relief was created, called the "Penance of Arjuna." The sculpted relief is 96 feet long and 43 feet high. Gods and goddesses converge on the central cleft (representing the Ganges River) adorned by *nagas,* or sacred snakes.

The Pallava established maritime links with Southeast Asia. They were even involved in the dynastic struggles of Sri Lanka and established diplomatic ties with China. But the kingdom was weakened by incessant struggles with the Chalukyas, one of the many regional kingdoms that prospered from 600 to 750 in the south part of India. Toward 900 the Pallava finally succumbed to their previous vassals and southern neighbors, the Cholas.

It was the Tamil Dynasty that flourished mostly during the tenth and eleventh centuries—the first successful dynasty since the Guptas. One of their greatest kings was Rajaraja (985), whose royal temple staffed 850 people, included 400 dancing girls, 67 musicians, and 174 priests, not to mention watchmen, treasurers, astrologers, and lamp bearers. The Cholas established diplomatic relations with China, Burma, and Malaysia. They took possession of the Maldives, occupied parts of Sri Lanka, and raided areas of Malaysia and Indonesia. On land their territory expanded to the northeast. They vanquished the eastern Chalukyas and took possession of the heartland of the Pallava, reaching Madras and beyond. They were unable to move further north, where the western Chalukyas offered firm resistance. Ultimately they were overwhelmed by the rise of the Pandyas to the south and the Hoysala.

Through all this, much of Southeast Asia was indianized. Ancient Sanskrit inscriptions have been found as far away as Champa (now the coast of South and Central Vietnam), Funan (Cambodia), Borneo (Indonesia), Thailand, and Malaysia.

The spread of Indian influence is also evident by the grand ruins of the Khmer temples in Cambodia. Angkor Wat, one of the largest religious buildings in the world, is in Cambodia and was dedicated to Vishnu. It was intended to serve as a funerary temple for King Suryavarman II (c. 1113–1152), the builder of this gigantic mausoleum/temple. The main entrance is 770 feet wide; the central sanctuary is 1309 feet high. One of the galleries of Angkor Wat features well-preserved and realistic reliefs depicting scenes from the epic poems the Ramayana and the Mahabharata.

For a while a Hindu dynasty controlled Central Java in Indonesia. Not far from Borobodur are the ruins of the Prambanam temple complex, which was built in 856 to honor Brahman, Vishnu, and Siva. In Thailand, Hinayana Buddhism prevails today, and there are still vestiges of Hinduism as well—such as the Erawan Shrine at a busy intersection in downtown Bangkok, dedicated to Brahma in 1956. Hinduism also still plays a role in court ceremonies.

The name *Harsha* has gained considerable luster as a champion of Buddhism. When King Grahavarman died childless, the nobles invited Harsha to the throne (606–647). He was 16 at the time. Thanks to his military ability, his small state became a large kingdom. The capital was established at Kanauj (643). In spite of his considerable administrative responsibilities, he managed to write several plays. He received recognition from China when the T'ang dynasty sent an embassy to his court. His kingdom was as large as the old Gupta dominion and shared identical weaknesses. Centralization was not feasible. The kingdom was only a loose federation, not a unified nation. The mostly feudal structure collapsed almost immediately upon his death, especially because he had no heirs. His appearance on the political horizon was as brilliant and evanescent as a comet.

In the ninth century, the philosopher Sankara (788–820) produced his commentaries on the Upanishads. He is one of the best-known expositors of the monistic philosophy, advocating the worship of an impersonal Brahman. This Brahman is beyond good and evil, and beyond all distinctions. "Hindu thinkers were inclined to make a big leap in their reasoning; they assume that *the existence of the Universal Self is known directly from the existence of the individual self.*"[64] The conclusion that Brahman exists because I exist is a huge leap of faith and an interesting example of retrospective reasoning, which goes from the effect back to the cause. I am, therefore One is. I might just as well reason that I am a person; therefore, God is a personal God. A philosophical abstraction is hardly an appropriate object for worship, and most people prefer a concrete deity. If the highest goal of ethics is a dissolving into the Brahman, who is beyond all words and beyond all silence, how can one conclude—as most Indians do—that Ultimate Reality is spiritual?

If the entire world is *maya,* or illusion—if all knowledge is nothing but an inconclusive illusion—then we have little incentive to understand the world.

Sankara saw the need to reclaim the essence of Hinduism and to strip away the accretions that had accumulated over the centuries. He advocated asceticism and

introduced monasticism into Hinduism. His goal was to reclaim the essence of the ancient Vedic teaching.

Ramanuja (c. 1100) was a Vaishnava philosopher who disagreed with Sankara that knowledge was the way to salvation. He taught that devotion, to give oneself entirely up to God, was the path to salvation. Ramanuja's god is one full of love and compassion, one who demanded a personal relationship, not a merging into the Absolute. Some of his followers taught that god himself selects those who will be saved. He is definitely involved in the process of salvation.

By the beginning of the twelfth century, the Cholas of southern India were frequently invaded by the Hoysalas of Mysore, India. In spite of the Hoysalas' intermittent warfare with the Cholas, the Hoysala king Narasimha III was able to erect the magnificent Keshava Temple around 1268. The construction took 40 years. The temple complex was built on a raised platform, and the ground plan is star-shaped so that the walls offer more space for sculpture. Narrow panels run horizontally around the temple walls, and intricate carvings represent episodes from the Ramayana. Animal and floral patterns abound, and dancers compete with battle scenes. Sculptures also present Vishnu in his many incarnations.

INCURSIONS AND INVASIONS INTO INDIA

THE MUSLIM ERA

One of the first Muslim incursions into India took place in 711. It was successful for the Muslims and ignored by the Indians.

Three hundred years later, Mahmud of Ghazni (998–1030) of Afghanistan raided northern India 16 times. Thanesar was defeated (1014), Mathura was sacked (1019), and Fort Somnath was destroyed (1025), and every raid yielded enormous spoils. Even Kanauj, the capital city, was not spared. Mahmud returned with 53,000 slaves and 350 elephants,[65] and carted away literally tons of gold and silver from Hindu temples. These military incursions were really raids and did not lead to occupation or annexation. Mahmud used the booty to maintain a distinguished court, to enlarge his army, and to patronize men of learning such as Firdausi, author of the Shah Namah, an epic celebrating Persian heroes, and al-Biruni, a historian and man of science.

When the Seljuks (recent converts to Islam from Central Asia) conquered Khorasan (now in northern Iran), the capital was moved from Ghazni in Afghanistan to Lahore (now in Pakistan). Part of India was now definitely lost. Indian dynasties had disregarded the raids and the Islamization of the strategic Indian borderlands and never united to face the intruder. Now it was too late. Mahmud, the sultan of the kingdom of Ghazna (998–1030), laid the foundation for the Muslim conquest of India. But the Ghaznavites had a rather short history in India. About 1150 a clan of Afghans rose against the Ghaznavid sultans. Muhammed of Ghor dethroned the last of the Ghaznavids. The new lords of the territory streamed across the Gomal Pass (a mountain pass on the border of Afghanistan) to annex the Punjab, and several Indian rulers acknowledged Muhammed's suzerainty. But Muhammed wanted to do more than just looting raids and thought in terms of permanent conquest. He now faced a strong army of Indian Rajputs who had temporarily put their differences aside to fight against Muhammed. They defeated Muhammed at the Battle of Tarain in 1191, but a year later, another battle was fought at the same place and the victory went to Muhammed. With only 12,000 horsemen, Muhammed achieved a crushing victory and took possession of Delhi. When he was assassinated in 1206, Qtub-ud-din, known as Aibak, became the sultan of Delhi. He had been appointed by Muhammed as successor and risen in the ranks till the former slave had attained the rank of general. Aibak razed Hindu temples and replaced them with Muslim mosques. Stones from 27 Jain and Hindu temples were incorporated into the Qutab Minar, a grandiose tower 240 feet high that was meant to proclaim the power of Islam. Geometric Muslim designs replaced Hindu statuary.

Aibak also conquered Bihar, far to the east, and had Buddhist monasteries destroyed and monks slaughtered. Buddhism was virtually extinguished in India. The invading Muslim armies were victorious because of superior military tactics and greater mobility. Their horses were easier to maneuver than the cumbersome Indian elephants. The Muslim army was also propelled by religious fervor. Aibak chose Delhi as the new capital for his autocratic government.

In spite of the Muslim conquest, the bulk of the population of India remained Hindu. At the most, one out of five people embraced Islam. The lower castes were attracted by a religion that proclaimed the equality of all believers before God. In time the boundaries between these two religions became more flexible. The Islamic sufis—mystics in search of oneness with God—adopted some Hindu ceremonies and yoga practices. Pilgrimage to sufi tombs became popular. The small Muslim military elite left the basic social structure of India intact. Even the caste system remained unchanged. But the status of the Hindu masses had to be defined. From the Muslim perspective, Hindus were idol worshippers, and the penalty for idolatry was death. Some kind of compromise had to be worked out. Hindus were granted the status of *dhimmis,* which was originally reserved for Jews and Christians, or "the people of the book," who believe in only one God. To include Hindus in this category was an extraordinary step. The Hanafi school of Islamic interpretation argued that a tax was an acceptable alternative to death. Still, in spite of these accommodations, friction between Hindus and Muslims was unavoidable.

Mongol Raiders

Mongol raiders appeared in India during the first half of the thirteenth century. They camped under the walls of Delhi for two months, then returned to Afghanistan. In 1304 another incursion with 40,000 horsemen ravaged the area north of Lahore, but fierce opposition and domestic trouble forced them to return to Central Asia in 1306. Occasionally an energetic Muslim leader emerged briefly, such as Ala-ud-din (1296–1316), who even conquered the great Rajput fortress of Chitor and killed 30,000, only to lose it later on.

In approximately 1322, Odoric of Pordenone, a Franciscan, sailed from Padua, Italy to western India. In Bombay he collected the remains of several Franciscans who had suffered martyrdom and took them to China for burial. Odoric visited the Malabar Coast (southwest coast of India) and went on to St. Thome or Myl-

apore, where he discovered a large Christian colony. He also went to Sri Lanka, Indonesia, and China, and wrote extensively about his travels.

Tughluq Dynasty

The Tughluq Dynasty seized power under Muhammad bin Tughluq (1325–1351), but the conquest was superficial. To celebrate his victories, engineers erected a pavilion, only to watch it collapse upon the conqueror at the first tread of an elephant. By the time of his death, most of the territory acquired was lost. Tughluq's cruelty stimulated opposition, and centralization was difficult because of the lack of communication. There were few good roads, and runners handled the postal service.

When Timur (or Tamerlane) conquered Delhi in 1398, the Hindu population was massacred or enslaved. Timur left within one year after destroying everything and establishing nothing, leaving the country in the grip of total anarchy.[66] Timur left India with 20,000 pack animals loaded with Indian treasures.

Fifty years later, in 1451, the Lodi from Afghanistan seized control of India, beginning the Lodi Dynasty. They developed a distinct architectural style and built square or octagonal tombs in open gardens. The tomb of Sikander Lodi was the first built with a double dome. The inner dome is a relatively low hemispheric ceiling that allowed the architect to raise the outer dome to a great height without causing the interior to be disproportionally high. The Taj Mahal followed the same pattern. The last Lodi sultan was Ibrahim, and his claim to absolute power alienated tribal chiefs, who appealed to an outsider for help. They invited Babur, the ruler of Kabul, to come to India, and he was willing to do so.

Babur

Zahir ad-Din Muhammad Babur (1483–1530) was born in Farghana, which is now in Uzbekistan. He claimed descent from Timur on his father's side and from Ghengis Khan on his mother's side. Babur lost his ancestral domain and became a fugitive at 11. He gained control of Kabul at 21. Although Babur ruled over a small kingdom, he was more than willing to bring his army from Afghanistan to India in response to the appeal of the governors of Punjab and Sind. Babur came with 12,000 men and—even though he was heavily outnumbered—defeated the Lodi army in 1526 at Panipat. Ibrahim was killed. The victory laid the foundation for the Mogul rule that lasted from the sixteenth to the nineteenth century. Babur went on from the battlefield at Panipat to Delhi and Agra. In Agra he faced 100,000 men led by Rana Sanga of the Rajput. Clan jealousy made these men largely ineffective. They could not withstand the tactics of Babur's cavalry and were defeated.

Humayun

Humayun, the eldest son of Babur, was 22 when Babur died. Humayun had moments of frenetic energy, followed by prolonged indolence, perhaps because of his addiction to opium. Sher Shah, a brilliant Afghan leader and great builder, forced Humayun to flee to Persia. In Persia, Humayun briefly accepted Shiite Muslim teachings. Meanwhile, Sher Shah outlined a basic administrative framework that subsequently inspired the future ruler Akbar, the son of Humayun. With help from the Shah of Persia, Humayun reclaimed Delhi. A year later he fell to his death. His widow supervised the building of his magnificent tomb, which featured a double dome.

Akbar

Akbar (ruled 1556–1605) ascended the throne at age 13. Four years later he dismissed the regent. Posterity rightly called him Akbar the Great. He was a contemporary of Elizabeth Queen of England, who granted a royal charter to the East India Company, which played a significant role in the history of India. But while Elizabeth ruled over five million, Akbar controlled one hundred million.

For political reasons, Akbar forged an alliance with Hindu rulers. The alliance was cemented by his marriage to a princess from a leading Rajput family. Akbar's wives were allowed to practice Hinduism. For a long time, and in spite of a harem of 300, Akbar had no sons. He sought the blessing of a famous sufi saint who predicted that he would have three sons—which he did. To honor the sufi, the city of Fatehpur Sikri was built where the saint lived. It took only nine years to build the new center, which became the capital for 12 years.

Akbar's palace was magnificent. The Panch Mahal has five floors and a small pavilion at the apex. It was a wind tower where the ladies could enjoy cool breezes. The astrologer's seat faced the Panch Mahal. Akbar, keen on astrology, always consulted both Hindu and Muslim specialists before engaging in a military campaign. The Diwan-i-Khas, or Hall of Private Audience, was used for legal, political, and religious discussions with Hindus, Jains, Zoroastrians, Jesuits, Daoists, Confucianists, and Buddhists. The sturdy sandstone pillar in the center upholds a circular platform—the seat of the emperor—linked to the four corners of the building. The decor on the pillar features emblems of the main religions.

Akbar created a new, syncretistic religion called Din Illahi, or the Divine Faith.

By combining elements of several different religions, he hoped to create a unifying ideology. Loyalty to the emperor would replace tribal affiliation or even religion. The emperor had a quasi-divine status. He recommended abstinence from meat and the slaughter of cows was made a capital offense. The nation was to be vegetarian for 100 days of the year. Pilgrimage to Mecca was banned and no new mosques were built. Perhaps influenced by the Persian court, Akbar saw himself as a monarch who ruled by divine right. He did not agree with the Islamic view that the emperor was God's deputy on earth and favored a doctrine of divine kingship. The *ulemas,* the Islamic theologians, agreed to reinterpret the Koran accordingly and gave Akbar the rank of interpreter of Islam—even though he was illiterate. Akbar recognized that compromise and tolerance were essential to maintaining the unity of the empire. He granted equality to Hindus and abolished the special tax imposed on non-Muslims. Hindus were free to build temples and the *ulemas* insisted in vain on the destruction of idolatry. They accused Akbar of heresy.

Akbar used local alliances with Hindu notables to create a counterweight to the small Turco-Muslim military elite. Raja Man Singh of Jaipur became a member of Akbar's round table. Akbar was also a brilliant general—once he and his army covered 600 miles in nine days and defeated a much larger but unsuspecting army. He made himself master of all of northern India and continuously extended the realm.

Akbar could also be ruthless. Exasperated by a four-month-long siege of a Hindu fortress, he massacred 20,000 noncombatants. But he abolished the enslavement of prisoners of war and many princes were allowed to keep their ancient possessions.

Although illiterate, Akbar owned 24,000 books. He ordered artists to prepare an illuminated manuscript of the legendary deeds of an adventurer from the days of Harun al-Rashid. One hundred painters labored 15 years to produce 12 volumes with more than 1,000 illustrations. Akbar was not concerned about Islamic strictures concerning painting and the reproduction of the human figure.

Akbar was a tireless builder. The Fort in Agra, completed in 1562, featured 500 buildings. His administration was brilliant—he created 33 levels of administrators, each one with clearly defined responsibilities from the commander of 5,000 down to the leader of 10. Akbar promoted on merit; titles and offices were not hereditary. Tenures were short, and he maintained absolute control.

After several false starts and 24 years of experience, the tax assessment was based on the average revenue of the previous 10 years. Uniform standards of weights and measures were developed. Nobles collected the assessed tax revenue. Upon the death of an official, the property reverted back to the emperor. The unintentional result was a disincentive to wealth accumulation and an encouragement to conspicuous consumption.

When Akbar died, his successors abandoned his policy of toleration and the empire began to decline. Jahangir (1605–1627) came to the throne at age 36 and ruled for 22 years. He was cruel and addicted to the hunt and luxury. His harem of 6,000 promoted his debauchery. On his birthday he was weighed and received his weight in gold. He grew attached to his favorite wife, Nur Jehan, who exerted much influence over the empire and amassed wealth for herself and her family. Over the course of his rule, Jahangir extended the frontiers of the empire.

THE BRITISH ERA

Few paid attention when Vasco da Gama, a Portuguese explorer, arrived in India in 1497. To his extreme surprise, Vasco da Gama "found a flourishing Christian community that traced its lineage back to the apostle Thomas."[67] Another Roman Catholic missionary, Francis Xavier, visited Goa. But the most interesting personality was Roberto de Nobili (1577–1656), who came from a distinguished Italian family. He accepted the lifestyle and dress code of the Brahmins and embraced every Brahmin practice that was not contrary to Christianity. He learned Tamil, Telugu, and Sanskrit and practiced his idea of "inculturation." It was highly successful, and thousands came to embrace Christianity. When others complained to Rome about this "Brahmin Christian Jesuit," Rome supported him.

During this era, Portugal's attention was focused on Brazil, not India, and thus Portugal did not exploit its advantage. The Dutch followed the Portuguese, then the French came, and finally the English. Indian officials welcomed the English, hoping to play them off against the Dutch. William Hawkins, the commander of the *Hector,* left his ship at Surat in 1608 and came to Agra, where he won the favor of Jahangir. The English gained a foothold at Surat, where they established a warehouse.

When Jahangir died, one of his sons, Shah Jehan, became the next ruler (1628–1666). Shah Jehan's first act was to execute all possible rivals, including brothers, uncles, and their male descendants. After two children by an earlier consort, Shah Jehan married Mumtaz Mahal, who died 18 years later at age 39 when she gave birth to child number 14. Shah Jehan built the majestic Taj Mahal in memory of his wife. It took 20,000 workers 22 years to build the structure. The builders used close to 1,000 pounds of gold, 750 pounds of pearls, and 5,000 gems. Special artists were brought in from Italy to teach the art of inlaying marble. Stonecutters, masons, and sculptors came from far away Baghdad and Constantinople. Upon the completion of the mausoleum, Shah Jehan ordered the hands of the craftsmen to be cut off to ensure that no one else used their abilities.

When Shah Jehan became ill, his four sons made attempts to take the throne. The son who succeeded, Aurangzeb, kept his father in prison till his death. The prison window allowed Shah Jehan to gaze across a river to see the Taj Mahal and reminisce. He had gained power through sheer brutality, and lost it through self-indulgence.

Meanwhile, the British established more and more warehouses in Surat and ended up with 23 by 1647. The British established Fort St. George—which later became Madras—on land acquired in 1640 from a Hindu ruler who had hoped to maintain his sovereignty with the help of the British in the face of enemies. People flocked to Fort St. George seeking both security in a turbulent era and commercial opportunities in the midst of growth. The British also established St. Mary, the first Protestant church in India.

Aurangzeb (1618–1707), who followed Shah Jehan, spoke Arabic, Turkish, Persian, and Hindi. He determined to restore Islam to its pristine purity. Music was banned from the court, portraits were obliterated, and even literature fell into disfavor. None of this prevented him from occupying the royal seat in the New Red Fort in Delhi and being called the Shadow of God. The fort was built in nine years and became the center of the Mogul Empire. Inside the Red Fort, Aurangzeb built his own private mosque. He was efficient and ruthless. Not only did he imprison his father for seven years; he also killed his three brothers and his nephews. His brutality was matched by his intolerance; he destroyed the precarious balance that Akbar had carefully established. Hindus were banned from court and excluded from public office, and their temples were razed. A special tax was levied on all non-Muslims, and taxes in general were raised to 50 percent. In some areas, peasants rebelled. Aurangzeb spent years away from Delhi to be with his army in the south. This weakened central authority and fostered regionalism, especially among the Rajputs and Marathas. Upon his deathbed Aurangzeb said, "I came alone; I am going alone. I have not done well to the country and to the people and of the future, there is no hope."

The Rise of Sikhism

According to Ninian Smart, the author of *World Religions,* Sikhism was "the result of the collision of Hindu and Islamic power."[68] The founder of Sikhism was Guru Nanak (1469–1539), a man from the merchant class. *Guru* means "enlightener." Nanak may have traveled to Sri Lanka, Afghanistan, Baghdad, and maybe even Mecca, in addition to crisscrossing India for 28 years. He married at 19 and had two children. We are informed that once Nanak went to bathe in a river and disappeared for three days because he was taken to God's court, where he received a cup of *amrit* (nectar)—hence the name of Amritsar, the great Sikh center in the Punjab. Upon his return his first words were, "There is no Hindu; there is no Muslim."

Nanak proclaimed "the unity of God, the brotherhood of man, the rejection of caste and the futility of idol worship."[69] He taught that the divine light dwells in every human being and that perfection is attained by developing love for God. The supreme object is union with God, a union that is not a merger or a loss of identity, but a link, an intimate connection. Nanak rejected ascetic practices such as fasting, celibacy, and begging. He deemed ritual unnecessary and ignored innumerable taboos. He accepted some of the basic Hindu traditions, including karma and reincarnation. Some Sikhs believe that there are 8,400,000 lives before one is born as a human being.[70] The patriarchal structure was also part of the culture and remained unchanged. Everything is subordinated to family interests. Daughters are a liability because sooner or later, a dowry has to be paid and the daughter is lost to another family. Intercaste marriages were disapproved. Although Sikhs were initially vegetarian and opposed to alcohol, over time, meat and alcohol became increasingly popular at weddings. Widowhood is seen as a state of perpetual pollution.

Guru Nanak's followers endowed him with celestial attributes. He was considered the embodiment of divine light. Initiation into the Sikh community was administered by drinking water in which the toe of a guru had been dipped. Today the baptismal waters are sweetened and stirred by a two-edged sword.

Nine other gurus, members of Nanak's immediate family, followed him. The third guru, Amar Das (1552–1574), offered community meals at Sikh centers where people ate together and ignored ritual pollution and caste distinctions.

The fifth guru, Arjun Dev (1581–1606), compiled the Granth Sahib, the Sikh sacred text. The book contains 5,594 hymns. The emphasis falls on *bhakti,* or devotion to God, a familiar Hindu theme. Nanak himself had composed 974 hymns, and 2,218 are from Arjun Dev. Some hymns were composed by Kabir, a Muslim sufi (not a Sikh) almost contemporary with Nanak. The Granth Sahib became the most sacred object and, in some instances, is accorded divine honor because it is "the abode of God." The sacred book is preserved in the Golden Temple in Amritsar.

Guru Arjan regulated the collection of contributions and decided that every Sikh should tithe. Jahangir killed him perhaps because he had supported another claimant to the throne. Aurangzeb publicly beheaded the ninth guru, Tegh Bahadur (1664–1675), when after severe torture, he refused conversion to Islam. The intransigent religious policy of Aurangzeb transformed the Sikh from a peaceful religious sect to a militant brotherhood of dedicated soldiers.

The tenth and last guru, Gobind Singh (1675–1708), was appointed at age 9. He added *singh* or "lion" to his name and created the Khalsa (the Pure), a brotherhood of soldier-saints. Members of this martial brotherhood had to adopt the five Ks: 1) *kesh* or uncut hair (making the tying of a turban compulsory) associated with holiness; 2) *kangha,* a comb to keep the hair tidy; 3) *kirpan,* a sword or dagger as an emblem of power; 4) *kara,* a steel bracelet, an insignia of "sternness and constraint"; and 5) *kachcha,* shorts reaching only to the knees, which were symbolic of readiness for action. In time the Sikhs became a military theocracy engaged in a struggle of liberation against the Moguls and later, the British.

The sons of Guru Gobind Singh (1675–1708), the tenth guru, had been killed or imprisoned, and thus he declared the line of the guru extinct. The status of guru was then bestowed upon the sacred scripture of the Sikhs (1708).

After the death of the last guru, a disciple called Banda Bahadur rose up against the Mogul power and for a few years established an independent state. He was finally defeated in 1716 when his last 700 soldiers were captured and slaughtered. A Mogul edict offered a choice of converting to Islam or death. Many Sikhs took refuge in the forests. After the collapse of the Mogul rule, the Sikhs re-emerged and took control of the Punjab till it was annexed by the British in 1849 after years of war.

The most famous Sikh maharaja was Ranjit Singh (1780–1839). He conquered Lahore and signed a treaty with the British that gave him a measure of security. He greatly expanded the boundaries of his domain and created a Sikh empire that extended to the borders of China and Tibet (invaded in 1840) in the north and from Afghanistan in the northwest to the Ganga River to the east. He was a military strategist and has been compared to Napoleon. In fact, he used a number of ex-Napoleonic officers.[71] He was noted enough abroad that he received gifts from the kings of France and England.

Ranjit Singh indulged in "bacchanalian revelries"—hardly appropriate for a Sikh—and was married more than 20 times. When he died at 58, four of his wives and seven maids mounted the funeral pyre. He had far too many potential successors given his many wives and concubines. Internal intrigues, dissent, and treachery facilitated the eventual British conquest, but it took eight battles and there were no easy victories. Once victorious, the British recruited Sikh soldiers to their ranks because of their extraordinary fighting spirit. The British allowed the Sikh soldiers to wear their turbans and keep their flowing beards.

Many students of Sikhism claim that it is only a branch of Hinduism, but Sikhs object vociferously to this "misrepresentation" and their claim seems to be confirmed by quotes from the earliest gurus, including Nanak, who wrote, "I am not a Hindu nor a Mussalman. I accept neither the Veda nor the Quran." On the other hand, the definition of Hinduism is so broad that it is difficult to rule out any Indian. Most Sikhs do not see themselves as Hindus. The official government classification of the Sikhs in India as part of Hinduism is perhaps more politically inspired than religiously justified.

The Breaking of the Mogul Empire

With the death of Aurangzeb in 1707 began the long decline and breakup of the Mogul Empire. The first six emperors had ruled 180 years, the next five only a dozen. As the central government disintegrated, rich provinces gained de facto independence. The great landowners opposed Imperial authority, but their efforts were uncoordinated. Princely rulers, especially those in remote territories, simply ceased to send tribute. Provincial governors appointed by the emperors declared de facto autonomy, including Oudh (Awadh) and Bengal. They took the title of *nawab*. In the chaotic situation, Nadir Shah of Persia conquered Delhi (1739) and killed more than 20,000 people. His spoils included the peacock throne. Years later Ahmad Shah

Abdali repeated the process. Between 1748 and 1767 he invaded India seven times and usually returned to Afghanistan with considerable booty. The Marathas suffered a disastrous defeat and lost 50,000 horses and 500 elephants. The repeated invasions undermined the tottering Mogul Empire and stopped the rampant imperialism of the Marathas.

The Growth of British Power
The Struggles for Power

Robert Clive (1725–1774) came to India at age 18 as a clerk at a time when the War of the Austrian Succession (1740–1748) spilled over into India. The British lost Madras to the French, but Clive managed to escape. In Europe the British and the French were at peace, but in India an undeclared (political) war continued between these archrivals. Clive, promoted to captain, was in charge of provisioning the troops of the East India Company. With only a handful of troops he conquered the fortress of Arcot (1751) and subsequently led a heroic defense of Arcot against overwhelming odds. The Indians hoped to batter down the high wooden gates of the fortress with elephants whose foreheads had been armed with iron plates. To escape the British bullets, the elephants turned and stampeded, trampling hundreds to death. This turned the tide against the French and their allies, and Clive's spirited defense at Arcot made him famous.

Clive later returned to England, but was sent out again in 1755. When the *nawab* of Bengal captured Calcutta, most of the British escaped. The rest were forced to spend the night in a cell called "the Black Hole of Calcutta." The next morning a few dozen Britishers were dead due to dehydration from the summer heat. It was perhaps an inadvertent atrocity because the *nawab* was asleep and his guards feared waking him to receive instructions. The political repercussions of the British deaths were enormous.

When war broke out again, the British were victorious in spite of the overwhelming Indian forces. It was another remarkable victory for Clive. He installed Mir Jafar as *nawab* of Bengal, Bihar, and Orissa. Mir Jafar was to pay a million sterling to the East India Company to help compensate for the company's losses in Calcutta, among other things. It was obvious who was really in charge.

In 1763 the Treaty of Paris ended the Seven Years' War and the French hopes in India. France was eliminated as a major player in India and confined to the city of Pondicherry, in south India, which was ceded to India in 1954.

Another battle loomed in the future with Mir Qasim, a successor of Mir Jafar. The Battle of Buxar (1764) pitched a large, disciplined Indian army against only 7,500 sepoys, Indians recruited into the British army. Under the command of Hector Monroe they fought brilliantly and, despite the odds, gained a hard-fought victory. It was the final blow to Mogul power in northern India.

In 1765 the British signed a treaty to take over the revenue collection rights for Bengal, Bihar, and Orissa. "The machine of administration remained Indian, with Mogul trappings and titles, but the control was in the hands of the [India] Company."[72] The British were the sovereign rulers of these large, prosperous, and heavily populated areas. The year 1765 marked the beginning of the British Empire in India as a territorial dominion. Clive had become the founder of British India. William Hastings, the first governor-general (1773–1784), was an excellent administrator. The two other British centers, Bombay/Mumbai and Madras, were now subordinated to Calcutta. The British Indian Empire emerged just when General Charles Cornwallis lost America for the crown.

It wasn't long before the British faced a powerful hostile coalition of Marathas, the *nawab* of Hyderabad and the *nawab* of Mysore. In 1783 Tipu Sahib, the sultan of Mysore, came to the throne. He modernized the army, trained the troops along European lines, and used French officers. He sent envoys to Louis XVI of France to secure an alliance. Tipu was a modernizer and reformer. Four wars were necessary before the British took control of Mysore.

In 1803 the British took the Mogul emperor under their protection, and Cornwallis placed Europeans in charge of the higher positions at the revenue collection and administrative agencies. Indian government participation was reduced to an absolute minimum because Cornwallis was convinced that "every native of Hindustan, I verily believe, is corrupt."

The Advent of Technology

With the British came railroads, the telegraph, the penny post, and modern conveniences. Missionaries appeared, but "throughout the eighteenth century missionaries were refused residence in the English settlements"[73] by the East India Company. One of the best-known missionaries was William Carey, a self-educated man with remarkable linguistic abilities. He studied Sanskrit, prepared a dictionary in Bengali, Sanskrit, and English; wrote a history of the Bengali kings with the help of Ram Basu (the first prose book in Bengali); and translated Sanskrit fables and the

Ramayana. He established the first printing press in India, opened schools for Indians, offered medical treatment, and helped establish the Agricultural and Horticultural Society of India to help improve farming. Missionaries also pioneered the study of modern Indian languages and created the first bilingual dictionaries and grammars in Bengali, Tamil, Hindi, and Telugu.

The Advancements Under Missionaries

The British governor-general did not condone missionary activity, but in 1813 a new charter for the East India Company lifted the ban on missionary activity and promoted Western education and the use of English. The practice of widows mounting funeral pyres (*suttee*) was outlawed. This had been opposed by William Carey and by men such as Ram Mohan Roy (1772–1833), who looked to Western learning and the Upanishads to create "a vision of a rationalist and monotheist 'modern' India."[74] Lord William Bentinck (1828–1835) also opposed "widow-burning" and hoped to end the "ritualized highway killing" of the *thuggee*. These "thugs" robbed and murdered in the name of Kali, the goddess of destruction. Bentinck's sympathies were on the side of the evangelicals. He made great efforts to reform the Indian legislation, especially regarding *suttee*.

In 1835 Thomas Macauley voiced the widely shared opinion that India should be English in taste, opinions, morals, and intellect. English now replaced Persian as the language of official documents and the law courts.

The Setback in Afghanistan

Fear of a possible Russian intervention in Afghanistan, unfounded rumors, faulty intelligence, superficial evaluations, and more contributed to the launch of the first Afghan War, one of the worst disasters ever to befall the British Empire. Most of the soldiers were sepoys. The British Indian army of 15,000 was trapped in Kabul, and there were few survivors. The image of British invincibility was shattered. The British tried to regain prestige by a quick invasion, but in the end evacuated Afghanistan. When the Sikhs lost the second Anglo-Sikh War they transferred Kashmir to the British as a war indemnity. That fact that a Hindu ruled over a predominantly Muslim population was not considered a serious problem, any more than the Muslim rule over a Hindu population. The British were still absorbing the Punjab and not ready to occupy such a vast new area. They sold Kashmir to Gulab Singh, a Hindu general who had served with distinction under Ranjit Singh. Gulab Singh (1792–1857) was the founder of the Dogra Dynasty, which ruled the area for a century.

Dalhousie (1848–1856) was one of the most effective British governors. He arrived just in time to receive the document of annexation from Maharaja Dhalip Singh that ended the Sikh kingdom of Ranjit Singh. Dalhousie developed the "doctrine of lapse," which stated that a ruler "manifestly incompetent" or one who "died without direct male heir" would see his realm annexed by the British. Aside from territory acquired through military conquests, Dalhousie added seven princely states to the Raj, the British dominion, under the doctrine of lapse. Shortly after the sepoy rebellion, the doctrine was abandoned.

INDUSTRIALIZATION AND INDEPENDENCE COME TO INDIA

THE INDUSTRIAL REVOLUTION IN England had a tremendous impact on India. At one point overseas textile demands provided jobs for 80,000 weavers in Bengal alone. But now, Indian goods were no longer able to compete with the machine-made goods made in Britain. Private merchants in India were ruined and opposed modernization. Ghandi later echoed some of these sentiments. Another technological advancement led to the Indian Mutiny of 1857, which was occasioned by Britain's new Enfield rifles. To load them, soldiers had to bite off the end of a greased cartridge and ram it down the barrel. Ordinance officers in England had decided that the best lubricants for doing this were cow and pig fat—both of which are unclean to Hindus and Muslims. This was the spark that started a one-year uprising. The offending grease was immediately withdrawn, and the cartridges were issued ungreased. It became the responsibility of the sepoys (the native Indian soldiers in the British army) to find beeswax and linseed oil as substitute lubricants for their weapons.

The underlying reasons for the Indian Mutiny were economic and social. People in India resented the many changes imposed by Western society. The independent princes and those in Madras and Bombay stood with the British, but Delhi fell and had to be reconquered. Atrocities took place on both sides. After 1857 the British distanced themselves from Indian society, and educated Indians wanted control over their own lives. British control over India was transferred from the British East India Company to the British Crown.

A key statistic in all this is that, according to the census of 1881, there were 253 million Indians and only 60,000 Britishers in India.

THE INDIAN NATIONAL CONGRESS

The Indian National Congress was formed in 1885 by some 70 English-educated Indians. The catalyst of the Congress was Allen Hume, an Englishman. Many of India's future leaders were key members of the Congress, including Dadabhai Naoroji (1825–1917), who was known as "the grand old man of India." He was also the first Indian elected to the British House of Commons. The National Congress never embraced, as a whole, a coherent policy to oust the British. Some members were more radical, including Bar Gangadhar Tilak, who called for strong action and ended up in prison for six years. He provoked a split in the Congress in 1907. Because the Indian National Congress didn't really represent the many Muslims in the country, a separate Muslim League was created in 1906 under the leadership of Ali Jinnah.

INDIA IN WORLD WAR I

In the First World War, 1.3 million Indians fought for the Allies and 60,000 were killed. After the war, hopes of greater freedom for India were disappointed. A terrible incident took place in Amritsar in 1919 when British General Dyer (who had left the Dublin Royal College of Surgeons because he could not stand the sight of blood) gave an order for soldiers to shoot into a dense crowd of unarmed Indians whom he said were conducting an unlawful assembly. It was a massacre pure and simple, with 379 persons killed and more than 1,000 wounded. Although the

Amritsar Massacre was an isolated incident, it gave ammunition to those who rejected British rule. Not only did General Dyer escape all censure for what he had done, he was lionized in England.

For a ten-year period, from 1921 to 1931, there were numerous clashes between Hindus and Muslims. Muslim festivals (such as the commemoration of the birth of Muhammed) complete with the sacrifices of goats or lambs, were seen as provocations by the Hindu majority.

At the same time, more and more people throughout India joined the struggle for independence from Britain. By far the most important personality was Ghandi, who exercised an extraordinary moral influence. He was called Mahatma, or "Great Soul." He advocated nonviolent opposition and suggested noncooperation, work stoppages, and the boycott of British imports. Some of Ghandi's key concepts were "inspired by early Christian concepts of love and self-effacing poverty."[75] Nonviolence had never been at the core of Hindu tradition,[76] and "many Western ideas and ideals were insinuated into Hinduism through Ghandi."[77] Ghandi not only opposed British control over India, but also rejected all their industrial developments. He said machinery "represents a great sin." He also never advocated a wholesale repudiation of the caste system or of the patriarchal family structure.

INDIA IN WORLD WAR II

During World War II, more than two million Indian volunteers served with distinction. Afterwards, Great Britain agreed to grant independence to India. Unfortunately—and in spite of Ghandi's earnest pleas—the ongoing distrust between Hindus and Muslims led to violent fighting.

In 1945 Ghandi, Muhammad Ali Jinnah, and the Indian National Congress leadership (many recently released from jail) met at Simla to discuss the future of India. Their hope to form a unified national government was not realized. The Indian National Congress insisted on its right to nominate Muslim representatives, whereas Jinnah and the Muslim League insisted on their exclusive prerogative to nominate all Muslim representatives. This disagreement led to the partitioning of India to create the Islamic Republic of Pakistan. The mostly Muslim western part of India split off to become Pakistan, and the easternmost part of India, which was also predominantly Muslim, became East Pakistan. India lay between these two parts of the new Pakistan.

The partition led to massacres and mass migrations. Exact numbers are impossible to ascertain, but perhaps as many as 12 million uprooted refugees crossed the India-Pakistan borders in both directions. Hundreds of thousands of people died before the violence was brought under control.

TERRITORIAL DISPUTES

Compromises between Hindus and Muslims settled some disputes, but no agreement was reached regarding the region of Kashmir, on the frontier between India and Pakistan. The disagreement led to the First Kashmir War (1948), and the problem continues to fester to this day.

In this climate of intense hatred, a fanatical Hindu assassinated Ghandi. Jawaharlal Nehru, who had been mentored by Ghandi, then came to power. On August 15, 1947, India became a self-governing nation. Up till then, one-third of the people had lived under the "indirect rule" of some

500 princes. They all joined the new India. And Pakistan proclaimed its independence as well, with Jinnah as first governor-general.

While British rule in India has received different evaluations in the years since, regardless of political or religious affiliations, most historians might agree that ultimately, the British administration helped to unify India by creating proper legal codification, facilitating the use of English as a language, and promoting public works and social reforms. That Britain's rule was not purely altruistic is self-evident and not to be expected. The British benefited, and so did India.

In 1958 a coup d'etat in Pakistan put Ayub Khan into power. Khan did not have good relations with India, and hostilities erupted with the Indo-Pakistani War of 1965. In East Pakistan, political unrest was met with repression and the tensions escalated into a civil war. Millions of refugees fled East Pakistan and entered India. The Indo-Pakistani war of 1971 ended with the secession of East Pakistan to become an independent state, Bangladesh. Another armed conflict in 1999 between India and Pakistan also involved Kashmir. India blamed the infiltration of the Pakistani army into Kashmir for the outbreak of hostilities, but Pakistan claimed that only Kashmiri militants were involved. Pakistan had to withdraw behind the "Line of Control."

MODERN-DAY INDIA

AN ECONOMIC POWER

India now boasts the fourth-largest economy in the world, and might soon surpass Japan. The growth of India is not based on exporting labor-intensive, low-priced manufactured goods to the West. Rather, India has relied on its domestic market, which is driven by consumption.[78]

As C. Raja Mohan pointed out, "India is arriving on the world stage as the first large, economically powerful, culturally vibrant, multiethnic, multireligious democracy outside of the geographic West."[79] At the same time, and perhaps unavoidably, there is a resurgence of Hindu consciousness that can easily degenerate into extreme nationalism and generate tensions with the Muslim population and other non-Hindu groups. Barring unforeseen events, the economic future looks bright for India.

A RELIGIOUS DIVERSITY

Over the last 150 years, Indian spirituality has continued to give birth to new types of religious thought. For example, there was Ramakrishna, a priest who experienced frequent ecstasies and claimed that meditation focused on Allah or Christ produced identical results. "This convinced him of the ultimate unity of all religions."[80] One of the first to promote his ideas in the United States was Vivekenanda (1863–1902). He was the key spokesman for India at the World Parliament of Religion held in Chicago in 1893 and founded the Ramakrishna Mission (1897). He saw God on two different levels—the higher being God as the One escaping all definitions, beyond all thought (cf. Brahman), and the lower being God appearing as Siva, Vishnu, or Kali, inadequate labels for the Ultimate. All religions, whether made up of idol worshippers or monotheists, are only preparatory for the time when all mankind rises to a higher, purer concept of the Ultimate One. Vivekenanda emphasized the potential divinity of every human being, yet at the same time he defended the caste system. He also made certain accommodations to Western thinking. For example, he played down the idea that all is *maya,* or illusion. He knew such an idea would not be easily accepted in the West. If all is *maya,* or as unreal as a dream, how can anything visible be taken seriously? To distinguish between "provisional reality" or ordinary "truth" and ultimate truth seems rather artificial.

Hans Ji Maharaj founded the Divine Light Mission in India in 1960. Instead of the oldest son, it was Prem Rawat, the fourth son of the founder, who at age eight, succeeded his father as the perfect master, an embodiment of God on earth, an object of veneration. He came to the United States in 1971, invited by a few Americans who were in search of spirituality. Soon, more than 20 religious communities *(ashrams)* were established. In 1973 an event was organized to celebrate the beginning of 1,000 years of peace and prosperity. It was a nonevent that left the movement broke and moribund. The family now endorsed the older brother, which led to a court battle. The brother remained a leader of the movement in India, and Prem Rawat was free to work in the rest of the world. In the 1980s the Divine Light Mission was disbanded, and Prem Rawat was no longer to be venerated as God and the *ashrams* were abandoned.

A new organization, Elan Vital, was created in 1983, and the trappings of Indian culture that had previously characterized the Divine Light Mission were set aside. Prem Rawat also married his secretary, said to be an incarnation of the goddess Durga. The teachings of Elan Vital are rooted in both Hinduism and Sikhism. They are also inspired by the Radhasoami tradition, founded by Shiv Dayal (1818–1878). He stressed God's communication through the essence of sound, or *shabd*—the audible life stream, the music of the spheres, the sustaining power of the universe. Meditation should focus on this internal spiritual melody so that we can detach the soul from material things and lead to a higher consciousness. Elan Vital is just one of the many movements centered on meditation techniques.

TM, or Transcendental Meditation, also focuses on meditation, as the title proclaims. TM is presented as an ancient Indian technique to develop brain potential and reach a higher level of consciousness, and it is even possible to take an advanced program that includes levitation. It has been promoted by Maharishi Mahi Yogi, the guru to the Beatles. The Maharishi now offers what is called a Vedic Astrology program, which allegedly helps followers to avert dangers to come. TM is the practice of twice-daily, 20-minute sessions of meditation and silent focus on a mantra. It only takes a few thousand dollars to learn this simple technique, and Maharishi advocates the use of a single mantra that is compatible with the nature and way of life of any particular individual.[81]

Although often presented as a simple meditation technique, a federal ruling (1978) has determined that TM is a religious practice. It is deeply rooted in Hinduism.

The Krishna Consciousness Movement, or ISKON, was founded in 1966 by A.C. Bhaktivedanta (1896–1977). He has written extensively and translated the Bhagavad Gita. The popular name of the group is Hare Krishnas because these words are uttered again and again by the devotees. They chant Krishna's name as a mantra, a vibration of sound that cleanses the mind. Once a person is in harmony with Krishna, it is possible for him to reach a pure state of consciousness. The soul is said to have fallen from the spiritual into the material realm, and once *maya* or illusion is destroyed, the soul is free to ascend to the heights.

Scandals, splits, and controversies have rocked the movement, with accusations of embezzlement, child abuse, and more. Most of the members are no longer involved in the monastic life, and communal arrangements have largely been abandoned.

The theoretical basis for this movement goes back to Chaitanya Mahaprabhu, an ascetic Vaishnava monk in the sixteenth century. He promoted an intense devotion to Krishna, the supreme lord who lives in paradise. The key to promoting Krishna consciousness is the utterance of his name and a devotion that clings to him with passion.

POINTS OF CONTACT

Since it is most difficult—if not impossible—to define Hinduism, it is a dubious undertaking to indicate points of contact. Still, almost all Hindus believe in the law of karma and reincarnation.

If karma cannot be evaded, if good deeds never cancel bad ones (which is true enough in itself), and if every seed must bear fruit, then escape is impossible, regardless of the number of incarnations someone goes through. One single bad thought or deed would be enough to create bad karma and necessitate yet one more incarnation. Has any human ever lived a perfect life? Is such even conceivable? For that matter, even an absolutely perfect life would not erase the bad karma of the past that must necessarily come to fruition.

And what about negative karma we might have inherited from the past? How much weighs on us from the moment of birth? How much has accumulated in the past? How can anyone know, when there is no recollection of the past? It seems that the idea of karma leaves no room for hope of escape.

There is a point of truth in the idea of karma, except that everything plays out either in this life or in the life to come—not through endless incarnations. "A man reaps what he sows" (Galatians 6:7). That is exactly why on the basis of "works" it is impossible to find salvation. God can break this "iron law of karma" and set us free…through grace. The incarnation of Christ takes the place of the innumerable human reincarnations that supposedly lead to a person's freedom. Christ broke the law of sin and death for us.

What's more, if God created the world, then matter is not evil in itself and there is no reason for the soul to "escape" the body. On the other hand, if there is no Creator, then the world has existed from all eternity, regardless of what scientists have to say. And if that's the case, wouldn't that mean evil (which equals matter) has been with us all along, perhaps in the very nature of things? If so, how can anyone escape? Why would matter be evil? Has it always been evil? Are sin and evil not moral issues, not connected to material entities? If the sacred slogan *tat tvam asi* is true—if the universal essence embraces all and if everything is Brahmin and all else illusion—should one conclude that evil is real and part of Brahmin or that it is only an illusion and does not exist?

Also, if all is *maya*, what has created or produced this illusion? Is it automatically linked to matter and therefore from all eternity? Or did it enter creation at some point? If all is *maya*, how do I know that I exist, and that my thoughts about illusion are not themselves illusions? How can anyone know anything unless there is a true God who has made himself known?

Unfortunately, Jains took over the idea of karma from Hinduism and thus inherited all the problems associated with the idea of karma. The Jains discovered some of these problems and tried to solve them. They taught that karma is a material substance, be it ever such refined material. But their answer raises more problems than it solves.

How strange it is that Jains, the most ardent advocates of nonviolence—who always live in fear of inadvertently eliminating life—have no other solution to the problems of life than to terminate it by starvation? Does that not count as a voluntary elimination of life? Is suicide the only exit? It is an extraordinarily pessimistic view of life, but it pervades Hinduism, Jainism, Buddhism, and Sikhism. If Jains advocate physical death through starvation, Buddhism demands mental or emotional suicide through elimination of all desire. Is it not a desire for one to want to enter the Pure Land or to reach nirvana (whatever it may be) to find extinction and release from karma? Is it not a desire to feel compassion or a compulsion to help others? Does this desire, in itself, not disqualify the seeker from the answer?

In light of these problems, Christianity is truly "good news" given its proclamation of salvation by the grace of God and its assurance that man is destined to die but once (Hebrews 9:27) and only once. A new birth is necessary, but it is not reached through reincarnation. Rather, it is achieved spiritually through repentance and faith in Christ. The good news is that Christ has overcome and broken the chains that hold mankind captive. He can set us free from illusions and false values. He can make us free to love and worship in the absolute assurance that anyone who calls on him is accepted "as is," solely on the basis of God's grace.

There are those who follow the highest teaching of the Bhagavad Gita, who endeavor to approach God through *bhakti,* or devotional love. In the Bible, however, when someone raised a question about the greatest commandment, Christ said that it is loving God with all your heart, soul, mind, and strength (not through mindless chanting) and your neighbor as yourself. The inquirer instantly recognized the truth and said that Christ was right. It was a wise answer and Jesus then said, "You are not far from the kingdom of God" (Mark 12:34).

To know this God is impossible unless he takes the initiative and makes himself known by descending to our level. The incarnation—in which God became man—is the culmination of divine communication. But the barrier of sin that stands between God and man can only be removed by the Son of God, Jesus Christ the Savior. Accepted in Christ, anyone can freely approach God to worship and love him.

JUDAISM

The order of the world rests upon three things:

on law, on worship, and on bestowal of favors.

Be a disciple of Aaron, love peace, pursue peace, love all men too, and bring them nigh unto the Law.

If I do not look to myself, who will do so? But if I look only to myself, what am I? And if not now, when?

Fix a time for study; promise little, and do much; receive everyone with friendly countenance.

All the days of my life have been passed among the sages and I have found never anything better for a man than silence; and the discussion of the law is not of such import as is the practice thereof. He who talks much, cannot avoid sin.

Do His will as if it were thy own, that he may do thy will as if it were His. Annul thy will before His, that he may annul the will of others before thy will.

TRACT ABOTH, TALMUD

JUDAISM

THE DETERMINATION OF WHO IS JEWISH

THIS SEEMINGLY SIMPLE QUESTION has ignited a passionate debate among Jewish people. Does the word *Jew* refer to religion, culture, tradition, race, or nationality?

In Bible times the word *Hebrew* was mostly used by foreigners to talk about the Israelites or by Jews speaking to foreigners. Literally it means someone "from the other side"—from across a river, for instance. Abraham had come to Canaan from beyond the River Euphrates, and was therefore called a Hebrew.[1] But the prophet Jeremiah used *Hebrew* and *Jew* interchangeably.[2] The dictionary agrees with Jeremiah and defines a Jew as a descendant from the ancient Hebrews of biblical times.

THE CHOSEN PEOPLE

The phrase "the Chosen People" refers to the election of Israel as God's special people. In the biblical context it speaks of a special relationship accompanied by responsibility. The chosen are recipients of a divine challenge by an act of grace. "The LORD did not set his affection on you and choose you because you were more numerous than other peoples, for you were the fewest of all peoples. But it was because the LORD loved you and kept the oath he

swore to your forefathers."[3] Israel was chosen to proclaim monotheism, to be a witness to all nations.[4]

After the Babylonian captivity, the word *Jew,* like the word *Israel,* was used as a national name for all the descendants of the 12 tribes. The word *Jew* was used to speak of all who returned from the exile as well as those who stayed behind. This is most noticeable in the book of Esther, which frequently speaks of "the Jews." After the Babylonian exile, from the perspective of the Chosen People, there were only Jews and Gentiles (or non-Jews).

THE DICTIONARY DEFINITION

The basic dictionary definition of *Jew* is "someone whose religion is Judaism." Since many Jews are not what one would call religious Jews, this definition raises more questions than it answers. One recent author wrote that Jews "practice the Jewish religion because they are Jews, not the other way around."[5]

None of this is very helpful for determining who is a Jew. One of the latest books on Judaism admits that "there is no single definition or criteria to determine who is a Jew. Jews still disagree over who should be considered a Jew and what is the essence of Judaism."[6] Huston Smith concurs that "it is impossible to name any one thing that of itself suffices to make one a Jew."[7]

A TRADITIONAL DEFINITION

The Law of Return, passed in Israel in 1950, states: "Every Jew shall have the right to come to this country as an immigrant." There was no definition given for the word *Jew*. Perhaps none was needed at the time. The traditional, orthodox definition is quite simple: A Jew is anyone born of a Jewish mother. It is a matter of biology and does not involve faith or a certain behavior. It means that even conversion to another religion does not affect one's status as a Jew.

Even from an orthodox position, however, this definition is problematic. Genesis informs us that Joseph married Asenath, daughter of Potiphera, the priest of On (Heliopolis) in Egypt.[8] Asenath, the Egyptian, gave birth to Manasseh and Ephraim, ancestors of two of the 12 tribes of Israel. It seemed incredible to the rabbis that Joseph should have married a heathen wife. They created the historic fiction that Asenath was the same person as Dinah, the daughter of Jacob who was raped by Hamor, a story related in Genesis 34. Although the Bible makes no mention of a child, we are told that Dinah's brothers wanted to kill the illegitimate child but were prevented by Jacob, who placed a talisman with the name of God around her neck and left her exposed under a thorn-bush. Perhaps the angel Gabriel transported the baby to the house of Potiphar. At any rate, his wife was childless and she reared the baby like it was her own daughter and called her Asenath. So, concluded the rabbis, Asenath was Jewish. Other stories—for one can hardly call them explanations—are even more convoluted. The reasoning is that Asenath somehow has to be Jewish or else the two tribes of Manasseh and Ephraim are not part of the Jewish nation.

There are other instances of intermarriage that are worthy of note. Genesis mentions in passing that Shaul, the son of Simeon, was the son of a Canaanite woman.[9] The Shaulite clan was part of the tribe of Simeon.[10] Intermarriage was not uncommon; even Moses married a Cushite.[11] And down through the ages, Jews and Gentiles have continued to intermarry. Emperor Theodosius II (408–450) forbade marriage between Christians and Jews. The Council of Orleans, in 538, issued a similar prohibition, which was echoed in Toledo in 589 and Rome in 743. Thus to assume the "racial purity" of any group is contrary to the facts of history.

The question of Jewish identity is an old one. John Hyrcanus (135–104 B.C.) conquered Edom (Idumea) and told the Idumites they would be permitted to stay in the country if they submitted to circumcision and accepted the Jewish way of life. Josephus comments that "they were hereafter no other than Jews,"[12] but many Jews looked upon them as semi-heathen. Nevertheless, who knows to what degree intermarriage took place?

THE ETHIOPIAN JEWS

The black Jews in Ethiopia, known as the Falasha, like to be called House of Israel. They are circumcised and observe some dietary and Sabbath laws, but their physical appearance is the same as that of other Ethiopians. According to tradition, they are descendants of Solomon and the Queen of Sheba. Even if this were remotely possible, the Queen of Sheba was hardly Jewish.

It has been suggested that the Falasha might descend from the tribe of Dan, a theory that appeared at some point in the ninth century. Supposedly the tribe of Dan migrated because they did not wish to be involved in the inter-tribal rivalry when the kingdom split into Judah and Israel (c. 920 B.C.). There is no historic data to confirm this migration of the tribe of Dan. Moving from tradition to fact, we know that some Jewish communities were settled in Upper Egypt near the border of Sudan by Ptolemy I (322–285 B.C.). Did they move to Ethiopia? Regardless of historic details, there must have been a great deal of intermarriage in Ethiopia for the Falasha to look like all other Ethiopians. Regardless of these unresolved questions, the State of Israel and the Jewish authorities officially accepted the Falasha as Jews in 1975, but controversy persists over their fitness to intermarry with other Jews.

MORE NONTRADITIONAL EXAMPLES

The exact status of Russian Jews is often in doubt. This is an important issue because of the large number of Russian immigrants who go to Israel. While in Russia, they were assimilated and religion did not play an important role in their lives. These immigrants do not easily meet orthodox legal standards. Some claim descent from a Jewish father only. It has been estimated that anywhere from eight to 30 percent—i.e., from 40,000 to 100,000 of these Russian immigrants are not really Jewish. No one really knows. According to Israeli newspapers, in 1994, churches in Nazareth saw a large influx of Russian immigrants.

The first serious challenge to the Law of Return was the notorious case of Father Daniel, a Polish Jew (complete with Jewish mother) who had become a Carmelite monk and requested citizenship under the Law of Return. Brother Daniel, born Oswald Rufeisen had saved many Jews during the holocaust. The Supreme Court of Israel, contrary to rabbinical law, decided that Father Daniel was not eligible to come to Israel under the Law of Return because he had adopted another religion. To be a Jew was no longer simply a matter of biology.

CONVERTS AND INTERMARRIAGE

In 1960 the new legal definition was that a Jew is "a person born of a Jewish mother *who does not belong to another religion,* or one who has converted [to Judaism] *in accordance with religious law*" (emphasis added). Two years later the Supreme Court of Israel upheld this new definition, although it is not in line with orthodox thinking. Legal debates followed and the law was amended in 1970 to read that a Jew is one born to a Jewish mother, or is one who has become converted to Judaism and who is not a member of another religion. What had been omitted, to the great consternation of Orthodox Jews, was a proviso that the conversion must be in accordance with religious law. This is a pivotal issue because Reform, Conservative, and Orthodox groups have different standards for conversion, and no branch accepts the converts of a less observant branch. For example, the Orthodox do not recognize the validity of conversions performed by Conservative or Reform rabbis. The latter may not insist on circumcision and baptism by immersion and make conversion easy. The Orthodox, by contrast, make conversion difficult. It can take one year to be accepted as Jewish. It is necessary to appear before a rabbinical court and face three rabbis who will determine if the potential convert has some basic knowledge and is sincere. If the rabbis are satisfied, the candidate is baptized and given a certificate regarding his new status.

The vast majority of Jews in the United States and Western democracies are affiliated with Reform and Conservative congregations, where the rate of intermarriage with non-Jews is high. In many cases the couples are lost to Judaism, but if a conversion takes place in a Reform or Conservative synagogue, it is not recognized in Israel, where the Orthodox are in control of all religious matters.

In 1970 the Law of Return granted the right of immigration to the children and grandchildren of a Jewish person, to non-Jewish spouses of Jews, to non-Jewish spouses of children of Jews, and even to non-Jewish spouses of non-Jewish grandchildren of Jews. According to newspaper reports and in line with this law, one Jewish woman from a Muslim country was able to bring her extended family of 170 practicing Muslems into Israel. The story sounds like a fairy tale, but apparently a Jew from a Muslim country came to Israel with his three sons but left his pregnant wife behind, who gave birth to a daughter. Since she was born of a Jewish mother, she emigrated to Israel. The abandoned wife stayed behind and married a Muslim and gave birth to nine sons. The Muslim sons married several wives each. Under the Law of Return, because the mother was Jewish, the nine sons were entitled to immigration along with their children, their grandchildren, and their children's spouses. In this fashion the total number reached 170. Even if the story is fictional, still, from a legal standpoint, this can be done.

A recent twist is the case of a Brazilian couple who converted to Judaism under Reformed auspices. The Supreme Court in Israel ruled that they could be registered in Israel. They were the first non-Orthodox converts to immigrate and receive Jewish identity cards in the state of Israel (1989).

VARYING DEGREES OF ACCEPTANCE

To complicate matters further, Reform Judaism decided in 1982 that anyone born of a Jewish father or mother is Jewish. This is absolutely not acceptable to Orthodox rabbis. The debate is not theoretical. Orthodoxy, although a minority, is the established religion in Israel.

In the United States, Orthodox, Reform, and Conservative rabbis can perform marriages, but only the Orthodox have that right in Israel. There are no civil marriages in Israel, and the Orthodox refuse to perform weddings between Jew and non-Jew unless the non-Jew has converted to Judaism.

Neither Conservative nor Reform groups have official standing in Israel, but population-wise, they comprise the vast majority of Jews in the United States. So which synagogue is authentically Jewish? Reform, Conservative, Reconstructionist, or Orthodox? Imagine the case of a boy born of a Jewish father and a converted non-Jewish mother, and reared in a Reform synagogue with a Jewish education and Bar Mitzvah. He considers himself completely and legally Jewish. The boy grows up and falls in love with an Orthodox girl only to be told by her rabbi that he is not Jewish according to Jewish law, and they cannot marry unless he formally converts to Judaism.[13]

Adoption can complicate matters even further. When a nonobservant couple in Israel adopted a baby from Uzbekistan, Orthodox rabbis refused to convert the child to Judaism unless the parents promised to follow an Orthodox lifestyle, which they rejected.

SECULAR JUDAISM UNDER ORTHODOX INFLUENCE

The official position of the Orthodox remains very strong in Israel because their vote is crucial in any coalition government. But the fact remains that the vast majority of Israeli Jews are secular. Nevertheless, when they wish to get married they have to use an Orthodox rabbi. The same is true in case of divorce, which is regulated by rabbinical law. As the law stands, only the husband can initiate a divorce. A woman cannot be divorced without her husband's consent. Unfortunately there are thousands of abandoned wives who cannot get a divorce because the husband may be 1) mentally ill, or 2) might have disappeared, or 3) is dead but his death cannot be established beyond doubt. To alleviate the problem to some degree, soldiers at risk have signed "conditional divorce" papers that become effective in case the soldier fails to return within a fixed period of time after demobilization. A forsaken husband is in a better legal position because he can receive a dispensation to take another wife. If an Orthodox court did not sanction the divorce, a child born of a second marriage is legally illegitimate. In other words, a letter of divorce granted by rabbinical authority is essential.

A child begotten in incest or adultery (but not the child of an unmarried woman) is considered illegitimate, a *mamzer.* This includes the child of an abandoned woman because legally, she is still married. A *mamzer* and his or her descendants are not allowed to marry for ten generations[14]—i.e., not allowed to marry a fellow Jew. But he or she can marry among themselves or a proselyte.[15] These are among the reasons that registers dealing with birth, marriage, divorce, and death records are most important.

An orthodox man thanks God each morning "for not making me a woman," whereas the woman praises God for making her according to His will. These civil/religious matters concerning identity and status continue to plague people in Israel and to create tension between Jews in Israel and those living elsewhere, especially in America.

SOME FINAL OBSERVATIONS

According to the dictionary, Judaism refers to the Jewish religion, but it can also mean conformity to Jewish rites, ceremonies, or customs. Judaism can be seen as a way of life or a culture that includes everything from art to literature. That definition fits a high percentage of Jews in the United States. They are nonobservant but think of themselves as Jews.

Whatever is meant by the word *Jew,* it is definitely not a racial term. There is no such thing as a Jewish race with distinguishing characteristics. This should no longer be an issue, except for hopelessly biased or ignorant people. The pseudoscientific racial theories advocated by the German Third Reich never had the backing of the scientific community. The very fact that Jews were forced to wear a special badge in the Middle Ages (and under Hitler) because they could not be distinguished from the rest of the population speaks for itself.

Because the definition of who is a Jew elicits different responses, statistical figures about the numbers of Jews in the world today should be regarded with caution. It is generally estimated that there are 5.9 million Jews in the United States today and five million in Israel. Russia, France, Canada, Argentina, and the United Kingdom are among the other nations with large Jewish populations.

THE SACRED BOOKS OF JUDAISM

THE TANAKH

If Judaism were defined in terms of a religion, it would involve the Bible, or the Tanakh. The Jewish Bible is divided into these basic sections:

- **T**orah or five books of Moses
- **N**evi'im or Prophets
- **TNK** or Tanakh
- **K**etuvim or Sacred Writings

The *Torah* or Law refers to the five books of Moses. These books are read in the synagogue either in a one-year or in a three-year cycle, usually the former.

The *Prophets* are subdivided into two categories: 1) the earlier prophets: Joshua, Judges, 1 and 2 Samuel, and 1 and 2 Kings; and 2) the later prophets: Isaiah, Jeremiah, Ezekiel, and the 12 minor prophets.

The *Sacred Writings* include three small collections: 1) Psalms, Proverbs, Job; 2) Song of Songs, Ruth, Lamentations, Esther, Ecclesiastes; and 3) Daniel, Ezra-Nehemiah, 1 and 2 Chronicles.

This ancient threefold division is mentioned in Luke 24:44, where mention is made of "the Law of Moses," "the Prophets" and "the Psalms," which is the first of the Writings.

In Jewish theology, these books have different values. By far the most important is the Torah. The other books in the Tanakh have lesser degrees of inspiration; the least important are the Writings.

THE TALMUD

The Talmud is of equal value with the Tanakh and has the same authority. According to the rabbis, the oral law was given at Mount Sinai and goes back to Moses. Because there were gaps of information in the written law, the oral law helped fill in the missing pieces. The oral tradition was "crucial...because the text was so manifestly cryptic."[16] For example, how could anyone obey the commandment not to work on the Sabbath without the help of further details? What activities are legal on the Sabbath? And what is illegal? The oral law provided these details. "Moses received the Law on Sinai and delivered it to Joshua; Joshua in turn handed it down to the Elders; from the Elders it descended to the prophets and each of them delivered it to his successors until it reached the man of the Great Assembly."[17] The "Great Assembly" of the days of Ezra and Nehemiah numbered 120 men, which is the same number of officials who sit in the Knesset, the Israeli parliament.

The oral tradition was transmitted from generation to generation and finally reached Rabbis Hillel and Shammai close to the beginning of our era, and they seldom agreed. The Talmud mentions 300 differences of opinion between these two schools of thought. Shammai followed a stricter interpretation than Hillel. Detailed interpretations of every word, letter, and even vowel points of the written law multiplied the differences of opinion.

The destruction of the Jewish temple in Jerusalem by the Romans in A.D. 70 and the death of many sages compelled Rabbi Jehuda to compile, select, and systematize the oral law. The result of his extraordinary effort is the Mishna, which is a compilation of legal opinions and debates. Jehuda finished his monumental work around A.D. 200–220.

Rodkinson, a translator of the Talmud, wrote that

reason compels us to admit, at least, that there were passages in the Mishna concerning Jesus and his teaching; for how is it possible that an occurrence which holds so important a place in the history of Israel, and which has spread its influence among the nations for centuries, should not even be hinted at in the Mishna? We must, therefore, conclude that Rabbi thought it well to clear the Mishna of any reference to the occurrence itself, as well to the adherents of the new faith.[18]

That is an interesting bit of speculation.

The second part of the Talmud is the Gemara, or commentaries on the Mishna. The Gemara includes stories and legends, folklore, homilies, and debates. It is a vast compendium of information and its size dwarfs the text of the Mishna. One commentary was compiled in Israel and, in combination with the Mishna, is called the Jerusalem Talmud, which was completed around 400. The more important Gemara was composed in Babylon about a century later and, combined with the same Mishna, is called the Babylonian Talmud. When the word *Talmud* is used without further specification, the reference is always to the Babylonian Talmud.

The Talmud follows the six major divisions of the Mishna: Seeds, Festivals, Women, Damages, Sacred Things (sacrifices), and Purification. Each section has further subdivision within them. The parts of the Talmud that are legally binding, are called *halakah* ("the going, or the direction, the way"). The moral stories, or *haggadah*, are not legally binding. About one third of the text is haggadah.

It takes a lifetime of study to grasp the essentials of the Talmud because it is so comprehensive. Joseph Caro (1488–1575) of Italy set himself to the task of producing a compact edition of the Talmud, called the *Shulchan Aruch*. This "essential Talmud" is still used today, although there have been digests of the digest created since the days of Caro.

Judaism has an enormous collection of rabbinical literature and although much of it is highly respected, none has the same authority as the Tanakh and the Talmud. The Midrash deserves to be mentioned. It is a collection of stories, homilies, commentaries, parables, and legends on biblical texts composed sometime between the fourth and the twelfth centuries. Most interesting are those on the last four books of Moses.

RABBINICAL PERSPECTIVES AND WRITINGS
The Law

According to the rabbis, there are 613 commandments in the Torah, of which 248 are positive injunctions ("do this") and 365 prohibitions ("don't do that"). About one third of these commandments cannot be observed because the temple is no longer standing or for some other reason. Some deal with the purification of priests, the offering of the showbread, the removal of ashes from the altar, and so on. As one Jewish author observed, it is disappointing that these 613 commandments "hardly included any purely spiritual demand. Even prayer was not regarded as properly performed unless one's lips moved during recitation."[19] Legalism prevails throughout. For example, there are specific rules about affixing the *mezuzah*. The text of Deuteronomy 6:9 was understood literally and the *mezuzah*, a piece of parchment, was created with the text of Deuteronomy 6:4-9 and

11:13-21 written in 22 lines. The paper was rolled up and put in a little case to be attached to the right-hand doorpost. The great rabbi Rashi thought that the *mezuzah* should be affixed vertically on the doorpost, but his grandson favored the horizontal position. A compromise has the *mezuzah* in a slanting position.

"Judaism is a religion of law" although it was founded on the concept of faith.[20] Abraham, father of the nation, heard the call of God and responded with trust. Faith, not law, was the definitive character of his life. King Jehoshaphat admonished the people, "Have faith in the LORD your God and you will be upheld," and Habakkuk proclaimed that "the righteous will live by his faith."[21] Dosick reminds us that "at least twice in the past 2,000 years, movements within Judaism have attempted to bring Judaism back to finding the spiritual, to celebrating faith." He refers to the kabbalists and the Hasidics, but adds that "their attempts were always stifled."[22] Not everyone understands faith as trust in God and a firm reliance on his word. According to Roth, "faith springs from moral integrity...rests on the authority of conscience."[23]

The commandment not to do any work on the Sabbath (Exodus 20:10) has been refined in the oral law to include 39 categories of work ("forty less one" chiefs or "fathers") listed in the Talmud.[24] They are plowing, sowing, reaping, binding sheaves, threshing, winnowing, sifting (selecting), grinding, sifting in a sieve, kneading, baking, shearing wool, washing it, beating it, dying it, spinning, weaving, making two loops, weaving two threads, separating two threads, tying a knot, untying a knot, sewing two stitches, tearing in order to sew two stitches, trapping deer, slaughtering it, skinning it, salting it, tanning, scraping hide, cutting hide to shape, writing two letters, erasing two letters, building, demolishing, extinguishing fire, lighting fire, beating with a hammer, and carrying from one possession to another.

These 39 activities are only the major categories. Each one has been carefully dissected into smaller parts. For example, carrying was divided into two separate acts: lifting up and putting down. It was also argued that something could be lifted up or put down from two different places—from a public to a private place, or vice versa. This, of course, requires a discussion to define what constitutes a private or public space. What about places like the ocean, which is neither public nor private? The details in these discussions are both fascinating and endless.

The permissible weight of an object to be carried gave rise to another discussion. Suppose the "lowest standard" is the weight of a dried fig. What about half a fig carried at two different times? Once again the possibilities for discussion are endless. What about an object thrown into the air with the left hand and caught with the right hand?

The seemingly simple act of writing underwent the same analytical torture. Was guilt incurred when a person wrote with fruit juice instead of ink? Or when a person wrote on skin or perhaps in the sand? What about writing one letter in the morning and one in the afternoon?

Women were told that on the Sabbath, they should not go out with ornaments that could be taken off because she might be tempted to show them to a friend and thus carry them—and such would be a "burden," which was unlawful on the Sabbath. Women were also forbidden to look into a mirror lest they discover a white hair and pull it out, which was yet another forbidden activity on the Sabbath. There are also the occasional hypothetical situations. What if a deer were to wander into a house through an open door on a Sabbath? Is it legal to close the door and entrap the deer, or would this be the equivalent of hunting, which was prohibited? Rules regarding the Sabbath take up a lot of space in the Talmud, yet it is impossible for rabbis to cover every eventuality, and thus commentaries continue to abound. Throughout history, leading rabbis have responded to these kinds of inquiries regarding the correct interpretation of the law.

The rules governing food have become increasingly complex. The Torah listed which animals are clean and unclean, but even the clean animals have to be slaughtered properly. This is the task of specialists because many rules must be observed. The blood of the animal must be removed by soaking and salting. Excess fat must be eliminated. The hindquarter is not used, thus, in the case of cows, disqualifying sirloin and porterhouse steak (at least in the United States). It is time consuming and costly to remove the sciatic nerve (Genesis 32:32), but it is done in Israel.

Many of the rules and regulations concerning food are based on the slender foundation of a single text: "Do not cook a young goat in its mother's milk."[25] The rabbis concluded from this passage that milk and meat should not be mixed. This is the basis of most of the kashrut (kosher) rules. It is necessary to use separate cooking utensils for meat and milk products and a different set of dishes and cutlery. In addition, a third set of everything is needed for the Passover to make sure that none of the kitchen utensils have ever been contaminated by leaven. And even if meat and milk

have been cooked separately, it is better to wait several hours (perhaps six) after eating meat before consuming milk products, but a shorter time lapse is enough for the reverse situation.

Archaeological excavations at the ancient site of Ugarit (now in Syria) have unearthed documents that have thrown new light on the enigmatic text of Exodus. We now know that the boiling of a kid in its mother's milk was a pagan custom and the Mosaic injunction is quite simply this: Do not imitate the customs of the heathen.

For orthodox Jews, the law is supreme and rules forever. As Maimonides put it, "I believe and affirm that this Torah will not be abrogated, nor shall another Torah come from God." This is one of the 13 articles proposed by Maimonides to sum up Jewish belief. These articles are a virtual creed of Judaism produced by one of its greatest scholars. Almost immediately Rabbi Joseph Albo objected to the idea that the law never changes. If two laws contradict each other, one has to be modified, and Rabbi Albo claimed to know several contradictory laws. Most Orthodox Jews agree with Maimonides. Nevertheless, according to Rabbi Abba Hillel Silver, "the Rabbis did permit much that was prohibited and in some instances prohibited things that were permitted."[26]

For example, the prophet Moses had stated that an emasculated person could not enter the assembly of the Lord (Deuteronomy 23:1). But Isaiah said eunuchs who keep the Sabbath, chose what pleases God, and hold fast to his covenant would be honored and received (Isaiah 56:4). The rabbis abrogated some biblical laws as early as the first century, including the ordeal by means of bitter water for the woman suspected of adultery.[27] The law was abolished on the authority of Jochanan ben Zakkai, who died in A.D. 80 (perhaps a contemporary of Christ) because adultery had become so common (Talmud, Sota 9:9 and Luke 18:11). The sages also discontinued the ritual of breaking a heifer's neck in case of an unsolved murder.[28] The rabbis "declared that under certain conditions a Sage or three private persons could declare a vow invalid and absolve the taker of the vow from its consequences."[29]

According to the law of Moses, when a man died without a son, his widow was to marry her brother-in-law. This was called a levirate marriage and commanded in the Torah.[30] The rabbis abolished that requirement. There are other cases in which the rabbis have effectively rendered the law inoperative. The ingenious but rather artificial extension of the Sabbath day's walk illustrates the point. The entire city, regardless of size, was considered the "house" of a person—as if four walls like a house surrounded the city. One could therefore walk throughout the city without restriction, even on the Sabbath day. The walking limit only applied to the distance beyond the (imaginary) city lines. Other commandments were surrounded by so many restrictions that for all practical purposes they were nullified. Chief Rabbi Kook (1865–1935) a strenuous advocate of religious Zionism, gave nonreligious Zionists a dispensation from letting the land lie fallow every seven years.

Maimonides and the Articles of Faith

There is no creed or formal statement on which all Jews agree, like the Apostles' Creed in Christianity. What comes closest to that are the 13 articles of faith listed by Maimonides. He is respected as one of the greatest scholars Judaism has ever produced. His primary focus was the person of God. In an effort to build a bridge between Greek philosophy and the Torah, Maimonides ended up with the God of the philosophers, a prime mover devoid of personality, not the God of Abraham, Isaac, and Jacob (cf. Pascal). Maimonides believed that God can only be described negatively, in terms of what he is not—he is not ignorant, he is not absent, etc. God is pure Mind, beyond anything finite. "This is more a confession of ignorance than description of God."[31] But the caution of Maimonides is understandable. If one affirms that God is love, the question might arise, Whom did God love before the creation of the earth? Yet from a biblical perspective, the picture of God as presented by Maimonides is both unsatisfactory and defective.

Maimonides's uncertainties regarding life after death also generated considerable controversy. It is true that the Tanakh does not have much to say about eternal life or the resurrection of the body. Rabbi Silver goes so far as to say that "the Torah shows no interest in the career of the soul after death."[32] This was one of the differences between two of the major Jewish sects in Jesus' day, the Pharisees and Sadducees. The latter rejected the idea of resurrection. But it was the Pharisees's understanding that prevailed and shaped the Talmud, in which life after death and the resurrection of the body are mentioned more than once. One passage even says, "The righteous among the Gentiles will have a portion in the world to come." While it is open to question whether "the world to come" designates the age of the Messiah or eternity, the text clearly presupposes life after death. It is a foregone conclusion, clearly stated in the Mishna, that "all Israel has a share in the world to come…the following have no share in the world to come: he who says that there is no allusion in the Torah concerning resurrection."[33] It is enough to be a child of Abraham to have a guarantee of eternal life.

Life after death is not a debatable issue in terms of Orthodox thinking, but other Jewish groups see it differently. They assume that the idea of life after death was adopted by Jews during the Babylonian exile and that these concepts originally came from Persia and Zoroastrians. Others, such as De Lange, opine that "this idea seems to have been borrowed from Greek thought." Some assume that it was in response to the political pressure of the Greeks and Romans that "the sages introduced the concept of afterlife, with God's reward and punishment for earthly behavior given in a world to come."[34] The rabbis created a new theological concept—namely, resurrection and a return to Israel—to be present when the perfection of the world is announced.[35] Along the same line, Rabbi Silver states that "it was not any spiritual evolution in Judaism which, toward the beginning of the common era, brought the doctrine of the resurrection and immortality within the framework of authoritative Judaism, but, quite simply, the inability of its leaders to withstand popular pressure."[36] If all references to life after death are foreign intrusions from Persia or Greece or elsewhere, and if the law of Moses is entirely this-worldly, then Judaism is not on a very high spiritual level.

In support of the afterlife Orthodox rabbis quote Genesis 25:8, where we are told that Abraham upon his death was "gathered to his people," or they mention Jacob, who anticipated rest with his fathers (Genesis 49:29), not to mention other such texts in the Psalms, Daniel, and Job. Rabbi

Epstein reminds us that "in a world largely dominated by the prospect of life after death, it would be strange if the Hebrews alone did not share this belief."[37]

Although occasionally Maimonides seemed to deny the immortality of the soul, in his 13 articles he wrote that he believed that a resurrection of the dead would take place at a time that would be well pleasing to the Creator. It seems that Maimonides held that only the soul could enjoy immortality and that the resurrected body will eventually die again.[38] Rabbi De Lange concludes that many religious Jews see Judaism as a this-worldly religion and do not believe in survival after death.

Maimonides embraced the idea of the Messiah: "I believe and affirm that the Messiah will come. Even should he tarry, I still long for his advent." This has remained the Orthodox position. As the Talmud put it, "All the prophets have prophesied only for the days of Messiah," and again, "The world was not created but only for Messiah." "Everyone has to wait for him, as it reads: 'Wait for him, because he will surely come.' "[39] The Orthodox are still waiting. Recently many thought that perhaps Menachem Mendel Schneerson (1902–1994) might reveal himself as the Messiah. He died in 1994, but some still believe that he continues to live in a fashion that eludes us and that he will reveal himself when the time is ripe.

Some have diluted and depersonalized the messianic hope held by some Jews. For Rabbi Mordecai Kaplan (1881–1983), founder of the Reconstructionists (one of the smaller Jewish groups), the Messiah is merely a symbol and God is not a person. He is only a "power that makes for salvation." The doctrine of the Messiah has been equated with belief in progress and hope, or an optimistic view of human nature. We are told that the idea of the Messiah is symbolic and expresses belief in the coming of a higher type of man than this world has yet to know. Some even see Zionism as a secular form of the messianic hope. For the ultra-Orthodox, only the Messiah can set up a true Jewish state.

Unfortunately there have been many pseudo-Messiahs across history who have only increased the sufferings of the Jews. All too often the idea of the Messiah was "inspiring as a hope [but] hopeless as a reality."[40] For Reform Judaism the *person* of the Messiah is not essential to messianism; it is a *golden age* when the vision of Isaiah will become reality and "the LORD will be king over the whole earth. On that day there will be one LORD, and his name the only name" (Zechariah 14:9).

As most Jews understand it, they have a mission to proclaim monotheism to the world (Isaiah 44:6-8). If monotheism has been proclaimed thanks to Christianity and Islam, what is left of the mission entrusted to Israel? If in the past Jews were prevented from spreading their faith, where are the Jewish missionaries today? Some tentative answers have been offered. Rabbi Silver admits that Judaism did not destroy paganism, but "through Christianity and, later, Islam, vital elements of its message [the monotheistic message of Judaism] spread through the world and carved new highways for the spirit of man."[41] The "daughter faiths," Christianity and Islam, "though with an imperfect vision of God" share in common many truths both religious and moral with the mother faith. "The improvement must come in God's own time."[42] The "improvement" is the better understanding of the unity of God—although

Judaism can hardly improve on this matter as far as Islam is concerned. Was the call of Israel to proclaim "an improved version of monotheism" to a pagan world? Whether the Jewish view of God is an improvement over against Christianity and Islam is, of course, a matter of debate.

Can anything be done to hasten the coming of the messianic era? Echoes of ancient discussions are found in the Talmud. Some thought that the Messiah would come after all hope has been renounced: others decided that it was impossible to know because there are passages in the Tanakh that "bore a hole to the depth"—that is, so deep that no one could fathom the depth. Said Rabh, "It depends only on repentance and good deeds" which is similar to the answer given to an inquiring rabbi: "[He will come] today, this day, if you will hearken to his voice."[43]

THE HISTORY OF THE JEWISH PEOPLE

IF NOTHING ELSE, JEWS are linked by a common history. It is essential to understand the great outlines of this ancient, tortured history to gain some insight into Judaism. Muslims, Christians, and Jews all point to Abraham as their spiritual ancestor. All three have been called religions of faith, in contrast to Confucianism, which emphasizes wisdom, or the religions of the Far East, which put people in search of a mystical union.

UNDER ABRAHAM

The approximate date of God's call to Abraham is 1920 B.C. Dates for the patriarchal period are uncertain, but "the stories of the patriarchs fit unquestionably and authentically in the milieu of the second millennium."[44] At some point the Lord appeared to Abram, and Abram obeyed the divine call, left his country and his father's house, and believed the promise that he would inherit a land he had never seen and become the ancestor of a great nation.[45] This was a monumental decision, and Abram moved forward with unshakable trust in the promise of God. The initiative rested with God. Monotheism was a matter of revelation, of disclosure, an unveiling. The choice of Abram was God's sovereign act. It was not motivated by unique qualities found in the person of Abram. Some ancient rabbis, in an effort to explain the choice, thought that Abram (who was later renamed Abraham) observed all the commandments—even the oral law.[46]

For some modern rabbis, it was the "genius of Israel" to invent monotheism. Did Jews rise "to a monotheistic conception of religion, head and shoulder above that of any other people"?[47] Was the discovery of monotheism a "gradual growth from more primitive conceptions, a primary irresistible intuition"?[48] Abba Eban raises the question, "In what were they [the Jews] so different from their contemporaries?" He supplies the answer: "Their greatest discovery and intuition was the idea of a single God."[49] Were Jews innately wiser than other people? "This much seems clear: the idea of a single, omnipotent, omniscient God is a Jewish invention, one that has changed the course of Western [and, therefore, world] history."[50] Other Jewish authors are more cautious in their assessments.

The historic reality presents a different picture. Terah, the father of Abraham, worshipped other gods.[51] Yet God took the initiative and revealed himself to Abraham, who walked in faith and obedience. But even Rachel, a member of the immediate patriarchal family, was attached to household gods.[52] At Mount Sinai, while Moses was in the presence of God, the people worshipped the golden calf. The prophet Elijah and his many successors fulminated against idol worship, but it was only after the excruciating Babylonian exile that the nation as a whole finally turned wholeheartedly to monotheism—although even a post-exilic prophet still denounced idols that speak deceitfully and visionary diviners and dreamers.[53] Not one of the many kings of Israel turned away from the worship of the golden calves at Bethel and Dan, and all too often the kings of Judah followed a similar pattern. Monotheism was not a Jewish idea; it was a divine revelation. It was proclaimed early but not practiced on a large scale till after the Babylonian exile.

UNDER MOSES

Sometime around the fifteenth century B.C., the towering personality of Moses appears, and he leads the people of Israel out of Egypt. The exodus is the decisive event of Jewish history; the national identity of Israel begins here. God says, "I will take you as my own people....I am the LORD your God who brought you out from under the yoke of the Egyptians."[54] Since then the great redemptive events of the exodus have been retold from generation to generation,[55] and year after year the Passover is celebrated as the "birthday" of the nation.

Fifty days after the Passover the festival of Weeks or Shavuot (Pentecost) takes place. It is probably the least observed of all the Jewish festivals. Originally it was a harvest festival.[56] Traditionally it is on that day that Moses received the Torah. Accepted by

Christianity and Islam, the Ten Commandments are the moral foundation of most of the Western world and had a significant impact on Western civilization.

The laws of Moses are an extraordinary collection of ethical principles and detailed ritual. The motive and principle of the entire legislation is to promote holiness, inspire godliness, and build character.[57] "Be holy, because I, the LORD your God, am holy."[58] With wonderful spiritual insight the rabbis taught that

> Isaiah came and reduced the 613 commands to six (Isaiah 33:15): "He that (a) walketh in righteousness, (b) speaketh uprightly, (c) despiseth the gain of oppressions, (d) shaketh his hands against taking hold of bribes, (e) stoppeth his ears against hearing of blood, and (f) shutteth his eyes against looking on evil."...Micah came and reduced them to three (Micah 6:8): "He hath told thee, O man, what is good and what the LORD doth require of thee: (nothing) but to do justice, and love kindness, and to walk humbly with thy God."...Isaiah again reduced them to two (Isaiah 56:1): "Thus saith the LORD, keep you justice and do equity." Amos then came and reduced them to one (Amos 5:4): "Seek ye for me, and ye shall live." Another Rabbi added: Habakkuk was the one who reduced them to one (2:4): "The righteous shall live with his faith."[59]

It was Moses who summed up the essentials in a few majestic words that are known to every Jew and are part of every ritual and private prayer: "Hear, O Israel: The LORD our God, the LORD is one. Love the LORD your God with all your heart and with all your soul and with all your strength."[60]

Moses established the cycle of the Jewish year. The Sabbath is the backbone of the rhythm of the year, which is punctuated by several festivals. The Passover has just been mentioned. Rosh Hashanah (the Jewish New Year) and Yom Kippur (the Day of Atonement) are High Holy Days, and the ten days separating these festivals are "days of awe." Rosh Hashanah is the Day of Judgment, characterized by the blowing of the shofar or ram's horn.[61] According to tradition, Rosh Hashanah was the birthday of both Isaac and Samuel, and it was on this same day that Abraham offered his son Isaac up to God.

On the tenth day of the month, on the day of Yom Kippur, "atonement will be made for you, to cleanse you. Then, before the LORD, you will be clean from all your sins."[62] It is a day of Sabbath rest and the same laws govern the day. Repentance involves acknowledgment of sin because "there is not a righteous man on earth who does what is right and never sins."[63] Confession, sorrow for sin, and the firm resolve to improve are key ingredients of repentance.

Yom Kippur is the most solemn day of the Jewish year. The keynote of the liturgy is repentance and confession of sins. It is appropriate that the Day of Atonement is a day of fasting. The next festival is called Succot, or the Feast of Tabernacles. The *sukkah* or booth is a reminder of the years Israel spent in the desert. A booth is erected at home as well as on the grounds of the synagogue. The roof is deliberately permeable so that some wind and rain can penetrate the booth. The last day of Succot coincides with the end of the annual reading of the Torah in the synagogue. Details about the feasts are found in Leviticus chapter 23.

UNDER THE MONARCHS

Though Moses led the people of Israel to the Promised Land, he never entered it. The task of conquering Canaan went to Joshua. After Joshua came the time of the judges, during which the nation of Israel was sporadic in its obedience to God and fell frequently into idol worship. Then came the prophet Samuel, who anointed Saul as Israel's first king. When Saul proved himself unfaithful to God's ordinances, David was chosen to be the next king.

The approximate date of David's reign was around 1000 B.C.. David was a military hero and effective king. He established the capital at Jerusalem, consolidated and expanded the state, and established an administrative machinery. As a man of war, he was not allowed to build the temple in Jerusalem—that job fell to his son Solomon. With the help of workers from King Hiram Solomon built the temple, but his building activity was not restricted to the house of the Lord. We have ample archaeological evidence that Solomon established a chain of fortified cities, including Hazor, Meguiddo (strategically situated near the main pass through the Carmel), Gezer, and other centers. Foreign trade was a royal monopoly, and Solomon's trading voyages reached Ophir. Merchants returned with apes and peacocks or baboons for the amusement of royalty.[64] The displays of magnificence, the incessant building activity, the costs of a large harem, and the many commercial ventures led to fiscal problems. Forced labor and heavy taxation were imposed and detested. New administrative districts replaced ancient tribal boundaries and were resented. Upon Solomon's death around 922 B.C. the kingdom split and Judah and Israel emerged as two separate entities. The empire was lost overnight. Damascus could not be held; the Philistine cities broke free. Ammon became independent, and Egypt was invaded.[65]

The ten tribes of the Northern Kingdom (called Israel) never embraced monotheism wholeheartedly and established sanctuaries in Bethel and Dan to worship "the gods who brought them out of Egypt" (1 Kings 12). The prophets, spokesmen for God, were usually in opposition to the king and the priests. The prophet Amos sounds a clarion call for social justice, and other prophets announce dire judgments to come. Elijah opposed the prophets of Baal and was temporarily successful, but nothing could stop the decline of the two kingdoms. Israel stumbled from crisis to crisis, often changing dynasties but always doomed to failure.

DURING THE EXILE

When Israel invaded Judah during Judean king Ahaz's reign, the king appealed to the Assyrians for help (2 Kings, chapter 16). They were happy to oblige, and soon afterwards, in 721 B.C., Samaria, the capital of Israel, fell to the Assyrians. According to Sargon II, more than 27,000 Israelites were deported to Upper Mesopotamia and Media and ultimately lost their identity. The "ten lost tribes of Israel" figure largely in fanciful legends and are variously placed in remote Asia or dark Africa or even identified with the Indians of North America or the British. Most of them are said to "simply assimilate and disappear, though some mingle with later exiles."[66]

The small kingdom of Judah had little chance to survive. Isaiah and Micah prophesied there and occasionally a godly king sat on the throne, but under King Manasseh, pagan cults and practices were allowed to flourish and were even tolerated in the Temple.[67] The prophet Ezekiel denounced the people's idolatry.[68] Denunciations from the prophets Jeremiah and Zephaniah went unheeded. Nebuchadnezzar, the great king of the Babylonian Empire, finally gave the coup de grace and the kingdom of Judah toppled. The temple was destroyed on the ninth of Ab in 587 B.C., and according to tradition, this was the very same calendar day on which the second temple was destroyed in A.D. 70. The people of Judah were taken into captivity.

The Tanakh makes it very clear why the temple was destroyed. Again and again God had sent messengers who pleaded for the people to turn away from idolatry and follow God alone, but the nation despised God's words and scoffed at his prophets till there was no remedy.[69]

After the destruction of the temple, the synagogue played an increasingly important role in Jewish religious life. The absence of the sacrificial cult gave renewed importance to the Sabbath celebrated in the synagogue. The focus of the people shifted to the study of the law. This was the beginning of rabbinic Judaism. Seventy years after the destruction of the first temple, under the benign rule of Cyrus, the Jews were allowed to return to Israel. The vast majority, however, stayed in Babylon. They were not enticed to return to a land in ruins and utter desolation and surrounded by enemies.

AFTER THE EXILE

Those Jews who returned under the leadership of Ezra and Nehemiah numbered into the tens of thousands. These people still remained under the overlordship of Persia. In time, the temple was rebuilt. In the absence of kings and prophets (except for Zechariah, Haggai, and Malachi), the priesthood loomed large.

At some point in the fifth century, in the days of the Persian king Ahasuerus (perhaps Xerxes, 485–464 B.C.), a Persian official named Haman denounced the Jews and had an anti-Jewish edict issued. Thanks to Esther, a Jewess who was one of the king's wives, the disaster was averted and Haman executed. To this day this deliverance of the Jewish people is celebrated yearly at the Feast of Purim, during which the book of Esther is read.

THE HELLENISTIC INFLUENCE

The coming of Alexander the Great in 333 B.C. marked the first time a European power appeared in Israel. There were lasting consequences. The successors of Alexander promoted Greek culture, which was anathema to Orthodox Jews. Palestine passed from Egyptian to Syrian domination. Antiochus IV Epiphanes (175–164 B.C.) was determined to impose Hellenism. This led to the Maccabean uprising.

In 167 B.C. some 40,000 Jews were massacred by the Syrian overlord and an equal number sold into slavery. The temple was desecrated and dedicated to Jupiter Olympus. Three years later, the victorious Maccabees pushed the Syrians out of Palestine. The temple was purified and order restored. Every year to this day, the Hanukkah feast, in which candles are aflame on a menorah, is a reminder of the triumph of light over darkness.

There were now two parties in Israel—the Grecians, so called because they favored Greek culture, and the Hasidim, or the

Orthodox Jews. They were the forerunners of the Pharisees. The Sadducees were the spiritual descendants of the priestly party and were inclined toward Hellenism. Their interests were primarily political. The office of the high priest was both political and religious and for sale to the highest bidder. Under John Hyrcanus I (135–105 B.C.) the rupture between Pharisees and Sadducees became public and permanent.

THE ROMAN CONQUEST

In 63 B.C. Pompey of Rome conquered Jerusalem, and Israel became a territory of Rome. This was resented by the Jews, and an intense yearning for political freedom pervaded the atmosphere. Hope centered on the Messiah that scripture had promised would bring deliverance. The Jews interpreted this to mean the Messiah would triumph over Rome, so messianic expectations ran high. Indeed, Jesus of Nazareth attracted multitudes during his ministry, but they were disappointed to discover that he had no political agenda. The message "Love your enemies"—including the Romans—was not well received. Rabbi Silver comments that to love enemies is "contrary to human nature."[70] But hopefully the limits of ethics are not determined by the limited capacity of human nature. Is religion not a call to transcendence?

Denounced by the Jewish priesthood, Jesus was turned over to the Roman authorities and crucified. His followers claimed that he rose from the dead. His mother, the apostles, and thousands upon thousands of Jews accepted him as the Messiah.[71] This explains why daily Jewish prayers included the twelfth benediction—in this case, a curse: "For the apostates let there be no hope...let the Nazarenes and the heretics be destroyed in a moment." The text is from the end of the first century and was found in a Cairo *genizah*, a depository for sacred texts no longer usable.[72]

Backtracking a bit to before Israel came under Roman rule, Rabbi Hillel was born in 70 B.C. He claimed descent from King David, and was one of the great sages of Israel and the leader of the Pharisees. The Mishna reports a few of his sayings, including, "If I do not look to myself, who will do so? But if I look only to myself what am I? And if not now, when?"[73] There was a story about two men stranded in the desert, and only one had a bottle of water. There was not enough water for both of them. Rabbi Akiba, another prominent rabbi, decided that the man with the bottle should keep it and drink all the water rather than save his neighbor and lose his own life. Why assume that your neighbor's affairs are worth more in God's eyes than yours? By contrast, Jesus declared, "Greater love has no one than this, that he lay down his life for his friends" (John 15:13).

Hillel is also known for his leniency on matters of divorce. According to the law, a man could divorce his wife if he found something indecent or shameful in her.[74] Hillel thus concluded that a man could divorce his wife for merely displeasing him, even for a trivial act such as putting too much salt in the soup. Rabbi Akiba went so far as to opine that it was enough if a man found a more beautiful woman. Was that really what Moses had in mind in Deuteronomy 24:1?

Hillel also thought of King Hezekiah as the Messiah. Hillel said, "There is no more any Messiah for Israel, as they have consumed him already in the days of Hiskia [Hezekiah]." Another rabbi, however—Rabbi Joseph—reasoned that: King Hezekiah could *not* have been the Messiah, for *after* Hezekiah's death, the prophet Zechariah announced the still-future coming of the Messiah.

A generation after Hillel, the voice of Jesus of Nazareth was heard. For centuries the Jews have ignored Jesus, but more recently some have tried to adopt him as one of the great Jewish rabbis. Max Nordau (1849–1923), a loyal Zionist leader alongside Theodor Herzl, the father of Zionism, wrote, "Jesus is the soul of our soul, as he is the flesh of our flesh. So who can exclude him from the Jewish people?"[75] Occasionally Hillel's sayings have been compared to those of Jesus, and efforts have been made to find rabbinical statements that parallel those found in Jesus' Sermon on the Mount. Here and there a similar thought has been discovered across a dozen different rabbinical writings, but all those same thoughts are found in one place in the New Testament Bible. As Rabbi Pinchas Lapide (1922–1997) put it, this is like the difference between a building and the stones of the quarry of which it is built. Isolated stones are not equal to an entire building. Hillel is rightly famous, but his reputation is largely confined to Jewish circles. By contrast, the words of Jesus of Nazareth circle the globe. There must be a significant reason for this difference.

THE FALL OF JERUSALEM

After Jesus' death and resurrection, the disciples continued to carry on his ministry. It didn't take long for false messiahs to start appearing on the scene. In A.D. 60, an Egyptian asked people to join him on the Mount of Olives and watch the walls of Jerusalem fall. He deluded a crowd of 30,000. Roman soldiers killed 400 and captured 200, but the Egyptian escaped and disappeared.[76]

Jewish sentiment against Rome continued to worsen. By A.D. 69–70, the situation got to the point that Rome sent Titus to besiege and destroy Jerusalem. The Jewish historian Josephus—who was biased in favor of Rome—wrote that one million Jews were killed and 97,000 were made prisoners. Some suspect those numbers are high, but still, there were many who lost their lives.

The fall of Jerusalem and destruction of the temple ended the Jewish commonwealth. The Essenes, a small group to begin with, vanished, and the Herodian party (those who supported Herod and Rome) became obsolete. The Sadducees lost the temple and the aristocracy and ceased to function. Only the Pharisees survived, in part thanks to Jochanan ben Zakkai, a disciple of Hillel who was known as a moderate Pharisee and peace advocate. During the Roman siege he was smuggled out of Jerusalem in a coffin, and the Romans allowed him to open a house of teaching in Jabneh.

The destruction of the temple was a devastating blow to Judaism. Again, the reason for the ruin of the first temple was clearly stated in the Tanakh: the rejection of God's messengers.[77] But what about the reasons for the destruction of the second temple? Some rabbis asked, "But the second temple, where the occupations were study of the Law, religious duties, and charity—why fell it?" According to the rabbis, that generation had been relatively innocent. The only reason that could be adduced was "unfounded hatred,"[78] or the fragmentation and internecine fighting Josephus describes in his accounts of the Roman conquest. Does it make sense that the second temple was destroyed and followed by an exile lasting for centuries all because hatred prevailed among the Jews themselves? Perhaps the question deserves more serious consideration.

The last fanatical holdouts against the Romans were zealots who took refuge in Masada, a fortress at the top of a high rock plateau. When it became impossible to defend the fortress, the 960 men, women, and children committed suicide.

A few years later, in A.D. 115, Jews in Egypt, Cyrenaica, Cyprus, and Syria took up arms against Rome and fought desperately for two years. A few years later, the homeland again erupted in violence. And in A.D. 135 Shimeon bar Cochba rose against Rome. Rabbi Akiba (c. 45–135) hailed bar Cochba as the Messiah. But bar Cochba was defeated by the Romans and fell in battle, and Rabbi Akiba was martyred. More than half a million Jews were killed, although the exact number is difficult to ascertain.

A MAJOR TRANSITION

By this time, the nation of Israel had been seriously decimated. The center of Jewish life shifted from Jerusalem to Safed, from the temple to the Torah. The rabbis focused on the law and created new walls firmer than those of Jerusalem. Tradition and law helped to cement the Jews together.

In the years that followed, oral tradition was put into writing. The Mishna was completed, and A.D. 350 saw the definitive formation of the Jerusalem Talmud. And A.D. 500 is the approximate date of the definitive formation of the Babylonian Talmud. Rabbinical rules regulated everything from hairstyle to sex.

Another false messiah emerged in A.D. 440, Moses of the island of Crete. He promised to bring the Jews to Palestine and cross the sea like Moses of old. Many drowned when he and his followers cast themselves into the ocean. This Moses then disappeared from the scene of history.

Some rabbis, in an attempt to calculate the date of the messiah's coming, taught that the world would "continue for six thousand years, the first two thousand of which were chaos, the second two thousand were of wisdom, and the third two thousand are the days of the Messiah."[79] Some fixed the date at 440; others favored 471. These speculations may have made it easier for Moses of Crete to present himself as the Messiah.

The increasing isolation of the Jews from those around them promoted prejudice. In the Roman Empire Jews were tolerated, but anti-Judaism lurked in the background because the Jews refused to worship the emperor and were "different" in their insistence on monotheism to the exclusion of all the other gods. The Sabbath observance set them apart as well. Dietary rules made it impossible for them to share a meal with non-Jews. Their opposition to mixed marriages was assumed to betray a sense of superiority. Echoes of these sentiments are found in Cicero, Seneca, and Tacitus. The latter wrote, "This race is detested by the gods," and added that their "customs are perverse and disgusting; they regard the rest of mankind with all the hatred of enemies."[80]

When the empire was converted en masse to Christianity under Constantine, anti-Jewish sentiments multiplied. Culturally the church was no longer Jewish, but Greco-Roman. The Old Testament was often interpreted allegorically. And the church blamed the Jews for the crucifixion. The same accusation was heard again and again across history and led to the slaughter of many Jews. Some anti-Jewish legislation was enacted in 434 under Theodosius II (401–450), emperor of the Eastern Roman Empire. It was decreed that Jews could not have Christian slaves. This spelled the end of Jewish agriculture because it was slaves who did the fieldwork.

THE MUSLIM CONQUEST

Nearly 200 years later, in A.D. 629, Dagobert (c. 603–639), king of the Merovingian Empire, gave the Jews of his realm a choice: Convert or be expelled. Many of the Jews opted for Christianity. The edict was not carried out rigorously, but locally the Jewish population suffered. Then in 637 the Muslim armies of Omar conquered Jerusalem. Christian pilgrims continued to visit the city and the Jews who remained there were left relatively unmolested. Although Muhammed had devastated the Jewish tribes in Arabia, by and large both Jews and Christians were treated respectfully by the Muslim conquerors because they were *dhimmi,* or "people of the book." Although subject to second-class citizenship and to special taxation, they were free to follow the precepts of their religion.

An important year in Muslim chronology was 711, when Muslim forces invaded and conquered Spain. They received help from the resident Jews, who had been the victims of several anti-Jewish decrees. Under the Muslims in Spain, Jews were free to pursue careers in finance, industry, and medicine. Some even became court physicians. These Jews also adopted the dress, language, and customs of the Arabs.

On a side note, it's important to observe that Spanish and North African Jews are called Sephardim Jews. Jews from Poland, Lithuania, and Germany are called Ashke-

nazim Jews. The former spoke Ladino, the latter Yiddish. Both Ladino and Yiddish are in steep decline. Currently there are two chief rabbis in Israel, one Ashkenazi the other Sephardi. Relatively small, liturgical differences between Sephardim and Ashkenazim have been magnified to the point where they worship in separate synagogues. The early pioneers in Israel were mostly Ashkenazim. It is only after the establishment of the State of Israel and increasing Arab hostilities that North African Jews emigrated to Israel. Given their large numbers in Israel, they have finally obtained political power commensurate with their number.

A most unusual situation developed in the eighth century when the Khazars, a Turkic-Mongol people in Russia, converted to Judaism. In an effort to escape pressure from Christian Byzantium on one frontier and the Muslim Empire on the other, the Khazars opted for Judaism. Two centuries later, in 965, the Russians conquered the Khazar Empire and forced the people to accept the Christian faith of Kiev. It has been suggested that some Ashkenazim Jews are descendants of the Khazars, but others are adamant that there is not a shred of evidence for this theory. What happened to the people after the fall of the Khazar kingdom? How deeply had Judaism penetrated the masses? Is it not reasonable to assume that at least some survivors might have migrated from the lower Volga to Poland or Lithuania and that some intermarriage took place? Evidence is scant, which allows speculation to abound.

In the same century Anan ben David, a nephew of the *exilarch* or political leader of the Jews, might have become the next *gaon,* or spiritual leader, but his opposition to the oral law prevented his nomination. He is the reputed founder of the Karaites (760), or "Scripturalists," who were opposed to the oral law and rabbinical additions and interpretations. They stood in line with the Sadducees of old, who had also rejected oral traditions. Anan received permission from the Muslim caliph to establish a second autonomous Jewish group that was free from Talmudic observation and rabbinical control. Anan moved to Jerusalem and separated himself from the mass of Jews by using a different calendar, changing the dietary rules (some of which were even stricter), using blue fringes on prayer shawls, refusing to affix the *mezuzah* on doorposts and refusing to wear phylacteries. In a significant departure from traditional Judaism, the Karaites defined Jews through matrilineal descent. The Talmudists declared that the Karaites were not Jews, and the Karaites retaliated by declaring marriage to a Talmudist sinful.[81] Over time, the Karaites split into many sects. The one thing they had in common was their detestation of the Talmudists. Today most of them reside in Israel, and estimates of their numbers vary from 30,000 to 50,000.

Meanwhile, in Europe, thanks to Charlemagne or Charles the Great (742–814), king of the Franks and emperor of the West, Jews enjoyed a certain degree of freedom and reached surprising levels of prosperity during the ninth and tenth centuries.

In the eleventh century, one Jew rose to the highest position of power in Spain. Samuel Ha-Nagid was born into a prominent family in Cordoba, Spain, but was forced to flee in 1013 in the wake of the Berber conquest under Chief Suleiman. Samuel fled to the port of Malaga, where he opened a spice shop near the palace. A maid who was a servant of the vizier asked Samuel to write certain letters because she liked the quality of his calligraphy. Samuel eventually came to the attention of the vizier, who often asked for and followed Samuel's advice. On his deathbed, the vizier confessed that much of his advice had been based on Samuel's counsel and recommended him as his successor. Samuel thus became the vizier of Granada and one of the most famous notables of Muslim Spain. Samuel was a linguist, well-versed in Arabic literature, a Talmudic scholar, a poet, a diplomat, and a distinguished soldier. Thanks to his capable administration, King Habbus (1019–1038) prospered. The Jewish vizier also led Muslim armies in decades of fighting, and he was of considerable help to Jews in other countries. Upon his death (1055) his son succeeded him, but was later murdered.

Under Muslim rule, Jews had a measure of autonomy. The political leader of the Jews carried the title of *exilarchate*, or "Head of the Exile." And the spiritual leader was called *gaon*. One of the most important *gaons* was Saadiah ben Joseph (882–942), the greatest Jewish authority of his time. According to him all laws, ethical or ritualistic, were to be observed regardless of their rational basis simply to ensure that honor was being conferred to God.

By and large the Babylonian Jews lived in peace, although sometimes edicts were enforced more energetically and Jews— along with Zoroastrians and Christians— had to wear a special badge that identified their heritage. In addition, rivalry led to conflicts between the Jewish political leader and the Jewish spiritual leader. This infighting made matters worse. Then the Mongol invasion of Baghdad in 1258 was the final nail in the coffin of Babylonian Jewry.

PERSECUTION IN EUROPE

Over in Europe, latent anti-Jewish feelings surfaced from time to time. The Church of the Holy Sepulcher in Jerusalem burned down in 1009. It was destroyed on orders of Caliph al-Hakim, and some years later the disaster was blamed on the Jews of Orleans in France, who supposedly had suggested the idea to the caliph. Reprisals were inevitable. Still, there were areas of Europe where the Jews continued to live more or less in peace, including Italy, Sicily, the Byzantine Empire, and Christian Spain. There were also periods of peace in England, France, and Germany. But life was always precarious, for hostility could arise unexpectedly from any direction. For example, in 1020, King Canute banished all Jews from England.

Twenty years later, in 1040, Rabbi Shelomo ben Yitzhak, affectionately known as Rashi, was born. He is one of the most famous Jewish commentators in history. He was a seller of wine in Troyes, France. His lucid commentary on the Five Books of Moses is still read today. His notes on the Talmud are so important that they are incorporated into many of the printed editions. Rashi died in 1105. Other luminaries were Abraham ibn Ezra (c. 1092–1167) of Spain and Rabbi David Kimkhi (1160–1235), who is famous for his excellent exegesis of the biblical text. Jehuda Halevi (1086–1147?) of Spain, whom historian Will Durant calls "the greatest European poet of his age,"[82] is the author of the famous line, "My heart is in the East, while I tarry in the West."

All through these centuries, the fires of persecution were never extinguished, only banked. At any time, slumbering embers could easily erupt into full-fledged flames. One such outbreak occurred in England in 1190. Attendance at the coronation of Richard I, Coeur de Lion (the Lionhearted) was by invitation only, and a proclamation excluded Jews and witches from the coronation banquet. Perhaps word had not reached a few wealthy Jews who came to Westminster with handsome gifts only to be forcibly ejected by the barons. Word circulated that Jews had hatched a plot to kill the king. Anti-Jewish feelings became more roused because the preaching of the First Crusade focused on the need to eliminate the infidels. Even a feeble excuse—such as the story of an imaginary plot—was enough to "justify" mob action. Jews were beaten, and a few were killed. "Their appetite for blood whetted, the people marched back to the city [of London], shouting, 'Death to the unbelievers!' Once rioting had started, nothing could stop it."[83] Two delegates from York were caught by the mob. York was the home of wealthy Jews, and many were happy to despoil them. About 1,000 Jewish survivors took refuge in the king's palace and attempted to defend themselves, but their situation was hopeless. They decided to kill themselves rather than surrender. The few who gave themselves up were butchered.

The Jews were also accused of being money-grubbers. It was claimed that they charged interest at the highest possible rate even though usury was prohibited. Because Christians were not allowed to charge interest (let alone usury), all financial transactions ended up being delegated to the Jews. Moneylending "was left to the Jews, as the necessary dirty work of society, and if they had not been available they would have had to be invented...excluded by the guilds from crafts and trades, they had been pushed into petty commerce and moneylending."[84] As tax collectors, Jews absorbed an added measure of popular hate. They served at the behest of the king, and a large share of their revenue went to the king as protector of the Jews. People were always glad to get rid of creditors, and the killing of Jews achieved this goal. And this was but a foretaste of things to come.

THE CRUSADES

The first crusade was launched in 1096 and the immediate result was the massacre of Jewish people. Why fight infidels in far-away countries when many were at hand? Jews in the Rhineland had reached a certain level of economic and even political influence and became the first victims of the Crusaders. Massacres in both Germany and France set in motion the great eastward migration of Jews toward Poland and Russia.[85] These persecutions were not systematic or government sanctioned; the Crusaders were a motley crew with any number of motives. Some were looking for adventure; others were anxious to leave debts behind. A few sought atonement for sin and many hoped for spoils and financial gain. Many of the Crusaders came from the lowest strata of society. To put the matter into a broader perspective, the Fourth Crusade never even reached the Holy Land but stopped in Constantinople, which was plundered because the people were not Latin but Orthodox Christian. The crusaders even desecrated the Church of St. Sophia, one of the greatest in Christendom. Not everyone agreed with the actions the Crusaders were taking. Bernard de Clairvaux, Abelard, and other Christian leaders discussed whether Jews should be tolerated in a Christian society and reached a positive conclusion. In a letter to the Archbishop of Mainz, Bernard protested that the Crusaders should not persecute Jews. He men-

tioned in passing that they would all be saved at the end of the world and should therefore be spared.

The fall of Jerusalem to the Crusaders in 1099 after a five-week siege was followed by the massacre of Jews. In such times of oppression, the Jewish desire for deliverance centered on the Messiah and invariably claimants appeared. In France (c. 1087), in Spain (c. 1117), and in Fez, Morocco (c. 1127) messianic claims were made. The Jewish rabbi and philosopher Maimonides mentions them and even admired Moses al-Dari of Fez because "his prophecies were true"—which goes to show that even a consistent rationalist can sometimes be inconsistent. We have virtually no information regarding these three messiahs.

THE HIGH MIDDLE AGES

Maimonides was born in Cordova, Spain in 1135. He was one of the most learned men of his time and perhaps the greatest Jewish scholar of all times. Tomas Aquinas and Albert the Great were both indebted to him. Aside from mastery of the enormous body of rabbinical literature written to that time, he was thoroughly versed in medicine, astronomy, mathematics, and philosophy. He left Spain in 1159 when fanatic Muslim Berbers forced the Jewish populace to choose between conversion or death. For nine years Maimonides lived in Fez pretending to be a Muslim. He then moved to Palestine and finally to Cairo. He became the court physician of Saladin, who reconquered Jerusalem from the Crusaders.

Maimonides's commentary on the Mishna is mandatory reading for anyone who hopes to understand the Talmud. In his *Guide to the Perplexed,* he sought to reconcile Aristotle with Moses and probably managed to displease both. Although absolutely certain of the existence of God, he did not think that anything definite could be said about him. He also said God can be spoken of only in negative terms. The moment one says God is omnipotent or omniscient, there is a division between the subject and the predicate, a plurality—God and his attributes. The God of Aristotle, the Prime Mover, is not the living God of scripture. Nevertheless, the 13 articles of faith elaborated by Maimonides have become the unofficial creed of Judaism. But, as De Lange points out, "What binds Jews together is not a creed but a history; a strong sense of a common origin, a shared past and a shared destiny."[86]

A child of his time—and in line with the Torah—Maimonides allowed Jews to marry four wives but limited cohabitation with each at once a month. He insisted on the death penalty for anyone who repudiated the Jewish law.

It was in the fateful year of 1144 that the accusation of blood libel was leveled against the Jews. Previously the early Christians had suffered similar accusations from those who misunderstood what the observance of communion was about. Other unorthodox groups, such as the Cathari or the Knights Templars, have also been accused of killing people in order to use their blood in secret rituals. And in 1144, for the first time, Jews were accused of ritual slaughter. It happened in England when William of Norwich, a tanner with frequent contact with Jews, disappeared. At the time, some believed that blood was used by Jews to prepare unleavened bread around the time of the Passover. Even though this myth was condemned by Pope Innocent IV and others, this superstitious belief could not be eradicated and caused untold damage

to the lives of countless Jewish people. Supposedly Jews reenacted the crucifixion to obtain the blood for their unleavened bread. Others believed that they tortured Christian children and drank their blood for unspeakably sinister reasons.

Once the idea of ritual slaughter was aired, it could not be contained. In 1171 rumors surfaced in France when Jews in Blois were accused of the crucifixion of a Christian child whose corpse was allegedly tossed into the Loire. Centuries later, in 1913, Menahem Mendel Beilis, a Ukrainian Jew, was tried for ritual murder because a 13-year-old boy had disappeared whose mutilated body was discovered one week later. And in July of 1946, about 200 Jews returned to Kielce in Poland. Some were holocaust survivors, other came out of hiding. When the old tired stories circulated once again, 40 were massacred and 80 wounded.

It was a moment of light when, in 1179, the Third Lateran Council called for toleration of the Jews "on grounds of humanity alone" or *pro sola humanitate*.[87] Unfortunately a bit later, in 1205, Pope Innocent III announced that Jews "were doomed to perpetual servitude as Christ-killers" and Aquinas concluded that "since Jews are the slaves of the Church, she can dispose of their possessions."[88]

The year 1215 signaled the beginning of the important Fourth Lateran Synod, convened by Pope Innocent III (1198–1216). The meetings were attended irregularly by 71 archbishops and more than 400 bishops, abbots, canons, and representatives of various secular powers. The deliberations altered the legal status of Jews, who were forbidden to go out during Holy Week, compelled to wear a special dress (sometimes welcomed by Jewish leaders as a barrier to assimilation), banned from taking public office, and subject to a special tax paid to the local Christian clergy. Canon 67 reads: "The more Christians are restrained from the practice of usury, the more they are oppressed in this matter by the treachery of the Jews." Jews were compelled to pay tithes to the church for property they seized from Christians. This bizarre legislation was enacted to ensure that the church would not suffer financial loss.

Canon 69 was enacted to prevent Christians from unknowingly having relations with Jewish or Muslim women. To make it easier to recognize Jews and Muslims, "a different character of their dress" was made mandatory. The synod insisted that in this matter they acted in line with the command of the Torah as stated in Numbers 15:37-41. As to the Holy Week, three days before Easter, "they shall not go forth in public at all." This was "justified" because Jews did not show signs of mourning on Good Friday, and they were accused of mocking Christians on that day.

Initially the Inquisition was launched against Albigensians and Cathari and entrusted to the Dominican order. Quickly Jews were included. Public disputations between Christians and Jews were held in 1241 but the victory of the Christians was surely a foregone conclusion. Wagonloads of Talmuds were burned in the streets of Paris. At first the archbishop intervened and the Talmuds were returned to their owners, but this was only a temporary respite. Upon the death of the archbishop, the book burning continued.

Edicts of expulsion pronounced against the Jews were not always carried out to the letter, which explains why in 1254 Louis IX banned all Jews from France, and in 1306 Phillip the Fair of France expelled them again. The Jews were called back by his son for financial reasons. They were used by the court to handle interest payments, of which the royal treasury took the major share. The king was, in effect, a silent partner of the moneylenders. This meant that public anger ended up being deflected from the court and focused on the Jews. The same situation prevailed in England.

In 1290, the Jews were expelled from England because they had outlived their usefulness as financiers. The English had come to learn how to handle all commercial transactions, including international ones, and used the great banking houses of Italy. Hundreds of Jews were hanged, thousands were imprisoned, and all were banished and their property confiscated. This meant that all debts owed to Jews were automatically cancelled. Regardless of the "official reasons" for the mass expulsion, economic issues played a dominant role.

In the late 1340s, the *Black Plague* raged through Europe. It has been estimated that one fourth or more of the European population fell victim to the plague. People looked for someone to blame, and Jews furnished a convenient scapegoat. They were accused of having poisoned wells and attempts were made to extract confessions from them through torture.

In 1348 Pope Clement VI (1342-1352) issued a bull prohibiting the forcible conversion of Jews and the looting and killing of them without trial, but in vain. In city after city, Jews were tortured and burned alive. Before the plague even reached Strasbourg, France, 2,000 Jews were taken to a cemetery and given the choice of conversion or death by fire. Hundreds killed themselves. Then in 1394 all Jews were expulsed from France. Many fled to Provence, which at the time, was not part of France.

At about that time, circa 1400, we come across the first mention of the Bar Mitzvah ceremony, when, at the age of 13, a Jewish boy is obligated to fulfill the commandment and is eligible to be counted as part of a *minyan*. The *minyan* was the necessary quorum of ten men needed in order to begin a public worship service. Women were not and still are not counted by the Orthodox. As of 1973, liberal synagogues have included women in the count. Rabbi Mordecai Kaplan (1881–1983) initiated a Bar Mitzvah ceremony for girls, called the Bat Mitzvah, and in 1922 his daughter was the first to experience the ritual that became more common after World War II, but has yet to be accepted by the Orthodox.

In 1492, Jews were expelled from Spain. This was a terrible blow; more than 100,000 emigrated and perhaps an equal or an even greater number were baptized and promptly called *marranos,* or pigs. A sharp eye was kept on these new converts. It was also in 1492 that Columbus reached the New World, which was to become a future haven for Jews. One of the new Spanish converts was Luis de Torres, who came with Christopher Columbus to the New World. In the meantime, the sultan of the Ottoman Empire invited Spanish Jews to come to Istanbul.

In 1502, a German named Asher Lemmlein, who appeared in the vicinity of Venice, proclaimed himself a forerunner of the Messiah and said that if Jews were to repent, the Messiah would appear within six months and a pillar of smoke would lead the Israelites to Jerusalem. He found believers in Germany and Italy (including some Christians). People fasted and gave alms, but Lammlein then either disappeared from the public scene or died. In 1524, David Reubeni claimed to be the forerunner of the Messiah. He was received by Pope Clement and the court of Portugal. He called upon Europeans to wage war against Sultan Selim, who had just conquered Egypt. Reubeni's presence at court and the flame of messianic hope emboldened a few Spanish pseudoconverts to fight, and it was feared a general uprising might follow. Reubeni left for France, moved on to Italy, and was arrested in Germany by the emperor. His main follower, Molko, was taken to Italy and burned at the stake. Reubeni was imprisoned in Spain, where he probably died.

THE REFORMATION ERA

The official date for the beginning of the Reformation is 1517. At first the Reformer Martin Luther had high hopes that Jews would turn to Christianity. After all, Luther preached the same message as the apostles, who saw thousands of Jews turn to Christ. Luther's pamphlet, *That Jesus Christ Was Born a Jew,* was well received, but mass conversions did not follow. Luther had overlooked the centuries of persecution against Jews in the name of Christ. Toward the end of life, bitterly disappointed, Luther turned violently against the Jews and published *Against the Jews and Their Lies.* In the typical brutal language of the day he suggested that synagogues should be burned and cash and jewelry confiscated. He said Jews should be condemned to hard physical labor, their teachings banned, and worship interdicted on pain of death. True, Luther used the same language when denouncing Turks or the pope, but his denunciation was resurrected by Hitler and has not been forgotten.

In every religion there are always some who turn to mysticism in the search of union with God. Judaism is no exception. With the publication of the *Zohar,* probably authored by Moses de Leon of Spain, the cabala or mystical interpretation of the scriptures gained momentum. Perhaps this was partly a reaction against the rationalism of Maimonides. Among the questions these searchers asked were, How does God interact with the world? How can the unchangeable Eternal One, who is Spirit, create a material world? What about the existence of evil? How is that explained?

Some speculated that the infinite God filled all space and had to withdraw or contract to create a void to make room for creation. The contraction was called *zimzum,* and the resulting void called *tehiru.* When the divine light streamed into the void it was supposed to be "contained" in vessels, but the process was flawed. The vessels were not strong enough and broke. As a result, sparks of God's creative impulse became scattered throughout the world. It is the task of the believer to "repair the world," or to mend the broken vessels, to correct the initial failure. The world can be redeemed through human deeds that rectify the primordial catastrophe, or the breaking of the vessels. This is accomplished through obedience to the 613 commandments. Thus obedience has cosmic consequences; it is possible to impact the world till good triumphs. And supposedly when the process is complete, the Messiah will appear.

Through the centuries, from the time Jerusalem was destroyed in A.D. 70 onward, many people came and went, claiming to be the Messiah. In 1626 the most famous of all false Messiahs, Sabbatai Zevi, was born. He attracted an enormous following throughout all of Jewry, from Morocco to Poland. His first teacher was a cabalist in the style of Luria, who believed in the transmigration of souls and claimed that the soul of

Messiah ben Joseph resided in him. Luria's cabalistic theories have had a tremendous impact on the entire hasidic movement. Sabbatai traveled to Greece, Palestine, and Egypt, but his support reached far beyond the areas visited. Perhaps it was not accidental that the messianic fever followed the Cossack massacres under Chmielnicki, when 100,000 to 200,000 Jews were killed in the Ukraine. At about that time and in the course of the Russo-Swedish war of 1655, thousands of Jews were massacred in Poland. It is even possible that Christian millenarians of England, who expected the apocalyptic year to be 1666, influenced the messianic fervor of this era.

Some cabalists expected the year 1648 to be decisive. This was the year when Sabbatai, age 22, chose to reveal himself as the long-expected Messiah. He had gained a significant following by now through his knowledge and charisma. Sabbatai began his travels and ended up in Salonica, an important cabalist center. His eccentric actions gained him new followers and more opposition. Sabbatai then went to Smyrna and publicly declared himself to be the Messiah. A circular introduced him in this way: "The first-begotten Son of God, Sabbatai Zevi, the Messiah and Redeemer of Israel...." He went on to Istanbul, perhaps expecting the sultan to crown him. The sultan failed to cooperate. Sabbatai was imprisoned, but he was treated leniently and his fame continued to spread. At the advice of a sultan's physician, Sabbatai converted to Islam. This pleased the sultan, who rewarded Sabbatai with a title and a high position. Many of Sabbatai's followers were disheartened, and others saw it as a holy apostasy. Cabalists believe that a spark of the divine is found in everything—even great evil.

Some of Sabbatai's followers also embraced Islam. On the one hand Sabbatai played the role of a godly Muslim, but at the same time he gave every indication of his faith in Judaism. He ended up forming a new sect, an amalgam of Judaism and Islam. In the end, he was banished to Dulcigno in Albania, where he died in 1676.

Several of Sabbatai's followers later claimed messiahship, including the brother of Sabbatai's fourth wife, who pretended to be Sabbatai's son. He and 400 followers accepted Islam in 1687 and made a pilgrimage to Mecca. By this time messianism had become epidemic. Claimants arose here and there. Some of the original followers expected Sabbatai to reveal himself within three years and refused to accept that he had died.

The last of the great messianic pretenders was born in 1726 and died in 1791. Jakob Frank claimed that the soul of King David resided in him. He opposed rabbinic Judaism and his followers were persecuted. At one point Frank converted to Islam while in Turkey, but upon his return to Poland in 1759 he accepted Christianity and 1,000 of his followers followed his example and became Polish gentry. Frank's Christianity was suspect, and he was jailed as a heretic. He ended up a Russian Orthodox—a remarkable career for a Messiah. Even while in jail he remained the head of the Frankist sect.

THE ENLIGHTENMENT ERA
The Reform Movement

Hans Kung called Moses Mendelsohn "the first modern Jew."[89] Born in 1729, Mendelsohn was influenced by the Enlightenment. To him the solution to the Jewish problem was emancipation—to live as free and equal citizens and to be assimilated into the dominant culture. Mendelsohn trans-lated the Tenakh into German and allowed prayers to be offered in the vernacular in an effort to bridge the gap with non-Jews. Mendelsohn is recognized as the founder of the Reform Synagogue. He "refused to admit any single article of faith save such as unaided reason could discover"[90]—a rather harsh judgment.

The first Reform temple was inaugurated in Hamburg in 1818, complete with organ and choral music, which were anathema to the Orthodox. The service was patterned after a typical Protestant church service, devoid of all traditional Jewish distinctives. The emphasis fell on ethical monotheism. The Reform movement is widespread in the United States. Reform rabbis met in 1873 and established the Union of American Hebrew Congregations (UAHC) as an umbrella organization. In 2000 they approved gay marriage and called same-sex relationships "worthy of affirmation through appropriate Jewish rituals."[91] As might be expected, they also ordain women.

Initially support for Zionism was weak, especially among the Reform Jews. The Pittsburgh Platform (1885) issued a document stating that they "expect neither a return to Palestine, nor a sacrificial worship under the sons of Aaron, nor a restoration of any of the laws concerning the Jewish state." But the Columbus Platform (1937), speaking of Palestine, reminds everyone of the obligation "to aid in its upbuilding as a Jewish homeland" and to create "a center of Jewish culture and spiritual life." As Wouk put it, only with the Six-Day War in 1967—50 years after the Balfour Declaration—did an abrupt mass turn to Zionism take place.[92]

Following a general conservative trend, the Reform synagogues have reintroduced a few Jewish symbols and feature Friday evening services complete with lighting of the Sabbath candles.

The Conservative Movement

In response to the rationalism of the Reform movement, the Conservative movement emerged in Germany in Breslau under Zacharias Frankl (1801–1875). They are seeking a middle ground between Reform and the Orthodox groups, a rather difficult position prone to attack from both sides. In search of a third way, they reject change just for the sake of innovation or adaptation and look for an internal logical evolution. Conservatives maintain many of the traditional laws and customs, but look positively upon modern culture. In 1950 they allowed the usage of cars to drive to the synagogue (prohibited by the Orthodox), where men and women usually sit together. In 1973 the Conservatives allowed women to count in the *minyan*. A few years later they approved the ordination of women.

EXPULSION, PERSECUTION AND ZIONISM

In 1789, during the French Revolution, a proclamation was issued regarding the emancipation of Jews. That same year, Jews were given full legal equality in the United States. In 1790 George Washington sent a letter to the Touro Synagogue in Newport, Rhode Island and wrote that the government of the United States "gives to bigotry no sanction, to persecution no assistance." Washington had received financial help from Hayyim Salomon (1740–1785), a Jew who was a member of the Sons of Liberty and had made a loan without charge to members of the Continental Congress.

A year later, Catherine II the Great came under intense pressure to expulse the Jews from her new Polish possessions. She followed her more liberal inclination and compromised by placing all Jews into the Pale of Settlement, a western border region of Russia including most of the Ukraine, Poland, Belarius, and Lithuania. At one point the Pale was home to five million Jews. Many lived in poverty because even in the Pale they suffered restrictions. The concentration of the Jewish population made them an easy target for pogroms. When Jews were blamed for the assassination of Alexander II, persecutions raged in both 1881 and 1884. The result was large-scale emigration. Between 1881 and 1914 two million left the Pale, mostly for the United States. A few Jews were allowed to live outside the Pale—mostly doctors, tailors, shoemakers, and veterans. Conditions remained precarious for the Jews even in the nineteenth century. Although full legal equality was obtained in Canada (1832), England (1856), and Germany (1871), new pogroms broke out in Russia (1881). Laws could not eliminate anti-Jewish prejudice. The celebrated Dreyfus Affair in France was a high-profile example of the anti-Semitism that prevailed throughout Europe.

Alfred Dreyfus was the highest-ranking Jewish artillery officer in the French army. In 1894, papers discovered in the wastebasket of a German military attache proved that French military intelligence had been supplied to the Germans. Dreyfus was accused and court-marshaled. The evidence was flimsy. Later it was established that important papers tending to exonerate Dreyfus never reached the judges. Dreyfus was stripped of his rank and sent to Devil's Island, the infamous French penal colony in French Guyana. Public opinion was divided. Right wing newspapers used the Dreyfus Affair to discredit the Jews, while other papers questioned what had happened.

The French army was shot through with anti-Semitism, but some officers thought Dreyfus had been railroaded. Lt. Col. Picquart (anti-Semitic himself) feared that the spy might be continuing to operate if the wrong man had been arrested and was increasingly convinced of a miscarriage of justice. He determined that the evidence pointed to Major Ferdinand Esterhazy, but the army was unwilling to admit a mistake. Emile Zola, a novelist, accused the army of a coverup with his famous headline *J'accuse!* and fled to England for safety. More evidence came to light and the army held another court-marshal, only to reaffirm the previous condemnation, but this time admitted that there were "extenuating circumstances." In 1899 the president of France pardoned Dreyfus, who returned to Paris, but Dreyfus had to wait till 1906 to be exonerated.

It is difficult, at more than 100 years removed from these events, to sense the passion that this affair ignited. One unexpected result was the impact these events had on Theodor Herzl, a journalist who covered the story for his Viennese newspaper *Neue Freie Presse.* That Vienna was a hotbed of anti- Semitism confirmed Herzl's conclusion that regardless of legislation, Jews would always be at risk unless they had their own country. That was why in 1897, Herzl convened the First Zionist Congress in Basel, Switzerland. He became a tireless apostle for the establishment of a Jewish homeland and met with world leaders in an attempt to get allies, but they failed to respond positively.

For years Russian Jews had moved to Palestine, but never thought of it as a homeland. Herzl himself was not necessarily committed to Palestine. The British government suggested Uganda (Kenya), and Herzl was interested. Perhaps he merely wanted to establish the principle of a Jewish homeland, or maybe he was influenced by renewed pogroms in Russia. The offer split the Zionists. To placate Herzl, they appointed a commission of inquiry. Herzl would have accepted Mozambique or perhaps Cyprus, from where Palestine might be taken by force. Tripoli came under consideration, and Herzl had an audience with the king of Italy. In seeking a homeland, Herzl had no religious motivation and was not interested in the rebirth of Hebrew. He had no ties with Orthodox Judaism. Perhaps he underestimated the emotional ties between Jewry and the Promised Land. Exhausted, he died in 1904 and never saw the realization of his dream.

Herzl's proposal regarding a Jewish homeland was a logical step in an era that breathed nationalism. Garibaldi in Italy and Bismarck in Germany pursued national unification. In the Jewish community there were dissenting voices. Zionist leader Ahad Ha-am believed that Jewish spiritual life had to be revived before the implementation of political Zionism. He was also sensitive to the presence of the Arabs in Palestine. He hoped that Zion would become a center of Jewish cultural life, a beacon to Diaspora Judaism. Others, especially the so-called ultra-Orthodox, opposed Zionism because they believed it is the Messiah who will bring the Jews back to the Holy Land.

THE MODERN DAY

After the "miracle" of the Six-Day War, more and more Jews came to embrace

Zionism. Some wondered about the exact meaning of the divine promise regarding the return to the land. Did it imply a modern state or a secure home? What might be the boundaries? They are variously given in the Scriptures as from El-Arish (the river of Egypt) to the Euphrates, an area that includes half of Iraq, part of Turkey, and Syria. Northern and southern frontiers are not clearly indicated (Genesis 15:18–21). According to Numbers 34:3-15 the southern line runs from the tip of the Dead Sea (the Salt Sea) to the Brook of Egypt and the northern frontier goes all the way up to Hamah (Hamath) in Syria. The eastern border is formed by the Jordan instead of the Euphrates (cf. Micah 7:11). The Talmud offers different opinions regarding the limits of the Promised Land.

Aside from geography, what does the promise of return mean? Jeremiah had predicted that the Babylonian captivity would last 70 years.[93] Although only about 50,000 finally returned, the promise of 70 years was fulfilled (Ezra 1:1). The territory occupied by the returning exiles was small—perhaps no more than 25 miles in a straight line. The area was small compared to the pre-exilic boundaries. How large an area would be occupied in the "second return"? Was political Zionism part of the fulfillment of ancient promises regarding the land, even though the leadership was not religious? How much land should they claim? Would the Messiah extend the boundaries? Should the temple be rebuilt and sacrifices restored? After all, when Israel returned from the Babylonian exile, the sacrificial ritual was resumed without the temple. It was the general opinion of the rabbis that the temple would be rebuilt in the days of the Messiah. Non-Orthodox Jewish groups, by contrast, have deleted references to the rebuilding of the temple from their prayer books.

Today rebuilding the temple is both a religious and a political issue. The Mosque of Omar occupies the Temple site, which makes rebuilding on the original site impossible at this time. There are some Jews today who belong to activist organizations that are committed to having the temple rebuilt. Israel's Supreme Court has restrained the activities of one such group, called "The Temple Mount Faithful."

By 1914 there were 90,000 Jews in Palestine, but not thanks to Zionism. Support for the settlers (mostly from Russia) came from one of the Rothschilds and other wealthy Jews. Their departure from Eastern Europe was stimulated by the massacres of Kichinev, Moldovia (1903), when the old accusation of ritual murder was resurrected and dozens of Jews were killed and hundreds wounded. The same accusation led to the highly publicized Beilis trial in Kiev (1913), which ended with an acquittal.

Martin Buber, a philosopher, educator, Bible commentator, and storyteller from Vienna (most famous for his *I and Thou*), was a protégé of Herzl but went his own way because of the political content of Zionism. Buber pursued spiritual values and, in his twenties, became involved with Hasidism. He published Hasidic Tales and brought the personality of Baal Shem Tov, the founder of Hasidism, to the attention of a broad audience. In 1938 he moved to Palestine, where he taught at The Hebrew University. He advocated Arab-Jewish cooperation and embraced the idea of a binational state. He died in 1965.

A major turning point in the history of Zionism took place in 1917. To gain the support of the Jews against the Ottoman Empire during World War I, the British

Foreign Secretary, Arthur Balfour, addressed a letter to Lord Rothschild on November 2, 1917, which read:

> Dear Lord Rothschild,
>
> I have much pleasure in conveying to you, on behalf of His Majesty's Government, the following declaration of sympathy with Jewish Zionist aspirations which has been submitted to, and approved by, the Cabinet.
>
> "His Majesty's Government views with favour the establishment in Palestine of a national home for the Jewish people, and will use their best endeavours to facilitate the achievement of the object, it being clearly understood that nothing shall be done which might prejudice the civil and religious rights of existing non-Jewish communities in Palestine, or the rights and political status enjoyed by Jews in any other country."
>
> I should be grateful if you would bring this declaration to the knowledge of the Zionist Federation.
>
> Yours sincerely,
>
> Arthur James Balfour

Then came the Churchill Memorandum in 1922, which hoped to reassure the Arabs and disclaimed any intention of creating "a wholly Jewish Palestine" or the "subordination of the Arab population, language, and culture in Palestine." According to this memorandum, the intention of the Balfour Declaration was "the further development of the existing Jewish community with the assistance of Jews in other parts of the world, in order that it may become a center in which the Jewish people as a whole may take, on grounds of religion and race, an interest and pride." Immigration would be limited to the "economic capacity of the country at the time to absorb new arrival."

Toward the end of World War I, in 1918, General Allenby captured Jerusalem for the victorious Allies. At the time there were about 56,000 Jews in Palestine, and they owned two percent of the land. The British controlled the area after World War I, but legally the British Mandate began in 1923, shortly after the Churchill Memorandum had been issued. But even before 1923, Arabs began rioting against Jewish immigration. The British Mandate of Palestine included the area east of the river Jordan, but—in spite of strenuous Zionist objections—Transjordan was detached and made into the Hashemite Kingdom of Jordan.

Anti-Semitism in Europe found especially fertile ground in Vienna. Many of the Jews in Austria became prominent in law and medicine even though they constituted only eight percent of the total population. In 1897 Vienna elected Karl Lueger as mayor. He accused Jews of both capitalism and communism; he was "the first European politician to ride to real power on this gathering wave of resentment"[94] against Jews. He was an inspiration for Hitler who was elected in Germany in 1933.

Hitler's contempt for the Jews was based not on religious prejudice but on his belief the Jews were an inferior race. In 1941 he enacted what was called the "Final Solution"—a systematic attempt to wipe out Judaism. The Holocaust was planned and implemented, and more than six million European Jews were killed. Some Jews prefer the Hebrew word *shoah* to Holocaust—*shoah* speaks of utter catastrophy and destruction.

In 1947, shortly after the Allied victory over the Axis powers, the United Nations General Assembly voted for the partition of Palestine into two independent states, linked by an economic union, and the creation of an International Zone in Jerusalem, which would include Bethlehem and the holy places in and around Jerusalem. Russia voted for the proposal, hoping to guarantee the exit of the British from the Middle East.

Of the available territory, roughly 55 percent of the total was to become the Jewish state for the 650,000 Jews in the land. The 1.3 million Arabs received the remaining 45 percent. It was perhaps an opportunity for peace and the establishment of an Arab state, which became the stated goal of Palestinians for the next few decades. Then in 1948 the state of Israel was born—and immediately the Arabs in the surrounding nations declared war on the fledgling nation. Israel won, and in 1949, became a member of the United Nations.

Though Israel's rebirth as a nation has a relatively short history, the nation has already endured five wars:

The War of Independence, May 15, 1948–February 24, 1949. One of the sad events was the Dir Yassin massacre by the Zionist militia known as Irgun, not to mention the destruction of 360 Arab villages and 14 cities.[95] The Haganah or Jewish defense force had about 50,000 men, plus a few thousand more from the Irgun and the Stern Gang. They faced and overcame overwhelming odds.

The Sinai Campaign, October 28– November 8, 1956. Egypt launched a naval blockade that prevented access to the Israeli port of Eilat, and then seized control of the Suez Canal. Britain and France sided with Israel to reopen the canal, and Israel seized the Sinai area. President Eisenhower of the United States pressured for a cease-fire and withdrawal.

The Six-Day War, June 5–11, 1967. The most threatening war Israel has faced to date could easily have ended in disaster for Israel. An awareness that Israel might have been destroyed and that a new holocaust might have taken place led to a re-evaluation by Jews in North America and elsewhere regarding Israel. Even the Orthodox turned pro-Zionist, except those who maintain that only Messiah can set up a true Jewish state. After the Six-Day War, more and more Jews came to actively support the State of Israel.

The Yom Kippur War, October 6–25, 1973. So-called because Arab nations, led by Egypt and Syria, carried out a surprise attack on Israel on the Jewish holiday of Yom Kippur. This strained Israeli military resources to the utmost limit. At the Syrian border 180 Israeli tanks faced 1,400 Syrian tanks, and at the Suez Canal only 500 Israeli soldiers were on guard when 80,000 Egyptians attacked. After the first two days, Israel regrouped and carried the war deep into Syria and Egypt. The Arab effort to regain all the lost territory failed. Only small territorial gains were achieved.

The Lebanon War, July 6, 1982. In response to an assassination attempt on an Israeli ambassador, Israeli military forces invaded southern Lebanon. In 1985, Israel withdrew unilaterally.

From a historic standpoint, it is too early to draw conclusions about these wars and the 2006 military engagement against Hezbollah in Lebanon. Tragically, peace continues to remain elusive in the Middle East. And anti-Semitism continues to be a very real problem in other parts of the world.

THE CONTRIBUTIONS OF JEWISH PEOPLE

JEWISH HISTORY IS UNIQUE. Even a most superficial review makes it patently clear that no other nation has suffered so greatly across the ages. It is astounding that in spite of a history marked by adversity, enmity, limiting decrees, persecution, and death, Jews have consistently made a significant contribution to world culture—a contribution that is totally out of proportion to their relatively small numbers when matched against the rest of the world's population. The United Nations Educational, Scientific and Cultural Organization (UNESCO) published a booklet entitled *Jewish Thought as a Factor in Civilization.* It acknowledges that Jews have made significant contributions in our world. For example, in medieval Europe, when Jews labored under enormous handicaps, people such as Ibn Gabirol of Spain and Maimonides emerged. More recently, other Jewish individuals have achieved international recognition—scientists such as Einstein and Oppenheimer and Jonas Salk, and composers such as Mahler and Shoenberg. The list of philosophers includes Bergson, Husserl, and Durkheim. From Benjamin Disraeli to Supreme Court justice Louis Brandeis, Jews have occupied prominent positions in world government. Names such as Freud or Chagall need no introduction. In the performing arts, from Hollywood to musicians, Jews have played a significant role. In the field of literature the list is surprisingly long and includes authors such as Kafka, Stephan Zweig, Chaim Potok, Saul Bellow, Shalom Aleichem, Marcel Proust, Danielle Steel, J.D. Salinger, Dorothy Parker, Isaac Asimov, and Isaac Bashevis Singer.

A people without a land, scattered across the world and persecuted relentlessly, has not only continued to exist but has triumphed over adversity and regained an ancient homeland. By any measurement, Jewish history has been exceptional when one would expect it to be as dead as the Hittites.[96] "There are two possibilities. Either the credit belongs to the Jews themselves, or it belongs to God."[97] From a Christian perspective there is only one possible answer—one that is in line with divine promises found in the Bible.

POINTS OF CONTACT

ONE CAN ONLY AGREE with Harvey Cox when he writes that Christians "will always have a special tie with Judaism that makes the Jewish-Christian relationship different from the interaction of Christians with any of the other faiths."[98] Along the same lines Stewart writes, "The roots of Christianity go deep into Jewish soil…. The very title he bears—the Christ—is meaningless apart from the background of Jewish history in which it had its origin."[99] *Christ* means "the anointed one, the Messiah." It is because of this historic connection that some key points must be observed regarding Christian dialogue with Jewish individuals.

Because Jews reject the *New* Testament, they cannot possibly speak of the *Old* Testament, a typically Christian expression. For Jews, the scriptures are the Tenakh. *The Bible* is a neutral term. If the topic arises, a reminder that the New Testament was written by Jews (with the possible exception of Luke) might not be out of place.

Jews do not pronounce the "sacred tetragram" consisting of four Hebrew letters, YHWH or Yahweh (erroneously Jehovah).

Many might agree with Abba Eban when he writes of the belief that Christians have replaced Jews as God's elect people.[100] But the apostle Paul makes it abundantly clear that God has not rejected his people (Romans 11:1). They have stumbled, but they are not beyond recovery. The wild branches (the Gentiles) are grafted in among (not in place of) the others. God's gifts and his call are irrevocable (Romans 11:11,17,29).

Apart from citing "messianic proof-texts" (and there are many), a Christian can focus on the problems of daily life. Is it true that "sin is failure to live up, in each given situation, to the highest moral potentialities in one's self"?[101] Should there not be a transcendent dimension in religion, going beyond one's self? Jews often repeat the words of Isaiah: "Holy, holy, holy is the LORD Almighty" (Isaiah 6:3). How can anyone face a holy God? David prayed, "Do not bring your servant into judgment, for no one living is righteous before you" (Psalm 143:2). Whoever believes in God's holiness must take sin seriously. *All* sacrifices were only for unintentional sins (Numbers 15:27ff). This is detailed in Leviticus 4:1,13,22,27, and other verses. There was no atonement for anyone who sinned deliberately or defiantly (Numbers 15:30). The blood of sacrifices only made atonement for unintentional sin or sins of ignorance. The center of the temple ritual, culminating in the Day of Atonement, was sacrifice related to sin. The offender placed his hand on the animal, identified with the animal, and knew that he had forfeited its life because of sin.

The sacrifice was a substitute. When the nation worshiped the golden calf, Moses offered his life to secure divine forgiveness (Exodus 32:32). According to Rashi, the death of Miriam is related immediately after the section regarding the red heifer to teach that sacrifice (of the red heifer) secures reconciliation and equally the death of the righteous (Miriam). The Talmud observes that those guilty of involuntary manslaughter can leave the city of refuge when the high priest dies because his death atones.[102]

Jews claim that the suffering servant depicted in Isaiah chapter 53 is Israel, suffering for the sins of the world. Although an erroneous interpretation, the idea of substitutionary sacrifice is obviously accepted. Rashi comments that the servant was chastised with pain so that the peoples should be forgiven through the sufferings of Israel. But the nation of Israel is hardly an appropriate unblemished sacrifice. Isaiah clearly refers to one person, not a nation—someone in a grave with the wicked and with the rich in his death. It is the suffering Messiah who made atonement for sin, the supreme sacrifice. It is he who became a guilt offering (Isaiah 53:10) to set mankind free from the power and guilt of sin. The idea of a suffering Messiah is already discussed in the Talmud: "The Rabbis say, the sufferer [or leprous one] of the house of Rabbi is His [Messiah's] name, as it is said, 'Surely he has borne our griefs...stricken, smitten of God and afflicted' (Isaiah 53:4)." Along the same line Rabbi Joshua said that the Messiah is "at the gate of Rome, among the poor people, inflicted with wounds."[103]

In Isaiah the servant 1) in the broadest sense designates the mass of the people, 2) but sometimes refers to the godly in the midst of the nation, and finally 3) refers to the servant par excellence, the ideal or true Israelite at the apex of the pyramid, the personal Messiah.

In the first few centuries when Jews mentioned Jesus, he was described as one who practiced magic—a tacit admission of his miracles.[104] It would be pointless to review the baseless accusations of the past. For centuries Jews have largely ignored Jesus of Nazareth, but finally some have decided to claim him as one of the great Jewish rabbis. To do this, however, much of the Gospel text has to be eliminated. If Jesus was so typically Jewish, why was he crucified? His contemporaries understood perfectly well that this man made extraordinary claims. He claimed pre-existence and was clearly understood when he made himself equal with God (John 5:18; 6:38). He also accepted the worship of those who said, "You are the Son of God" (Matthew 14:33; John 1:49), and he meant this in an exclusive sense. He forgave sins, which no one but God could do (Mark 2:5-7). No wonder He claimed to be the Messiah (Matthew 26:63-64) and proclaimed his death, resurrection, and return. Either this man was indeed the Messiah or he was one of the first in a long line of pretenders. He was and claimed to be far more than just a gifted Jewish rabbi. If he was nothing more, how is it possible that a different religion, Christianity, came into being? Christianity was not the work of Paul (as is sometimes claimed), because without Christ, there would be no Paul.

Maimonides opined that "the Creator is one, with a oneness which is absolutely unique." Again and again Jews across the ages have recited the words "Hear O Israel: The LORD our God, the LORD is one" (Deuteronomy 6:4). What exactly does that mean? Maimonides, to preserve this "absolute oneness," could only define God negatively and rob him of all personality. If God is love, then for him, love is more than an attribute; it is part of his very essence. He could never be God without a relationship (love)—the mysterious relationship between the persons of the Godhead. Maimonides was well aware of this and preferred to speak of God like the prime mover of Aristotle, devoid of all personality. We can only accept what God reveals about himself and in our own anthropomorphic terms. God is always a mystery, but he is all that personality means and more. He is not "hanging as a shapeless vapor or an undifferentiated ooze."[105]

A translation of the Tenakh published in 1985 by the Jewish Publication Society translated Deuteronomy 6:4 this way: "Hear O Israel! The Lord is our God, the Lord *alone*." It is not a matter of mathematics, but of uniqueness. The word translated "one" is also used in Genesis 2:24, where we are told that man and wife "become one flesh"—not a mathematical unity. The fact of the matter is that we only know of God what he has been willing to reveal.

Here and there significant hints appear in the Tenakh. When God declares, "Here is my servant...I will put my Spirit on him" (Isaiah 42:1), the three persons of the Trinity seem to be in view. Speaking of God, the prophet declares that in the distress of Israel "he too was distressed, and the angel of his presence saved them.... Yet they rebelled and grieved his Holy Spirit" (Isaiah 63:9-10). The angel of his presence is a mysterious reminder of the Angel of the Lord, who appears frequently and is sometimes identified with and yet distinctly from God (Exodus 3:1-6, among other texts). Who is the child called "Mighty God"? (Isaiah 9:6). The deity of the Messiah is mentioned in one of the last messianic prophecies in the Old Testament: "I will send my messenger.... suddenly the Lord you are seeking will come to his temple" (Malachi 3:1).

As to the virgin birth, did not God bring about another miraculous birth for Sarah, who was barren? Only the mother of Messiah is mentioned in the Tenakh, never his father (Psalm 22:9; Isaiah 49:1,5). The first reference to the Messiah appears in Genesis 3:15, a text that also speaks of the death of the Messiah. And the list of messianic texts runs through the entire Tenakh. In Proverbs 30:4 the question is raised, "Who has established all the ends of the earth? What is his name, and the name of his son?" As Franz Delitzsch observed, "he would not have ventured this question if he did not suppose that God was not a *monas* [unity] who was without manifoldness in Himself."[106]

The rabbis of old discussed the destruction of the second temple and failed to discover a valid reason. The prophets insisted on the judgment of God and vindicated the moral element of history.[107] The Bible offers an explanation for the cataclysmic event. The first temple was destroyed because Israel refused to listen to the voice of the Lord (2 Chronicles 36). The long and painful exile followed. Then came the destruction of the second temple in A.D. 70. But God remains faithful to His promise to the people of Israel. The nation of Israel has been re-established physically, and will ultimately receive the rejected Messiah as its one and only Savior.

CHRISTIANITY

Faith is a living, bold trust in God's grace, so certain of God's favor that it would risk death a thousand times trusting in it. Such confidence and knowledge of God's grace makes you happy, joyful, and bold in your relationship with God and all creatures. The Holy Spirit makes this happen through faith. Because of it, you freely, willingly, and joyfully do good to everyone, suffer all kinds of things, love and praise the God who has shown such grace. Thus, it is just as impossible to separate faith and works as it is to separate heat and light from fire.

MARTIN LUTHER

CHRISTIANITY

THE TEACHINGS OF CHRIST cannot be evaluated separately from his person and claims. And the person of Christ is firmly anchored in world history. He lived under the reign of Tiberius Caesar, a Roman emperor, when Pilate was governor of Judea.[1] And his crucifixion is documented as both a historical event and a religious doctrine. Ultimately, Christianity is Christ.

THE BEGINNING OF CHRISTIANITY

JESUS WAS BORN IN Bethlehem and never traveled more than 100 miles from his birthplace. He was brought up in Nazareth, an insignificant village in Galilee, in the house of a carpenter. We know next to nothing of his childhood. He began his public ministry with a call to repentance. He was an extraordinary communicator. The guards sent to arrest him came back without the prisoner, saying, "No one ever spoke the way this man does."[2] He taught "as one who had authority."[3] His message was revolutionary. In a country under occupation by the hated Romans he told people to love their enemies, turn the other cheek, volunteer to walk an extra mile, cultivate meekness, be merciful, and forgive unconditionally even as God forgives. He healed a paralytic and claimed to have the authority to forgive sin, a divine prerogative. When Nathaniel, Martha, Peter, and the disciples said, "You are the Son of God,[4] he accepted their affirmation. Naturally he was accused of blasphemy.[5]

Jesus disregarded the innumerable laws governing the Sabbath and declared that the Son of Man is Lord even of the Sabbath.[6] He touched lepers and remained undefiled. He disregarded dietary laws. "What goes into a man's mouth does not make him 'unclean,' but what comes out of his mouth, that is what makes him 'unclean.'"[7] His listeners picked up stones to kill him because they understood perfectly well that he made himself equal with God.[8] Jesus told the Samaritan woman and the high priest of the Jews that he was the promised Messiah.[9] Israel expected a Messiah who would effect political liberation, but Jesus offered spiritual freedom and declared, "My kingdom is not of this world."[10] Israel, disappointed, handed Jesus over to the Romans to be crucified. Pilate, who was indifferent, thought Jesus innocent. Jesus' enemies, present in every crowd, had watched him day and night but found no valid accusation of wrongdoing. One of the disciples was a spy, Judas. Even he failed to find one act of sin in Jesus and, in the end, confessed, "I have betrayed innocent blood."[11] Peter, a disciple and friend, exclaimed, "Go away from me, Lord; I am a sinful man!"[12] Peter's confession "was the spontaneous effect on a sensitive conscience of the proximity of the Divine."[13] Peter testified that Jesus committed no sin, and John, who knew him intimately, wrote, "In him is no sin."[14] Sin had no claim on him; death could not hold him.

A small group of disheartened followers hiding behind locked doors for fear of the Jews became exuberant and energetic because Jesus, after having risen from the dead, appeared to them. The resurrection of Christ transformed the disciples from abject discouragement to jubilant strength. It moved them from despair to joyful affirmation. They went out to proclaim the message throughout the world and gave their lives for Christ. The central message was not a new system of ethics, but the resurrection of Christ, which validated his life and death. The disciples saw the resurrection as the triumph of Christ. For them, it was the beginning of a new age, the beginning of the end. His future return would be the end of the end.

THE SPREAD OF CHRISTIANITY

THAT CHRISTIANITY BECAME A world religion owes much to the intense labor of a Jew called Saul, who was born in Tarsus, a cosmopolitan center. Saul studied under Rabbi Gamaliel and became a Pharisee, a member of a spiritual elite. He went from being an ardent persecutor of Christians to a devoted follower of Christianity because he saw the risen Christ—a story related three times in the book of Acts, in chapters 9, 22, and 26. Saul, now called Paul, became "the colossus of the Church, the most striking and powerful human being in its history."[15]

He had the advantage of being a Roman citizen, which meant he had the protection of Roman law. Some Roman officials were even friends of Paul.[16] He traveled over the excellent Roman roads (some 50,000 miles had been paved by this time) that linked the far-flung borders of the empire. The Pax Romana prevailed everywhere; the Roman world was at peace. Communication was greatly facilitated all throughout the empire because the common language was Greek.

Paul started his missionary journeys from Antioch, the third most-important city in the empire, and reached out to Jews and Jewish proselytes scattered everywhere, especially Syria, Egypt, and Rome. When most of them rejected the message, he went on to proclaim Christ to the Gentiles. Over and over again Paul stressed the point that the Gentiles could become Christians without circumcision, without observance of the Jewish law, on the sole basis of faith in Christ as Lord and Savior. In Israel, thousands of Jews turned to Christ (Acts 21:20). There were Jewish believers in virtually every church. For example, Evaristus (A.D. 97–105), the fifth bishop of Rome, was born in Bethlehem of Jewish parents. But the vast majority of Christians had non-Jewish backgrounds and had converted from other religions.

When Paul proclaimed the good news in the Roman Empire, a vague sense of monotheism was in the atmosphere, but adherence to eastern mystery religions was widespread. There was the orgiastic worship of Cybele, a vegetarian goddess with promises of immortality. The blood of a bull was used to purify initiates from sin and symbolized new life. Isis of Egypt, the goddess of fertility, also offered immortality and was extremely popular. Mithraism, linked to Persian sun worship and connected to Zoroastrianism, was favored by the military. The followers would sacrifice a bull and pour its blood over the worshipper so he or she could achieve new birth. Eastern religions were all about searching for immortality and redemption.

When emperor worship became required in the Roman Empire, the Jews were granted a tacit dispensation from having to participate in this worship—as long as they were loyal subjects. Christians operated in the shadow of Judaism, which was sanctioned by Rome as lawful, a *religio licita*. The moment Christians were no longer seen as a Jewish sect but as a distinct religious movement, they became a *religio illicita,* or an unlawful organization no longer protected by Roman law.

THE HISTORY OF CHRISTIANITY

THE EARLY CHURCH

Once Christianity was recognized as a distinct religion, Christians became fair game for the Romans. They no longer had a legal footing. Meetings had to be clandestine. Emperor Nero (54–68) blamed Christians for the fire that engulfed Rome in A.D. 64 and launched a cruel but limited persecution. Some Christians were covered with the skins of wild beasts and left for dogs to devour, others were crucified, and still others were set afire to serve as living torches.[17] For all that went wrong, Christians became convenient scapegoats. As Tertullian (145–220) put it, "If the Tiber rises as high as the city walls, if the Nile does not send its waters up over the fields, if the heavens give no rain, if there is an earthquake, if there is a famine or pestilence, straightway the cry is, 'Away with the Christians to the lion!' "[18]

One of the early Christian martyrs was Polycarp of Smyrna (modern Izmir in Turkey), who was "instructed by the apostles, and conversed with many who had seen Christ."[19] Justin Martyr (c. 100–165) studied philosophy and after he became a Christian, continued to dress like a philosopher. He wrote an apology or vindication of Christianity. His *Dialogue with Trypho,* addressed to Jews, was an exposition of the reasons that Jesus is the Messiah. There were many other capable apologists in this time period as well, such as Athenagoras, Theopilus of Antioch, Minucius Felix, and Clement of Alexandria, to name only a few.

Christians throughout the empire suffered sporadic persecutions, mostly on a local level. In 202 Septimus Severus was sufficiently concerned about the large number of Christians in Egypt that he issued an edict forbidding conversions. Under Decius (249–251), imperial edicts ordered all citizens of the Roman Empire to sacrifice to the gods. Once this was done, the worshipper received a certificate of compliance. Some Christians bought certificates to avoid persecution, while others suffered imprisonment, Origen among them, along with the bishops of Rome and Jerusalem. Some Christians were killed for their refusal to comply. So when Decius was later slain in battle, some Christians saw it as divine judgment upon him. Severe edicts were issued in 258 under Emperor Valerian (253–260) and were directed strategically against the clergy. Among the victims was Cyprian, a bishop in North Africa. A major persecution began in 303 under Emperor Diocletian (284–305). Churches were destroyed and copies of the Scriptures were burnt. According to some sources, even Marcellinus, the bishop of Rome, offered incense to idols to escape death.

In spite of this state-mandated persecution, the church expanded rapidly. "During the first six centuries of its existence, Christianity had spread outward in roughly concentric fashion from its cradle-land in Palestine"[20] Tertullian cried triumphantly, "We are but of yesterday, and we have filled every place among you—cities, islands, fortresses, towns, market places, the very camp, tribes, companies, palace, senate, forum—and we have left nothing to you but the temples of your gods."[21] The heaviest concentrations of Christians were in Asia and North Africa in spite of the severe persecution of A.D. 211. In Edessa (modern Urfa in southeast Turkey), Christianity became a state religion till the Romans took over in A.D. 216. There were Christian communities in Persia and churches in Mesopotamia and Armenia. In 238, King Tiridates III of Armenia made Christianity the official state religion. It is perhaps true that the apostle Thomas reached India.

In Egypt, the gospel spread among the Coptic population and traveled south to Nubia and Ethiopia. In Europe the dissemination of the Christian faith was much slower. In circa A.D. 150, only 12 bishops attended a provincial synod in Italy. Only a handful of bishops attended the council of Elvira in Spain in A.D. 306. Bishops from Trier and Cologne, Roman colonies in Germany, and three other bishops from Britain came to a synod in Arles, France, in 314.

The early church's rapid growth was due mostly to the ardent witness of the church and the extraordinary perseverance of those who were persecuted, as well as the courage of the martyrs (some have said that the blood of the martyrs is the seed of the gospel). The world was also impressed by the charitable deeds the church extended to all, including widows, the aged, the sick, orphans, and prisoners. The early church "produced an endless succession of Christian schools, hospitals, and programs to help the poor, the broken and the oppressed."[22]

Missionaries from Asia Minor planted the church in Gaul. One might have expected them to come from Rome, which was so much closer geographically. The first bishop of Lyon, a western outpost of the church, was Photinus from Asia Minor, who died a martyr. Persecutions raged in Lyon in 175 and 177 (the martyrdoms of Blandina and Perpetua). Irenaeus escaped because he had been dispatched to carry documents to the church in Rome. Upon his return to Lyon he was installed as the second bishop (178–202).

Early Heresies

Not only did the early church have to contend with persecution, but it also faced the spread of heresies, among them Montanism. Montanus, who was active in Asia Minor (c. 156), believed that he was the *paraclete* or comforter spoken of in John 14:16 and the bearer of the final revelation from God. He practiced extreme austerity, fell into trances, and uttered strange sounds. He condemned all second marriages and insisted on extensive fasting. He also announced that the heavenly Jerusalem would be set up at Pepuza in Phrygia and urged his disciples to gather there. The movement continued after his death and was vigorously opposed by Irenaeus.

Irenaeus's main effort, however, was directed against Gnosticism, which was "an attempt to combine Christian ideas and phraseology with ideas drawn from Greek and Oriental religions."[23] The Gnostics found inspiration in pagan myth, magic, and mysticism in an effort to transform religion into theosophy. For the most part, the Gnostics embraced dualism. They assumed a tension between matter (inherently evil) and spirit (good). This led to endless speculations that attempted to explain how a good God had created the material (evil) universe. The incarnation was equally mysterious. How could the Son of God dwell in a material body? The apostle John, in his epistles, opposed the incipient Gnosticism of those who denied that Jesus is the Christ. He declared that Jesus is the Christ come in the flesh.[24]

Marcion, an early Gnostic, was a wealthy shipowner who came to Rome c. 140 and taught for 20 years. He assumed the existence of two gods—one the creator of the world, whom he identified with the god of the Old Testament, and one the father of Jesus Christ, whom he said was a god of mercy. Marcion saw the creator as just or maybe evil, a somewhat lower being, a secondary deity or demiurge. According to Marcion, the God of mercy was unknown till Jesus came. He descended to earth in an assumed a body, and matter did not pollute him. To Marcion, salvation was attained through *gnosis,* or knowledge.

Later Marcion's movement merged into the Manichaens (a gnostic group) of the third and fourth centuries. Marcion rejected the Old Testament and his New Testament contained only the gospel of Luke and ten of Paul's letters:

> He mutilates the Gospel which is according to Luke, eliminating all that is written respecting the generation of the Lord…. he dis-membered the epistles of Paul, removing all that is said by the apostle respecting that god who made the world…. [Marcion] was truly speaking with the mouth of the devil.[25]

Another gnostic whose teachings threatened the church was Valentinus (c.100– c. 175), a well-educated Egyptian who was closer to Plato than the Gospels. He accepted absolute dualism between spirit and matter and maintained that the universe came into being through a series of emanations of spiritual entities. The God of the Old Testament was a demiurge far removed from the Supreme God. And a spark of light remained in some humans, who can be redeemed through Christ, who brought the necessary knowledge or *gnosis.* The heavenly Christ descended upon the man Jesus at his baptism and left him at the cross, which means that Christ did not die. Irenaeus dedicates the first seven chapters of his book *Against Heresies* to the description of this complex pseudo-Christian system that "neither the prophets announced, nor the Lord taught, nor the apostles delivered."[26]

Approximately contemporary with Valentinus was Basilides from Syria. None of his writings have survived, and we know his teaching only through his opponents. Basilides taught that Jesus did not suffer death. Rather, his place was taken by Simon of Cyrene, while "Jesus himself received the form of Simon, and standing by [the cross] he laughed at them." Since Jesus was an "incorporeal power," he transformed himself as he pleased.[27] The early church responded to heresies, Gnosticism, and persecutions in the following three ways:

1. *By affirming the canon of scripture.* Marcion had questioned which books of

the Bible were truly inspired. It was urgent, then, for the church to establish a canon or standard (literally, measuring rod) of which books were recognized as authoritative. With or without Marcion "there was an increasing tendency to cite apostolic writings as authoritative, and there seems to have been the beginnings of collections of the writings."[28] Barnabas (c. 70–100) had already quoted the Gospel of Matthew as scripture.[29] According to Beare, "it is beyond dispute that the collection of Paul's letters had been formed and published before the end of the first century."[30]

The Gnostics created "gospels" and legend-makers added more writings, some of which covered the childhood of Christ. They copied existing models and created the gospels of Peter, Thomas, and Philip and the acts of John, Peter, and others.

Because Christianity was an illegal religion in the early church era under the Roman Empire, it wasn't readily possible for the leaders to hold a council with representatives from the four corners of the empire to help settle the question. One old list, the so-called Muratorian Fragment (c. 170–200), listed most of the books of the New Testament as authoritative. By A.D. 180, most issues about which books belonged in the New Testament had been settled. Clement of Alexandria quotes all the New Testament books as authoritative. Tertullian also included 1 John, 1 Peter, and Jude among the canonical books of the New Testament.

When New Testament scriptures were used to refute the Gnostics, the Gnostics replied that "the truth was not delivered by means of written documents" and fell back on secret oral traditions. Irenaeus reminded them that the correct apostolic tradition was preserved in the scriptures and publicly in the churches.[31]

2. *By affirming the trusted leaders.* To refute heresies and resist persecution, the church needed more structure. The role of the bishops became more important. In the New Testament the Greek word *episkopos,* translated "overseer" or "bishop" (KJV), is synonymous with *presbyteros,* which is usually translated "elder."[32] The two words "did not imply any distinction, let alone antithesis," but the words, widely known as titles, were "not precisely defined and therefore in their very breadth of meaning capable of new and specific use."[33]

In A.D. 97, when Clement sent a letter from Rome to the Corinthians, he used the words *bishop* and *presbyter* interchangeably.[34] Perhaps it was unavoidable that one of the elders would become "the first among equals." Slowly differences developed between bishops and elders. Already Ignatius (c. 110) wrote, "Do nothing without the bishop."[35] The idea of a "monarchical episcopacy" developed when a single bishop gained authority over a group of presbyters. Irenaeus wrote, "Let no man do anything connected with the Church without the bishops...whatsoever he shall approve of, that is also pleasing to God, so that everything that is done may be secure and valid."[36]

The larger churches of that era established lists to show the connections between their bishops and the apostles. It was assumed (perhaps correctly) that these lists went all the way back to "those who were by the apostles instituted bishops in the Churches, and [to demonstrate] the succession of these men to our time."[37] The bishops were seen as successors of the apostles and as those who maintained the truth of the gospel against heretics and Gnostics.

3. *By affirming specific doctrines.* In view of the many heresies spreading throughout the early church, it was necessary for the church to specify the basic Christian doctrines. It is possible that the New Testament contains early traces of a creed. To confess "Jesus is Lord"[38] might have been the shortest formula. Paul speaks of a "form of teaching"[39] and a type of creedal statement might appear in 1 Corinthians 15:3-7 (see also 8:6) and 1 Timothy 3:16. The well-known Apostles' Creed incorporates the text of an older Roman creed that might go back to the first century. According to Irenaeus, a creed was produced by the apostles[40] (hardly likely), and Tertullian believed that such a creed was "taught by Christ"[41] (equally unlikely). Tertullian speaks of the immovable "rule of faith" and offers the following text: I believe "in one only God omnipotent, the Creator of the universe, and His Son Jesus Christ, born of the Virgin Mary, crucified under Pontius Pilate, raised again the third day from the dead, received in the heavens, sitting now at the right hand of the Father, destined to come to judge living and dead through the resurrection of the flesh."[42] Elsewhere he offers a slightly different text. These early creeds were bulwarks against heretics and Gnostics.

A Surge of Roman Persecution

The last great persecution under the Roman Empire took place under Diocletian (284–305), who hoped to reinforce the political unity of the empire. The persecution began in 303. Church services were banned and places of worship were destroyed. Edicts insisted on the destruc-tion of the scriptures and commanded the burning of incense to idols. Many Christians became martyrs, while others compromised. Those who gave up the scriptures were called *traditores*. In actual fact, it was difficult for the emperor to enforce the edict throughout the empire. The persecution reached its peak under Galerius (305–311), till he became convinced of the futility of this effort. Shortly before he died, he issued an edict of toleration (A.D. 311). His death unleashed wars of succession that pitted Maxentius against Constantine.

THE CHANGES UNDER CONSTANTINE

Constantine, born in Serbia, served at the court of Emperor Diocletian and became a member of his bodyguard. When passed over for a promotion, he rejoined his father. Together they fought the Picts and Scots (305) in Britain. Upon the death of Constantine's father the troops in Britain hailed Constantine as the next Augustus (306), but in Rome the favorite was Maxentius. Constantine had married Fausta, the sister of Maxentius, which made the two contenders brothers-in-law. Constantine decided to settle the succession issue once for all by meeting Maxentius in Rome. Constantine's relatively small army faced Maxentius in front of the Milvian Bridge. Constantine was a skillful general and won the battle. When the bridge collapsed, Maxentius drowned.

The Conversion Experience

It was prior to this crucial battle that Constantine had a vision. There are several versions of the story. One relates that at noon on the day of the battle, a cross appeared in the sky and bore the inscription "By this sign you will conquer." Another version mentions a dream. Historian Michael Grant opines that "it was hardly unexpected that such a highly charged man should have a meaningful dream on the night before a decisive battle" and it seems likely that he had such a dream.[43] Dream or vision, "there is no reason why both events, vision and dream, should not have occurred, or have been believed to occur."[44] At any rate, there "is no doubt that Constantine became wholeheartedly converted to Christianity....[he] genuinely felt that he was in continuous touch with God."[45] He brought up his children in the faith and refused to participate in the "ascent to the Capitol to sacrifice to Jupiter."[46]

Constantine issued an edict of toleration that put Christianity on an equal footing with other religions and made it a *religio licita* in 313. This act did not make him immensely popular: it has been estimated that at that time, only three to five percent of the population was Christian. Paganism was the religion of the majority and was endorsed by most of the Roman senate members.

A State Religion

Thanks to Constantine, almost overnight the church went from being a persecuted minority to a governing minority. The church was no longer a pilgrim community. The new position of the church contained subtle dangers that were not as easy to perceive as outright persecution or heresy, but equally perilous. The clergy was honored and made immune from public burdens, an extraordinary privilege. All too soon, rivalries evolved.

Constantine "chose every bishop when a vacancy arose,"[47] and the state controlled the church. This had far-reaching and negative consequences. In 321 Sunday became a public holiday. This pleased the Christians as well as those who honored the sun. Among other things, Constantine humanized criminal law, abolished crucifixion, and mitigated slavery.

Conquest and Controversy

Licinius, the emperor of Eastern Rome, was defeated repeatedly even when Constantine was greatly outnumbered. When Licinius was assassinated in 315, Constantine became the sole, uncontested ruler of the Roman Empire. If he had hoped that Christianity would unify the empire, he was to be disappointed. Right after toleration had been granted, the Donatists of North Africa appealed to the emperor and asked him to help settle an ecclesiastical controversy. During the persecution under Diocletian, many believers had given up the sacred scriptures. How to deal with these lapsed believers became a major issue. The majority of Christians in North Africa deemed these lapsed individuals unfit to occupy positions of leadership. When Caecilian was appointed bishop, many objected because Felix, the consecrating bishop, had been a *traditore*. They promptly appointed another bishop, Majorinus, and a schism was born. At issue here were both the nature of the church and the effectiveness of the sacraments. Was the church an assembly of people living blameless lives? Did the validity of the sacraments (baptism, for instance) depend on the moral character of the administrator or upon the holiness of God?

A council of bishops ruled against the Donatists, who promptly appealed to Constantine. He referred the matter to a synod at Arles (314) where, once again, the Donatist position was rejected. But the Donatists outnumbered the orthodox Christians in

North Africa. They rebaptized believers on the theory that their original baptisms were invalid because they had been administered by clergy consecrated by a lapsed bishop. Only after the council of Carthage (411)—and thanks to the influence of Augustine—did the influence of the Donatists wane.

Constantine rejected the Donatist claim and tried to enforce his view by force of arms. This persecution only fueled the movement and prompted the Donatists to turn against the state. Constantine tired of the controversy and left the Donatists to their own devices (321). Though the Donatists took the high moral ground, they showed a lack of understanding regarding the nature of sin and the grace of God.

The next controversy involved the deity of Christ. Arius, a presbyter from Alexandria, taught that there was a time, prior to creation, when the Son did not exist. Constantine, more concerned about unity than theology, wanted to settle the matter and summoned a council of the church in Nicea (modern-day Iznik in Turkey). He took part in the deliberations, although he was hardly a theologian and not even baptized—an action postponed till the time of his death. Anywhere from 220 to 250 bishops attended (including four with Jewish names from Persia[48]). Only six were from the West, including two who represented the bishop of Rome. The center of gravity of the church was in the East. Arius had been excommunicated by an assembly of bishops in Alexandria (320) but had found refuge with some sympathizers. The controversy grew till it engulfed most of the East. Arius was roundly condemned at Nicea and exiled to Illyria. The wording of the Nicene Creed is explicit: Jesus Christ is "God from God, Light from Light, true God from true God, begotten not made, one in being *(homoousion)* with the Father, through whom all things came into being." The word *homoousion* was carefully chosen—Christ was not *homoiousion,* or merely of similar substance. Toynbee speaks of "the translation of Christian faith into the technical terms of ancient Greek philosophy."[49] Arius was recalled from exile in 336, but died later that year.

Frequently important theological issues in the church were determined by the inclination of an emperor. For example, Julian the Apostate exiled the orthodox and reinstated the Donatists. Constantinus (337–361), the son of Constantine and emperor of Eastern Rome, recalled all exiled clergy. In 356 he decreed that all pagan temples should be closed. By 380 Christianity became the official religion of the empire by decree of Theodosius (379–395). He proscribed all non-Christian religions and banned pagan cults. He also had the first heretic executed by the Christian state.[50]

Solidifying Christianity's Presence

To eliminate factions in the empire, the state enforced religious uniformity by upholding Christianity and declaring all other religions heretical. Constantine carried the old title of *pontifex maximus,* or chief priest of the pagan state cult (now an official title of the pope), and saw himself as the vicar of God on earth. The church was not separated from the state. In the East, the emperor dominated the church. In the West, the invasion of the barbarians and the collapse of the Roman Empire left the bishop of Rome in charge. When the imperial residence was moved from Rome to Ravenna, the bishop remained the sole authority in Rome and his power continued to grow. The bishops of the provincial capitals had taken the title of *metropolitan. Patriarchs* (or supermetropolitans) headed Rome, Alexandria, Antioch, and Constantinople. Jerusalem was added to the list on an honorific basis, for historic reasons. With the Muslim conquest Alexandria, Antioch, and Jerusalem lost significance and only Constantinople and Rome survived as important patriarchal seats. The Roman patriarch wanted recognition in the East, a struggle that lasted for centuries and led to the split between the Orthodox and Roman Catholic churches.

Constantine moved the capital to Byzantium, which was renamed Constantinople (A.D. 330). He was an enthusiastic builder, and church structures first appeared toward the end of the second century. Constantine built churches in Rome (St. Peter, Lateran Basilica), Constantinople (the Church of the Holy Apostles), and Palestine. For the most part these buildings no longer exist. Meanwhile, outside of the frontiers of the Roman Empire, persecution of the church continued, especially in Persia under King Shapur in 339 and 344.

Fausta, the wife of Constantine, unjustly accused the son of his first wife, and Constantine had the son executed. When he learned the truth, he also executed Fausta. The emperor was not baptized until shortly before his death because it was felt that no sin should be committed after baptism. Constantine's mother, Helena, made a pilgrimage to the Holy Land and thought that she had discovered the true cross and other remarkable relics. Pilgrimages to the tombs of famous martyrs multiplied, and most churches sought to acquire sacred relics because they were thought to protect and heal. Millions of pagans entered the church during this era and with them came a number of non-Christian customs:

genuflection, devotion to relics, and the use of candles and incense.[51]

THE MONASTIC PERIOD

Monasticism emerged as a reaction against the secularization of the church. The early hermits simply removed themselves from society and dwelled in the desert. Best-known is Anthony, who discovered that isolation did not eliminate temptation. He was over 100 years old when he died in 356. Many others had moved into the desert, and Pachomius (c. 285–346) grouped isolated anchorites into communities. The rules were simple: obedience to the abbot, common meals, regular spiritual exercises, no private property, and helping to do the manual labor (weaving mats, farming). There was no lifelong commitment. Pachomius's sister started a cloister just for women.

Debates about the person of Christ dominated the next few councils. The Greek churches, not Rome, hammered out the details of orthodoxy. Debates about the incarnation shook the Eastern churches to the core, to the neglect of practical Christianity. Theological speculation dominated the day and unleashed ferocious passions that rallied around formulas.

The Council of Chalcedon (451), with 520 bishops in attendance, was the largest synod of the ancient church. These bishops recognized the three previous ecumenical councils: Nicea (325), Constantinople (381), and Ephesus (431). (The seven ecumenical councils were Nicea [325], Constantinople [381], Ephesus [431], Chalcedonia [451], Constantinople [553], Constantinople [680], and Nicea [787].) They also specified that the relationship between the divine and the human nature of Christ is indivisible and inseparable.

The distinction of two natures does not take away the union. The property of each nature is preserved in one Person—in other words, Christ is both fully God and fully man. They carefully distinguished Person and nature, which was an explicit condemnation of monophysitism, which taught that Christ had only one nature.

Nestorius (c. 386–c. 451), the bishop of Constantinople, was in the center of the controversy about the exact relationship between the divine and the human natures of Christ. He objected to the word *theotokus,* "mother of God," to speak of Mary and insisted on "mother of Christ." It is sometimes difficult to determine what he really taught, but his view was clear enough that Cyril of Alexandria felt compelled to accuse him of error. Cyril sent a deferential letter to the pope, who also received one from Nestorius, which was, unfortunately less flattering. The pope ruled against Nestorius, who was exiled and 16 years later died in poverty in Egypt.

These debates were often more politically motivated than theologically oriented. Alexandria and Rome resented the influence of Constantinople and almost automatically opposed Nestorius. The Nestorians found refuge in Persia, the chronic enemy of Rome. Churches excommunicated each other and pronounced anathemas. The Nestorians kept moving east and reached China in 635.

Monasticism spread like wildfire and was introduced into the Hellenistic world by Basil of Caesaria. His rules are still observed. The Council of Chalcedonia (451) placed the monasteries under the authority of the bishop. In the fifth century the ascetics known as "pillar saints" appeared in Syria. Most famous is Simeon Stylites, who spent 30 years on a column

(d. 459). In the West, Jerome became an ardent advocate of the monastic life. He believed that virginity was the original state of man and that sexual intercourse was an inferior option and a consequence of sin. He saw celibacy as a superior state of life and advocated it with his typical "ferocious intolerance and bigotry, his nasty explosions of temper, his uncouth displays of vanity...."[52] The pagan idea that sexual intercourse produced ceremonial uncleanness entered the church. In the third century bishops, presbyters, and deacons were prohibited from marriage after ordination. The formal prohibition of marriage for priests was not enacted until the eleventh and twelfth centuries, and never in the Eastern churches.

Martin of Tours, a bishop, opened a monastery in the North of Gaul. He is best known for the story that he cut his cloak in half and shared it with a beggar. He spent his life proclaiming the love of God. The West embraced the rules of Saint Benedict, who was deeply influenced by the Eastern hermits. He stressed learning and culture, and monks were expected to read and study two hours a day. Care for the poor was rare in Western Rome, and monasteries filled the gap with a strong social outreach to help the needy. In the East, monasteries were dedicated to prayer, and the primary emphasis was placed on the search for holiness.

An unexpected problem was the spread of Manicheism, which originated in Persia. Mani (215–c. 274) hoped to replace Zoroastrianism with his new religion. He embraced a radical dualism between light and darkness and saw them not only as symbols, but light as good and darkness as evil. He taught that an evil god created man, who somehow retained sparks of light. Salvation is attained when this light is set free through abstinence. His theology was a bizarre mix of ancient mythology, extreme dualism, and strict morality. Mani's teachings were initially welcomed at the Persian court till the priests of Zoroaster imprisoned and crucified him. The teachings gained popularity in the Roman Empire around A.D. 330 and found many followers in North Africa, including, for a while, Augustine (354–430).

Augustine was born in North Africa. His father was a man of violent temper, and his mother, Monica, was a devout Christian. Augustine took a mistress at age 17 and had a son, Adeodatus. Reading Cicero turned Augustine's mind to philosophy. He read the old Latin Bible but, as a student of rhetoric, he despised the crude language. He taught rhetoric in Carthage, but hoped to find better students in Italy. He admired the sermons of Ambrose, who was the bishop of Milan (in Italy). In 386, while lying under a fig tree in deep turmoil, he heard the voice of a child repeating over and over again, *"Tolle lege"*—take it and read. He opened the scripture and read Romans 13:13–14 and said that "the light of faith flooded into my heart." A short time later Augustine's son died, and Augustine returned to Thagaste in North Africa and set up a monastery with the specific purpose of combating false doctrines and heresies, especially Donatism and Manicheism and, of course, the pagans. When he visited Hippo the people seized Augustine and ordained him to the priesthood so that he could become their bishop.

Augustine produced 232 titles, not to mention innumerable letters and sermons. In answer to the Donatists he pointed out that the holiness of the church is not derived from the perfection of each member, but from her purpose and direction. In response to the pagans who blamed the church for the decline of the empire he wrote *The City of God*. And his famous book *Confessions* details his own spiritual struggle.

Augustine's influence on the church is perhaps only second to the apostle Paul. Luther was an Augustinian monk, and Calvin found inspiration in Augustine's theory of predestination. And many people through the ages have been influenced by Augstine's writings.

Augustine died when the Vandals invaded Hippo. The Vandals, of Arian persuasion, had invaded southern France, moved on to the Iberian Peninsula, and crossed over into North Africa, where they maintained a kingdom (429–534) with Carthage as the capital. The Romans were no longer able to defeat the Gauls, Franks, Visigoths and Ostrogoths, Jutes, Angles, Saxons, and other Germanic tribes.

Attila the Hun, a fearsome enemy of the Roman Empire, came into Italy "inflamed with fury," as an old chronicler put it. Pope Leo bribed him not to attack Rome and Attila left. A few years later Rome was sacked by the Vandals from Africa (455). This time the pope extracted only minimal concessions. Western Rome collapsed under the barbarian onslaught, and in time, its population was a fraction of what it used to be. The Goths entered the city in 546, and the Lombards, who captured Milan, headed the next wave of invaders. Some of the Germanic tribes were pagans, while others had accepted Arianism. The only organized body left more or less intact was the church under the leadership of the pope. The remaining centers of culture in the West were the monasteries. The Barbarians respected monks, who tamed the wilderness and were able to read and write. And the

Christians who lived under the barbarians looked to Rome as the final authority.

THE PAPACY AND MISSIONARY ENDEAVORS

Even in these dark days missionary work never ceased. Ulfilas (c. 310–382) was dedicated in Constantinople (341) to undertaking the conversion of the Goths. The Gothic alphabet is attributed to him, and he translated the Bible into Gothic. The mass conversion of Goths followed.

The Eastern church suffered severe losses when the Muslim armies exploded out of the Arabian desert and conquered Jerusalem, Antioch (638), and Alexandria (641). The old patriarchal centers lost significance. Only Constantinople and her patriarch survived as a center of influence. The Muslim invasion was greatly facilitated by the divisions that took place within the church. Some loathed "heretics" more than Muslims. Between the Muslim conquests and the barbarian invasions, the church had been reduced to a small geographic area.

The Rise of Papal Power

In 381 the Council of Constantinople declared that their bishop had "the prerogative of honor" after the bishop of Rome because Constantinople was the New Rome, the capital of the empire. Nevertheless, Pope Siricus (384–399) implicitly claimed the right to make decisions that had universal application, and Leo (440–461) openly asserted the supreme authority of the papacy. He advanced the argument that Peter was the rock on whom Christ built the church and that the popes were the direct successors of Peter. Pope Gelasius (492–496) stressed the primacy of the spiritual over the temporal and concluded that priestly authority is greater than the

temporal power of kings. His epistle to the emperor was a milestone in the interaction between church and state. All through the Middle Ages, the tension between the papacy and emperors remained constant. Below are some of the statements in Gelasius's letter to the emperor:

> …the powers that chiefly govern this world are two: the sacred power of the bishops and the temporal power of the kings. Of these two powers, the ministry of the bishops has the greater weight, because they must account to the tribunal of God also for the kings of the mortals. You are also aware that, to take part in the divine mysteries, you have to fulfil the precepts of religion, which are not given to you to determine, because in such matters you depend on the judgment of the ministers of the sanctuary whom you cannot bend to your own will. In temporal matters, on the other hand, concerning the State, those dedicated to the worship of God also obey your laws because they know that, by divine power you were given imperial power so that with regard to temporal matters all resistance is to be excluded. And if it is fitting that all of the faithful submit themselves to the bishops, who correctly administer sacred matters, how much more necessary it is to proceed with the head of that see which God has set above all the others and which has always been venerated with filial devotion by the Universal Church.[53]

The Spread into Other Lands

The great task of Western Christendom was the conversion of the barbarian invaders who had embraced Arianism or remained pagans. The Franks, one of the most powerful of the Germanic tribes, were among the first to accept Christianity. King Clovis (481–511) was baptized in 496, perhaps under the influence of his Christian wife and probably not without political considerations. He, like Constantine, called upon Christ to win a battle against the Alemanni. He was victorious, redeemed his promise, and was baptized with 2,000 of his men. The king (not the pope) controlled the church. Edicts of the bishop of Rome were enacted only if confirmed by the king. Between 500 and 750, church and monasteries controlled one-third of the land.

Meanwhile, Roman administration had been withdrawn from England in 410. The country fractured into many small Anglo-Saxon kingdoms. When Ethelbert of Kent married the daughter of a Frankish king, Pope Gregory seized the opportunity and sent Augustine to convert the English. He arrived in 597 and the same year, the king became a Christian and allowed the mission to be established in Canterbury, the capital. Augustine was instructed to handle the transition from paganism to Christianity with tact and consideration. Pagan idols were destroyed, but the temples were simply sprinkled with holy water and rededicated.

Though the "reign" of Gregory the Great on "the throne of Peter" was brief (590–604), his impact was tremendous. He had been Prefect of Rome, the highest civil servant position, and renounced everything to become a Benedictine. His ancestral home became a monastery and his inherited wealth was given to the poor. As a papal legate he spent several years in Byzantium. He then returned to Rome, became the papal secretary, and was elected pope by popular acclaim. He laid the foundation of medieval Christendom and was the *de facto* ruler of central Italy. He raised armies and negotiated with the Arian Lombards, whom he converted to the Catholic faith. And he used his administrative gifts to manage papal estates, feed the poor, and redeem slaves.

The Arian Visigoths established a kingdom centered in Toledo, Spain (507–711) and accepted the Catholic creed in 589. Patrick, a Roman Britain, was the most famous missionary to Ireland. Legends about him abound. Although there were Christians in southeast Ireland before Patrick, he is hailed as the apostle to the Irish. At age 16 Patrick was carried away captive to Ireland, where he remained enslaved for six years. We know little about the intervening years till he reappears while heeding a call to evangelize Ireland. Consecrated a bishop, he returned to Ireland and converted thousands.

Winfrid, known as Boniface (c. 675–754), the "Apostle to Germany," was born in Britain, the descendant of a noble family. He entered the Order of Saint Benedict and was ordained priest at age 30. His first mission to Friesland (716) was hindered by political circumstances. While visiting Rome in 718, Winfrid, now called Boniface, received a mandate from Pope Gregory II to convert the heathen who lived east of the Rhine. He labored in Frisia for three years with the pioneer Willibrord, then returned to Germany. Christians in Thuringia and elsewhere had relapsed into semipaganism, and for five years Boniface labored in Hesse, Thuringia, and Frisia. Thousands turned to Christ. During another visit to Rome he was consecrated a regional bishop. In 723 in Geismar in lower Hessia, in the presence of a large number of pagans, he felled an oak tree sacred to Thor, the God of thunder. Boniface used the wood to erect a chapel. The fall of the oak stood symbolically for the fall of heathenism. Toward the end of his life Boniface once again took up the work of converting the Frisians and reached thousands. Converts had assembled for confirmation when a band of pagans fell upon them and murdered Boniface and his companions.

The Controversy over Icons

The Orthodox churches continued in an unbroken line since the days of the apostles and rightly thought that they were the source of Western Christianity. Unfortunately they were deeply divided by the iconoclastic controversy. To most Orthodox Christians, the icon was more than the picture of a saint painted on wood. It was a presence, a "window to heaven." Through an icon, the sacred became visible, and the saint becomes both visible and accessible. But to Byzantine emperor Leo III (717–741), who was famous for his brilliant victories against the Muslims, the veneration of icons was nothing but idolatry, and he published a decree demanding the destruction of icons. Perhaps he was influenced by Muslims or Jews and hoped to win them for Christ. Another factor may have been the loss of vast areas of the Byzantine Empire to the Muslims. Both Leo III and his son, Constantine V, thought this might be an expression of God's anger, a punishment for permitting the making of icons.

The controversy regarding icons lasted for over 100 years and sapped the remaining power of the Byzantine Empire. It became a contest between the church and the emperor. Party-spirit displaced rational thought. Anathemas were hurled, and zealous monks fought pitched battles. The most famous Byzantine theologian, John of Damascus (c. 700–c. 753), came out in favor of icons. The seventh ecumenical council also allowed the veneration of icons, a decision that was reinforced in a synod in Constantinople in 843. The controversy finally ended and ever since, the Orthodox Church has celebrated the Feast of Orthodoxy in memory of the final defeat of iconoclasm and the restoration of the icons.

The Beginnings of the Papal State

Charlemagne (768–814) built an empire that reached from the Atlantic to the Danube. By the time of his death it also included Saxony and Lombardy. Because he retained the reins of the church in his hands, he became the protector of the church in the West. Charlemagne married the daughter of Desiderius, king of the Lombards in Italy, but then he repudiated the princess and earned the enmity of her father. In the ensuing war, Charlemagne conquered Pavia (in northern Italy) and afterwards took the title King of the Lombards.

A document entitled *Donatio Constantini* ("the Donation of Constantine") purported that Pope Silvester I had not only converted Constantine but also healed him from leprosy. The document asserted that out of gratitude Constantine had donated a vast tract of land to the church, including the city of Rome and all the provinces. In 1440, the Italian Lorenzo Valla exposed the document as a forgery. Meanwhile, however, Pepin the Short (714–768), son of Charles Martel, who had defeated the Muslims, had ratified the donation. The document became the foundation of the papal state in Italy. In 800 the clergy, the nobles, and Frankish and Roman citizens were summoned by Charlemagne to a congress to examine the charges against Leo III. The pope was to appear before the king's court like any common subject. He had been accused of adultery and perjury. For three weeks the evidence was reviewed till Leo took an oath of purgation on the Gospels. His opponents were then recognized as guilty of the crime of *lèse majesté* (injury against the majesty) and condemned to death. The conspirators were exiled into Frankish territory.

Two days later Charlemagne attended Christmas mass at St. Peter's. When he finished his prayers and rose to his feet, Leo III placed a crown of gold on his head. Charles was then acclaimed as universal Roman emperor. It appeared spontaneous, but the immediate response of the crowd indicated careful orchestration. This was a splendid demonstration of the supremacy of the church over kings.

Charles accepted what had happened and defined to his own satisfaction the meaning of the imperial title. He appointed bishops, made ecclesiastical decisions, and intervened in the internal affairs of the church. He hoped to improve the moral level of the people and insisted that the clergy should familiarize the common people with the basic articles of the faith. He took steps to improve the education of the clergy. He drew scholars to his court, including the Anglo-Saxon Alcuin (c. 730–804), perhaps the most learned man of the empire at that time. Alcuin became a trusted royal adviser and headed the palace school. He developed a minuscule script, the basis of the way letters of the Roman alphabet are written today. Later he served as abbot of the Abbey of St. Martin at Tours.

Alcuin was one of the few who objected to the onslaught on the Saxons, whom Charles fought for 25 years in attempts to convert them. Rebellions were punished without mercy. After an uprising in 782, as many as 4,500 were beheaded and others sold into slavery or moved to the Rhineland. In spite of such an inauspicious beginning, the Saxons became staunch supporters of the church. Through Saxony the empire came in touch with the Avars, who had settled in the Hungarian steppes. The Avars, too, were subjected and came to accept Christianity.

The Continued Expansion
To Scandinavia

Sweden heard the gospel from Anskar (801–865), whom Pope Gregory IV named the papal legate for the north. Anskar's success was limited; perhaps the chief reason was political. To accept a Carolinian missionary might bring the nation into the orbit of the Franks. The Danes were more willing to accept missionaries from England because close contact had been established when the Danes conquered England. Denmark was the first Scandinavian country to accept the gospel when King Bluetooth was baptized.

Canute (1014–1035), the king of England and Denmark, was resolutely Christian. Norway was converted to Christianity under King Olaf Tryggvason (995–1000), a colorful personality. And finally, in the eleventh century a Swedish king was baptized and the christianization of the three Scandinavian countries was completed. What these mass conversions meant on an individual basis is impossible to determine. No one knows how much paganism was absorbed or how many non-Christian traditions were incorporated into Christianity.

To the Slavs

When in the eighth century Greece was decimated by pestilence, Slavs invaded and settled in Greek territories. They became Hellenized and accepted Christianity. Two brothers from Thessalonica, Constantine (later called Cyrill) (827–869) and Methodius (c. 815–885), were missionaries among the Slavs in Moravia, now the Czech Republic. They were well received by Prince Ratislav of Moravia. Much of their success was due to the usage of Slavonic (instead of Latin) in the church worship services. Cyrill is credited with the Cyrillian alphabet used in Russia and elsewhere. He was familiar with Greek, Latin, Hebrew, and Arabic and translated parts of the Bible. When Germans claimed jurisdiction over the area they kept Methodius in a monastery for more than two years, away from his mission field. Released thanks to the pope, Methodius was ultimately made an archbishop.

To Eastern Europe

Dynastic connection with Moravia brought the gospel to Poland, where Prince Miecislav was baptized (966). He organized the Polish church, which flourished under the reign of his son. In Hungary, Vajk, an important tribal leader, was baptized and married a Bavarian princess. He accepted a crown sent by the pope and is now known as St. Stephen (980–1015). Hungary became a monarchy and the royal family was instrumental in the mass conversion of the people.

At about the same time (c. 864) the gospel message reached Bulgaria. Their leader, Boris, was personally baptized by Photius, patriarch of Constantinople, and remained faithful to the Orthodox Church. The greatest Orthodox gain, aside from Bulgaria and Serbia, was Russia. Vladimir the Great (980–1015), the ruler of Kiev, married a Byzantine princess, Anna, who was the sister of the Byzantine emperor. Vladimir was baptized (987) and the mass conversion of his subjects followed. They used the Slavonic liturgy and adopted the Cyrillic alphabet. Although linked to Byzantium, the church developed along nationalistic lines.

Decline of the Papacy

The geographic spread of Christendom during this era could not possibly make up for the severe losses due to Muslim invasions. At the same time, the papacy reached new lows. Pope John VIII (872–882) was offered a poisoned drink by a relative but death came so slowly that a hammer was used to fracture his skull. "Of the forty-one Popes and anti-Popes who followed him, a third had unnatural deaths, by strangulation, suffocation, or mutilation. Stephen VIII had his ears and nose cut off…. Benedict IX was a teenager when he was enthroned."[54] John XII (955–964) "continued to gratify his unbridled pleasures, and the Lateran palace became a real bordello, with the Pope surrounded by beautiful women and handsome boys in a depraved lifestyle completely at variance with ecclesiastical duties."[55] Pope Stephen VI (896–897) exhumed the remains of the previous pope and put the rotting corpse on trial. The corpse was found guilty and deprived of three fingers, then quickly buried only to be re-exhumed and thrown in the Tiber River. Religion was primitive and attracted to things visible, associated with tangible things such as a tree, a stone, a grove—perhaps the remnant of old pagan beliefs.

East/West Differences

There were profound linguistic (Greek/Latin), cultural (East/West), theological (speculative/practical), and political factors (East/West Rome) that had long separated Byzantium from Rome. So it is surprising that the open break between the churches did not come until 1054. The structure of the Orthodox Church was conciliar (patriarchs), whereas the Roman Catholic Church was monarchical (popes). The Orthodox disliked the Roman Catholic emphasis on purgatory and indulgences, and the immaculate conception and bodily assumption of Mary. The lower clergy were allowed to marry, and the Orthodox did not accept the idea of the procession of the Holy Spirit from the Father and the Son and objected to the insertion of the word *filioque* ("and the Son") into the creed. The *filioque* was added at the Synod of Toledo (589).

The Eastern or Orthodox Church preferred the mystical to the legal approach to God. The spiritual discipline of *hesychasm,* the quiet prayer of the heart, was encouraged and practiced in many monastic communities. The official break came in 1054 under Pope Leo IX, who did much to correct abuses. At that particular time the reasons for the schism were more political than theological. The Latin or Roman Catholic churches in Constantinople had been closed, and the papal legate in Constantinople had deposited the papal excommunication of the Orthodox Church on the altar of St. Sophia. The patriarch then promptly launched a bull of excommunication against the Latin Church. The mutual excommunications were repealed in 1964.

Introduction of Reform

The reforms initiated by Pope Leo IX were continued by his successors. To avoid mob action or popular pressure, Nicholas II (1058–1061) decreed that popes should be elected by the College of Cardinals. Disregarding the new regulation, Hildebrand, known as Pope Gregory VII (1073–1085), was acclaimed as pope by people and clergy during the funeral of Pope Alexander. The new pope made every effort to eliminate the buying or selling of a church office and clerical marriage. Gregory was determined to assert the supremacy of the Church of Rome over its bishops, over other churches, and over the empire. He claimed the right to depose emperors and to release subjects from their oath of loyalty. His position was strengthened by the so-called Donation of Constantine, a spurious edict attributed to Constantine, which strengthened the power of the pope.

Pope Gregory forbade the German king Henry IV (1056–1106) to appoint bishops. Henry ignored the pope and continued to appoint bishops, including one in Milan. These German bishops had the dual role of both pastor and vassal, and as vassals, they controlled large territories and generated considerable revenue. The Pope invited Henry to appear before him in order to exonerate himself under pain of excommunication. Henry declared the pope unfit, and many of the German bishops sided with Henry. In response, Gregory excommunicated the king and 24 rebellious bishops (1076). Some princes saw this as an opportunity to diminish imperial authority and opposed Henry in the name of religion. They asked Pope Gregory to preside over a meeting to either absolve or condemn Henry. Because bishops and princes had deserted Henry, the king had no choice but to humble himself. He went to Canossa to meet Gregory, who kept him waiting in the snow for three days before receiving him. Henry then willingly submitted royal authority to the pope—and swore vengeance.

When Henry's conduct did not improve, many of the German princes turned against him and elected Rudolph of Swabia to be king. The pope also supported Rudolph. Henry stood in danger of losing the throne, but then Rudolph died. Henry then convened a council of bishops and replaced the pope with the archbishop of Ravenna, who took the name of Clement III. Henry went on to invade Italy and appeared before Rome. The pope took refuge in the castle of San Angelo and called upon an old ally, Norman Robert Guiscard, founder of the Norman state of the Two Sicilies. Henry left under the pressure of the advancing Normans and Guiscard was able to successfully free the pope, but all of this ended up turning the people of Rome against the pope, who ended up a virtual prisoner of the Normans and died defeated and alone.

THE CRUSADES

The Muslim Seljuks decisively defeated the Byzantine armies at the Battle of Manzikert (now Malazgirt in eastern Turkey) in 1071 and even captured Emperor Romanus IV Diogenes. They continued their advance toward Constantinople, and Emperor Alexius Comneus sent an urgent plea to Pope Urban II (1088–1099) to come to the rescue. The pope was at a council at Clermont-Ferrand, France, which was attended by 14 archbishops, 250 bishops, 400 abbots, and countless knights. A huge multitude met east of the city and listened to an impassioned speech by Urban. The crowd shouted, "God wills it!" and the Crusades were launched. But it was hardly a Christian crusade; it began with massacres of Jews in Europe. If the pope was hoping to reestablish the unity between Orthodox and Catholics, this attempt was an abysmal failure. The promise of plenary indulgence was perhaps enough motivation for many crusaders, but the majority came from humble dwellings in search of adventure, wealth through plunder, escape from creditors, or because they were attracted to the mysterious East and the romantic idea of liberating Jerusalem from the infidels. Stories about the mistreatment of pilgrims fired their imagination, and economic reasons swayed Italian cities hoping to increase trade.

The First Crusade was relatively successful. Jerusalem was captured in 1099, and Muslims and Jews were killed indiscriminately. When Muslim forces recaptured Edessa (1144), the Second Crusade was launched and ended in failure before Damascus. To retrieve the losses, the Third Crusade was launched with Richard I the Lionheart, Frederick I of Germany and Phillip II of France. They only managed to recapture Acre.

The Fourth Crusade (1204) was disastrous. The crusaders never reached the Holy Land or faced the Saracens. Instead, they sacked Constantinople and allowed the troops the freedom to pillage for three days. St. Sophia was plundered and desecrated (a prostitute was installed on the patriarchal seat) and a Latin kingdom was created (1204–1261). This was a fatal blow from which the Byzantine Empire never fully recovered, and it greatly facilitated the future Muslim conquest of Constantinople. East Rome had always stood as a Christian bulwark against the Islamic onslaught, but never recognized the supremacy of the pope. The "Latin" crusaders treated them like the enemy, and the schism between East and West became irrevocable. Michael VIII, a Byzantine emperor, finally regained control of Constantinople (1261). In 1291 Acre, the last crusader stronghold, fell—and this effectively ended the crusades.

THE MIDDLE AGES
A New Spirituality
Bernard of Clairvaux

Bernard of Clairvaux (1091–1153), the great Cistercians abbot, played a key role in the Second Crusade. His preaching was so effective that villages and towns became largely deserted as a result of his urging people to fight in the Crusades. Bernard has been called the uncrowned head of Europe, the religious genius of the twelfth century. No one wielded more influence in Western Europe in his day. Born of a noble family in southern France, he was deeply religious from an early age. With irresistible zeal he gathered a band of 30 companions, including his brothers and friends, who together with him joined the Cistercians monks at Cisteaux. In 1115 Bernard was appointed abbot of a small monastery in a desolate and forbidding valley that he christened *Clairvaux,* or "the beautiful valley."

Bernard was a brilliant preacher and a person of great moral force. Again and again he was called away from his cell to settle disputes among the mighty. Following the death of Pope Honorius II in 1130, a disputed election left two competing popes, Anacletus II and Innocent II. Bernard thought Innocent II the better

man and decided in his favor. His great task was to persuade the sovereigns of Europe who supported Anacletus II to transfer their allegiance to Innocent II. He was able to secure the allegiance of most of the rulers of Europe. When Anacletus died, Bernard persuaded his successor to resign.

One of Bernard's own monks was elected pope as Eugenius III (1145–1153), and Bernard continued to advise and chide him as if he were still his abbot.

Richard Rolle

Among the key individuals in this time period were Richard Rolle (c. 1300–1349) of England, who "broke the hard crust that had gathered round the heart of Christianity, by formalism and exteriority, and restored the free flow of spiritual life."[56] In an age of dry scholasticism he wrote,

> Love is a burning yearning after God, with wonderful delight and certainty. God is light and burning. Light clarifies our reason; burning kindles our will, that we desire naught but Him. Love is a life joining together the loving and the loved…love makes us one with God. Love is the beauty of all virtues…. Truth may be without love: but it cannot help without it…. whoso will love wisely, it behooves him to love lasting things, lastingly; and passing things, passingly; so that his heart be settled and fastened on nothing but God.[57]

Lady Julian of Norwich

Lady Julian of Norwich, England (1342–c. 1416) was a visionary with a focus on the passion of Christ. In spite of the Black Death and widespread corruption within the church she was certain of the triumph of the love of God, a theme she expounds in *Showing of Love*.

Hildegard of Bingen

One of the earlier mystics was another woman, Hildegard of Bingen, Germany (1098–1179), who came from a noble family. She hesitated to share her visions till at age 42 it came to pass "that the heavens were opened and a blinding light of exceptional brilliance flowed through my entire brain." She was overcome by feelings of inadequacy, but the pope encouraged her to finish her writings. She became an adviser to the pope and the emperor.

Other Contemplatives and Mystics

John Tauler (c. 1300–1361) was a Dominican preacher influenced by Eckhardt (1260–1327) but avoiding his pantheistic tendency. Ruysbroeck (1293–1381) was a contemplative who labored in Brussels for 26 years then retired to a small hermitage to enjoy solitude but was followed by friends and admirers. He influenced Gerhard Groote (1340–1384) of Deventer, Holland, founder of the Brethren of the Common Life. Groote was a friend of Tauler. Groote abandoned his superficial life of fame and fortune and created religious communities to cultivate the interior life. The groups were largely composed of laymen in search of practical mysticism, personal devotion, and service to others. The movement spread to Germany and Switzerland. Groote wanted people to read the Bible and began to translate it into the vernacular. He did not believe that man could be saved through good works and foreshadowed Luther in this regard. The Brethren created many schools. Thomas à Kempis, the author of *The Imitation of Christ,* was among the Brethren of the Common Life. His direct appeal to Christ made the clergy feel threatened.

Francis of Assisi

Another influential mystic from this era is Giovanni Barnardone, also known as Francis of Assisi (1182–1226), who was born into a wealthy Italian family. In 1208 he followed the admonition of Christ to care for the sick and the lepers and to possess nothing.[58] He distributed his possessions to the poor and, surrounded by a few friends, began his pilgrimage. Some went to Morocco, Syria, and Spain. Francis traveled to Egypt and preached to the sultan there.

Of the many hymns Francis composed, the most famous is his *Canticle of the Sun*. Francis was "one of the most winsome figures of Christian history."[59] The order of the Poor Clares followed shortly when devoted women insisted on a similar lifestyle. Members of the so-called Third Order of St. Francis embraced a simple lifestyle but remained in the world and retained property. All too soon the original idealism was discarded and poverty was no longer observed.

Dominic

Dominic (c. 1170–1221) followed a typical clerical career. In southern France he discovered the popularity of the Cathari (also known as Albigensians), a sect that embraced a dualism reminiscent of the old Manichaens. The Cathari gained many followers, in part because their morality was better than that of the Catholic clergy. Dominic's goal was to erase heresy. His mendicant order was sanctioned by Innocent III, with a special emphasis on teaching and preaching. The order became responsible for the enforcement of the Inquisition that had been introduced by Gregory IX

(1227–1241). Tens of thousands of Cathari were killed as heretics.

The Flagellants

The Flagellants movement began in Italy (1259), perhaps influenced by Joachim of Flora, who announced the coming of the age of the Spirit. The Flagellants were active in Italy and Germany, but disappeared within a hundred years. Their self-flagellation did not help prevent the plague that, in the late 1340s, wiped out between one-fourth and one-third of the entire population of Europe.

Peter Waldo

Peter Waldo, a wealthy businessman in Lyon, determined to follow Christ and was the founder of what became known as the Waldensians. He made adequate provisions for his wife and daughters, then distributed the rest of his wealth and began a life of itinerant preaching (c. 1173). He commissioned translations of the Bible from Latin into vernacular French. Pope Alexander III allowed him to preach only in the unlikely event of an invitation by a local priest. Waldo preached anyway and was promptly excommunicated (1184). He allowed women to preach and developed small training centers for his followers. They opposed masses for the dead and purgatory, and in time were persecuted by the Catholic Church. The Waldensians survived mostly in Italy and once freedom of religion was granted (1859), their influence began to spread again.

The Beginning of Scholasticism

Pope Innocent III (1198–1216), was a key player in European history, the first to call himself *Vicar of Christ*. He never doubted that absolute dominion over all powers on earth belonged to the papacy. Even as the soul is superior to the body, so the spiritual must dominate the material…. the emperor receives his authority from the pope, even as the moon receives light from the sun.[60] Karl Heussi speculated that the political success of Innocent III undermined the spiritual respect of European nations for the see of St. Peter.[61]

The Fourth Lateran Council (1215) took place under Innocent III. It was attended by more than 2,000, including 400 bishops and 800 abbots. At this council, transubstantiation became a dogma. First seriously advocated by Paschasius Radbertus around 831, this doctrine teaches that once the bread and wine of communion have been consecrated by the priest, though they may appear unchanged, in reality they have become the substance of the body and blood of Christ. The body that was Christ's while on earth is now present in the element and is crucified. The mass is a bloodless sacrifice; this ritual takes place "in a sacred realm, an eternal realm where time as we know it does not exist."[62]

Around this same time, universities began springing up in Paris, Rome, Bologna, Oxford, Cambridge, and elsewhere, and scholasticism flourished. Most famous among the scholars was Thomas Aquinas (1225–1274), who combined Augustine with Aristotelian logic and mysticism. He was not an innovator, but presented a solid intellectual foundation for Catholicism. Bonaventura (1221–1274), another scholar, was more partial to Augustine and mysticism. Both Dominicans were opposed in certain areas by John Duns Scotus (c. 1265–1308), a Franciscan who taught mostly in Oxford and Paris.

Parallel with this intense intellectual activity (950–1350) was the construction of cathedrals. According to Moynahan, "between 1050 and 1350, eighty cathedrals, five hundred large churches, and tens of thousands of smaller ones were built in France alone."[63] Although that count seems rather high, the overall picture that many churches were being built is undoubtedly correct.

Not everyone in this era was under the sway of dry scholasticism. An example of practical mysticism is Raymond Lull (c. 1232–c. 1315), who was born in Majorca in an aristocratic family. He distributed his wealth to the poor and dedicated his life to missionary service. He learned Arabic, advocated the creation of linguistic schools for missionaries, and authored over 250 books. As he approached 60 years of age, he took the bold step of traveling to North Africa and disembarking at Tunis, the western center of the Muslim world in those days. He invited Muslim leaders to a debate. When some accepted Christ, Lull was imprisoned and banished. He wasn't killed due to the respect the Muslims had for his intellectual ability.[64] In all, he made three journeys to North Africa, and then was stoned in Algiers about 1315. This kind of punishment was also fashionable in the Inquisition—even more so after Pope Innocent IV approved of torture.

The Inquisition became a permanent fixture from the time of Gregory IX (1232). The Dominicans controlled it, and the horrors of the Inquisition were revived in Spain under Torquemada (1483–1498), also known as the Grand Inquisitor. This persecution was brought against *conversos,* or Jews and Muslims who had become converts to Christianity under duress. About 9,000 people were burned. Accusations were fueled by greed, because those who fingered potential victims received material benefits—usually the possessions that had belonged to the accused who were seized. No reason was given to victims for their arrest. There were no formal trials, only the rack and burning for those who were arrested. The Spanish Inquisition continued until 1834.

THE EARLY REFORMATION PERIOD
The Key Individuals
John Wycliffe

John Wycliffe, sometimes called "the Morning Star of the Reformation," was born around 1330. He was educated at Oxford and earned his doctor of divinity degree in 1372. Two years later he was appointed rector to those in Lutterworth. He held that all "dominion" or lordship belongs to God and can be forfeited by sin. Given the ungodly state of the clergy—so many of the church's leaders were living in sin—Wycliffe thought that the king had the necessary authority to deprive them of what they held unlawfully. This was a bold move toward attacking the corruption present in the church. Wycliffe taught that the popes erred in claiming to be the successors of the apostle Peter. He denied transubstantiation and opposed the cult of saints, the veneration of relics, the endless pilgrimages to certain sites, and masses for the dead. He advised the English court that it was legal to withhold the traditional payments made to Rome, and he led the movement for the translation of the Bible into English and encouraged traveling preachers.

Though Wycliffe received much opposition and was declared a heretic, he died in peace, not at the stake. His many followers, who were called Lollards, were severely persecuted. John Oldcastle, a leader of the Lollards was burned at the stake. Nevertheless the Lollards survived, though they suffered much. As late as 1521 the bishop of London arrested 500 Lollards.[65]

John Hus

Wycliffe's teachings were carried to Bohemia and influenced John Hus (c. 1369–1415). Hus was an ordained priest and became dean of the philosophy department at the University of Prague. He was a popular preacher in both Latin and Czech at the Church of Bethlehem in Prague. Because Hus came to accept most of Wycliffe's teachings, Pope John XXIII excommunicated him in 1411. But the authority of the popes became further undermined when a third one was elected and all three claimed to be the Vicar of Christ on earth.

Hus was summoned to appear before the Council of Constance (1414–1418) and received a letter of safe-conduct from the emperor, but he was imprisoned anyway. Hus refused to recant but prepared to submit his judgment to the council if he could do it without offending God or his conscience. The council condemned Hus and had him burned at the stake.

The very idea of a general council called for the purpose of healing the papal schisms implied that such a council had authority over the pope. This was stated explicitly in a declaration dated April 6, 1415. The Council of Constance deposed John XXIII, who fled but was caught. Gregory XII resigned, and Benedict XIII faded into obscurity. With all three papal contenders disposed of, the Council of Constance elected Martin V (1417–1431) as the new pope. The great schism that had begun under Urban VI (1378–1389) finally ended. It had begun when Urban VI added Italian cardinals as a counterweight to the French cardinals. They, in turn, declared

the papal seat vacant, accused Urban of apostasy, and elected Clement VII (1378–1394), who decided to reside in Avignon to ensure his safety among his French allies. So began the "Babylonian captivity" of the papacy. Urban, fearful of opposition, imprisoned and tortured six cardinals, five of whom simply disappeared.[66] They were probably slain at his orders.[67] The fact that there were contending popes had greatly diminished the spiritual authority of the Catholic Church.

Girolamo Savonarola

Girolamo Savonarola (1452–1498), a Dominican, came to Florence, Italy in 1481. Ten years later, enthusiastic crowds thronged to hear him announce impending judgments that condemned corruption. Florence, at the heart of the Renaissance, repented and changed. Religious fervor replaced the carnival. Savonarola's enemies denounced him and the pope excommunicated him. Florence, under threat of interdict, turned against the reformer. He was tortured, hung, and burned. He had been "orthodox in doctrine, ruthless in morality, and reckless and ambitious in politics."[68]

John Wessel

John Wessel (1420–1489), a Dutch theologian who belonged to the Brethren of the Common Life, has been called a precursor of the Reformation. He opposed indulgences, denied the infallibility of the pope and encouraged the study of the original languages of the Bible, Greek and Hebrew. He was never threatened by the Inquisition, but his writings were placed on a list of forbidden books. Luther once said, "if I had read his books before, my enemies might have thought that I had borrowed everything from Wessel, so great is the agreement between our spirits."[69]

The Geographic Circumstances

Sporadic efforts were made to reunite the Orthodox and the Roman Catholics. The advance of the Ottomans in the Balkans created a new urgency. Hundreds of Byzantine delegates came to Italy in search of compromise. In 1438 the pope announced that union with the Greek bishops had been achieved. But upon returning to Constantinople, popular resistance forced the Orthodox bishops to recant.

The conquest of Constantinople by the Ottomans (1453) was a deadly blow to the Orthodox Church. In Russia, Ivan III (1462–1505) took as his second wife Sophia, the niece of Constantine XI, the last emperor of Byzantium. The idea of Russia as "the third Rome" (successor to ancient Rome and East Rome) gained ground. When Ivan IV or Ivan the Terrible (1547–1584) was crowned in 1547, he took the title of *tsar,* which was derived from the Roman title *Caesar.* The tsars were thought of as successors of the Byzantine rulers and therefore as guardians of the Orthodox faith. In 1589, Job of Moscow became the first Patriarch of Moscow and All Russia and was recognized as such by Constantinople.

In the sixteenth century, France, Spain, and England were united kingdoms. Italy was divided into five states and many small principalities. Germany had a bewildering number of ecclesiastical and secular principalities (some 300 independent states), imperial cities, and a few larger feudal states. The election of the emperor of the Holy Roman Empire was in the hands of seven prince-electors. Beginning in 1356, these electors chose a succession of kings from the house of Hapsburg. When they voted for Charles V, the king of Spain (1519–1556) rather than Francis I of France, it led to wars between Charles V and France. The Ottomans, under Suleiman the Magnificent (1519–1566), took advantage of the strife and conquered Belgrade and Hungary and threatened Vienna, but failed to conquer the city. At this point Suleiman declared victory and retreated.

The 1400s ushered in the age of the humanists, none more famous than Desiderius Erasmus of Rotterdam, Holland. Both John Calvin and Ulrich Zwingli also had humanist backgrounds. Erasmus (1466–1536) lived in Holland, Italy, England, and Switzerland. He corresponded with the emperor and the pope and counseled princes and clergy. Erasmus saw Christ preeminently as teacher and the Sermon on the Mount as the essence of religion. He saw the need for reform and hoped to achieve it through a renovation of morals. To reach this goal he contributed negatively through wit and satire (*In Praise of Folly*) and positively through the publication of a Greek edition of the New Testament.

THE REFORMATION PERIOD
The Key People
Martin Luther

Erasmus was a teacher when the times needed a prophet. Such a man was Martin Luther (1483–1546). He spent his childhood in a small mining town. He was a "poor scholar" who received a free education and lodging and sang for his food. He attended the University of Erfurt and while there entered an Augustinian convent in search of salvation. He fasted and scourged himself and confessed so often that he was told to stop and wait till he had something to confess. In his cell he read the apostle Paul's letter to the Romans. His struggle lasted two years till he came to the glorious understanding that he could have fellowship with God because he was justified in the sight of God by faith in Christ. Justification by faith (not works) became the rock-solid foundation of his life and teaching.

In 1508, Luther began to teach theology at the new University of Wittenberg. He was more interested in the practical side of theology than the speculative aspects. His lectures drew students from all over Germany. Luther opposed the sale of indulgences as a moral evil that was detrimental to spiritual life. On October 31, 1517 he proposed 95 theses for an academic debate regarding indulgences. The fact that the theses were nailed to a church door was not unusual. It communicated that Luther was committed to defending the opinions he had expressed and was willing to enter an academic debate. He had no idea that in doing this, he had lit a match that almost instantly created an enormous conflagration.

In summary, Luther opposed the belief that the pope had access to a storehouse of merits gained by the saints and the death of Christ. The saints had a superabundance of good deeds (more than they needed) that could be added to the infinite merits of Christ. It was rather difficult to understand why the "merits" of the saints were needed since those of Christ were infinite. Out of this great treasury the pope could dispense merits to the faithful, or indulgences. Though a believer may have escaped eternal punishment thanks to absolution by the priest, he still had to face temporal punishment here on earth or hereafter in purgatory. This punishment could be shortened or escaped altogether through indulgences.

In 1517, Pope Leo X declared that those who gave monetarily to the rebuilding of St. Peter's Basilica could receive indulgences. It was this that prompted Luther to write and circulate his 95 theses.

The dissemination of the 95 theses across Germany was extraordinary. From 1500 until the Reformation in 1517, German printers produced an average of 40 books a year. But between 1517 and 1520, approximately 350,000 copies of Luther's 30 publications were printed. A disputation was arranged in Leipzig (1519) between Luther and Johann Eck, one of the ablest Catholic controversialists. Eck's sole purpose was to force Luther to admit that he shared some of the same views as Hus or Wycliffe, both of whom had already been condemned as heretics. In this Eck succeeded. Luther published the debate and in 1520 authored three books that are at the heart of the matter: *The Liberty of a Christian Man, To the Christian Nobility of the German Nation,* and *On the Babylonian Captivity of the Church.* The pope issued a bull with the threat of excommunication. Luther dismissed the bull, and because ecclesiastical measures had failed to silence Luther, secular authorities now became involved. Luther was summoned to appear before the emperor at the Diet of Worms in 1521. All the secular electors and great princes were present, as well as the Catholic Church's cardinals and ambassadors. Luther's books were spread out on a long table and he was asked to recant his writings. Luther refused and ended his brief response with the words, "Here I stand." Asked to give an unambiguous answer, he said, "It is impossible for me to recant unless I am proved to be in the wrong by the testimony of the Scriptures or by clear reasoning; I cannot trust the decisions of councils or popes, since it is well known that they have often erred and contradicted themselves. My conscience is captive to the Word of God. I cannot and I will not retract anything, since it is neither safe nor honest to go against one's conscience."

Luther affirmed the authority of the Bible interpreted by a sanctified conscience, rather than the authority of the Catholic Church. He rediscovered the teaching of the priesthood of all believers in the New Testament, which automatically invalidated the necessity of priestly mediation. He based salvation on God's initiative of grace and the response of faith, eliminating the concept of salvation by good works or the mysterious efficacy of sacraments. In a few words, *sola scriptura, sola gratia, sola fides*—only scripture, only grace, only faith. For Luther, faith was a living, busy, active, powerful thing. It is impossible for it not to do good works continually, because good works are the *result* of faith and forgiveness.

Luther opposed simony, or the sale of ecclesiastical appointments (including the appointments of cardinals), a significant source of papal income. Unfortunately, unprecedented corruption marked the papal reign of Sixtus IV (1471–1484) and nepotism reigned supreme. Nine of his relatives became cardinals. Innocent VIII (1484–1492) officially recognized his bastard children, who were even married in the Vatican. Historians agree that the election of Alexander VI (1492–1503) was also tainted by simony. He was one of the Borgias of ill fame. He sired two more children while he was pope, and his mistress was a married woman. Julius II (1503–1513) was a patron of Michelangelo. Like the Renaissance princes, he enjoyed the arts, donned armor to lead his troops, and brooked no insubordination. Leo X (1513–1521) was a Medici, "an elegant dilettante,"[70] with 700 courtiers, an orchestra, a theater company, and a menagerie. "Lasciviousness and moral corruption reached the highest levels with Leo X."[71]

When Luther denounced the indulgences, a key source of papal revenue was seriously threatened. Luther suggested that the pope should use the inexhaustible treasure of merits he claimed to have at his disposal and immediately empty purgatory free of charge and release everyone. This would surely be an act of mercy befitting a pope.

An imperial edict against Luther threatened his followers with extermination. Friends of Luther sheltered him in the Wartburg Castle. Luther used the time to translate the Bible into German. In his absence, extreme groups gained influence and the Reformation threatened to degenerate into mindless fanaticism. Some went so far as to reject all civil government. Because some of the wild-eyed fanatics rejected infant baptism, the entire Anabaptist movement was tainted by association. Luther left the safety of the castle and returned to Wittenberg to help restore calm.

One of the most disastrous events for the Reformation was the outbreak of the Peasant's War. It was one in a long series of almost chronic uprisings. The people's demands were primarily economic, and not so much religious. The extreme violence on the part of the peasants prompted Luther to write the tract *Against the Murdering, Thieving Hordes of Peasants*. Afterwards he was forever distrustful of the concept of democracy.[72] In the end, the peasants were subdued ferociously, and their situation remained unchanged.

Soon after Luther's death a religious war broke out that ended with the Peace of Augsburg treaty (1555) on the basis of *cuius regio, eius religio*—the ruler's religion binds his subjects. Thanks to a few Protestant princes, Protestantism gained official recognition in their realms. There were small tentative steps toward toleration dictated by political realities such as 1) the religious divisions in Germany, 2) the emperor and pope being at war, and 3) the threat of the Ottomans. Unfortunately, this tolerance only covered Lutherans and was not extended to Reformed or Anabaptist churches.

Several factors were at work in Germany that helped to facilitate the Reformation, but the key element was the spark provided by Luther. People were intensely religious and saw the need for change, but someone like Luther was needed to speak the prophetic word. The Reformation was helped by the rise of nationalism (although there was no such thing as a German state till centuries later) and changing economics, but it was the printing press more than anything else that was responsible for Luther's success compared, for instance, to Wycliffe. Luther's translation of the Bible was both a linguistic masterpiece and an act of daring, and his other writings were able to circulate widely with thanks to the printing press. Luther also promoted education and insisted that all cities, towns, and villages establish schools supported by public funds and that children be compelled to attend. This was the first great impetus to free compulsory education. Philip Melanchthon (1497–1560) a close friend of Luther and fellow reformer, proposed the division of schools into classes. Melanchthon, a brilliant theologian of gentle temperament, played a significant

but often overlooked role in the Protestant reformation. He was easily eclipsed by the large shadow Luther cast.

Though Luther was a tremendously positive force for needed change, his legacy is still marred by his intemperate language in denouncing the peasants and his violent diatribes against the Jews toward the end of his life.

Zwingli and Calvin
Ulrich Zwingli

Ulrich Zwingli (1484–1531) led the Reformation movement in Switzerland—more precisely, in the cantons of Zurich and Bern. Zwingli received an excellent humanistic education and slowly—independently of Luther—found his way to the truth of the gospel while serving as a priest in Einsiedeln (1516–1519). In 1523 he presented 57 theses and persuaded the civic authorities of Zurich to accept the Reformation. In time, more cantons (territorial divisions) turned to Protestantism, which led to civil war. Zurich was unprepared for war and lost. Zwingli, the army chaplain, was killed at the Battle of Kappel (1531).

The Reformation gave birth to four basic groups: Lutherans, Anabaptists, Reformed, and Anglicans. Between 1542 and 1546, almost 60 Anabaptists were executed in Switzerland. In Germany and Holland, Mennonites were not tolerated. The extravagance and radicalism of Thomas Munzer, who finally joined the peasant uprising and was beheaded, besmirched the Anabaptist reputation beyond redemption. Another negative incident was the brief establishment of the "New Jerusalem" in Munster (1534–1535), when Jan Matthys, a baker from Harlem, Holland, saw himself as the successor of King David. He introduced the community to polygamy. Matthys had

16 wives and killed one. His fanaticism only served to further damage the reputation of the Anabaptists. By and large they were peaceful and devout and did not indulge in fanaticism. They favored tolerance, advocated pacifism, and abstained from participation in public life. Conrad Grebel (c. 1498–1526), who came from a prominent Swiss family, and Menno Simons (1496–1561), an ex-priest, were among the group's early leaders.

John Calvin

John Calvin (1509–1564) was born into an upper-middle-class family and received the typical humanistic education of his day. Calvin speaks of his "sudden conversion," which led him to Protestantism and being forced to leave Paris. In Basel, at 26, he published the first edition of *Institutes of the Christian Religion,* which he continued to revise and enlarge throughout his life. His commentaries cover most of the books of the Bible. His learning was extraordinary. "He knew the ancient Fathers as no one else in the century."[73]

While Calvin was passing through Geneva in 1536, Guillaume Farel (a local reformer) adjured him to stay in the city, which had just embraced the Reformation. But Calvin's stern moral principles forced him to move on to Strasbourg. The Geneva city council recalled him in 1541. Calvin then spent the rest of his life reinforcing ecclesiastical discipline and government. His enormous correspondence extended his influence to England, Scotland, Hungary, and Poland. And his academy trained clergy for France, where his influence was extraordinary.

The writings of Luther reached France under Francis I (1515–1547), a man who was essentially indifferent to religion and who even allied himself with the Ottomans to oppose Charles V of Spain. The sister of Francis I, Margaret of Navarre, was well-disposed toward Protestants. In France they were called *Huguenots,* a word of uncertain derivation, perhaps a French mispronunciation of the German *Eidgenossen* (Iguenots = Huguenots), which means "conspirators." In 1555 the Huguenots began to organize churches, and the first national synod was held in 1559. Although many members of the higher aristocracy were won for the Reformation, Huguenots still suffered severe persecution. For example, in Toulouse, 3,000 men, women, and children were massacred. Eight religious wars inevitably followed, and they ended with the Treaty of St. Germain-en-Laye in 1570.

The marriage of Henry of Navarre (1553–1610), the nominal Huguenot leader, to Margaret de Valois (1553–1615), the youngest sister of Charles IX, was arranged to help cement the peace. When the leaders of the Huguenots came to Paris for the marriage celebration, they were killed in the Massacre of St. Bartholomew. This betrayal, reenacted in the surrounding provinces, led to 70,000 deaths, the death of Protestant leadership, and yet another religious war. In Rome the pope called for a *Te Deum* (a hymn of praise) to celebrate the massacre. When a monk slew King Henry III, Henry of Navarre, a Protestant, was compelled to become Catholic to accept the crown. He issued an edict of toleration in 1598, and the Huguenots grew in number and influence again—until Louis XIV of France abrogated the edict and persecution resumed (1785).

It was Max Weber who proposed a definite linkage between Calvinism and economics in his groundbreaking book *The Protestant Ethic and the Spirit of*

Capitalism[74] (1930). Luther had proclaimed the priesthood of all believers which eliminated the priest as an intermediary between God and man and placed the believer face to face with God. Calvin added that what the believer discovered at that point was God's inscrutable decree of predestination. How could anyone be certain to be among the elect? Calvin's answer was simple: perseverance in good works not in order to be saved, but to demonstrate that salvation had been received. To do all things for the glory of God produced intense worldly activity that, combined with a nonworldly attitude, led inevitably to capitalism. Money received from earnest and honest labor (with the glory of God in mind) was not spent on frivolities (elegant clothing, jewelry, etc.) or on worldly entertainment (gambling, alcohol, etc.) and simply accumulated. Calvinism (and later, Puritanism) induced a form of asceticism that avoided ostentation and all unnecessary expenditure. The struggle was not against acquisition, but against the irrational use of wealth.[75] In this way, capitalism was born. And this attitude was not limited to Calvinism. According to John Wesley, "religion must necessarily produce both industry and frugality, and these cannot but produce riches." For Methodism to survive intact, "we ought not to prevent people from being diligent and frugal; *we must exhort all Christians to gain all they can, and to save all they can; that is, in effect, to grow rich.*"[76] According to Weber, Calvinism led almost inevitably to the accumulation of capital, making funds available for capitalism. In addition, Calvin rejected the medieval interpretation of Deuteronomy 23:19-20, which was said to prohibit all forms of interest. He made his position clear in a letter to Claude de Sachins. Huguenots were free

to charge (moderate) interest without fear of offending God.[77]

Some Key Developments

In the fifteenth century, Spain finally achieved political consolidation. With the conquest of Grenada, King Ferdinand and Queen Isabella expelled the last Moorish kingdom from Spanish soil. Ferdinand no longer needed the Jews to help finance his war against the Moors. In 1492, the same year that Columbus sailed across the Atlantic, all Jews—some 400,000—were exiled. Ten years later, the Moors shared a similar fate. The Inquisition that had established in Spain in 1480 under the Grand Inquisitor, a Dominican named Tomás de Torquemada, could now focus the government's efforts on *conversos* and *moriscos,* or Jews and Moors "converted" under duress. Over the next 15 years, Torquemada condemned thousands to torture and death at the stake. Although strict orthodoxy was enforced in line with papal decrees, Spain retained a large measure of independence from the papacy.

Francisco Ximénez de Cisneros (1436–1517) emerged as a key figure at this time. When he was about 50, Ximénez became a friar. His extreme austerity attracted large crowds of penitents. He was called to the royal court as confessor to Queen Isabella, and three years later he was named archbishop of Toledo. He launched a thoroughgoing reform of the Spanish clergy. He was a patron of the new learning and founded the University of Alcalá (1500) to provide clerical education. With the help of other scholars, Ximénez edited a Polyglot edition of the entire Bible in Hebrew, Greek, and Latin in parallel columns with accompanying translations. Through his dedicated labor, Ximénez helped to purify the Spanish church. He enlisted the best scholarship of the Renaissance in his campaign to renew the life of the church.

ENGLAND, SCOTLAND, AND THE NEW WORLD
England

In England the reformation took a unique direction and gave birth to the Anglican Church. "It would be a mistake, however, to think that Henry's eagerness to be divorced from Catherine accounts for the English Reformation. No king, however despotic, could have forced such a revolution unless there was much in the life of the people that reconciled them to the change."[78]

At 17, when Henry VIII (1491–1547) became king, he married Catherine of Aragon, the widow of his older brother. Henry had received a special papal dispensation for this, but later he became convinced that his marriage to Catherine had been invalid. However, he failed to convince Pope Clement. Henry asked for an annulment, which was often routinely granted, but in this particular case it was denied because the pope feared retribution from Charles V, a member of Catherine's family. The pace of negotiations between King Henry VIII and Pope Clement VII accelerated toward the end of 1532. During this time, Anne Boleyn, whom Henry wanted to marry, became pregnant. For the child—hopefully a boy—to be legitimate and a recognized heir to the throne, Henry had to marry Anne without delay. But the pope withheld his consent because he needed Charles's political support. Catherine was an aunt of Charles, who was determined that her honor remain intact.

At this impasse, Henry VIII had to find someone who would give him what he needed. If this meant that England's church must break away from the Roman Church, then that was the price to pay. Henry's attitude was not altogether unreasonable. The pope had already granted the Spanish government the right to set up and direct the Inquisition and issued a bull in 1508 granting the Spanish crown the right to name bishops in the Americas. The kings of France and England also controlled the appointment of church bishops. Thomas Cranmer (1489–1556), the Archbishop of Canterbury, believed that royal supremacy might be good for the church and lead to reform. He too rejected the validity of Henry's first marriage, and the ecclesiastical court justified the king and the pope was defied. The English Parliament voted on the Act of Supremacy (1534) whereby the king became the supreme head of the Church of England. Later, under the weak Edward VI (1547–1553), royal protectors hoped to introduce Protestantism. With reform in mind, the Book of Common Prayer was issued and the essential beliefs of the Anglican Church were written in the 42 Articles (precursor of the 39 Articles), in which Calvinistic tendencies were published.

With the death of King Edward VI, Mary ascended the throne (1553–1558) and initiated a strong Catholic reaction. Papal jurisdiction was reestablished, and 300 Protestant martyrs were burned at the stake, including Latimer and Cranmer. In 1555 the pope's supremacy was restored by an act of Parliament. The persecutions of Protestants, combined with a pro-Spanish foreign policy, led to ever-deepening resentment of the queen. Upon her death, Elizabeth (1558–1603) took over the throne. Her supremacy over the church was enacted by Parliament (1559), although 15 out of 16 bishops refused to accept the parliamentary verdict. The same year, the pope declared Elizabeth illegitimate because she had been conceived out of wedlock by Henry VIII and Anne Boleyne. A confession of faith in 39 articles, moderately Calvinistic, was accepted in 1563 and approved by Parliament in 1571. The pope excommunicated Elizabeth, and plots against her multiplied. One of the last acts of the drama was Protestant England's defeat of the pro-Catholic forces of the Spanish Armada in 1588.

Scotland

Scotland was not a major power in this era, but the country played a significant role in the Reformation. The first Scottish Protestant martyr was Patrick Hamilton (1528), who was burned at the stake in St. Andrews. The movement toward reform grew and pro-Catholic government opposition intensified. A Protestant uprising was defeated with the help of a French fleet. In the process, Protestant Scotsman John Knox (c. 1505–1572) was imprisoned and spent almost two years as a slave on a French galley. Upon his release he went to England and then Geneva, where he was deeply influenced by Calvin. In the meantime, the Reformation continued to grow in Scotland and some Protestant nobles entered a covenant to establish "the Word of God and his Congregation" (1556). After a civil war the Scottish Parliament adopted a confession of faith drafted by John Knox. Church organization under the leadership of the reformer was largely Calvinistic. In 1567, with the abdication of Mary, the Reformers triumphed. The throne of Scotland went to Mary's son, James VI, who followed the pro-Protestant Elizabeth as James I of England. Under his rule, 54 scholars produced the Authorized

Version of the Bible, otherwise known as the King James Version.

The New World

Beginning in 1564, there were some Reformers called Puritans who wanted to cleanse the church of *all* vestiges of popery. They thought that the reforms of the Anglican Church had not gone far enough. Elizabeth persecuted these nonconformists or dissidents and many left for Holland (1608) but then returned to England to obtain the backing of the Virginia Company. They then set out for America to find "a better and easier place of living" with the "great hope, for the propagation and advancing of the gospel of the kingdom of Christ in those remote parts of the world." Most settled in New England.

Though the Puritans had a significant part in settling New England, much of the population was not Puritan. Between 1761 and 1800, one-third of all first births occurred after less than nine months of marriage between the parents, and only one out of five New Englanders had a religious affiliation.[79] Free schooling was offered for all children. The first American college was established (Harvard), and Boston became the second largest publishing center in the British Empire. Today the word *Puritan* often has negative connotations, in part because of the Salem witch trials. But in those days, no one questioned belief in witches. Although the witch trials are regrettable, they have to be kept in perspective. If 40 were executed in Salem, then more than 100,000 were burnt alive in the persecutions that took place in Europe.[80]

THE COUNTER-REFORMATION

The most significant leader of what has been called the counter-Reformation was Ignatius of Loyola (1491–1556), the youngest of 13 children born to a noble Basque family. He served as a page at the court of Ferdinand and became a soldier. At the siege of Pamplona (1521), he and his fellow Spaniards were outnumbered by the invading French, and a cannonball shattered his leg. During his recovery his readings on Jesus and the saints inspired him to enter a convent at Manresa and practice extreme, self-imposed austerity. His spiritual struggle is inevitably compared with Luther's. Ignatius threw himself upon the mercy of God to find peace. A combination of mystic experience and introspection produced the *Spiritual Exercises,* a collection of meditations that give spiritual direction. He entered the University of Alcala, but ended up studying in Paris. Twice he was imprisoned during the Spanish Inquisition and accused of teaching without proper authorization. He and a few disciples hoped to preach in Jerusalem. The mission failed because war broke out between Venice and Turkey and the road was closed. The group decided to present themselves to Pope Paul III, who, in 1540, allowed them to form a new order. The order had a military structure, with Loyola elected as the first general. The members of the order were called Jesuits, and in addition to the normal vows of poverty, chastity, and obedience, they pledged unconditional obedience to the pope. According to the *Spiritual Exercises,* we should be ready "to believe that what seems to us white is black, if the hierarchical church so defines it."

In the *Spiritual Exercises,* Ignatius developed techniques for working with mental imagery. The course extended over a four-week period of time. Meditation was to help the person attain self-control. To stimulate contrition for sin, Ignatius recommended five meditations on hell that affected the five senses. Imagination could *see* the flames of hell, *hear* the shrieks of the damned, *smell* the stench of burning sulfur, *taste* the tears cried in vain, and *touch* the scorching flames. Ignatius insisted that it was essential for a person to imagine the physical aspects of hell. It was crude; it was effective.

The Jesuit order played the leading role in counteracting Protestantism in Europe, and their missionary activity, especially in the New World (Brazil and Paraguay), expanded the frontiers of the church. The Jesuits were not the only such order. The Oratorians, founded by Philip Neri (1515–1595), worked in France and gave birth to what were called *oratorios.* The Barnabites hoped to deepen their spiritual life, and the brothers of the Hospitallers of St. John opened hospitals in France and Italy.

Other Spaniards fought heresy by cultivating mystical spirituality. Teresa of Avila (1515–1582), descended from a family of *conversos,* or Spanish Jews forcibly converted to Christianity. She reformed the Carmelite order of nuns and established 16 convents dedicated to countering heresy through contemplative prayer. She heard interior voices, saw visions, and experienced revelations. Her classic text, *The Interior Castle,* provides an imaginative account of the soul's journey toward union with God. Her Carmelite colleague, John of the Cross (1541–1591), developed the vivid imagery of the "dark night of the soul" to portray the struggle to reach internal union with God. Thanks to conflicts within the Carmelite order, John wrote many of his mystical texts while confined in prison.

The mystic spirituality of Ignatius of Loyola, Teresa of Avila, and John of the Cross had a profound impact on revitalizing Catholic spirituality. Francis de Sales

(1567–1622), scion of a noble family, was the quintessential French confessor who introduced quietist mysticism into the salons of Paris. His contemporary was Vincent de Paul (1576–1660), who was captured by pirates, sold as a slave, and ended up as a slave to a Christian renegade. Vincent convinced his master to return to his faith, and together they returned to France. Ever after Vincent desired to ransom captives and became the shepherd of galley slaves. He headed up the visitation order whose sisters nursed the sick.

The Council of Trent (1545–1563) met off and on over the course of 18 years. Charles V had hoped for conciliation toward Protestants, but this was not to be. Decisions were made in small committee meetings and the official sessions were largely decorative. Among the many decisions of the council, the following are of special interest.

1. The apocryphal books were included in the canon of scripture. They were never part of the canon prior to this time; both Jews and the Reformers had excluded them from the Bible.

2. Trent also affirmed that the Vulgate version of the Bible contained the authoritative text of Holy Scripture, setting aside the scholarship of the Renaissance.

3. Tradition was placed on a par with the Scriptures. The Bible must be interpreted in line with tradition and the unanimous consensus of fathers of the church—not that an authoritative list of "fathers" was offered or that the "church" was defined. For that matter, the "fathers" were seldom unanimous on any particular topic.

4. The belief in purgatory was reaffirmed.

5. Justification was declared to be by faith *and works*.

6. A list, or Index, of prohibited books was issued (1564) and censured almost 75 percent of all existing titles. The Index was abolished in 1966. At Trent, traditionalism triumphed over the spirit of reform.

An area of significant Catholic success during this era was the field of foreign missions. Francis Xavier (1506–1552) met Loyola in Paris and became an ardent disciple of him. He then went off to Goa, India, East Indonesia, then Japan. He died on a small island off the coast of China. Matteo Ricci (1552–1610), born of a noble Italian family, went to China, where he became a court mathematician. Jesuits in China were men of science who made significant contributions in the fields of mathematics, astronomy, and cartography. The greatest missionary success was in the Philippines, reached via Mexico. Hundreds of thousands were baptized. Meanwhile, Antonio de Andrade, a Jesuit priest, crossed the Himalayas and was one of the first Europeans to enter Tibet (1624).

Meanwhile, in Europe, the last and bloodiest segment of the Thirty Years' War (1618–1648) played out between 1635–1648. To call it a series of religious wars is an oversimplification. In the closing years of the war, religion faded into the background. When Protestant Sweden entered the war, it was supported by the Pope to act as a counterweight to the power of the Hapsburg monarchy. In the end, very little changed in Germany, and neither Catholics nor Protestants made significant gains. In

1648 things reverted back to the situation of 1529. The war began as a religious struggle with political overtones and ended as a political struggle with religious overtones.[81]

THE GROWTH OF PROTESTANTISM
In Europe

In the following century, the Protestant church in Germany discussed minutia of orthodoxy and became ossified in creedal controversies. In Holland, the Arminian controversy (1604–1619) regarding predestination ended in a victory for the strict Calvinists at the Synod of Dordt. The revocation of the edict of toleration by Louis XIV in 1685 re-ignited extreme Huguenot persecution. These hard-working, industrious, sober citizens scattered to England, Germany (Berlin), Switzerland, Holland, and the New World. Entire industries were lost to France as more than 200,000 artisans left the country. Toleration was not restored till the French Revolution (1789).

A book by Bishop Jansenius (published posthumously) regarding the teachings of Augustine concerning sin and grace was immediately denounced by the Jesuits, but heartily embraced by the Cistercians of Port-Royal (Paris) and Blaise Pascal (1623–1662). Pascal was an eminent philosopher, mathematician, and scientist. Upon his death, a note was found in the lining of his coat recording his experience of God in 1654: "God of Abraham, God of Isaac, God of Jacob, not of the philosophers and scholars. Certainty, certainty, heartfelt, joy, peace. God of Jesus Christ...." Two years after writing this note he published his *Lettres Provinciales,* which denounced the Jesuits. His incomplete *Pensees* is still worth reading.

Archbishop Fenelon (1651–1715) was greatly influenced by Madame Guyon (1648–1717), a quietistic mystic who ended up in the Bastille prison. The pope condemned the writings of Fenelon, who accepted the judgment and burned his books.

In England

In England, James I (1603–1625) upheld the theory of the divine right of kings (the view that a monarch's powers are endowed by God's will—so anyone who opposes the king is, in effect, opposing God), as well as the right of kings to make laws without consultation with the Parliament. James tried to limit the old liberties of Parliament and was staunchly opposed by the Puritans, who advocated political freedom. Charles I (1625–1649) followed his father's footsteps. It was well known that Archbishop William Laud, who served under Charles, favored the high-church wing in the Anglican Church. The Puritans feared his Catholic tendencies and felt threatened. They were fined for failing to attend Anglican services. Charles tried to force religious reforms upon Scotland, and the general assembly of the Church of Scotland rejected the English Book of Common Prayer. Charles initiated military action against the Scottish Covenanters to force the issue. The so-called First Bishops' War (1639) was not popular in England. To raise money for the second one, Charles was compelled to call a meeting of Parliament. They could raise the needed funds, but not without obtaining concessions.

King Charles's marriage to a Catholic wife did nothing to enhance his popularity. The Parliament, concerned about what they perceived as "popery" in Laud, had him arrested and executed in 1645 for high treason. Parliament also forced Catholic bishops out of the Upper House;

the Lower House was predominantly Presbyterian. Independents created a new party advocating freedom of religion, abolition of the state church, and the autonomy of local congregations. Their energetic leader was Oliver Cromwell (1599–1658), a deeply religious man who was passionately fond of music and a military genius.[82] He has been accused of worshipping expediency,[83] but not many biographers would agree. No one questions his military ability. In one battle, more than 2,000 royalists were killed while Cromwell lost less than 100 men.

The English Civil War was actually a series of three armed conflicts between Parliamentarians and Royalists between 1642 and 1651. Cromwell defeated the royal armies and Charles fled to Scotland but was later handed over to the English Parliament. Accused of high treason, Charles was executed and Cromwell became Lord Protector of the realm. The restoration of the Stuarts followed. It was among the independents that the General Baptists emerged—*General* because they rejected a narrow interpretation of predestination (versus the Particular Baptists).

After Cromwell's death, the monarchy was restored and Charles II ascended to the throne (1660–1685). He dismissed 2,000 Puritan preachers from their ministries, including Richard Baxter. Over 8,000 dissenters ended up in jail (John Bunyan for 12 years), and 60,000 others were punished in some fashion.

In Early America

A significant movement called the Society of Friends developed during this time under the leadership of George Fox (1624–1691). They were derisively called Quakers because of the way they trembled in the course of ecstasy (first mentioned in 1654). Few were carried away to the extent James Naylor was, who entered Bristol claiming to be the Messiah (1656). Persecution raged. Fox was imprisoned eight times but remained a fervent preacher. The Society of Friends dismissed creeds and the sacraments (baptism and the Lord's Supper) along with professional clergy and focused on the "inner light" available to all and on practical Christianity. A simple lifestyle, truthfulness, the rejection of the oath and military service distinguished them. William Penn (1644–1718) joined the movement. Son of an English admiral, brilliant and educated, he received a proprietary province in the New World to cancel a debt (1681). He called Pennsylvania a "holy experiment" allowing freedom of religion. It became a haven not only for Quakers, who were tortured in New York and hanged in Boston, but also for Mennonites and many German sectarians. Penn also "made a worthy and successful effort to be just to the Indians of his province."[84]

Roger Williams (1603–1683) a brilliant linguist who had even learned Indian languages, became a clergyman with Low Church sympathies. In 1630 he and his wife, Mary Barnard, sailed for Massachusetts. He became the pastor of the church at Salem. He spoke out on behalf of the Indians and was usually at odds with the Puritans. Warned by Governor Winthrop that he would be deported to England, he fled the Massachusetts jurisdiction, bought some land from the Indians, and founded Providence, where he was joined by a few people, including a few Jews from Latin America. He advocated the separation of church and state, founded the first Baptist church in America, and returned to England twice to obtain and confirm a charter for the new colony. Charles II granted it in 1663. Williams became the governor of Rhode Island, and his ideas regarding the separation of church and state and religious freedom were later incorporated into the U.S. Constitution.

Other key figures in early American Christianity include John Eliot (1604–1690), who translated the Bible into the Algonkian Indian language and taught the American Indians to read. David Brainerd (1718–1747) was a missionary extraordinaire to the Indians until he died of tuberculosis. Brainerd had ministered to Indians in New York and New Jersey, and his published journals have long inspired generations of young people. Jonathan Edwards (1703–1758), who knew Brainerd and preached Brainerd's funeral sermon, was perhaps the most important early American theologian. He sparked a revival in New England and wrote prolifically and is famous for the sermon "Sinners in the Hands of an Angry God."

Eusebio Kino, a Jesuit missionary among the Pima Indians of Arizona, was an astronomer, mathematician, mapmaker, linguist, and above all, a successful missionary.

Commenting on this time period, church historian Kenneth Scott Latourette wrote, "One of the most striking features of the two hundred and fifty years between 1500 and 1750 was the resumption of the world-wide spread of Christianity."[85]

THE RISE OF PIETISM

Back in Germany, Pietism, a movement among Lutherans, reacted against wooden orthodoxy and stressed orthopraxis. The difference was not theological but practical. Philipp Spener (1635–1705), who started the movement, encouraged Bible study, active Christianity, and preaching for edification rather than oratorical effect.

August Francke (1663–1727), a professor at the University of Halle, was a renowned founder of orphanages with a keen missionary interest. Through his contact with the Danish court, arrangements were made to send missionaries to Tranquebar (a Danish seaport in India), where Bartholomaeus Ziegenbald translated the Bible into Tamil. A great missionary impetus came from Count von Zinzendorf (1700–1760), who allowed followers of the Moravian Brethren on his estates. With the approval of the Danish king, missionaries went to St. Thomas (Danish at the time) in 1732 and to the Eskimos, where Hans Egede had already been at work since 1721.

In Russia, liturgical innovations introduced by Patriarch Nikon (1605–1681) of the Russian Orthodox Church met with bitter resistance. The conservatives called themselves Old Believers and fought change to the point of committing mass suicide. The anathema against them was lifted in 1971. Peter the Great (1672–1725) abolished the Moscow patriarchate (1721) and replaced it with the Holy Synod, a council of ten clergymen who were nominated by the emperor himself. Catherine II (1761–1796), who ruled longer than any other emperor since the start of the Russian Empire, issued a decree of religious toleration. Nicolas I (1796–1855) held to the motto One Tsar, One Faith, One Nation.

Cyril Suchanov established a church in Siberia (1776) in the same year when a Lutheran missionary baptized the first Eskimo in Labrador. Veniaminov (1797–1879), a priest born in Siberia, volunteered for service in the Aleutian Islands, where he was well received. He proclaimed the Christian message in Alaska, Japan, the island of Sitka, and in the far reaches of Russia's vast Eastern Empire. At age 70 he retired to a monastery, but was elected patriarch of Moscow. For another decade he guided the Russian church and greatly expanded its missionary vision.[86] He helped found the Orthodox Missionary Society (1870). Ivan Kasatkin, known as Nikolai (1836–1912), was on his way to Japan when he met Veniaminov. Nikolai learned Japanese and studied the culture. Within a few years, thousands turned to Christ. In 1911 after 50 years of missionary work, the Orthodox Church counted more than 250 communities. Nikolai was elevated to the office of archbishop of Japan in 1907.

Meanwhile, the gradual collapse of the Ottoman Empire ("the sick man of Europe") gave new life to the Orthodox churches of Bulgaria, Romania, Macedonia, and Serbia. Greece became independent, and the church was free to develop on its own.

FROM COLONIALISM TO INDEPENDENCE

Between the 1880s and World War I European powers, motivated by imperialistic dreams and greed, scrambled for a piece of Africa, each one hoping to gain a strategic advantage. At the Berlin Conference (1894–1895), these powers drew and finalized the boundaries of the countries in Africa. The participants were largely ignorant of actual conditions in Africa and of realities on the ground. This required new exploration, and missionaries quickly entered the scene. In 1787 Granville Sharp founded a settlement for freed slaves. He was able to secure a land grant that became what is now known as Sierra Leone. The settlement, however, fell the victim to attacks by neighboring tribes and by a French squadron. Thus, the burden of defense and settlement was transferred

to the British crown in 1808. The growth of the church in Africa continued to take place largely under the auspices of various missionary societies.

After World War II, when colonialism ended and most African countries achieved independence, Christian churches flourished and their leadership became primarily African. Churches have since continued to grow at a rapid pace.

Colonialism—be it in Africa or elsewhere—did not necessarily benefit missionaries. Sometimes it had an adverse effect. For example, the East India Company banned all missionary work till 1813. Adoniram Judson (1788–1850) and his bride were refused entrance to India and thus ended up in Rangoon, Burma. There were no known Christians in Burma, and for six years no one turned to Christ. At one point Judson was even imprisoned for 21 months as a British spy and condemned to die. Spared thanks to his wife's pleading, he completed his monumental translation of the Bible into Burmese. Shortly after his death, there were no less than 200,000 Christians in Burma.

Worldwide missionary activity continued to increase remarkably. Father Damian (1840–1889), a Belgian priest, went to Hawaii as a missionary and, at his own request, went to the leper colony of Molokai, where he improved the lot of the lepers till he himself was infected by the disease and died. William Wade Harris (c. 1865–1928), who was from Liberia, preached to and baptized 120,000 in a single year in the Ivory Coast. "Villages destroyed symbols of the old religion, built churches and elected their own leaders to conduct Christian worship. Harris inspired the greatest Christian mass movement in West Africa history."[87]

RATIONALISM AND SOCIALISM

The second half of the seventeenth century saw the triumph of rationalism. In England, Deism—which recognizes God as Creator and human reason as authoritative—became fashionable. Divine revelation was deemed unnecessary and miracles were dismissed or explained away, although the explanations were often more incredible than the miracles! "The integrity of the disciples was saved only at the expense of their intelligence."[88] Unitarianism, which denies the trinitarian view of God, was promoted by Joseph Priestley (1733–1804). In France, Voltaire (1694–1778) led the charge against the church. The culmination was the Reign of Terror (1793–1794). About 40,000 priests were exiled. In 1798, the Papal States (Italy) were invaded and Pius VI died a year later in exile in France. The Papal States were restored in 1800, invaded again in 1808, and restored again when Napoleon fell. Italian nationalists eliminated them in 1870 and the Lateran Treaty of 1929 formally established the State of Vatican City.

Other trends of thought surfaced during the seventeenth through nineteenth centuries, among them classicism and romanticism. Socialism in the persons of St. Simon (1760–1825) and Pierre-Joseph Proudhon (1809–1865) emerged. His dictum "Property is theft!" gained him fame. He called himself an anarchist and corresponded and disagreed with Karl Marx (1818–1883), who believed that economic factors dominated history and offered a materialistic interpretation of life. In the age of reason, mysticism and occultism flourished, especially the Freemasons and Swedenborgians. In Europe Christianity declined (1750–1815), but a conservative reaction followed.

REVIVALS AND WORLDWIDE EXPANSION

Revivalists

John Wesley's (1703–1791) ancestors were Puritans on both sides of the family. At age ten, Wesley attended the Charterhouse School in London. At age 16 he enrolled in Oxford, where he obtained his masters degree and founded the Holy Club. He met George Whitefield at Pembroke College, and the two remained friends in spite of their dogmatic differences. The Society for the Promotion of Christian Knowledge asked Wesley to minister in Georgia and to convert the Indians. On his voyage to the New World, Wesley was deeply impressed by a group of Moravian Christians who remained fearless in the midst of a severe tempest. Upon his return to Britain, he attended a Moravian meeting. Someone read the preface to Martin Luther's *Epistle to the Romans,* and Wesley said, "I felt my heart strangely warmed."

Wesley continued his ministry and imitated George Whitefield, who preached to huge outdoor audiences. A building was erected in Bristol to hold the large crowds that Wesley's preaching attracted. Wesley did not dispose of enough ordained clergy to meet all the demands; he allowed laypersons to preach in cases of necessity.

From the beginning, Wesley's actions revealed a strong social conscience. The Holy Club he had organized fed up to 150 people a day, and taught some how to spin and provided spinning wheels for them.[89] They also established the first free dispensary in London.

Wesley was a born organizer. Methodist societies were united into regional preaching circuits that expanded rapidly and involved 21 preachers. Wesley was "a passionate supporter of the established church,"[90] and he hoped to revive the Anglican Church. Unavoidably, the movement became a church within the Church. When the Anglican Church failed to supply preachers to meet the need of the many circles Wesley had organized, he decided to use women as leaders of classes. He created a rather thin distinction between exhortation and preaching and involved women in the former.

By the time Wesley died, he had traveled some 250,000 miles and preached countless sermons. (Francis Asbury [1745–1816] equaled the feat when he traveled 300,000 miles on horseback in the United States, where he arrived in 1771.) Wesley opposed slavery and proclaimed the virtues of industry and of a sober lifestyle. "Wesley did more than anyone to reintroduce the religion of the heart into 18th-century England."[91]

George Whitefield (1714–1770) was an Anglican priest but excluded from the pulpit because of his enthusiasm—a cardinal sin in the Anglican Church. He spoke in open-air meetings to immense crowds. The fact that he was cross-eyed did not impede his enormous oratorical skills. He was passionate and energetic and reached thousands with the message of Christ. He crossed the Atlantic 13 times and sparked the Great Awakening in the United States.

"The religious revivals that took place in the eighteenth century had a dramatic influence on the social and political structures of the following decades."[92] Roland Bainton made a similar observation, stating that "on the social life of England their influence was unparalleled."[93] William Carey created the Baptist Missionary Society and sailed to India, becoming the first Protestant missionary in that country.

He translated parts of the Bible into 24 languages. The Anglican London Missionary Society was organized in 1795 and the British Foreign Bible Society followed in 1804. Lord Mansfield's famous judgment (1772) was the first victory for slaves. Small pressure groups composed mainly of evangelical Christians proceeded to organize a relentless campaign against the British slave trade.[94] They were spearheaded by William Wilberforce (1759–1833), a strong evangelical voice in Parliament. The law abolishing slavery was passed in 1807.

During the nineteenth century, organizations focused on social concerns proliferated. George Müller (1805–1898), a German pietist, sheltered orphans. Thomas John Barnardo (1845–1905), while preparing to be a missionary in China, reached out to the underprivileged in London and in his lifetime rescued 60,000 children. William Booth (1829–1912) came from a poor family, worked in a pawnshop, became a Methodist lay preacher, and found his mission field in the slums of East London. When he changed the name of the mission to Salvation Army—using the army as a model for the mission—it became enormously successful. Before Booth died, the Salvation Army was active in 58 countries. George Williams (1821–1905) organized the Young Men's Christian Association (YMCA). He had been influenced by Charles Finney (1792–1875), a Congregationalist minister whose book *Lectures on the Revival of Religion* had a profound influence. Finney became the president of Oberlin College in Ohio, where for the first time women and blacks sat in the same classroom as whites. And Charles Spurgeon (1834–1892), London's most popular preacher during his pastorate at the Metropolitan Tabernacle (which sat 6,000 people), sponsored orphanages and outreaches to poor ministers and needy people.

For the popes, however, the eighteenth century was difficult. Elections took place under pressure from France, Spain, and Austria, and the office of pope was filled mostly with mediocre personalities. But things were much better for the Catholic Church's missionary endeavors. Back in 1622, the Congregation for the Propagation of the Faith had been created to coordinate missionary activity. Temporarily disbanded in 1808 (thanks to opposition from Napoleon), the society was reestablished in 1814. One of their cardinal tenets was to accept local customs as much as possible and to ordain indigenous people. Robert de Nobili (1577–1656), who came from a distinguished Italian family, spearheaded Catholic missionary efforts in India. He not only learned Sanskrit and Indian languages, but adopted the Brahmin manner of life. When the pope was challenged about this, the pope justified Nobili's approach. The caste system in India created problems and the Jesuits saw no alternative but to build different church entrances for each caste and to separate the castes in the church by low walls.

Missionaries

Among the notable Protestant missionaries is Robert Morrison (1782–1834), the first Protestant missionary in China. He was sent out by the London Mission Society. His preparation included the study of medicine and astronomy. Morrison learned Chinese, which by Imperial edict was illegal for non-Chinese individuals. Nevertheless Morrison translated the Bible into Chinese and created a Chinese-English dictionary that was published in 21 volumes. James Hudson Taylor arrived in China in 1853

and understood the importance of cultural adaptation. He was the founder of the China Inland Mission, which became the largest mission agency in the world.

Christians in China, including missionaries, suffered severe persecution during the Boxer Uprising (1899–1901). And when the Communists took over China, thousands of missionaries—two-thirds of them Protestant and one-third of them Catholic—were expulsed. The Communist regime launched an anti-religion campaign, and Christians were forced into the Three-Self Patriotic Movement, which began in 1951. Those who refused had no option but to go underground. After the death of Mao Zedong in 1976, 6,375 churches were opened, but antireligious laws have not yet been repealed, and everything depends on enforcement. After decades of economic development, life has become a bit easier for most Christians in China. Their number has been estimated at anywhere from 30 to 80 million.

By contrast, Christianity has made relatively little progress in Japan. Townsend Harris was the first U.S. Consul General to Japan after the door had been forced open by Commodore Perry. Townsend held Christian services in his home. The Meiji Restoration brought about social reforms that, among other things, granted religious freedom (1873). Since then, Christianity has grown gradually, with the most significant growth taking place after World War II. But in South Korea, since the 1960s, the church has experienced dynamic growth and roughly one-third to one-half the population claims to be Christian.

In the United States, the Catholic missionary efforts on the West Coast moved forward under Junipero Serra (1713–1784), a Franciscan friar who established

21 missions along the coast of California. It was King Charles who granted Lord Baltimore a slice of northern Virginia. And Maryland became a proprietary colony, a refuge for Roman Catholics in the same way New England had become a haven for the Puritans.

Those who assume that there were more churched people in the past than there are today are incorrect. It has been estimated that in 1800, church membership in the United States was only 6.9 percent of the total population. On the eve of the Revolution, perhaps 17 percent of Americans were churched. By 1906, more than half had a religious affiliation, and by 1980, about 62 percent. This extraordinary growth came about for many reasons and people were reached in many different ways. The "camp meetings" of the nineteenth century were an innovation and combined a family vacation with spiritual renewal. Farm families were often isolated and suffered from loneliness. The camp meeting was an excellent opportunity for people to socialize and to hear the Word of God. The frontier, "short on churches and long on crime,"[95] attracted adventurers and people without social ties. The law was largely absent. But the frontier also offered economic opportunity, anonymity, and greater freedom. Few ministers came to the frontier because highly educated seminary graduates were ill-equipped to serve the needs of the frontier people. Methodist circuit riders who—like the Baptists—spoke the language of the people were the most effective.

The New World attracted Roman Catholic immigrants, especially the Irish, Germans, Italians, and Poles. The trickle became a flood in the 1820s. John Carroll was confirmed as the first American Catholic bishop in 1789. Between 1820 and 1865, about two million Catholic immigrants came to the United States—mostly from Ireland, Italy, and Mexico. In the 20 years between 1870 and 1890, Catholics doubled their number largely through immigration—and so did the Methodists through outreach. Both added foreign language services (German, Italian, and Polish) in their churches. In 1915, the traditional Catholic territorial parish design was altered to allow the formation of "national parishes" that cut across parish lines. This allowed members of a specific nationality or linguistic group to meet together. [96]

The first black denomination in America was the African Methodist Episcopal Church (1787), founded by Richard Allen (1760–1831) in Philadelphia to allow for greater self-expression. It was one of the very few denominations that came into being not for theological reasons, but sociological.

Strangely enough, the so-called "social gospel," prominent at the end of the nineteenth century and the beginning of the twentieth, ignored blacks and failed to speak up for women's rights. It was a utopian dream that spoke of correcting social evils and bringing in the kingdom, but it fell on hard times after World War I.

Entering the Twentieth Century

A significant movement began in 1906 with the Azusa Street Revival. This marked the beginning of Pentecostalism, which emerged out of the Methodist Holiness movement. William Seymour (1870–1922), an African American, preached that speaking in tongues was evidence of the baptism of the Holy Spirit. The meetings attracted people from around the world. The revival was multiracial and encouraged the leadership of women. Azusa Street in

Los Angeles was not the only place where glossolalia, or speaking in tongues, occurred, but the three-year revival became seminal for the worldwide Pentecostal movement.

In the tradition of Whitefield and Finney, D.L. Moody (1837–1899) reached out to the unchurched. A successful shoe salesman, he had minimal education yet dedicated himself to evangelism when he was in his early twenties. He and Ira Sankey, a singer and musician, preached to multitudes both in the United States and Britain. Moody "worked happily with men of quite different religious convictions" and "had a wide and profound influence through the length and breadth of Protestantism in the English-speaking world, especially that of the Evangelical tradition, and through it upon much of mankind."[97] His meetings were largely interdenominational.

MODERN-DAY CHRISTIANITY

THE CATEGORIES OF PROTESTANTISM

Protestant churches today can be broken down into three basic categories: fundamentalist, liberal, or evangelical.

The most conservative churches are *Fundamentalist.* Between 1910 and 1915, some conservative Christian leaders published a series of tracts entitled *The Fundamentals,* and by 1920 sponsored a congress of Fundamentalists. They demand a high level of commitment from their members and are characterized by separation from the world. Dogmatic certainty "has its greatest appeal in times and places where values and ways of life are changing."[98] Fundamentalists have a high view of biblical inspiration (inerrancy), usually embrace a dispensational understanding of the Scriptures, and expect a pretribulation rapture and the return of Christ before the millennium. Fundamentalists have also tried to influence the direction of politics in the United States.

The label of *liberal* has theological implications and often refers to the so-called mainline denominations. "Liberal Protestantism tends to evanesce into secularism" and the net result is that these denominations "are now shrinking—quickly." Again and again, researchers have made the point that "while the number of American Christians has grown, membership in the mainline denominations has sharply dropped."[99] To quote Roger Finke and Rodney Stark, "We will repeatedly suggest that as denominations have modernized their doctrines and embraced temporal values, they have gone into decline."[100] It is also true that even liberals have become more conservative and that the unbounded optimism that liberal theologians have expressed about human reason has been shattered by the atrocities of World War II and subsequent human disasters from genocide in Rwanda to racial cleansing in Serbia. Karl Barth is perhaps more acceptable than Harry Emerson Fosdick.

Evangelicals may not have theological differences with Fundamentalists (although there may be some disagreement regarding dispensationalism and the prophetic outlook), but they pursue a different lifestyle and the emphasis does not fall on separation. Evangelicals too find themselves at odds with the secular world but draw the boundaries differently. They are perhaps the fastest-growing group in the United States. Their membership growth by far exceeds the losses of the mainline denominations and the population increase of the

United States. "The churching of America was accomplished by aggressive churches committed to vivid otherworldliness."[101]

THE ORTHODOX CHURCHES

The Greek Orthodox Church in the United States was the largest of the new autonomous churches that include, among others, the Rumanian Orthodox, the Serbian Orthodox, and the Ukrainian Orthodox. The first Greek people came under the English "indentured servant" law and landed in the St. Augustine area of Florida in 1768. Further immigration from Greece led to the creation of multiple churches, and by 1920, the Greek Orthodox Church was firmly established. In 1940, most of the Orthodox churches formed a federation. The most distinguishing aspect of the Orthodox churches is the liturgy, a form of prayer and responses that has not changed for centuries. It is a unique form of worship.[102] "Historically Protestants have emphasized the salvation of the individual, Catholics the salvation of the world, and Orthodox the salvation of the cosmos, including the natural world."[103]

The Coptic Church, the Ethiopian Church, the Jacobite Syrians, and the Christians of St. Thomas in India accept only the first three Catholic ecumenical councils and, in the past, have been largely isolated for either political or theological reasons. Some have become Uniate churches, acknowledging the pope while maintaining their own rituals. Nestorians in Iran, hoping for protection, have joined the Russian Orthodox Church.

THE PERSECUTED CHURCH

If Christianity has registered tremendous gains worldwide, it has been at a heavy cost, all too often overlooked. For example, toward the end of the eighteenth century, 25,000 Korean Christians suffered persecution and martyrdom. Catholicism continued underground. Protestant missionaries arrived in 1876 and rapidly gained converts. Today, with the sole exception of the Philippines, Korea is the most Christian country of the Asian continent and even sends missionaries to other nations. In Vietnam there have been sporadic persecutions, especially under King Toi Nouc (1848–1883). It is impossible to know how many Christians perished in China in the days of the Boxer Uprising. Half a century later, China came under the control of Communism and created new martyrs.

Few people are aware of the massacre of Maronite Christians in Lebanon by the Druze in 1860, which let up only after French intervention. In Spain, anticlericalism was given free reign during the Spanish Civil War (1936–1939). Almost 8,000 "religious" people were killed, including 12 bishops. More than 5,000 priests were killed before the end of the Spanish Civil War. In Germany, the Confessing Church (a Christian resistance movement) was persecuted ruthlessly. Both Martin Niemoller and Dietrich Bonhoeffer ended up in World War II concentration camps. No one knows how many priests and ministers were executed or how many Christians sacrificed their lives.

In Russia, the church was intimately linked to the regime and suffered serious consequences when the Communist revolution broke out in 1917. In 1914, there were in excess of 100,000 priests in Russia, 550 monasteries, and 475 nunneries. The Communist era offers grim statistics. Only during the Great Patriotic War against Germany did persecution abate. Joseph Stalin

(1878–1953) knew that he needed the support of the church to mobilize and inspire the masses. It was a significant although tacit admission not only of the importance of the church, but also that Communism, in spite of relentless anti-Christian propaganda, had not been able to eradicate Christianity. In 1988 the Russian ban on religious television was lifted. Most Russians identify themselves with the Orthodox Church, but it is difficult to know if it is a cultural or religious identification.

In Yugoslavia, Josip Broz Tito, a more moderate Communist, closed over 4,000 places of worship and had scores of priests executed and many more people imprisoned. And news reports from places such as Egypt and Indonesia continue to report the deaths of Christians. In spite of these enormous obstacles and others like them, the church continues to grow worldwide.

THE CATHOLIC CHURCH

The Catholic Church has seen a remarkable renewal thanks to the Second Vatican Council convened by Pope John XXIII. Concrete steps have been taken to heal ancient wounds between Catholics and Orthodox and even Protestants. In *Lumen Gentium,* a document from Vatican II, the world was informed that the church of Christ "subsisted in" rather than "was" the Roman Catholic Church. The statement is not to be taken lightly, because it signals an important shift in viewpoint. Olive branches have been offered to Jews and Muslims. Of course, all this has occurred so recently that it is too early to know what the final results might be.

In Latin America, many Catholics have embraced liberation theology, in which emphasis falls on social action in this world instead of waiting patiently for the next.

Liberation theology is an effort to redress economic injustice here and now. In 1960 this theology of liberation evolved to a new level and advocated revolution. Christ the Savior became Christ the Warrior. The utopia of changing the world, of creating a just society, was taken seriously. Anthropology replaced ecclesiology. All the while, Catholic ecclesiastical authorities were told that the basis of their beliefs remained intact and that liberation theology was only a new emphasis.

THE "INDIGENIZATION" OF CHRISTIANITY

OVER THE LAST CENTURY, Christianity has become truly worldwide. It is no longer seen as Middle Eastern or European and does not necessarily appear in American style. One can truly speak of the "indigenization" of Christianity in countless regional cultures around the world. People in North America tend to forget that Christianity was "founded in the Near East [and] Christianity for its first thousand years was stronger in Asia and North Africa than in Europe."[104] The message continues to spread and have an enormous impact. Various translations of the Bible—from Jerome's Latin Vulgate to Luther's translation to the King James Version and others since—have shaken the world. The Bible or portions thereof are now available in more than 1,800 languages.

Over the last century the center of gravity of the Christian world has shifted away from Europe and North America at least in terms of sheer numbers, although not in terms of economics. Africa and Latin America have registered enormous gains over recent decades. In Africa alone the Christian population grows by eight million a year.

Christianity should no longer be equated with Western civilization. Christianity existed long before Western civilization and will "continue to be a living spiritual force in the world for thousands of years after our Western civilization has passed away."[105] The message is unchanged, regardless of cultural trappings. It is still the old Apostle's Creed centered in the person of Christ—his life, his death, his resurrection, and his return. The response of faith to the offer of salvation in Christ remains an essential component of Christianity. The survival of the church of Christ and the worldwide expansion of that church can only be understood in the light of him who said to the Twelve, "I will build my church, and the gates of Hades will not overcome it" (Matthew 16:18).

NOTES

INTRODUCTION

1. Samuel P. Huntington, *The Clash of Civilizations and the Remaking of the World Order* (New York: Simon & Schuster, 1996), p. 47.

ISLAM

1. Samuel P. Huntington, *The Clash of Civilizations and the Remaking of the World Order* (New York: Simon and Schuster, 1996), pp. 47, 66.

2. Christine Ollivier, "Chirac Threatens Nuclear Response to Attack by State-backed Terrorists," *Naples Daily News,* January 20, 2006, p. 17A.

3. Philip Jenkins, *The Next Christendom: The Coming of Global Christianity* (Oxford, UK: Oxford University Press, 2002), p. 161.

4. Jenkins, *The Next Christendom,* pp. 168-72.

5. Daniel Pipes, (Converts to Violence?" *New York Post,* October 25, 2002.

6. Jenkins, *The Next Christendom,* p. 163.

7. Arnold Toynbee, *Christianity Among the Religions of the World* (New York: Charles Scribners' Sons, 1957), p. 87.

8. Lumen Gentium, article 16.

9. Koran 29:61.

10. Koran 29:65.

11. Koran 93:8.

12. Koran 7:157.

13. Koran 93.

14. Koran 97:1.

15. Koran 96.

16. Koran 10:16.

17. Koran 111:1-5.

18. Ameer Ali Syed, *The Spirit of Islam* (London: W.H. Allen, 1891), p. 35.

19. Koran 17:75; 22:52.

20. Koran 2:142-44.

21. Koran 2:217.

22. Koran 8:60.

23. Koran 59:5-6.

24. Koran 33:26-27.

25. Koran 48:24.

26. Koran 80:1.

27. Ali Abdullah Yusuf, *The Meaning of the Holy Quran* (Beltsville, MD: Amana Publications, 2003), commentary on 80:1.

28. Koran 33:49.

29. Koran 33:50ff.

30. Koran 33:36.

31. Koran 33:52.

32. Koran 66:1-2.

33. Koran 17:1.

34. Koran 26:105.

35. Koran 33:40.

36. Koran 61:5-6.

37. Koran 7:157.

38. Koran 8:30.

39. Koran 34:43.

40. William H. McNeill, *The Rise of the West: A History of the Human Community* (Chicago: The University of Chicago Press, 1963), p. 421.

41. J.N.D. Anderson, *The World's Religions* (Grand Rapids, MI: Eerdmans, 1953), p. 60.

42. Koran 38:29.

43. Koran 43:3; 56:76.

44. William E. Phipps, *Muhammed and Jesus: A Comparison of the Prophets and Their Teachings* (New York: The Continuum Publishing Company, 1996), pp. 223–26.

45. Koran 52:34.

46. A. J. Arberry, *The Koran* (New York: Macmillan, 1976), p. 17.

47. Will Durant, *The Age of Faith* (New York: Simon & Schuster, 1950), p. 175.

48. Hans-Joachim Schoeps, *The Religions of Mankind: Their Origin and Development* (Garden City, NY: Doubleday & Co., 1968), p. 253.

49. A.C. Bouquet, *Sacred Books of the World* (Harmondsworth, UK: Penguin Books, 1954), p. 282.

50. Koran 3:6.

51. Koran 16:105.

52. Koran 40:25, 39.

53. Koran 2:249.

54. Koran 38:34.

55. Koran 38:43.

56. Koran 5:60; 7:166.

57. Koran 3:3.

58. Koran 2:40.

59. Koran 5:14.

60. Koran 5:45-50.

61. Koran 31:14-19.

62. Koran 26:165.

63. Koran 17:27.

64. Koran 70:29.

65. Koran 16:67.

66. Koran 2:219.

67. Koran 5:90.

68. Koran 83:25.

69. Koran 13:39.

70. Koran 2:106.

71. Koran 16:103.

72. Koran 44:54; 55:56; 78:33.

73. Koran 93:1; 103:1; 84:16; 74:35.

74. Koran 3:45-46.

75. Koran 42:13.

76. Koran 4:155-157.

77. Irenaeus, The Ante-Nicene Fathers, *Against Heresies,* Book I, chap. 24.4 (Grand Rapids, MI: Eerdmans, 1951).

78. Ali Abdullah Yusuf, *The Meaning of the Holy Quran,* Commentary on *Sura* 4:157.

79. Koran 3:53.

80. Koran 43:61.

81. Koran 28:88 and 55:16-27.

82. Koran 5:115.

83. Koran 19:37,90.

84. Koran 3:60; 16:123.

85. Koran 62:9.

86. Koran 2:125-126.

87. Koran 33:21.

88. Koran 4:115.

89. Koran 9:24 (Arberry's translation), 9:41,73.

90. Koran 4:74-75.

91. Koran 9:29.

92. Koran 9:5.

93. Koran 47:4 and 4:93,89.

94. Koran 9:111.

95. Koran 2:190.

96. Koran 6:125; 16:37.

97. Koran 17:31.

98. Koran 33:59 and 24:31.

99. Koran 4:3.

100. Koran 5:5.

101. Associated Press release on September 22, 1996.

102. Koran 2:115.

103. Koran 50:16.

104. Koran 49:14.

105. Koran 49:9.

106. Koran 16:106.

107. Rene Grousset, *The Empire of the Steppes: A History of Central Asia* (New Brunswick, NJ: Rutgers University Press, 1997), p. 120.

108. Koran 3:159; 42:38.

109. Koran 13:11.

110. Bukhari 3:48:819-820.

111. Toynbee, *Christianity Among the Religions of the World,* p. 12.

112. Hans Kung, *Der Islam* (Munchen, Germany: Piper, 2004), pp. 538ff.

113. Pipes, *Militant Islam Reaches America,* p. 94.

114. Bill Powell, "Generation Jihad," *Time* (Oct. 3, 2005), p. 56.

115. Pipes, *Militant Islam Reaches America,* pp. 3-14.

116. Walter Russell Mead, "God's Country?" in *Foreign Affairs* (Sept./Oct. 2006), p. 42.

117. 1 Peter 3:15.

118. John 15:26; 16:8-9.

119. Genesis 17:20; cf. 21:13,18.

120. Genesis 21:12-13,18.

121. Matthew 21:42; Luke 20:17-18.

122. Deuteronomy 18:15-18.

123. John 14:16-17,26.

124. Koran 33:5.

125. Numbers 15:27-30.

126. Koran 16:61.

SHINTOISM AND BUDDHISM

1. *The Kojiki,* English translation by B.H. Chamberlain.

2. *Holy Nihongi,* English translation by W.G. Ashton.

3. *Nihongi,* Part 2.

4. Sokyo Ono, *Shinto* (Boston: Tuttle Publishing, 1962), p. 8.

5. C. Scott Littleton, 2002, *Shinto* (New York: Oxford University Press, 2002), p. 6.

6. *Kasuga Taisha* (Nara, Japan: Kasuga Shrine Society).

7. Ono, *Shinto,* p. 92.

8. Ninian Smart, *The World's Religions* (Cambridge, MA: Cambridge University Press, 1998), p. 147.

9. Ibid., p. 60.

10. *The Teachings of the Buddha* (Tokyo, Japan: Bukkyo Dendo Kyokai—Society for the Promotion of Buddhism, 1999), p. 30.

11. Ibid., p. 104.

12. *The Cause and Effect Sutra* (Singapore: Internal Printers), pp. 67, 73, 99, 101, 159.

13. *The Teachings of the Buddha,* p. 272.

14. Ibid., p. 144.

15. William H. McNeill, *The Rise of the West* (Chicago: University of Chicago Press, 1963), p. 188.

16. Ibid., p. 186.

17. David K. Wyatt, *Thailand: A Short History* (New Haven, CT: Yale University Press, 1984), pp. 176, 213.

18. *The Teachings of the Buddha,* p. 386.

19. Ibid., p. 448.

20. *The Kofuku-ji Temple* (Nara, Japan: Hosso Headquarters).

21. Ibid., p. 42.

22. Samuel C. Morse, *Todai-ji* (Nara, Japan, 1996).

23. Hajime Nakamura, *Ways of Thinking of Eastern Peoples: India-China-Tibet-Japan* (Honolulu, HI: East-West Center Press, 1964), p. 308.

24. *The Teachings of the Buddha,* pp. 202-08.

25. Nakamura, *Ways of Thinking of Eastern Peoples,* p. 377.

26. Ibid., p. 214.

27. *The Sutra of the Master of Healing,* translated into Chinese from Sanskrit by Hsuan Tsang and into English from Chinese by Chow Su-Chia (Singapore: Internal Printers), pp. 6, 12.

28. Nakamura, *Ways of Thinking of Eastern Peoples,* p. 21.

29. *The Teachings of the Buddha,* p. 554.

30. *Daibutsu, the Great Buddha of Kamakura* (Kamakura, Japan: Mitsuo Sato), p. 12.

31. The Golden Pavilion (Kyoto, Japan: Rokuonji), p. 1.

32. *The Teachings of the Buddha,* p. 550.

33. David Scott and Tony Doubleday, *The Element of Zen* (New York: Barnes & Noble, 1992), p. 6.

34. Ibid., p. 7.

35. Daisetz Teitaro Suzuki, *An Introduction to Zen Buddhism* (New York: Grove Press, 1964), Introduction.

36. Mumon Yamada, *How to Practice Zazen* (Kyoto, Japan: Institute for Zen Studies), p. 4.

37. Ibid., p. 4.

38. Suzuki, *An Introduction to Zen Buddhism,* p. 10.

39. Nakamura, *Ways of Thinking of Eastern Peoples,* p. 194.

40. Yamada, *How to Practice Zazen,* p. 12ff.

41. Ibid., pp. 21, 48-55.

42. Ibid., p. 19.

43. Suzuki, *An Introduction to Zen Buddhism,* p. 7.

44. Ibid., pp. 8, 91-92.

45. Scott and Doubleday, *The Element of Zen,* p. 23.

46. Mary Elizabeth Berry, *Hideyoshi* (Cambridge, MA: Harvard University Press, 1982), p. 193.

47. *Hideyoshi and Osaka Castle: A Look into Its History and Mystery* (Osaka, Japan: Osaka Castle Museum, 1988).

48. *The Treasures of the Toyotomi Family* (Osaka, Japan: Osaka Castle Museum, 1997).

49. Berry, *Hideyoshi,* p. 1.

50. Bradley Smith, *Japan: A History in Art* (Garden City, NY: Doubleday & Co., 1964), p. 175.

51. R.H.P. Mason and J.C. Caiger, *A History of Japan* (Rutland, VT: Charles E. Tuttle Co., 1997), p. 173.

52. Hans Kung and Julia Ching, *Christianity and Chinese Religions* (New York: Doubleday, 1989).

53. Harvey Cook, *The Story of a Warrior Tradition* (New York: Sterling Publishing, 1993), p. 6.

54. James McClain, *Japan in Modern History* (New York: W.W. Norton, 2002), p. 44.

55. Ibid., p. 75.

56. Kurozumi Munetada, *The Living Way* (Walnut Creek, CA: Rowman & Littlefield, 2000), pp. xxv, 9.

57. Robert N. Bellah, *Tokugawa Religion* (Boston, MA: Beacon Press, 1957). Bellah, a disciple of Max Weber, wrote his thesis on the Singaku movement and the impact of the movement on the economic changes that took place in Japan.

58. Ibid., p. 150.

59. Kenneth Scott Latourette, *A History of Christianity* (New York: Harper & Row, 1953), p. 1329.

60. McClain, *Japan in Modern History,* p. 272.

61. Ono, *Shinto,* p. 75.

62. John 20:11ff. and Revelation 21:1.

63. Genesis 2:15 and Romans 8:21.

64. 1 Corinthians 9:19-23.

65. Bellah, *Tokugawa Religion,* p. 70.

66. Piers Vitebsky, *The Shaman* (Boston, MA: Little, Brown and Company, 1995), p. 133.

67. Suzuki, *An Introduction to Zen Buddhism,* p. 13.

68. Romans 12:1; Colossians 3:10; Philippians 1:9.

CONFUCIANISM AND DAOISM

1. D.C. Lau, *The Analects* (London: Penguin Books, 1979), p. 19. The translation of the Analects quoted from time to time is the one produced by D.C. Lau, published by the Penguin Group.

2. Shigaki Kaizuka, *Confucius: His Life and Thoughts* (Mineola, NY: Dover Publications, 2002), p. 48.

3. H.G. Creel, *Confucius and the Chinese Way* (New York: Harper & Row, 1949), p. 7.

4. Ibid., p. 312.

5. Analects 2:4.

6. Analects 7:22.

7. Analects 7:19.

8. Analects chapter 10.

9. Analects 19:4,7.

10. 2 Thessalonians 3:10.

11. Analects 14:38.

12. Analects 7:1.

13. Creel, *Confucius and the Chinese Way,* p. 312.

14. Analects 7:8.

15. Analects 16:9.

16. Analects 4:10,16.

17. Rodney L. Taylor, *The Way of Heaven* (Leiden, Holland: E.J. Brill), p. 53.

18. Kaizuka, *Confucius: His Life and Thoughts,* p. 99.

19. Lau, *The Analects,* p. 198.

20. Analects 12:2,15.

21. Liu Wu-Chi, *Confucius: His Life and Time* (New York: Philosophical Library, 1966), p. 174.

22. Tu Wei-ming, *Confucianism in Our Religions* (San Francisco, CA: Harper Collins Publishers, 1993), p. 193.

23. Wu-Chi, *Confucius: His Life and Time,* p. 174.

24. Ibid., p. XIV.

25. Analects 17:25.

26. Creel, *Confucius and the Chinese Way,* p. 125.

27. Analects 4:19; 2:5.

28. Analects 1:11; 17:21.

29. Analects 8:21.

30. Analects 11:12; 6:22.

31. Analects 5:13; 7:21.

32. Smith, *The World's Religions,* p. 154. Huston Smith has taught at Washington University, MIT, Syracuse University, and Berkeley. He is a leading authority on comparative philosophy of religion.

33. Samuel Huntington, *The Clash of Civilizations and the Remaking of the World Order* (New York: Simon & Schuster, 1996), p. 225.

34. Smith, *The World's Religions,* p. 154.

35. Hans Kung and Julia Ching, *Christianity and Chinese Religions* (New York: Doubleday, 1989), p. 118.

36. Analects 3:5.

37. Analects 4:6; 7:26; 9:18.

38. *Book of Mencius,* Book VI, Part I.

39. Shang Yang, *The Book of the Lord Shang* (Ware, UK: Wordsworth Editions, 1998), p. 147.

40. Max Weber, *On Charisma and Institution Building* (Chicago: University of Chicago Press, 1968), p. 66; also Max Weber, *The Religion of China* (New York: The Free Press, 1951), p. 149.

41. Analects 2:12.

42. Sun Tzu, *The Art of War* (Ware, UK: Wordsworth Editions, 1998), p. 22.

43. Hans-Joachim Schoeps, *The Religions of Mankind* (Garden City, NY: Doubleday & Co., 1968), p. 197.

44. Liu Xiaogan, *Taoism in Our Religions* (San Francisco, CA: Harper Collins Publishers, 1993), p. 231.

45. Lao-Tzu, *Tao Te Ching* Washington, DC: Counterpoint, 2000), chapter 2.

46. Lao-Tzu, *Tao Te Ching* (Washington, DC: Counterpoint, 2000), chapter 2.

47. Ibid., chapters 64, 8, and 29.

48. Ibid., chapter 20.

49. Ibid.

50. Schoeps, *The Religions of Mankind*, p. 200.

51. Lao-Tzu, *Tao Te Ching*, chapter 17.

52. Chuang Tzu, On Tolerance, at http://www.religiousworlds.com/taoism/cz.text2.html.

53. Tzu, *Tao Te Ching*, chapter 16.

54. Xiao Xiaoming, *Taoism* (Beijing: Foreign Language Press, 2002), p. 18.

55. Kung and Ching, *Christianity and Chinese Religions*, p. 140.

56. "Once-taboo Feng Shui Makes a Comeback in China," *Japan Times*, August 23, 2001.

57. Hajime Nakamura, *Ways of Thinking of Eastern Peoples: India-China-Tibet-Japan* (Honolulu, HI: East-West Center Press, 1964), pp. 175-76.

58. Massac Abe, *Buddhism in Our Religions* (San Francisco: Harper Collins Publishers, 1993), p. 72.

59. Harvey Cox, *Christianity in Our Religions* (San Francisco: Harper Collins Publishers, 1993), p. 368.

60. Abe, *Buddhism in Our Religions*, p. 106.

61. Kenneth Scott Latourette, in the *Encyclopaedia Britannica* (Chicago: William Benton, 1962), s.v. "China: History."

62. Rene Grousset, *The Empire of the Steppes, a History of Central Asia* (New Brunswick, NJ: Rutgers University Press, 1997), p. 120.

63. Jacques Gernet, *A History of Chinese Civilization* (Cambridge, UK: Cambridge University Press, 1996), p. 344.

64. A.C. Bouquet, *Sacred Books of the World* (Harmonsworth, UK: Penguin Books, 1954), p. 180.

65. Grousset, *The Empire of the Steppes*, p. 586.

66. Ibid., p. 191.

67. Dalai Lama (Tenzin Gyatso), *The World of Tibetan Buddhism* (Boston, MA: Wisdom Publications, 1995), p. 99.

68. Ibid., p. 99.

69. Ibid., p. 65.

70. Latourette, *A History of Christianity*, p. 941.

71. Kung and Ching, *Christianity and Chinese Religions*, p. 103.

72. Tien-wei Wu, *Lin Bao and the Gang of Four* (Carbondale, IL: Southern Illinois University Press, 1983), pp. 75-76.

73. Latourette, *A History of Christianity*, p. 1448.

74. Richard Madsen, "Demystifying Falun Gong," *Current History*, Sept. 2000, p. 246.

75. Jacques Gernet, *A History of Chinese Civilization* (Cambridge, UK: Cambridge University Press, 1999), p. 679.

76. James D. Seymour, Human Rights, Repression and "Stability," *Current History*, Sept. 1999, p. 284.

77. Tien-wei Wu, *Lin Bao and the Gang of Four*, pp. 14, 26.

78. Analects 1:1.

79. Cheu Hock-Tong, *Confucianism in Chinese Culture* (Selangor, Malaysia: Pelanduk Publications, 2000), p. 94.

80. Alasdair Clayre, *The Heart of the Dragon* (Boston, MA: Houghton Mifflin Company, 1984), p. 30.

81. Kung and Ching, *Christianity and Chinese Religions,* pp. 87,89.

82. Weber, *The Religion of China,* p. 229.

83. Aristotle, *The Nichomachean Ethics,* Book Four, chapter 3.

84. Weber, *The Religion of China,* p. 164.

85. Tien-wei Wu, *Lin Bao and the Gang of Four,* p. 71.

86. Weber, *The Religion of China,* p. 152.

87. Ibid., p. 87.

88. Minta C. Wang, *The Essentials of Chinese Thought* (Westbury, NY: About Face Press, 1983), p. 36.

89. Creel, *Confucius and the Chinese Way,* pp. 196-97.

90. John R.W. Stott, *The Epistles of John* (London: The Tyndale Press, 1964), p. 93.

91. Ibid., p. 94. It is the meaning of the Greek word translated "true."

HINDUISM, JAINISM, AND SIKHISM

1. William H. McNeill, *The Rise of the West* (Chicago: University of Chicago Press, 1963), p. 169.

2. Arthur Llewellyn Basham, *The Wonder That Was India* (New York: Hawthorn Books, 1963), p. 36.

3. *The Laws of Manu,* translated by G. Buhler, Chapter 1:87.

4. Ibid., Chapter 2:103.

5. bid., Chapter 2:52.

6. Arvind Sharma, *Our Religions* (San Francisco: Harper San Francisco, 1993), p. 25, s.v. "Hinduism."

7. Will Durant, *Our Oriental Heritage* (New York: Simon & Schuster, 1954), p. 488.

8. Bhagavad Gita, trans. Juan Mascaro (Harmondsworth, UK: Penguin Books, 1962), 4:13; 18:41-45.

9. Rig Veda, trans. Ralph T. Griffith (New York: History Book Club, 1992), Book 10, Hymn 129. The translation of Max Muller is quoted by Will Durant in *Our Oriental Heritage,* p. 409.

10. Ibid., Book 1, Hymn 50.

11. P. Masson-Oursel & Louise Morin, *New Larousse Encyclopedia of Mythology* (Feeltham, UK: The Hamlyn Publishing Group Ltd., 1972), p. 326. S.v. "Indian Mythology."

12. Dharam Vir Singh, *Hinduism: An Introduction* (Jaipur, India: Travel Wheels, 1991), p. 71.

13. Rig Veda, Book 4, Hymn 53.

14. Ibid., Book 5, Hymn 82.

15. Ibid., Book 7, Hymn 89.

16. Masson-Oursel & Morin, "Indian Mythology," p. 335.

17. McNeill, *The Rise of the West,* p. 170.

18. Rig Veda, Book 1, Hymn 164:46.

19. Rig Veda, Book 3, Hymn 54:8b.

20. Ninian Smart, *World Religions* (Cambridge, UK: Cambridge University Press, 1998), p. 59.

21. Bhagavad Gita 10:25.

22. James B. Robinson, *Hinduism* (Philadelphia: Chelsea House Publishing 2004), p. 108.

23. Ibid., p. 26.

24. A.C. Bouquet, *Sacred Books of the World* (Harmondsworth, UK: Penguin Books, 1954). The quote of the *Mundaka Upanishad* appears on p. 130.

25. Robert Brow, *Religion: Origins and Ideas* (Chicago: InterVarsity Press, 1966), p. 27.

26. Smart, *World Religions,* pp. 73-74.

27. Sharma, "Hinduism," p. 24.

28. Huston Smith, *The World's Religions* (San Francisco: Harper, 1958), pp. 63-64.

29. Narayan Vasudha, *Hinduism in Eastern Religions* (Oxford, UK: Oxford University Press, 2005), p. 65.

30. Singh, *Hinduism: An Introduction,* p. 1.

31. Sharma, "Hinduism," p. 5.

32. Ibid., p. 6.

33. Singh, *Hinduism: An Introduction,* p. 53.

34. Juan Mascaro, trans., Bhagavad Gita (Harmondsworth, UK: Penguin Books, 1962), p. 22.

35. Bhagavad Gita 1:28; 2:31; 3:35.

36. Ibid., 2:57; 3:43; 4:21; 5:24.

37. Ibid., 6:11-13.

38. Ibid., 6:47; 11:54; 9:31.

39. Ibid., 6:42.

40. Ibid., 2:11,16.

41. Narayan, *Hinduism in Eastern Religions,* p. 91.

42. Basham, *The Wonder That Was India,* p. 337.

43. Narayan, *Hinduism in Eastern Religions,* p. 28.

44. *Laws of Manu,* Book 2:103 and 101.

45. Rig Veda, Book 3, Hymn 72:10.

46. Nagin J. Shah, *Jaina: Philosophy and Religion* (Delhi, India: Motital Banarsidass Publishers, 1998), p. 1.

47. Ibid., pp. 6-7, 20, 31.

48. Ibid., p. 9.

49. Ibid., p. 31.

50. Smart, *World Religions,* p. 70.

51. Shah, *Jaina: Philosophy and Religion,* p. 32.

52. Ibid., p. 144.

53. Ibid., p. 8.

54. Ibid., p. 67.

55. Narayan, *Hinduism in Eastern Religions,* p. 65.

56. John Ross Carter and Palihawadana Mahinda, *Buddhism: The Dhammapada* (New York: The History Book Club, 1992), p. xvi.

57. Basham, *The Wonder That Was India,* p. 278.

58. Ibid., p. 274.

59. Romans 3:8.

60. John Keay, *India, a History* (New York: Grove Press, 2000), p. 83.

61. Ibid., p. 101.

62. Romila Thapar, *A History of India* (London: Penguin Books, 1990), p. 134.

63. Ibid., p. 134.

64. Hajime Nakamura, *Ways of Thinking of Eastern Peoples: India-China-Tibet-Japan* (Honolulu, HI: East-West Center Press, 1964), p. 99 (emphasis in original).

65. Keay, *India, a History,* p. 209.

66. Rene Grousset, *The Empires of the Steppes: A History of Central Asia* (New Brunswick, NJ: Rutgers University Press, 1997), p. 445.

67. David Chidester, *Christianity: A Global History* (San Francisco: HarperSanFrancisco, 2000), p. 343.

68. Smart, *World Religions,* p. 398.

69. Choor Singh, *Understanding Sikhism* (Singapore: Central Sikh Gurdwara Board), p. 1.

70. Sewa Singh Kalsi, *Sikhism* (Philadelphia: Chelsea House Publishers, 2005), p. 50.

71. Keay, *India, a History,* p. 422.

72. Percival Spear, *A History of India* (London: Penguin Books, 1990), p. 86.

73. Barbara D. Metcalfe and R. Thomas, *The Concise History of India* (Cambridge, UK: Cambridge University Press, 2002), p. 46.

74. Ibid., p. 85.

75. Stanley Wolpert, *Ghandi's Passion: The Life and Legacy of Mahatma Ghandi* (New York: Oxford University Press, 2001), p. 61.

76. Metcalfe, *The Concise History of India,* p. 172.

77. Sharma, "Hinduism," p. 17.

78. Gucharan Das, "The India Model," *Foreign Affairs,* July/August 2006, p. 2.

79. C. Raja Mohan, "India and the Balance of Power," *Foreign Affairs,* July/August 2006, p. 18.

80. Smart, *World Religions,* p. 410.

81. James R. Lewis, *Cults: A Reference Handbook* (Santa Barbara, CA: ABC-CLIO, 2005), pp. 167-69.

JUDAISM

1. Genesis 14:13.

2. Jeremiah 34:9.

3. Deuteronomy 7:7-8.

4. Isaiah 44:1-8.

5. Nicholas De Lange, *An Introduction to Judaism* (Cambridge, UK: Cambridge University Press, 2000), p. 1.

6. Kenneth Atkinson, *Judaism* (Philadelphia: Chelsea House Publishers, 2004), p. 3.

7. Huston Smith, *The World's Religions* (San Francisco: Harper, 1958), p. 312.

8. Genesis 46:19-20.

9. Genesis 46:10.

10. Numbers 26:13.

11. Numbers 12:1.

12. Josephus, trans. William Whiston, *The Antiquities of the Jews* (Grand Rapids, MI: Kregel Publications, 1963), Book XIII, Chapter 9.

13. Wayne Dosick, *Living Judaism* (New York: Harper Collins, 1995), p. 57.

14. Deuteronomy 23:2.

15. J.F. Schroeder, *Satzungen und Gebrauche des Talmudisch-Rabbinischen Judenthums* (Bremen, Germany: A.D. Geisler, 1851), p. 539. This is negative commandment number 354 of the law as codified by Maimonides.

16. David Klinghoffer, *Why the Jews Rejected Jesus* (New York: Doubleday, 2005), p. 139.

17. Michael L. Rodkinson, *The New Edition of the Babylonian Talmud* (Boston, MA: The Talmud Society, 1918), Mishna, Aboth I:1.

18. Ibid., Volume 1, pp. 14-15.

19. Joseph Dan, *Kabbalah: A Very Short Introduction* (New York: Oxford University Press, 2006), p. 53.

20. Dosick, *Living Judaism,* p. 106.

21. 2 Chronicles 20:20; Habakkuk 2:4.

22. Dosick, *Living Judaism,* p. 110.

23. Cecil Roth, *The Haggadah* (Boston, MA: Little, Brown and Company, 1965), p. 62.

24. Rodkinson, *The New Edition of the Babylonian Talmud,* Mishna, Sabbath 7:2.

25. Exodus 23:19.

26. Abba Hillel Silver, *Where Judaism Differed* (New York: The Macmillan Company, 1956), p. 143.

27. Numbers 5:11ff.

28. Deuteronomy 21:1ff.

29. Silver, *Where Judaism Differed,* p. 104.

30. Deuteronomy 25:5ff.

31. Neil Gillman, *The Jewish Approach to God* (Woodstock, VT: Jewish Lights Publishing, 2003), p. xii.

32. Silver, *Where Judaism Differed,* p. 312.

33. Rodkinson, *The New Edition of the Babylonian Talmud,* Sanhedrin XI:1.

34. Dosick, *Living Judaism,* p. 12.

35. Ibid., p. 46.

36. Silver, *Where Judaism Differed,* p. 320.

37. Isidore Epstein, *Encyclopaedia Britannica* (Chicago: William Benton, 1962). S.v. "Judaism."

38. De Lange, *An Introduction to Judaism,* p. 211.

39. Rodkinson, *The New Edition of the Babylonian Talmud,* Sanhedrin 99a and 98b.

40. Silver, *Where Judaism Differed,* p. 140.

41. Silver, *Where Judaism Differed,* p. 83.

42. Epstein, *Encyclopedia Britannica,* s.v. "Judaism."

43. Rodkinson, *The New Edition of the Babylonian Talmud,* Sanhedrin 98.

44. John Bright, *A History of Israel* (Philadelphia: The Westminster Press, 1959), p. 70.

45. Genesis 12:1-3.

46. The Talmud, Yoma 28b.

47. Silver, *Where Judaism Differed*, p. 90.

48. Roth, *The Haggadah*, p. 27.

49. Abba Eban, *Heritage: Civilization and the Jews* (New York: Summit Books, 1984), p. 28.

50. George Robinson, *Essential Judaism: A Complete Guide to Beliefs, Customs, and Rituals* (New York: Simon & Schuster, 2000), p. 7.

51. Joshua 24:2.

52. Genesis 31:34.

53. Zechariah 10:2.

54. Exodus 6:7.

55. Exodus 13:1-8.

56. Exodus 23:16; Leviticus 23:16-23; Numbers 28:26.

57. Numbers 15:40.

58. Leviticus 19:2.

59. Talmud: Maccoth, Gemara on Mishna IX.

60. Deuteronomy 6:4-5.

61. Leviticus 23:23-25.

62. Leviticus 16:30.

63. Ecclesiastes 7:20.

64. 1 Kings 10:22.

65. 2 Kings 14:25-28.

66. Herman Wouk, *The Will to Live On* (New York: Harper Collins Publishers, 2000), p. 39.

67. 2 Kings 21:7.

68. Ezekiel 8:14,16.

69. 2 Chronicles 36:15-16.

70. Silver, *Where Judaism Differed*, p. 159.

71. Acts 21:20.

72. Hans Kung, *Judaism: Between Yesterday and Tomorrow* (New York: Continuum, 1992), p. 359.

73. Rodkinson, *The New Edition of the Babylonian Talmud*, Aboth I:14.

74. Deuteronomy 24:1.

75. Kung, *Judaism: Between Yesterday and Tomorrow*, p. 309.

76. Josephus, *Antiquities of the Jews*, XX.8.6; Acts 21:38.

77. 2 Chronicles 36:15-17.

78. Talmud, Yoma 9b.

79. Rodkinson, *The New Edition of the Babylonian Talmud*, Sanhedrin 97.

80. Tacitus, History V/1ff.

81. Rodkinson, *The New Edition of the Babylonian Talmud*, vol. 1, p. 28.

82. Will Durant, *The Age of Faith* (New York: Simon & Schuster, 1950), p. 398.

83. B. Thomas Costain, *A History of the Plantagenets: The Conquering Family* (New York: Doubleday & Co., 1949), p. 137ff.

84. Barbara Tuchman, *A Distant Mirror: The Calamitous 14th Century* (New York: Alfred A. Knopf, 1978), pp. 38, 110-11.

85. Friedrich Heer, *The Medieval World* (New York: New American Library, 1962), p. 312.

86. De Lange, *An Introduction to Judaism*, p. 26.

87. Heer, *The Medieval World*, p. 311.

88. Tuchman, *A Distant Mirror*, 310.

89. Kung, *Judaism: Between Yesterday and Tomorrow*, p. 196.

90. Epstein, *Encyclopaedia Britannica*, s.v. "Judaism."

91. Samuel G. Freedman, *Jew vs. Jew* (New York: Simon & Schuster, 2000), p. 356.

92. Wouk, *The Will to Live On*, p. 26.

93. Jeremiah 25:12.

94. Wouk, *The Will to Live On*, p. 69.

95. Kung, *Judaism: Between Yesterday and Tomorrow*, p. 300.

96. Herbert Butterfield, *Christianity and History* (London: G. Bell & Sons, 1967), p. 100.

97. Smith, *The World's Religions*, p. 309.

98. Harvey Cox, as cited in *Our Religions*, ed. Arvind Sharma (San Francisco: HarperSanFrancisco, 1993), p. 416.

99. G. Wauchoppe Stewart, in *A Dictionary of Christ and the Gospels*, vol. 2 (Edinburgh, UK: T & T Clark, 1924), s.v. "Originality."

100. Eban, *Heritage: Civilization and the Jews*, p. 108.

101. Silver, *Where Judaism Differed*, p. 129.

102. Numbers 35:25 and in the Talmud, Maccoth 11.

103. Talmud, Sanhedrin 98b.

104. Talmud, Sanhedrin 107b.

105. Butterfield, *Christianity and History*, p. 155.

106. Franz Delitzsch, *Biblical Commentary on the Proverbs of Solomon*, vol. II (Edinburgh, UK: T&T Clark, 1875), p. 276.

107. Ibid., p. 78.

CHRISTIANITY

1. Luke 3:1.

2. John 7:46.

3. Mark 1:22.

4. See John 1:49; 11:27; Matthew 16:16; 14:33.

5. John 19:7.

6. Mark 2:28.

7. Matthew 15:11.

8. John 5:18.

9. John 4:26; Matthew 26:64.

10. John 18:36.

11. Matthew 27:4.

12. Luke 5:8.

13. James Stalker, *Dictionary of Christ and the Apostles*, vol. II (Edinburgh, UK: T&T Clark, 1923), s.v. "Sinless."

14. 1 Peter 2:22 and 1 John 3:5.

15. Brian Moynahan, *The Faith: A History of Christianity* (New York: Doubleday, 2002), p. 25.

16. Acts 19:31.

17. Tacitus XV:44.

18. Tertullian, *Apology*, Ante-Nicene Fathers, vol. III (Grand Rapids, MI: Eerdmans Publishing Co., 1951), chapter 40. His earlier writings are more in line with Christianity than those from his Montanist period.

19. Irenaeus, *Against Heresies*, Ante-Nicene Fathers, vol. I (Grand Rapids, MI: Eerdmans Publishing Co., 1951), Book III, 3/4.

20. William H. McNeill, *The Rise of the West* (Chicago: The University of Chicago Press, 1963), p. 441. This is an excellent and readable presentation in one single volume.

21. Tertullian, *Apology*, chapter 37.

22. Michael Collins and Matthew A. Price, *The Story of Christianity: 2000 Years of Faith* (New York: Dorling Kindersley, 1999), p. 10.

23. A.R. Whitham, as cited in *Dictionary of Christ and the Gospels*, vol. II (Edinburgh, UK: T & T Clark, 1924), p. 850, s.v. "Christ in the Early Church."

24. 1 John 2:22; 4:3.

25. Irenaeus, *Against Heresies*, Anti-Nicene Fathers, vol. I (Grand Rapids: Eerdmans Publishing Co., 1951), Book I, 27/2 and 3.

26. Irenaeus, *Against Heresies*, Book I, 8/1.

27. Irenaeus, *Against Heresies*, Book I 24/4.

28. Jaroslav Pelikan, *The Christian Tradition: The Emergence of the Catholic Tradition* (Chicago: The University of Chicago Press, 1971), p. 79. This is part of a scholarly five-volume history of the development of doctrine.

29. *The Epistle of Barnabas* in Ante-Nicene Fathers, vol. I (Grand Rapids: Eerdmans Publishing Co., 1951), Barnabas 4/14.

30. F.W. Beare, as cited in *The Interpreter's Dictionary of the Bible,* vol. 1 (Nashville, TN: Abingdon Press, 1962), s.v. "Canon of the New Testament."

31. Irenaeus, *Against Heresies,* Book III, 2/1 and 2.

32. Acts 20:17,28; Titus 1:5-7.

33. *Theological Dictionary of the New Testament,* ed. Gerhard Kittel (Grand Rapids: Eerdmans Publishing Co., 1964), vol. II, pp. 616, 619.

34. Clement, *First Epistle of Clement to the Corinthians,* Ante-Nicene Fathers, vol. I (Grand Rapids, Eerdmans Publishing Co., 1951), chapter 44.

35. Ignatius, *Epistle to the Philippians,* Ante-Nicene Fathers, vol. I (Grand Rapids: Eerdmans Publishing Co., 1951), 2/7.

36. Ignatius, *Epistle to Smyrna,* Ante-Nicene Fathers, vol. I (Grand Rapids: Eerdmans Publishing Co., 1951), chapter 8.

37. Irenaeus, *Against Heresies,* Book III, 3/1.

38. Romans 10:9.

39. Romans 6:17.

40. Irenaeus, *Against Heresies,* Book I, 10/1.

41. Tertullian, *On Prescription Against Heresies,* Ante-Nicene Fathers, vol. III (Grand Rapids: Eerdmans Publishing Co., 1951), chapter 13.

42. Tertullian, *On the Veiling of Virgins,* Ante-Nicene Fathers, vol. III (Grand Rapids: Eerdmans Publishing Co., 1951), chapter 1.

43. Michael Grant, *Constantine the Great* (New York: Charles Scribner's Sons, 1994), p. 141.

44. Ibid., p. 145.

45. Ibid., pp. 146, 151.

46. Ibid., p. 154.

47. Grant, *Constantine the Great,* p. 159.

48. Mark A. Noll, *Turning Points: Decisive Moments in the History of Christianity* (Grand Rapids: Baker Books), p. 50.

49. Arnold Toynbee, *Christianity Among the Religions of the World* (New York: Charles Scribner's Sons, 1957), p. 61.

50. Owen Chadwick, *A History of Christianity* (New York: St. Martin's Press, 1995), p. 64.

51. Thomas Bokenkotter, *A Concise History of the Catholic Church* (New York: Doubleday, 2004), p. 46.

52. Claudio Rendina, *The Popes: Histories and Secrets* (Santa Ana, CA: Seven Locks Press, 2002), p. 75.

53. Bokenkotter, *A Concise History of the Catholic Church,* p. 76.

54. Moynahan, *The Faith: A History of Christianity,* p. 213.

55. Rendina, *The Popes: Histories and Secrets,* p. 226.

56. Carl Horstman, as cited in Richard Rolle, *The Form of Perfect Living* (London: Thomas Baker, 1910), p. xxiii.

57. Rolle, Richard, *The Form of Perfect Living,* pp. 55-56.

58. Matthew 10:5-10.

59. Kenneth Scott Latourette, *A History of Christianity* (New York: Harper & Row, 1953), p. 429.

60. Rendina, *The Popes: Histories and Secrets,* p. 311.

61. Karl Heussi, *Kompendium der Kirchengeschichte* (Tubingen, Germany: J.C.B. Mohr, 1922), p. 175.

62. Ann Marie B. Bahr, *Christianity* (Philadelphia: Chelsea House Publishers, 2004), p. 62.

63. Moynahan, *The Faith: A History of Christianity,* p. 265.

64. Samuel M. Zwemer, *Raymond Lull, First Missionary to the Moslems* (New York: Funk & Wagnalls Co., 1902), pp. 87,91.

65. Thomas M. Lindsay, *A History of the Reformation,* vol. II (Edinburgh, UK: T&T Clark, 1908), p. 317.

66. Collins and Price, *The Story of Christianity: 2000 Years of Faith,* p. 119.

67. Rendina, *The Popes: Histories and Secrets,* p. 391.

68. Moynahan, *The Faith: A History of Christianity,* p. 333.

69. Lindsay, *A History of the Reformation,* vol. I, p. 58.

70. Roland H. Bainton, *Here I Stand: A Life of Martin Luther* (Nashville, TN: Abingdon Press, 1950), p. 223.

71. Rendina, *The Popes: Histories and Secrets,* p. 444.

72. Lindsay, *A History of the Reformation,* vol. I, p. 337.

73. Ibid., vol. II, p. 104.

74. Max Weber, *The Protestant Ethic and the Spirit of Capitalism* (London: Allen and Unwin, 1930). The edition published by Routledge Classics (1992) features an introduction by Anthony Giddens.

75. Ibid., p. 115.

76. Ibid., p. 119 (emphasis in original).

77. Benjamin Nelson, *The Idea of Usury from Tribal Brotherhood to Universal Otherhood* (Chicago: The University of Chicago Press, 1969), pp. 63-69. The book is an outstanding contribution to the topic of usury and presents a historic analysis of the relevant texts in Deuteronomy.

78. Lindsay, vol. II, p. 316.

79. Roger Finke and Rodney Stark, *The Churching of America, 1776–1990* (New Brunswick, NJ: Rutgers University Press, 2002), p. 22.

80. Moynahan, *The Faith: A History of Christianity,* p. 479.

81. Stephen Thompson, *Turning Points in World History* (San Diego, CA: Greenhaven Press, 2002), p. 196.

82. Antonia Fraser, *Cromwell: Our Chief of Men* (Frogmore, UK: Granada Publishing Ltd., 1973), pp. 104, 106. A brilliant biography of Cromwell that illuminates an important period in English history.

83. Mary Lee Settle, *I Roger Williams* (New York: W.W. Norton Co., 2002), p. 204.

84. Samuel Eliot Morison, *The Oxford History of the American People* (New York: Oxford University Press, 1965), p. 129.

85. Latourette, *A History of Christianity,* p. 923.

86. Noll, *Turning Points: Decisive Moments in the History of Christianity,* p. 276.

87. J.B. Webster and A.A. Boahen with M. Tidy, *West Africa Since 1800: The Revolutionary Years* (London: Longman Group Ltd., 1980), p. 243.

88. Roland Bainton, *Christianity* (Boston, MA: Houghton Mifflin, 1985), p. 331.

89. Stephen Tomkins, *John Wesley, a Biography* (Grand Rapids, MI: Eerdmans Publishing Co., 2003), pp. 86, 92.

90. Ibid., p. 148.

91. Ibid., p. 196.

92. Collins and Price, *The Story of Christianity: 2000 Years of Faith,* p. 169.

93. Bainton, *Christianity,* p. 341.

94. Roland Oliver and J.D. Fage, *A Short History of Africa* (Baltimore, MD: Penguin Books, 1962), p. 136.

95. Finke and Stark, *The Churching of America, 1776–1990,* p. 32. A lucid presentation buttressed with detailed statistical data.

96. Ibid., p. 130.

97. Latourette, *A History of Christianity,* p. 1255.

98. Nancy Tatom Ammerman, *Bible Believers: Fundamentalists in the Modern World* (New Brunswick, NJ: Rutgers University Press, 1987), p. 192.

99. Walter Russell Mead, "God's Country?," *Foreign Affairs,* September/October 2006, pp. 32, 36. An insightful article.

100. Finke and Stark, *The Churching of America, 1776–1990,* p. 1.

101. Ibid., p. 18.

102. Demetrios J. Constantelos, *Understanding the Greek Orthodox Church* (Brookline, MA: Hellenic College Press, 1998), p. 184.

103. Ann Marie B., Bahr, *Christianity* (Philadelphia, PA: Chelsea House Publishers, 2004), p. 5.

104. Philip Jenkins, *The Next Christendom: The Coming of Global Christianity* (New York: Oxford University Press, 2002), p. 15.

105. Toynbee, *Christianity Among the Religions of the World,* p. 63.

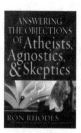

ANSWERING THE OBJECTIONS OF ATHEISTS, AGNOSTICS, AND SKEPTICS
Ron Rhodes

With clear reasoning and understandable language Ron Rhodes provides readers with the explanations and scriptural background they need to respond confidently to common arguments against the foundations of Christianity.

THE BARE BONES BIBLE HANDBOOK
Jim George

This is the perfect resource for a fast and friendly overview of every book of the Bible. It explores the key themes, characters, events, and verses of Scripture, and highlights important lessons for everyday life.

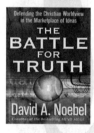

THE BATTLE FOR TRUTH
David Noebel

Now, David Noebel's landmark guide, *Understanding the Times,* in an abridged, easier-to-read version! Compares the views of Humanism, Marxism/Leninism, and the New Age movement with biblical truths, affirming the coherence and truthfulness of Christianity.

BIBLE ANSWERS TO LIFE'S BIG QUESTIONS
Bruce Bickel and Stan Jantz

Bruce Bickel and Stan Jantz offer clear, biblical answers to the biggest questions their readers ask about faith and the Christian life including, "Is the Bible true?" and "How do we know God exists?"

CHRISTIANITY ACCORDING TO THE BIBLE
Ron Rhodes

Popular Bible scholar Ron Rhodes lays out the clear teaching of Scripture on 12 essential elements of biblical Christianity. Each chapter is thorough yet easy-to-understand, informative yet highly inspirational.

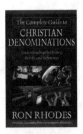

THE COMPLETE GUIDE TO CHRISTIAN DENOMINATIONS
Ron Rhodes

An easy-to-use manual that provides readers with accurate, straightforward information about various churches. Includes each denomination's brief history, its most important doctrinal beliefs, and distinctive teachings.

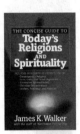

THE CONCISE GUIDE TO TODAY'S RELIGIONS AND SPIRITUALITY
James K. Walker

Biblical, evangelical, and orthodox, this comprehensive, A-to-Z source provides the basics for evaluating belief systems and spiritual phenomena—Christian, quasi-Christian, and non-Christian—and people connected with them. Thousands of entries with cross references make this an excellent resource for individuals—parents, church leaders, counselors—and study groups and church libraries.

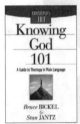

KNOWING GOD 101
Bruce Bickel and Stan Jantz

Readers of all backgrounds will enjoy the inspiring descriptions of God's nature, personality, and activities. Curious inquirers and earnest seekers will find straightforward responses to essential questions about God.

KNOWING THE BIBLE 101
Bruce Bickel and Stan Jantz

With extensive biblical knowledge and a contemporary perspective, Bruce Bickel and Stan Jantz provide a manageable approach to understanding God's written message—its origin, themes, truth, and personal relevance.

HARVEST HOUSE
PUBLISHERS